Essential
CHRISTIAN
CLASSICS

Essential
CHRISTIAN
CLASSICS

BARBOUR
PUBLISHING

Member of the
Evangelical Christian
Publishers Association

CONTENTS

WELCOME TO ESSENTIAL CHRISTIAN CLASSICS

Every year, hundreds of new Christian books are published. And though the advance of technology has increased this output over recent decades, Christian books have been prominent in publishing since Johannes Gutenberg christened his world-changing invention—the moveable type press—by printing a Bible.

Since that event in 1455, countless Christian books have been written, edited, printed, and distributed. Whether doctrinal works, gospel tracts, or hymn books, practical living titles, histories and biographies, or fictional stories that teach biblical truths, this literature has spanned the width and breadth of Christian experience.

But what makes some of these books *classics*? And what constitutes an "essential Christian classic"?

Certainly, a classic must stand the test of time. While many bestselling books address pressing issues for readers of their time, they are not read fifty, twenty, or even ten years after their release. For a book to be read and appreciated a hundred, or two hundred, or four hundred years after it was written clearly indicates its message goes beyond the need of the day. This kind of book can be described as "timeless."

And that's the type of book you'll find in *Essential Christian Classics*. In the pages to follow, you'll be introduced (or reintroduced) to four very different books that have spoken deeply to readers for at least a century—and in some cases, several centuries:

The Christian's Secret of a Happy Life: The beloved Christian living title by Hannah Whitall Smith, first published in 1870.

Foxe's Christian Martyrs: The shocking—yet encouraging—history first published by John Foxe in 1563.

In His Steps: The 1897 novel that first asked the question, "What Would Jesus Do?" written by Charles M. Sheldon.

The Pilgrim's Progress: John Bunyan's allegory—one of the most significant Christian books of all time—first published in 1678.

Though the message of these books is timeless, their language (and their readers) have changed over the centuries. So *Essential Christian Classics* presents these four titles in carefully abridged versions, with language lightly updated for ease of understanding. But the powerful, primary thoughts of each book have been maintained—with the expectation that these "essential Christian classics" will continue to change lives in our unsettled and often unsettling twenty-first century.

Each book is preceded by a brief historical and biographical note to place its message into a clear context.

We hope you'll find challenge, encouragement, and inspiration from these four books. They are truly essential Christian classics.

THE EDITORS

The Christian's
Secret of a
Happy Life

Hannah Whitall Smith is best remembered as the author of one of the most popular devotional/Christian living books of all time, *The Christian's Secret of a Happy Life*.

Born into a strict Quaker home in Pennsylvania in 1832, Hannah Whitall suffered from deep spiritual doubts during her early years. Her inner struggle continued into her marriage to Robert Piersall Smith in 1851, but in 1858 the couple committed their lives to Christ and decided to leave the Quaker faith to join the Plymouth Brethren.

A further spiritual experience in 1867 led Hannah and Robert to undertake a speaking tour on the "Higher Christian Life" in the United States and Europe. As Robert's health declined, the couple stayed in England and observed the 1874 founding of the Keswick Convention. It was at a Keswick conference in 1887 that Amy Carmichael would feel the call of God to the mission field.

Hannah Whitall Smith penned *The Christian's Secret of a Happy Life* in 1875 and wrote eighteen other books, as well, including *The Unselfishness of God and How I Discovered It* in 1903. She was active in the Women's Christian Temperance Union, supported woman's suffrage and other issues of sexual equality, and studied the various religious movements that blossomed in the late nineteenth century.

Smith was stricken with arthritis for the last seven years of her life and was ultimately confined to a wheelchair, but she still entertained admirers of her writings. She died in 1911.

PART I
The Life

CHAPTER 1

Is It Scriptural?

No thoughtful person can question the fact that, for the most part, the Christian life, as it is generally lived, is not entirely a happy life. A keen observer once said, "You Christians seem to have a religion that makes you miserable. You are like a man with a headache. He does not want to get rid of his head, but it hurts him to keep it. You cannot expect outsiders to seek very earnestly for anything so uncomfortable." For the first time I saw that Christianity ought to make its possessors, not miserable, but happy. I asked the Lord to show me the secret of a happy Christian life. I shall share this secret.

In moments of illumination, God's children feel that a life of rest and victory is their birthright. Remember the shout of triumph your souls gave when you first met the Lord Jesus and glimpsed His mighty saving power? How easy it seemed to be more than conquerors through Him who loved you! Under the leadership of a captain who had never been foiled in battle, how could you dream of defeat!

And yet, to many of you, how different your real experience has been! Your victories have been few and fleeting, your defeats many and disastrous. Christ is believed in, talked about, and served, but He is not known as the soul's actual and very life, abiding there forever and revealing Himself there continually in His beauty. You have found Jesus as your Savior from the penalty of sin, but you have not found Him as your Savior from sin's power. You have carefully studied the holy scriptures and have gathered much precious truth from them, which you hoped would feed and nourish your spiritual life. But in spite of it all, your souls are starving and dying within you, and you cry out in secret, again and again, for that bread and water of life that you see promised in the scriptures to all believers.

Your early visions of triumph have seemed to grow dimmer and dimmer, and you have been forced to settle down to the conviction that the best you can expect from your religion is a life of alternate failure and victory, one hour sinning and the next repenting, and then beginning again, only to fail again, and again to repent.

But *is* this all? Had the Lord Jesus only this in His mind when He laid down His precious life to deliver you from your difficult and cruel bondage to sin? Was there a hidden reserve in each promise that was meant to deprive it of its complete fulfillment? Can we dream that the Savior, who was wounded for our transgressions and bruised for our iniquities, could possibly see of the travail of His soul and be satisfied in such Christian lives as fill the Church today? The Bible tells us that "for this purpose the Son of God was manifested, that he might destroy the works of the devil"; and can we imagine for a moment that this is beyond His power and that He finds Himself unable to accomplish the thing He came to earth to do?

In the very beginning, then, settle down on this one thing, that Jesus came to save you, now, in this life, from the power and dominion of sin and to make you more than conquerors through His power. If you doubt this, search your Bible and collect together every announcement or declaration concerning the purposes and object of His death on the cross. His work is to deliver us from our sins, from our bondage, from our defilement; and not a hint is given anywhere that this deliverance was limited and partial, one with which Christians so continually try to be satisfied.

When the angel of the Lord appeared unto Joseph in a dream and announced the coming birth of the Savior, he said, "And thou shalt call his name Jesus: for he shall save his people from their sins."

When Zacharias was "filled with the Holy Ghost" at the birth of his son, and "prophesied," he declared that God had visited His people in order to fulfill the promise and the oath He had made them, "that we being delivered out of the hand of our enemies might serve him without fear, in holiness and righteousness before him, all the days of our life."

When Peter was preaching in the porch of the temple to the wondering Jews, he said, "Unto you first God, having raised up his Son Jesus, sent him to bless you, in turning away every one of you from his iniquities."

When Paul told the Ephesian church the wondrous truth, that Christ had so loved them as to give Himself for them, he went on to declare that His purpose in doing this was "that he might sanctify and cleanse it with the washing of water by the word, that he might present it to himself a glorious church, not having spot, or wrinkle, or any such thing; but that it should be holy and without blemish."

When Paul was seeking to instruct Titus, his own son after the common faith, concerning the grace of God, he declared that the object of that grace was to teach us "that, denying ungodliness and worldly lusts, we should live soberly, righteously, and godly, in this present world." He then added the reason—that Christ "gave himself for us, that he might redeem us from all iniquity, and purify unto himself a peculiar people, zealous of good works."

When Peter encouraged the Christians, to whom he was writing, to walk holy and Christlike, he tells them that "even hereunto were ye called: because Christ also suffered for us, leaving us an example, that ye should follow his steps: who did not sin, neither was guile found in his mouth." He added, "Who his own self bare our sins in his own body on the tree, that we, being dead to sins, should live unto righteousness: by whose stripes ye were healed."

In Ephesians when Paul contrasted the walk suitable for a Christian with the walk of an unbeliever, he set before them the truth in Jesus as being this: "That ye put off concerning the former conversation the old man, which is corrupt according to the deceitful lusts; and be renewed in the spirit of your mind; and that ye put on the new man, which after God is created in righteousness and true holiness."

In Romans 6, Paul brought up the fact of our judicial death and resurrection with Christ as an unanswerable argument for our practical deliverance from sin. For a child of God to continue sinning is utterly foreign to the whole spirit and aim of the salvation of Jesus. He says, "God forbid. How shall we, that are dead to sin, live any longer therein? Know ye not, that so many of us as were baptized into Jesus Christ were baptized into his death? Therefore we are buried with him by baptism into death: that like as Christ was raised up from the dead by the glory of the Father, even so we also should walk in newness of life," and adds, "Knowing this, that our old man is crucified with him, that the body of sin might be destroyed, that henceforth we should not serve sin."

Sometimes we overlook the fact that there are far more references made of a present salvation from sin than of a future salvation in a heaven beyond.

Can we for a moment suppose that the holy God, who hates sin in the sinner, is willing to tolerate it in the Christian, and that He has even arranged the plan of salvation in such a way as to make it impossible for those who are saved from the guilt of sin to find deliverance from its power?

Dr. Chalmers says, "Sin is that scandal which must be rooted out from the great spiritual household over which the Divinity rejoices. Now that the penalty is taken off, do you think it is possible that the unchangeable God has so given up His antipathy to sin that man, ruined and redeemed, may now indulge in sin, which under the old order destroyed him? Does not the God who loved righteousness and hated iniquity six thousand years ago bear the same love to righteousness and hatred to iniquity still? The cross of Christ, by the same mighty and decisive stroke that moved the curse of sin away from us, also surely moves away the power and the love of it from over us."

The redemption accomplished for us by our Lord Jesus Christ on the cross at Calvary is a redemption from the power of sin as well as from its guilt.

He *is* able to save to the uttermost all who come unto God by Him.

A quaint old Quaker divine of the seventeenth century says: "There is nothing so contrary to God as sin, and God will not suffer sin always to rule His masterpiece, man. When we consider God's inexhaustible power for destroying that which is contrary to Him, who can believe that the devil must always stand and prevail?

"It is inconsistent and disagreeable with the true faith for people to be Christians and yet to believe that Christ, the eternal Son of God, to whom all power in heaven and earth is given, will allow sin and the devil to have dominion over them.

"If you say sin is deeply rooted in man, I say so, too. But Christ Jesus has received power to destroy the devil and his works and to recover and redeem man into righteousness and holiness. Or else it is false that 'He is able to save to the uttermost all that come unto God by Him.' We must throw away the Bible if we say that it is impossible for God to deliver man out of sin.

"So, then, I do expect the benefit of my redemption and that I shall go out of my captivity. But still they say you must abide in sin as long as you live. What! Must we never be delivered? Must this crooked heart and perverse will always remain? Must I be a believer and yet have no faith that reaches to sanctification and holy living? Is there no mastery to be had, no getting victory over sin? Must it prevail over me as long as I live? What sort of a redeemer is this, or what benefit of my redemption do I have in this life?"

This isn't a new doctrine in the Church; however, much of it may have been lost sight of by the present generation of believers. It is the same old story that has filled the daily lives of many saints of God with songs of triumph throughout all ages; and it is now being sounded forth again to the unspeakable joy of weary and burdened souls.

Do not reject it until you have prayerfully searched the scriptures to see whether these things be indeed so. Ask God to open the eyes of your understanding by His Spirit that you may know "what is the exceeding greatness of his power toward us who believe, according to the working of his mighty power, which he wrought in Christ, when he raised him from the dead, and set him at his own right hand in the heavenly places." And when you have begun to have some faint glimpses of this power, learn to look away utterly from your own weakness, and, putting your case into His hands, trust Him to deliver you.

CHAPTER 2

God's Side and Man's Side

There are two very decided and distinct sides to this subject, and like all other subjects, it cannot be fully understood unless both of these sides are kept constantly in view. I refer of course to God's side and man's side; or in other words, to God's part in the work of sanctification and man's part. These are very distinct and even contrasting, but they are not really contradictory, although to a casual observer they may appear so.

Suppose two friends go to see some celebrated building and return home to describe it. One has seen only the north side and the other only the south.

The first says, "The building was built in such a manner, and has such and such stories and ornaments."

"Oh no," says the other, interrupting him, "you are altogether mistaken. I saw the building, and it was built in quite a different manner, and its ornaments and stories were so-and-so."

A lively dispute might follow upon the truth of the respective descriptions until the two friends should discover that they had been describing different *sides* of the building, and then all would be reconciled at once.

I believe there are two distinct sides in this matter. But only looking at one without seeing the other is certain to create wrong impressions and views of the truth. In brief, man's part is to trust, and God's part is to work. There is certain *work* to accomplish. We are delivered from the power of sin and are made perfect in every good work to do the will of God. This real labor is worked in us and upon us. Besetting sins are conquered, evil habits are overcome, wrong dispositions and feelings are rooted out, and holy tempers and emotions are birthed. A positive transformation takes place. So at least the Bible teaches.

Most of us tried to do it for ourselves at first, and have grievously failed. Then we discover that we are unable to do it. But the Lord Jesus Christ has come on purpose to do it, and He will do it for all who put themselves wholly into His hands and trust Him without reserve.

Plainly the believer can do nothing but trust, while the Lord, in whom he trusts, actually does the work entrusted to Him. *Trusting* and *doing* are certainly contrasted things, often indeed contradictory, but are they contradictory in this case? Obviously not, because it is two different parties that are concerned. The preacher, who is speaking on man's part in the matter, cannot speak of anything but surrender and trust, because this is positively all the man can do. Such preachers are constantly criticized as though, in saying this, they had meant to imply there *was* no other part. The cry goes out that this doctrine of faith does away with all realities, that souls are just told to trust, and that they sit down from now on in a sort of religious easy chair, dreaming away a life, fruitless of any actual result. This misapprehension arises, of course, from the fact that either the preacher has neglected to state, or the hearer has failed to hear, the other side of the matter, which is, that when we trust, the Lord works, and that a great deal is done, not by us, but by Him. Actual results are reached by our trusting, because our Lord undertakes the thing entrusted to Him and accomplishes it. *We* do not do anything, but *He* does it. And it is all the more effectually done because of this. As soon as this is clearly seen, the difficulty as to the preaching of faith disappears entirely.

On the other hand, the preacher who dwells on God's part in the matter is criticized on a totally different ground. He does not speak of trust, for the Lord's part is not to trust but to work. The Lord's part is to *do* the thing entrusted to Him. He brings to bear upon us all the refining and purifying resources of His wisdom and His love, causing us to grow in grace and conforming us, day by day and hour by hour, to the image of Christ. Sanctification is both a step of faith and a process of works. It is a step of surrender and trust on our part, and it is a process of development on God's part. By a step of faith, we put ourselves into the hands of the divine Potter. By a gradual process, He makes us into a vessel unto His own honor. Suppose I were to describe to a person, who was entirely ignorant of the subject, the way in which a lump of clay is made into a beautiful vessel. I tell him first the part of the clay in the matter. All I can say about this is that the clay is put into the potter's hands and then lies passive there, submitting itself to all the turnings and overturnings of the potter's hands upon it. The potter takes the clay thus abandoned to his working and begins to mold and fashion it according to his own will. He kneads and works it; he tears it apart and presses it together again; he wets it and then suffers it to dry. Sometimes he works at it for hours together; sometimes he lays it aside for days and does not touch it. And then, when by all these processes he has made it perfectly pliable in his hands, he proceeds to make it up into the vessel he has proposed. He turns it upon the wheel, planes it, and smoothes it, and dries it in the sun, bakes it in the oven, and finally turns it out of his workshop, a vessel to his honor and fit for his use.

This is the clay's part in the matter. I now speak of the potter's part. These two are necessarily contrasted, but not in the least contradictory. The clay is not expected to do the potter's work, but only to yield itself up to his working.

Nothing, it seems to me, could be clearer than the perfect harmony between these two *apparently* contradictory sorts of teaching.

What *can* be said about man's part in this great work but that he must continually surrender himself and continually trust? When we come to God's side of the question, what is there that may not be said as to the many and wonderful ways in which He accomplishes the work entrusted to Him? It is here that the growing comes in. The lump of clay could never grow into a beautiful vessel if it stayed in the clay pit for thousands of years. But when it is put into the hands of a skillful potter, it grows rapidly, under his fashioning, into the vessel he intends it to be. And in the same way the soul abandoned to the working of the heavenly Potter is made into a vessel unto honor, sanctified, and meet for the Master's use.

Having, then, taken the step of faith by which you have put yourself wholly and absolutely into His hands, expect Him to begin to work. His way of accomplishing that which you have entrusted to Him may be different from your way, but He knows, and you must be satisfied.

I knew a lady who had entered into this life of faith with a great outpouring of the Spirit and a wonderful flood of light and joy. She supposed, of course, this was a preparation for some great service and expected to be put forth immediately into the Lord's harvest field. Instead of this, almost at once her own husband lost all his money, and she was shut up in her own house to attend to all sorts of domestic duties with no time or strength left for any gospel work at all. She accepted the discipline and yielded herself up as heartily to sweep and dust and bake and sew, as she would have done to teach, or pray, or write for the Lord. And the result was that, through this very training, He made her into a vessel "meet for the Master's use, and prepared unto every good work."

Another lady, who had entered this life of faith under similar circumstances of wondrous blessing and who also expected to be sent out to do some great work, was shut up with two peevish invalid children to nurse and humor and amuse all day long. Unlike the first one, this lady did not accept the training, but chafed and fretted, and finally rebelled, lost all her blessing, and went back into a state of sad coldness and misery. She had understood her part of trusting to begin with, but, not understanding the divine process of accomplishing that for which she had trusted, she took herself out of the hands of the heavenly Potter, and the vessel was marred on the wheel.

The maturity of a Christian experience cannot be reached in a moment but is the result of the work of God's Holy Spirit, who, by His energizing and transforming power, causes us to grow up into Christ in all things. And we cannot hope to reach this maturity in any other way than by yielding ourselves up, utterly and willingly, to His mighty working.

All that we claim, then, in this life of sanctification is that by an act of faith we put ourselves into the hands of the Lord, for Him to work in us all the good pleasure of His will, and then, by a continuous exercise of faith, keep ourselves there. When we do it, and while we do it, we are, in the scripture sense, truly pleasing God, although it may require years of training and discipline to mature us into a vessel that shall be in all respects to His honor and fitted to every good work.

Our part is the trusting; it is His to accomplish the results. And when we do our part, He never fails to do His, for no one ever trusted in the Lord and was destroyed. Do not be afraid, then, that if you trust or tell others to trust, the matter will end there. Trust is the beginning and the continuing foundation.

And this explains that apparent paradox that puzzles so many. They say, "In one breath you tell us to do nothing but trust, and in the next you tell us to do impossible things."

They are to reconciled, just as we reconcile the statements concerning a saw in a carpenter's shop, when we say, at one moment, that the saw has sawn asunder a log, and the next moment declare that the carpenter has done it. The saw is the instrument used; the power that uses it is the carpenter's.

In the divine order, God's working depends upon our cooperation. Of our Lord it was declared that at a certain place He could do there no mighty work because of their unbelief. It was not that He would not, but He could not. Just as the potter, however skillful, cannot make a beautiful vessel out of a lump of clay that is never put into his hands, so neither can God make out of me a vessel unto His honor unless I put myself into His hands. In this book, I shall of course dwell mostly upon man's side, as I am writing for human beings, in the hope of making it plain how we are to fulfill our part of this great work. But I wish it to be distinctly understood all through, that unless I believed with all my heart in God's effectual working on His side, not one word of this book would ever have been written.

CHAPTER 3

The Life Defined

The experience sometimes called the "higher Christian life" is the only true Christian life and is best described in the words "the life hid with Christ in God." The scriptures do set before the believer in the Lord Jesus a life of abiding rest and of continual victory, which is very far beyond the ordinary run of Christian experience. In the Bible we have presented to us a Savior able to save us from the power of our sins as really as He saves us from their guilt.

The chief characteristics of a life hid with Christ are an entire surrender to the Lord and a perfect trust in Him, resulting in victory over sin and inward rest of soul. It differs from the lower range of Christian experience in that it causes us to let the Lord carry our burdens and manage our affairs for us instead of trying to do it ourselves.

Most Christians are like a man who was toiling along the road, bending under a heavy burden, when a wagon overtook him, and the driver kindly offered to help him on his journey. He joyfully accepted the offer but, when seated in the wagon, continued to bend beneath his burden, which he still kept on his shoulders.

"Why do you not lay down your burden?" asked the kindhearted driver.

"Oh!" replied the man, "I feel that it is almost too much to ask you to carry me, and I could not think of letting you carry my burden, too."

And so Christians who have given themselves into the care and keeping of the Lord Jesus still continue to bend beneath the weight of their burdens and often go weary and heavy laden throughout the whole length of their journey.

When I speak of burdens, I mean everything that troubles us, whether spiritual or temporal.

First of all, the greatest burden we have to carry in life is self, and the most difficult thing we have to manage is self. Our own daily living, our frames and feelings, our special weaknesses and temptations, our peculiar temperaments, our inward affairs of every kind—these are the things that perplex and worry us more than anything else and that bring us most frequently into bondage and darkness. You must hand yourself, with your temptations, your temperament, your frames and feelings, and all your inward and outward experiences, over into the care and keeping of your God and leave it all there.

He made you, and therefore He understands you and knows how to manage you. You must trust Him to do it. Say to Him, "Here, Lord, I abandon myself to You. I have tried in every way I could think of to manage myself and to make myself what I know I ought to be, but I have always failed. Now I give it up to You. Take entire possession of me. Work in me all the good pleasure of Your will. Mold and fashion me into such a vessel as seems good to You. I leave myself in Your hands, and I believe You will, according to Your promise, make me into a vessel unto Your own honor, 'sanctified, and meet for the Master's use, and prepared unto every good work.' " And here you must rest, trusting yourself to Him, continually and absolutely.

Next, lay off every other burden—your health, your reputation, your Christian work, your houses, your children, your business, your servants— everything, in short, that concerns you, whether inward or outward.

It is generally much less difficult for us to commit the keeping of our future to the Lord than it is to commit our present. We know we are helpless as regards the future, but we feel as if the present was in our own hands and must be carried on our own shoulders; and most of us have an unconfessed idea that it is a great deal to ask the Lord to carry ourselves, and that we cannot think of asking Him to carry our burdens, too.

I knew a Christian lady who had a very heavy temporal burden. It took away her sleep and her appetite, and there was danger of her health breaking down under it. One day, when it seemed specially heavy, she noticed lying on the table near her a little tract called *Hannah's Faith*. Attracted by the title, she picked it up and began to read it, little knowing, however, that it was to create a revolution in her whole experience. The story was of a poor woman who had been carried triumphantly through a life of unusual sorrow.

She was giving the history of her life to a kind visitor on one occasion, and at the close the visitor said feelingly, "Oh, Hannah, I do not see how you could bear so much sorrow!"

"I did not bear it," was the quick reply; "the Lord bore it for me."

"Yes," said the visitor, "that is the right way. We must take our troubles to the Lord."

"Yes," replied Hannah, "but we must do more than that: *leave* them there. Most people," she continued, "take their burdens to Him, but they bring them away with them again and are just as worried and unhappy as ever. But I take mine, and I leave them with Him and come away and forget them. If the worry comes back, I take it to Him again; and I do this over and over until at last I just forget I have any worries and am at perfect rest."

It was a very simple secret she found out: it was possible to obey God's commandment contained in those words, "Be careful for nothing; but in every thing by prayer and supplication with thanksgiving let your requests be made known unto God"; and that in obeying it, the result would inevitably be, according to the promise, that the "peace of God, which passeth all understanding, shall keep your hearts and minds through Christ Jesus."

The soul who has discovered this secret of simple faith has found the key that will unlock the whole treasure-house of God.

Some child of God who is hungering for just such a life as I have been describing is reading this book. You long unspeakably to get rid of your weary burdens. You would be delighted to hand over the management of your unmanageable self into the hands of one who is able to manage you. Do you recollect the delicious sense of rest with which you have sometimes gone to bed at night after a day of great exertion and weariness? How delightful was the sensation of relaxing every muscle and letting your body go in a perfect abandonment of ease and comfort! You no longer had to hold up an aching head or a weary back. You trusted yourself to the bed in absolute confidence, and it held you up, without effort or strain or even thought on your part. You rested!

Suppose you had doubted the strength or the stability of your bed and had dreaded each moment to find it giving way beneath you and landing you on the floor. Could you have rested then? Would not every muscle have been strained in a fruitless effort to hold yourself up, and would not the weariness have been greater than if you had not gone to bed at all?

Let this analogy teach you what it means to rest in the Lord. Let your souls lie down upon the couch of His sweet will, as your bodies lie down in their beds at night. Relax every strain, and lay off every burden. Let yourself go in a perfect abandonment of ease and comfort, sure that, since He holds you up, you are perfectly safe. Your part is simply to rest. His part is to sustain you, and He cannot fail.

Take another analogy, which our Lord Himself has abundantly sanctioned—that of the child-life. For "Jesus called a little child unto him, and set him in the midst of them, and said, . . . Except ye be converted and become as little children, ye shall not enter into the kingdom of heaven."

What are the characteristics of a little child, and how does he live? He lives by faith, and his chief characteristic is freedom from care. His life is one long trust from year's end to year's end. He trusts his parents, he trusts his caretakers, he trusts his teachers. He even trusts people sometimes who are utterly unworthy of trust, out of the abounding trustfulness of his nature. The child provides nothing for himself, and yet everything is provided. He lives in the present moment and receives his life unquestioningly, as it comes to him day by day from his father's hand.

I was visiting once in a wealthy home where there was a little adopted child upon whom was lavished all the love and tenderness and care that human hearts could bestow or human means procure. And as I watched that child running in and out day by day, free and lighthearted with the happy carelessness of childhood, I thought what a picture it was of our wonderful position as children in the house of our heavenly Father. How much more must the great, loving heart of our God and Father be grieved and wounded at seeing His children taking so much anxious care and thought! Who is the best cared for in every household? Is it not the little children? And does not the least of all, the helpless baby, receive the largest share? We all know that the baby toils not, neither does he spin; and yet he is fed and clothed and loved and rejoiced in more tenderly than the hardest worker of them all.

This life of faith consists in just this—being a child in the Father's house.

Let the ways of childish confidence and freedom from care, which so please you and win your hearts in your own little ones, teach you what should be your ways with God. Leaving yourselves in His hands, learn to be literally "careful for nothing," and you shall find it a fact that the peace of God, which passes all understanding, shall keep (as with a garrison) your hearts and minds through Christ Jesus.

It is no speculative theory. Neither is it a dream of romance. There *is* such a thing as having one's soul kept in perfect peace, now and here in this life; and childlike trust in God is the key to its attainment.

CHAPTER 4

How to Enter In

This blessed life must not be looked upon in any sense as an attainment but as an obtainment. We cannot earn it; we cannot climb up to it; we cannot win it; we can do nothing but ask for it and receive it. It is the gift of God in Christ Jesus. And where a thing is a gift, the only course left for the receiver is to take it and thank the giver. In order, therefore, to enter into a practical experience of this interior life, the soul must be in a receptive attitude, fully recognizing the fact that it is God's gift in Christ Jesus, and that we cannot gain it by any efforts or works of our own. He can bestow it only upon the fully consecrated soul, and it is received by faith.

I was once trying to explain to a physician who had charge of a large hospital the necessity and meaning of consecration, but he seemed unable to understand. At last I said to him, "Suppose, in going your rounds among your patients, you should meet a man who entreated you earnestly to take his case under your special care in order to cure him. At the same time he refused to tell you all his symptoms or to take all your prescribed remedies. Suppose he should say to you, 'I am quite willing to follow your directions as to certain things, because they commend themselves to my mind as good, but in other matters I prefer judging for myself and following my own directions.' What would you do in such a case?" I asked.

"Do?" he replied with indignation. "Do? I would soon leave such a man as that to his own care. For, of course," he added, "I could do nothing for him unless he would put his whole case into my hands without any reserves and would obey my directions implicitly."

"It is necessary, then," I said, "for doctors to be obeyed, if they are to have any chance to cure their patients?"

"Implicitly obeyed!" was his emphatic reply.

"And that is consecration," I continued. "God must have the whole case put into His hands without any reserves, and His directions must be implicitly followed."

"I see it," he exclaimed. "I see it! And I will do it. God shall have His own way with me from now on."

An entire surrender of the whole being to God means that spirit, soul, and body are placed under His absolute control, for Him to do with us just what He pleases. We mean that the language of our hearts, under all

27

circumstances and in view of every act, is to be "Thy will be done." We mean the giving up of all liberty of choice. We mean a life of inevitable obedience.

To a soul ignorant of God, this may look hard; but to those who know Him, it is the happiest and most restful of lives. He is our Father, and He loves us, and He knows just what is best, and therefore, of course, His will is the very most blessed thing that can come to us under any circumstances. But it really would seem as if God's own children were more afraid of His will than of anything else in life—His lovely, lovable will, which only means loving-kindnesses and tender mercies, and blessings unspeakable to their souls! I wish I could only show to everyone the unfathomable sweetness of the will of God. Heaven is a place of infinite bliss because His will is perfectly done there, and our lives share in this bliss just in proportion as His will is perfectly done in them. He loves us—*loves us*, I say—and the will of love is always blessing for its loved one. Could we but for one moment get a glimpse into the mighty depths of His love, our hearts would spring out to meet His will and embrace it as our richest treasure; and we would abandon ourselves to it with an enthusiasm of gratitude and joy that such a wondrous privilege could be ours.

A great many Christians seem practically to think that all their Father in heaven wants is a chance to make them miserable and to take away all their blessings; and they imagine, poor souls, that if they hold on to things in their own will, they can hinder Him from doing this.

A Christian lady who had this feeling was once expressing to a friend how impossible she found it to say, "Thy will be done," and how afraid she should be to do it. She was the mother of an only little boy, who was the heir to a great fortune and the idol of her heart.

After she had stated her difficulties fully, her friend said, "Suppose your little Charley should come running to you tomorrow and say, 'Mother, I have made up my mind to let you have your own way with me from this time forward. I am always going to obey you, and I want you to do just whatever you think best with me. I will trust your love.' How would you feel toward him? Would you say to yourself, 'Ah, now I shall have a chance to make Charley miserable. I will take away all his pleasures and fill his life with every hard and disagreeable thing that I can find. I will force him to do just the things that are the most difficult for him to do and will give him all sorts of impossible commands'?"

"Oh no no no!" exclaimed the indignant mother. "You know I would not. You know I would hug him to my heart and cover him with kisses and would hasten to fill his life with all that was sweetest and best."

28

"And are you tenderer and more loving than God?" asked her friend. "Ah no!" was the reply. "I see my mistake. Of course I must not be any more afraid of saying, 'Thy will be done,' to my heavenly Father, than I would want Charley to be of saying it to me."

Faith is an absolutely necessary element in the reception of any gift. Let our friends give a thing to us wholeheartedly; it is not really ours until we believe it has been given and claim it as our own. Above all, this is true in gifts that are purely mental or spiritual. Love may be lavished upon us by another without stint or measure, but until we believe that we are loved, it never really becomes ours.

I suppose most Christians understand this principle in reference to the matter of their forgiveness. They know that the forgiveness of sins through Jesus might have been preached to them forever, but it would never really have become theirs until they believed this preaching and claimed the forgiveness as their own. But when it comes to living the Christian life, they lose sight of this principle and think that, having been saved by faith, they are now to live by works and efforts. Instead of continuing to *receive*, they now begin to *do*. This makes our declaration that the life hid with Christ in God is entered into by faith seem perfectly unintelligible to them. And yet it is plainly declared that "*as* ye have therefore received Christ Jesus the Lord, *so* walk ye in him." We received Him by faith, and by faith alone; therefore we are to walk in Him by faith and by faith alone. *Then* we believed that Jesus was our Savior from the guilt of sin, and according to our faith it was unto us. *Now* we must believe that He is our Savior from the power of sin, and according to our faith it shall be unto us. *Then* we trusted Him for forgiveness, and it became ours; *now* we must trust Him for righteousness, and it shall become ours also. *Then* we took Him as a Savior in the future from the penalties of our sins; *now* we must take Him as a Savior in the present from the bondage of our sins. *Then* He was our Redeemer; *now* He is our Life. *Then* He lifted us out of the pit; *now* He is to seat us in heavenly places with Himself.

God "hath blessed us with all spiritual blessings in heavenly places in Christ," but until we set the foot of faith upon them, they do not practically become ours. "According to our faith" is always the limit and the rule.

But this faith of which I am speaking must be a present faith. No faith that is exercised in the future tense amounts to anything. No faith that looks for a future deliverance from the power of sin will ever lead a soul into the life we are describing. Perhaps no four words in the language have more meaning in them than the following, which I would have you repeat over and over with your voice and with your soul, emphasizing each time a different word:

Jesus saves me now—It is He.
Jesus *saves* me now—It is His work to save.
Jesus saves *me* now—I am the one to be saved.
Jesus saves me *now*—He is doing it every moment.

To sum up, then: In order to enter into this blessed interior life of rest and triumph, you have two steps to take—first, entire abandonment, and second, absolute faith. No matter what may be the complications of your peculiar experience, no matter what your difficulties or your surroundings or your "peculiar temperament," these two steps, definitely taken and unwaveringly persevered in, will certainly bring you out sooner or later into the green pastures and still waters of this life hid with Christ in God. If you will let every other consideration go and simply devote your attention to these two points and be very clear and definite about them, your progress will be rapid, and your soul will reach its desired haven far sooner than you can now think possible.

A lady, now very eminent in this life of trust, when she was seeking in great darkness and perplexity to enter in, said to the friend who was trying to help her, "You all say, 'Abandon yourself and trust, abandon yourself and trust'; but I do not know how. I wish you would just do it out loud, so that I may see how you do it."

Shall I do it out loud for you?

"Lord Jesus, I believe You are able and willing to deliver me from all the care and unrest and bondage of my Christian life. I believe You died to set me free, not only in the future, but now and here. I believe You are stronger than sin, and that You canst keep me, even me, in my extreme of weakness, from falling into its snares or yielding obedience to its commands. And, Lord, I am going to trust You to keep me. I have tried keeping myself and have failed most grievously. I am absolutely helpless. So now I will trust You. I give myself to You. I keep back no reserves. Body, soul, and spirit, I present myself to You as a piece of clay to be fashioned into anything Your love and Your wisdom shall choose. And now I *am* Yours. I believe You accept that which I present to You; I believe that this poor, weak, foolish heart has been taken possession of by You, and that You have even at this very moment begun to work in me to will and to do of Your good pleasure. I trust You *utterly*, and I trust You *now*."

Are you afraid to take this step? Does it seem too sudden, too much like a leap in the dark? Do you not know that the step of faith always "falls on the seeming void, but finds the rock beneath"? If ever you are to enter this glorious land, flowing with milk and honey, you must sooner or later step into the brimming waters, for there is no other path; and to do it now may save you months and even years of disappointment and grief. Hear the word of the Lord: "Have not I commanded thee? Be strong and of a good courage; be not afraid, neither be thou dismayed: for the LORD thy God is with thee whithersoever thou goest."

PART II
Difficulties

CHAPTER 5

Difficulties Concerning Consecration

Christians should not be ignorant of the temptations that seem to stand ready to oppose every onward step of their progress heavenward and that are especially active when the soul is awakened to a hunger and thirst after righteousness and begins to reach out after the fullness that is ours in Christ.

The one chief temptation that meets the soul at this juncture is the same that assaults it all along the pathway, at every step of its progress; namely, the question as to *feelings*. Because we do not feel that God has taken us in hand, we cannot believe that He has. As usual, we put feeling first and faith second, and fact last of all. Now, God's invariable rule in everything is fact first, faith second, and feeling last of all. The way to meet this temptation is to adopt His order by putting faith before feeling. Give yourself to the Lord definitely and fully, according to your present light, asking the Holy Spirit to show you all that is contrary to Him, either in your heart or life. If He shows you anything, give it to the Lord immediately, and say in reference to it, "Thy will be done." If He shows you nothing, then believe that there is nothing and conclude that you have given Him all. Then recognize that it must be the fact, that, when you give yourself to God, He accepts you; and at once let your faith take hold of this fact. If you are steadfast in this reckoning, sooner or later the feeling will come. Is this the way in which you have been acting toward God in this matter of consecration? You have given yourself to Him over and over daily, perhaps for months, but you have invariably come away from your seasons of consecration wondering whether you really have given yourself after all and whether He has taken you. And because you have not *felt* any change, you have concluded at last, after many painful tossings, that the thing has not been done. Do you know, dear believer, that this sort of perplexity will last forever unless you cut it short by faith? Come to the point of considering the matter an accomplished and settled thing, and leave it there before you can possibly expect any change of feeling whatever.

The Levitical law of offerings to the Lord settles this as a primary fact, that everything given to Him becomes, by that very act, something holy, set apart from all other things, something that cannot without sacrilege be put to any other uses. The giver might have made his offering very grudgingly and halfheartedly, but, having made it, the matter was taken out of his hands altogether, and the devoted thing, by God's own law, became "most holy unto the Lord." It was not made holy by the state of mind of the giver but by the holiness of the divine receiver. All Israel would have been aghast at the man who, having once given his offering, should have reached out his hand to take it back. Yet, day after day, earnest-hearted Christians, with no thought of the sacrilege they are committing, are guilty in their own experience of a similar act, by giving themselves to the Lord in solemn consecration and then, through unbelief, taking back that which they have given.

Because God is not visibly present to the eye, it is difficult to feel that a transaction with Him is real. What we need, therefore, is to see that God's presence is a certain fact always, and that every act of our soul is done before Him, and that a word spoken in prayer is as really spoken to Him as if our eyes could see Him and our hands could touch Him. Then we shall cease to have such vague conceptions of our relations with Him and shall feel the binding force of every word we say in His presence.

I know some will say here, "Ah yes, but if He would only speak to me and say that He took me when I gave myself to Him, I would have no trouble then in believing it." No, of course you would not; but then where would be the room for faith? Sight is not faith, and hearing is not faith, neither is feeling faith; but believing when we cannot see, hear, or feel *is* faith; and everywhere the Bible tells us our salvation is by faith. Therefore we must believe before we feel, and often against our feelings, if we would honor God by our faith. It is always he who believes who has the witness, not he who doubts. When we surrender ourselves to the Lord, according to His own command, He does then and there receive us, and from that moment we are His. A real transaction has taken place that cannot be violated without dishonor on our part, and that we know will not be violated by Him.

In Deuteronomy 26:17–19, we see God's way of working under these circumstances. "Thou hast avouched the LORD this day to be thy God, and to walk in his ways, and to keep his statutes, and his commandments, and his judgments, and to hearken unto his voice: and the LORD hath avouched thee this day to be his peculiar people, as he hath promised thee, and that thou shouldest keep all his commandments. . .and that thou mayest be an holy people unto the LORD thy God, as he hath spoken."

When we declare the Lord our God and that we will walk in His ways and keep His commandments, He declares us to be His and that we *shall* keep all His commandments. And from that moment He takes possession of us. This has always been His principle of working.

Look at a New Testament declaration that approaches the subject from a different side, but which settles it, I think, quite as definitely. It is in 1 John

5:14–15, and reads, "And this is the confidence that we have in him, that, if we ask anything according to his will, he heareth us: and if we know that he hear us, whatsoever we ask, we know that we have the petitions that we desired of him." Is it according to God's will that you should be entirely surrendered to Him? There can be, of course, but one answer to this, for He has *commanded* it. Therefore, on God's own word, you are obliged to know that He hears you. And knowing this much, you are compelled to go further and know that you have the petitions that you have desired of Him. That you *have*, I say—not will have, or may have, but have now in actual possession. It is thus that we "obtain promises" by faith. It is thus that we have "access by faith" into the grace that is given us in our Lord Jesus Christ. It is this way, and this way only, that we come to know our hearts "purified by faith" and are enabled to live by faith, to stand by faith, to walk by faith.

You have trusted the Lord Jesus for the forgiveness of your sins and know something of what it is to belong to the family of God and to be made an heir of God through faith in Christ. Now you feel the longing to be conformed to the image of your Lord. You know there must be an entire surrender of yourself to Him, that He may work in you all the good pleasure of His will. And you have tried over and over to do it but up until now without any apparent success. Come once more to Him, in a surrender of your whole self to His will, as complete as you know how to make it. Ask Him to reveal to you, by His Spirit, any hidden rebellion; and if He reveals nothing, then believe that there is nothing. You have wholly yielded yourself to the Lord, and from henceforth you do not in any sense belong to yourself. Never listen to a suggestion to the contrary. If the temptation comes to wonder whether you really have completely surrendered yourself, meet it with an assertion that you have. Do not even argue the matter. Repel any such idea instantly and with determination. You meant it then; you mean it now; you have really done it. Your emotions may clamor against the surrender, but your will must hold firm. It is your purpose God looks at, not your feelings about that purpose. And your purpose, or will, is therefore the only thing you need to attend to.

Believe that God takes that which you have surrendered and consider that it is His. There is nothing more for you to do, except to be from now on an obedient child, for you are the Lord's now, absolutely and entirely in His hands. He has undertaken the whole care and management and forming of you, and will, according to His Word, "work in you that which is well pleasing in his sight through Jesus Christ." If you begin to question your surrender or God's acceptance of it, then your wavering faith will produce a wavering experience. You will find it a great help to put your reckoning into words and say over and over to yourself and to your God, "Lord, I am Yours. I yield myself up entirely to You, and I believe that You accept me. I leave myself with You. Work in me all the good pleasure of Your will, and I will only lie still in Your hands and trust You."

Make this a daily, definite act of your will, and many times a day recur to it, as being your continual attitude before the Lord. Confess it to yourself. Confess it to your God. Confess it to your friends. Sooner or later, you will find that you are being made into "a holy people unto the LORD, as he hath spoken."

CHAPTER 6

Difficulties Concerning Faith

The next step after consecration in the soul's progress is that of faith. And here, as in the first step, the soul encounters at once certain forms of difficulty and hindrance.

The subject of faith is involved in such a hopeless mystery to his mind that this assertion, instead of throwing light upon the way of entrance, only seems to make it more difficult and involved than ever.

"Of course it is by faith," he says, "for I know that everything in the Christian life is by faith. But that is just what makes it so hard, for I have no faith, and I do not even know what it is nor how to get it." Baffled at the very outset by this insuperable difficulty, he is plunged into darkness and almost despair.

This trouble arises from the fact that the subject of faith is very generally misunderstood; for, in reality, faith is the simplest and plainest thing in the world and the easiest of exercise.

Your idea of faith is either a religious exercise of soul or an inward, gracious disposition of heart, something tangible. When you have secured it, you can look at and rejoice over it and use it as a passport to God's favor or a coin with which to purchase His gifts. And you have been praying for faith, expecting all the while to get something like this; and never having received any such thing, you are insisting upon it that you have no faith. Now faith, in fact, is not the least like this. It is nothing at all tangible. It is simply believing God. You see something and thus know that you have sight; you believe something and thus know that you have faith. For as sight is only seeing, so faith is only believing. If you believe the truth, you are saved; if you believe a lie, you are lost. Your salvation comes, not because your faith saves you, but because it links you to the Savior who saves.

Recognize, then, the extreme simplicity of faith—that it is nothing more nor less than just believing God when He says He either has done something for us or will do it; and then trusting Him to keep His word. What does it mean to trust another to do a piece of work for me? I can only answer that it means committing the work to that other and leaving it without anxiety in his hands. All of us have many times trusted very important affairs to others in this way and have felt perfect rest in this trust because of the confidence we have had in those who have undertaken them.

How constantly do mothers trust their most precious infants to the care of babysitters and feel no shadow of anxiety! How continually we are all of us trusting our health and our lives, without a thought of fear, to cooks and coachmen, engine drivers, railway conductors, and all sorts of paid servants who have us completely at their mercy and who could, if they chose to do so, or even if they failed in the necessary carefulness, plunge us into misery or death in a moment. All this we do and make no demur about it. Upon the slightest acquaintance, often we thus put our trust in people, requiring only the general knowledge of human nature and the common rules of human intercourse as the foundation of our trust, and we never feel as if we were doing anything in the least remarkable.

Try to imagine yourself acting in your human relations as you do in your spiritual relations. When you sat down to breakfast, you would say, "I cannot eat anything on this table, for I have no faith, and I cannot believe the cook has not put poison into the coffee, or that the butcher has not sent home diseased or unhealthy meat," so you would go starving away. When you went out to your daily avocations, you would say, "I cannot ride in the railway train, for I have no faith, and therefore I cannot trust the engineer, nor the conductor, nor the builders of the carriages, nor the managers of the road." When your friends met you with any statements or your business agent with any accounts, you would say, "I am very sorry that I cannot believe you, but I have no faith and never can believe anybody." If you opened a newspaper, you would be forced to lay it down again, saying, "I really cannot believe a word this paper says, for I have no faith. I do not believe there is any such person as the queen, for I never saw her; nor any such country as Ireland, for I was never there. I have no faith, so of course I cannot believe anything that I have not actually felt and touched myself. It is a great trial, but I cannot help it, for I have no faith."

Just picture such utter folly. Ask yourself: If this want of faith in your fellowmen is so dreadful and such utter folly, what must it be when you tell God that you have no power to trust Him, nor believe His word; that it is a great trial, but you cannot help it, for you "have no faith"?

Is it possible that you can trust your fellowmen and cannot trust your God, that you can receive the "witness of men" and cannot receive the "witness of God," that you can believe man's records and cannot believe God's record, that you can commit your dearest earthly interests to your weak, failing fellow creatures without a fear and are afraid to commit your spiritual interests to the Savior who laid down His life for you and of whom it is declared that He is "able also to save them to the uttermost that come unto God by him"?

You say, I cannot believe without the Holy Spirit. Very well; will you conclude, then, that your want of faith is because of the failure of the Holy Spirit to do His work? In taking up the position that you have no faith and cannot believe, you are not only "making God a liar," but you are also showing an utter want of confidence in the Holy Spirit.

God is always ready to help our infirmities. We never have to wait for Him; He is always waiting for us. And I for my part have such absolute confidence in the Holy Ghost and in His being always ready to do His work, that I dare to say to every one of you, that you *can* believe now, at this very moment. If you do not, it is not the Spirit's fault, but your own. Put your will, then, over on the believing side. Say, "Lord, I will believe; I do believe," and continue to say it. Insist upon believing in the face of every suggestion of doubt that intrudes itself. Out of your very unbelief, throw yourself unreservedly on the Word and promises of God, and dare to abandon yourself to the keeping and saving power of the Lord Jesus. If you have ever trusted a precious interest in the hands of an earthly friend, I entreat you, trust yourself and all your spiritual interests now in the hands of your heavenly Friend, and never, *never*, *never*, allow yourself to doubt again.

Remember always that there are two things that are more utterly incompatible even than oil and water, and these two are trust and worry. Would you call it trust if you should give something into the hands of a friend to attend to for you and then should spend your nights and days in anxious thought and worry as to whether it would be rightly and successfully done? And can you call it trust when you have given the saving and keeping of your soul into the hands of the Lord if day after day and night after night you are spending hours of anxious thought and questionings about the matter?

When a believer really trusts anything, he ceases to worry about the thing he has trusted. And when he worries, it is a plain proof that he does not trust. Tested by this rule, how little real trust there is in the church of Christ! No wonder our Lord asked the pathetic question, "When the Son of man cometh, shall he find faith on the earth?" He will find plenty of work, a great deal of earnestness, and doubtless many consecrated hearts; but shall He find faith, the one thing He values more than all the rest? I remember, very early in my Christian life, having every tender and loyal impulse within me stirred to the depths by an appeal I met within a volume of old sermons, to all who loved the Lord Jesus, that they should show to others how worthy He was of being trusted by the steadfastness of their own faith in Him. As I read the inspiring words, there came to me a sudden glimpse of the privilege and the glory of being called to walk in paths so dark that only an utter recklessness of trust would be possible!

You have trusted God in a few things, and He has not failed you. Trust Him now for everything, and see if He does not do for you exceeding abundantly above all that you could ever have asked or even thought, not according to your power or capacity, but according to His own mighty power, working in you all the good pleasure of His most blessed will.

It is not hard, you find, to trust the management of the universe and of all the outward creation to the Lord. Can your case then be so much more complex and difficult than these that you need to be anxious or troubled about His management of you? Away with such unworthy doubtings! Take your stand on the power and trustworthiness of your God, and see how quickly all difficulties will vanish before a steadfast determination to believe. It is a law of spiritual life that every act of trust makes the next act less difficult, until at length, if these acts are persisted in, trusting becomes, like breathing, the natural unconscious action of the redeemed soul.

Therefore put your will into your believing. Your faith must not be a passive imbecility but an active energy. You may have to believe against every appearance, but no matter. Set your face like a flint to say, "I will believe, and I know I shall not be destroyed." If you are a child of God at all, have at least as much faith as a grain of mustard seed, and therefore you dare not say again that you "cannot trust because you have no faith." Say rather, "I can trust my Lord, and I will trust Him. And none of the powers of earth or hell shall be able to make me doubt my wonderful, glorious, faithful Redeemer!"

Be patient and trustful, and wait. This time of darkness is only permitted that "the trial of your faith, being much more precious than of gold that perisheth, though it be tried with fire, might be found unto praise and honour and glory at the appearing of Jesus Christ."

CHAPTER 7

Difficulties Concerning the Will

When the child of God has, by entire abandonment and absolute trust, stepped out of himself into Christ and has begun to know something of the blessedness of the life hid with Christ in God, there is one form of difficulty that is especially likely to start up in his path. After the first emotions of peace and rest have somewhat subsided, or if, as is sometimes the case, they have never seemed to come at all, he begins to feel such an utter unreality in the things he has been passing through that he seems to himself like a hypocrite when he says or even thinks they are real. It seems to him that his belief does not go below the surface, that it is a mere lip-belief and therefore of no account, and that his surrender is not a surrender of the heart and therefore cannot be acceptable to God. He is afraid to say he is altogether the Lord's, for fear he will be telling an untruth; and yet he cannot bring himself to say he is not.

But there is nothing here that isn't easily overcome when the Christian once thoroughly understands the principles of the new life and has learned *how* to live in it. The common thought is that this life hid with Christ in God is lived in the emotions, and consequently all the attention of the soul is directed toward them. Because emotions are satisfactory or otherwise, the soul rests or is troubled. Now the truth is that this life is not lived in the emotions at all but in the will. Therefore, if man's will is kept steadfastly abiding in its center, God's will, the varying states of emotion do not in the least disturb or affect the reality of the life.

Fenelon says that "pure religion resides in the will alone." By this he means that, as the will is the governing power in the man's nature, if the will is set right, all the rest of the nature must come into harmony. The will is the deliberate choice, the deciding power, to which all that is in the man must yield obedience.

It is sometimes thought that the emotions are the governing power in our nature. But I think all of us know, as a matter of practical experience, that there is an independent self within us, behind our emotions and behind our wishes, that decides everything and controls everything. Our emotions belong to us and are put up with and enjoyed by us, but they are not our true selves. If God is to take possession of us, it must be into this central will or personality that He enters. If, then, He is reigning there by the power of His

43

Spirit, all the rest of our nature must come under His sway, and as the will is, so is the man.

A young man of great intelligence, seeking to enter into this new life, was utterly discouraged at finding himself the slave to a chronic habit of doubting. Nothing seemed real or true to his emotions. The more he struggled, the more unreal it all became. Someone told him this secret concerning the will: that if he would only put his will over on the believing side, if he would choose to believe, he need not then trouble about his emotions, for they would find themselves compelled, sooner or later, to come into harmony.

"What!" he said. "Do you mean to tell me that I can *choose* to believe in that bold way, when nothing seems true to me? Will that kind of believing be real?"

"Yes," was the answer. "Simply put your will over on God's side, making up your mind that you will believe what He says because He says it." The young man paused a moment and then said solemnly, "I understand and will do what you say. I cannot control my emotions, but I can control my will. The new life begins to look possible to me, if it is only my will that needs to be set straight in the matter. I can give my will to God, and I do."

From that moment, disregarding all the pitiful clamoring of his emotions, which continually accused him of being a wretched hypocrite, this young man held on steadily to the decision of his will, answering every accusation with the continued assertion that he chose to believe, he meant to believe, he did believe, until at the end of a few days he found himself triumphant, with every emotion and every thought brought into captivity to the power of the Spirit of God. At times it drained all the willpower he possessed to his lips, to say that he believed, so contrary was it to all the evidence of his senses or of his emotions. But he caught the idea that his will was, after all, himself, and that if he kept that on God's side, he was doing all he could do. God alone could change his emotions or control his being. The result has been one of the grandest Christian lives I know of in its marvelous simplicity, directness, and power over sin.

A lady who had entered into this life hid with Christ was confronted by a great prospective trial. But she had learned this secret of the will, and knowing that, at the bottom, she herself did really choose the will of God for her portion, she did not pay the slightest attention to her emotions but persisted in meeting every thought concerning the trial with the words, repeated over and over, "Thy will be done! Thy will be done!" In an incredibly short space of time, every thought was brought into captivity, and she began to find even her very emotions rejoicing in the will of God.

Again, there was a lady who had a besetting sin. But she learned this secret concerning the will, and going to her closet, she said, "Lord, You see that with my emotions I love this sin, but in my real central self I hate it. Until now my emotions have had the mastery; but now I put my will into Your hands and give it up to Your working. I will never again consent in my will to yield to this sin. Take possession of my will and work in me to will and to do of Thy good pleasure." Immediately she began to find deliverance.

How do you apply this principle to your difficulties? Cease to consider your emotions, for they are only the servants. Simply regard your will, which is the real king in your being. Is that given up to God? Is that put into His hands? Does your will decide to believe? Does your will choose to obey? If this is the case, then *you* are in the Lord's hands, and you decide to believe, and you choose to obey; for your will is yourself. Get hold of this secret and discover that you can ignore your emotions and simply pay attention to the state of your will. Scripture commands you to yield yourself to God, to present yourself a living sacrifice to Him, to abide in Christ, to walk in the light, to die to self. When this feeling of unreality or hypocrisy comes, do not be troubled by it. It is only in your emotions, and it is not worth a moment's thought. Only see to it that your will is in God's hands, that your inward self is abandoned to His working, that your choice, your decision, is on His side, and leave it there.

The will is like a wise mother in a nursery. The feelings are like a set of clamoring, crying children. The mother, knowing that she is the authority figure, pursues her course lovingly and calmly in spite of all their clamors. The result is that the children are sooner or later won over to the mother's course of action and fall in with her decisions, and all is harmonious and happy. But if that mother should for a moment let in the thought that the children were the masters instead of herself, confusion would reign unchecked. In how many souls at this very moment is there nothing but confusion, simply because the feelings are allowed to govern instead of the will?

The real thing in your experience is what your will decides, not your emotions. You are far more in danger of hypocrisy and untruth in yielding to the assertions of your feelings than in holding fast to the decision of your will. I am convinced that throughout the Bible the verses concerning the "heart" do not mean the emotions, that which we now understand by the word *heart*. They mean the will, the personality of the man, the man's own central self. The object of God's dealing with man is that this "I" may be yielded up to Him and this central life abandoned to His entire control. It is not the feelings of the man God wants, but the man himself.

Do not let us make a mistake here. I say we must "give up" our wills, but I do not mean we are to be left will-less. We are not so to give up our wills as to be left like limp, nerveless creatures, without any will at all. We are simply to substitute the higher, divine, mature will of God for our foolish, misdirected wills of ignorance and immaturity. Is your face set as a flint to will what God wills? He wills that you should be entirely surrendered to Him and that you should trust Him perfectly. If you have taken the steps of surrender and faith in your will, it is your right to believe that no matter how much your feelings may clamor against it, you *are* all the Lord's, and He *has* begun to "work in you both to will and to do of His good pleasure."

The following letter is a remarkable, practical illustration of this chapter's teaching. Pasteur Theodore Monod of Paris handed it to me. It details the experience of a Presbyterian minister:

Newburgh, Sept. 26, 1842

Dear Brother,—Since I last saw you, I have been pressing forward, and yet there has been nothing remarkable in my experience of which I can speak. Indeed, I do not know that it is best to look for remarkable things. Instead, we should strive to be holy, as God is holy, pressing right on toward the mark of the prize.

The Lord deals differently with different souls, and we shouldn't attempt to copy the experience of others. Yet everyone who is seeking after a clean heart should pay attention to certain things.

There must be a personal consecration of all to God, a covenant made with God that we will be wholly and forever. I pledged myself to the Lord and laid my all upon the altar, a living sacrifice, to the best of my ability. After I rose from my knees, I was painfully conscious that there was no change in my feelings. But yet I was sure that I had, with all the sincerity and honesty of purpose of which I was capable, made an entire and eternal consecration of myself to God. I did not then consider the work as done by any means, but I determined to abide in a state of complete devotion to God, a living perpetual sacrifice. And now came the effort to do this.

I knew also that I must believe that God accepted me and dwelled in my heart. I was conscious I did not believe this, and yet I desired to do so. I read with much prayer John's first epistle and endeavored to assure my heart of God's love to me as an individual. I finally hit upon the method of living by the moment, and then I found rest.

I felt shut up to a momentary dependence upon the grace of Christ.

I would not permit the adversary to trouble me about the past or future. I agreed that I would be a child of Abraham and walk by naked faith in the Word of God and not by inward feelings and emotions. I sought to be a Bible Christian. Since that time the Lord has given me a steady victory over sins which before enslaved me. I have covenanted to walk by faith and not by feelings.

Your fellow-soldier,
William Hill

CHAPTER 8

Difficulties Concerning Guidance

You have now begun the life of faith. You have given yourself to the Lord to be His wholly and completely, and you are now entirely in His hands to be molded and fashioned according to His own divine purpose into a vessel unto His honor. Your one most earnest desire is to follow Him wherever He may lead you and to be very pliable in His hands. You are trusting Him to "work in you both to will and to do of His good pleasure." But you find a great difficulty here. You have not yet learned to know the voice of the Good Shepherd and are therefore in great doubt and perplexity as to what really is His will concerning you.

There is a way out of all these difficulties to the fully surrendered soul. The first thing is to be sure that you really do *purpose* to obey the Lord in every respect. If this is your purpose and your soul only needs to know the will of God in order to consent to it, then you surely cannot doubt His willingness to make His will known and to guide you in the right paths. There are many very clear promises in reference to this:

John 10:3–4: "'He calleth his own sheep by name, and leadeth them out. And when he putteth forth his own sheep, he goeth before them, and the sheep follow him: for they know his voice.'"

John 14:26: "'But the Comforter, which is the Holy Ghost, whom the Father will send in my name, he shall teach you all things, and bring all things to your remembrance, whatsoever I have said unto you.'"

James 1:5–6: "If any of you lack wisdom, let him ask of God, that giveth to all men liberally, and upbraideth not; and it shall be given him."

Our faith must confidently look for and expect God's guidance. This is essential, for in James 1:6–7, we are told, "Let him ask in faith, nothing wavering. For he that wavereth is like a wave of the sea driven with the wind and tossed. For let not that man think that he shall receive any thing of the Lord." God promises His divine guidance, and if you seek it, you are sure to receive it.

Next, remember that our God has all knowledge and all wisdom and that it is very possible He may guide you into paths wherein *He* knows great bless-

49

ings are awaiting you. Nevertheless, to the shortsighted human eyes around you, everything seems to result in confusion and loss. His very love for you may perhaps lead you to run counter to the loving wishes of even your dearest friends. Luke 14:26–33 and similar passages state that in order to be a disciple and follower of your Lord, you may perhaps be called upon to forsake inwardly all that you have—father or mother, or brother or sister, or husband or wife, or maybe your own life. Unless the possibility of this is clearly recognized, you will very likely get into difficulty, because it often happens that the child of God who enters upon this life of obedience is sooner or later led into paths that meet with the disapproval of those he loves best. Unless he is prepared for this and can trust the Lord through it all, he will scarcely know what to do.

How does God's guidance come to us? And how do we know His voice? There are four ways in which He reveals His will to us—through the scriptures, through providential circumstances, through the convictions of our own higher judgment, and through the inward impressions of the Holy Spirit on our minds. Where these four harmonize, it is safe to say that God speaks. If God tells me in one voice to do or to leave anything undone, He cannot possibly tell me the opposite in another voice. Therefore my rule for distinguishing the voice of God is to bring it to the test of this harmony.

The scriptures come first. If you are in doubt upon any subject, you must, first of all, consult the Bible about it and see whether there is any law there to direct you. Until you have found and obeyed God's will as it is there revealed, you must not ask nor expect a separate, direct, personal revelation. Where our Father has written out for us a plain direction about anything, He will not of course make a special revelation to us about that thing. And if we fail to search out and obey the scripture rule, where there is one, and look instead for an inward voice, we open ourselves to delusions and almost inevitably get into error. The Bible does not always give a rule for every particular course of action, and in these cases we need and must expect guidance in other ways. But the scriptures are far more explicit, even about details, than most people think, and there are not many important affairs in life for which a clear direction may not be found in God's book.

If, therefore, you find yourself in perplexity, first of all search and see whether the Bible speaks on the point in question, asking God to make plain to you, by the power of His Spirit, through the scriptures, what is His mind. And whatever shall seem to you plainly taught there, obey. No special guidance will ever be given about a point on which the scriptures are explicit, nor could any guidance ever be contrary to the scriptures.

Remember that the Bible is a book of principles and not a book of disjointed aphorisms. Isolated texts can be made to give approval to things to which the principles of scripture are totally opposed.

If, however, upon searching the Bible you do not find any principles that will settle your special point of difficulty, then seek guidance in the other ways mentioned, and God will surely voice Himself to you, by a conviction of your judgment, by providential circumstances, or by a clear inward impression. If any one of these tests fails, it is not safe to proceed, but wait in quiet trust until the Lord shows you the point of harmony, which He surely will, sooner or later, if it is His voice that is speaking. Anything that is out of this divine harmony must be rejected as not coming from God.

Never forget that "impressions" can come from other sources as well as from the Holy Spirit. The strong personalities of those around us are the source of a great many of our impressions. Impressions also arise often from our wrong physical conditions, which color things far more than we dream. And finally, impressions come from spiritual enemies. These spiritual enemies, whoever or whatever they may be, must by necessity communicate with us by means of our spiritual faculties, so their voices will be, as the voice of God is, an inward impression made upon our spirits. It is not enough to have a "leading." We must find out the source of that leading before we give ourselves up to follow it. It is not enough, either, for the leading to be very "remarkable," or the coincidences to be very striking, to stamp it as being surely from God. In all ages of the world, evil and deceiving agencies have been able to work miracles, foretell events, reveal secrets, and give "signs." And God's people have always been emphatically warned about being deceived thereby.

It is essential, therefore, that our "leadings" should all be tested by the teachings of scripture. But this alone is not enough. They must be tested as well by our own spiritually enlightened judgment or what is familiarly called "common sense."

Some, however, may say here, "But I thought we were not to depend on our human understanding in divine things." We are not to depend on our unenlightened human understanding but upon our human judgment and common sense enlightened by the Spirit of God. That is, God will speak to us through the abilities He has Himself given us and not independently of them. The third test to which our impressions must be brought is that of providential circumstances. If a "leading" is of God, the way will always open for it. Our Lord assures us of this when He says, in John 10:4, "And when he putteth forth his own sheep, *he goeth before them*, and the sheep *follow* him: for they know his voice." Notice here the expressions "goeth before" and "follow." He goes before to open a way, and we are to follow in the way He opens. It is never a sign of a divine leading when the Christian insists on opening his own way and riding roughshod over all opposing things. If the Lord "goes before" us, He will open the door for us, and we shall not need to batter down doors for ourselves.

The fourth point is that just as our impressions must be tested, as I have shown, by the other three voices, so must these other voices be tested by our inward impressions. If we feel a "stop in our minds" about anything, we must wait until that is removed before acting. A Christian who had advanced with unusual rapidity in the divine life gave me, as her secret, this simple direction: "I always mind the checks." We must not ignore the voice of our inward impressions. When the spiritual world is opened to a soul, both the good and the evil there will meet it. But we must not be discouraged by this. With the four tests I have mentioned and a divine sense of "oughtness" derived from the harmony of all of God's voices, there is nothing to fear. And to me it seems that the blessedness and joy of this direct communication of God's will to us is one of our grandest privileges. That God *cares* enough about us to desire to regulate the details of our lives is the strongest proof of love He could give. God's law, therefore, is only another name of God's love; and the more minutely that law descends into the details of our lives, the surer we are made of the depth and reality of the love. We can never know the full joy and privileges of the life hid with Christ in God until we have learned the lesson of daily and hourly guidance.

God's promise is that He will work in us to *will* as well as to do of His good pleasure. This means, of course, that He will take possession of our will and work it for us. His suggestions will come to us, not so much as commands from the outside as desires springing up within. This makes it a service of perfect liberty. It is always easy to do what we desire to do, no matter how difficult the accompanying circumstances may be. He "writes his laws on our hearts and on our minds," so that our affection and our understanding embrace them, and we are *drawn* to obey instead of being *driven* to it.

It sometimes happens, however, that in spite of all our efforts to discover the truth, the divine sense of "oughtness" does not seem to come, and our doubts and perplexities continue unenlightened. In such a case there is nothing to do but to wait until the light comes. But we must wait in faith and in an attitude of entire surrender, saying a continual yes to the will of our Lord, let it be what it may. If the suggestion is from Him, it will continue and strengthen; if it is not from Him, it will disappear. If it continues, if every time we are brought into close communion with the Lord it seems to return, if it troubles us in our moments of prayer and disturbs all our peace, and if it conforms to the test of the divine harmony, we may then feel sure it is from God, and we must yield to it or suffer an unspeakable loss.

In all doubtful things stand still and refrain from action until God gives you light to know more clearly His mind concerning them. Very often you will find that the doubt has been His voice calling you to come into more perfect conformity to His will. But sometimes these doubtful things are only temptations, or morbid feelings, to which it would be most unwise for you to yield. The only safe way is to wait until you can act in faith, for "whatsoever is not of faith is sin."

Take all your present perplexities, then, to the Lord. Tell Him you only want to know and obey His voice, and ask Him to make it plain to you. Promise Him that you will obey, whatever it may be. Believe implicitly that He is guiding you according to His Word. In all doubtful things, wait for clear light. Look and listen for His voice continually. And the moment you are sure of it, then, but not until then, yield an immediate obedience. Trust Him to make you forget the impression if it is not His will. And if it continues and is in harmony with all His other voices, do not be afraid to obey.

Above everything else, trust Him. Nowhere is faith more needed than here. He has promised to guide. You have asked Him to do it. And now believe that He does, and take what comes as being His guidance. No earthly parent or master could guide his children or servants if they should refuse to take his commands as being really the expression of his will. And God *cannot* guide those souls who never trust Him enough to believe that He is doing it.

Above all, do not be afraid of this blessed life, lived hour by hour and day by day under the guidance of your Lord! If He seeks to bring you out of the world and into very close conformity to Himself, do not shrink from it. It is your most blessed privilege. Rejoice in it. Embrace it eagerly. Let everything go that it may be yours.

CHAPTER 9

Difficulties Concerning Doubts

A great many Christians are slaves to a chronic habit of doubting. I do not mean doubts as to the existence of God or the truths of the Bible, but doubts as to their own personal relations with the God in whom they profess to believe, doubts as to the forgiveness of their sins, doubts as to their hopes of heaven, and doubts about their own inward experience. Their lives are made wretched, their usefulness is effectually hindered, and their communion with God is continually broken by their doubts.

Many of us remember our childish fascination, and yet horror, in the story of Christian's imprisonment in Doubting Castle by the wicked giant Despair and our exultant sympathy in his escape through those massive gates and from the cruel tyrant. Little did we suspect then that we should ever find ourselves taken prisoner by the same giant and imprisoned in the same castle. But I fear that each one of us, if we were perfectly honest, would have to confess to at least one such experience and some of us perhaps to a great many.

It seems strange that people, whose very name of believers implies that their one chief characteristic is that they believe, should have to confess that they have doubts. And yet it is such a universal habit that if the name were to be given over again, the only fitting and descriptive name that could be given to many of God's children would have to be that of doubters. In fact, most Christians have settled down under their doubts as to a sort of inevitable malady from which they suffer acutely but to which they must try to be resigned as a part of the necessary discipline of this earthly life; and they lament over their doubts as a man might lament over his rheumatism, making themselves out as "interesting cases" of special and peculiar trial, which require the tenderest sympathy and the utmost consideration.

This is too often true even of believers who are earnestly longing to enter upon the life and walk of faith and who have made, perhaps, many steps toward it. They may have gotten rid of the old doubts that once tormented them—whether their sins are really forgiven and whether they shall, after all, get safe to heaven—but they have not gotten rid of doubting. They have simply shifted the habit to a higher platform. This includes an interminable array of doubts concerning most of the declarations and promises our Father has made to His children. One after another they fight with these promises and refuse to believe them until they can have some more reliable proof of their being true than the simple word of their God; and then they wonder why they are permitted to walk in such darkness and look upon themselves almost in the light of martyrs and groan under the peculiar spiritual conflicts they are compelled to endure.

Doubts would be better named spiritual rebellions! Our fight is a fight of faith; and the moment we let in doubts, our fight ceases and our rebellion begins.

To drunkards and doubters alike, I would dare to do nothing else but proclaim the perfect deliverance which the Lord Jesus Christ has in store for them. I would beseech, entreat, and beg them, with all the power at my command, to avail themselves of that deliverance and be free from the bonds of their sin. In the sight of God, I truly believe doubting is in some cases as displeasing as lying. It certainly is more dishonoring to Him, for it attacks His truthfulness and defames His character. John says that "he that believeth not God hath made him a liar," and it seems to me that hardly anything could be worse than thus to fasten on God the character of being a liar! Have you ever thought of this as the result of your doubting?

I remember seeing once the indignation and sorrow of a mother's heart deeply stirred by a little doubting on the part of one of her children. She had brought two little girls to my house to leave them while she did some errands. One of them, with the happy confidence of childhood, abandoned herself to all the pleasures she could find in my nursery and sang and played until her mother's return. The other one, with the wretched caution and mistrust of maturity, sat down alone in a corner to wonder, first, whether her mother would remember to come back for her and to fear she would be forgotten and then to imagine her mother would be glad of the chance to get rid of her anyhow because she was such a naughty girl. She ended with working herself up into a perfect frenzy of despair. I shall not easily forget the look on that mother's face when upon her return the weeping little girl told what was the matter with her. Grief, wounded love, indignation, and pity all strove together for mastery, and the mother hardly knew who was most at fault, herself or the child, that such doubts should be possible.

Have you ever indulged in hard thoughts against those who have, as you think, injured you? Have you ever brooded over their unkindnesses, pried into their malice, and imagined all sorts of wrong and uncomfortable things about them? It made you wretched, of course; but it is a fascinating sort of wretchedness that you could not easily give up.

The luxury of doubting is very similar. Things have gone wrong with you in your experience. Your temptations have been strange. Your "case" is different from others. What is more natural than to conclude that for some reason God has forsaken you and does not love you and is indifferent to your welfare? How irresistible is the conviction that you are too wicked for Him to care for or too difficult for Him to manage! You do not mean to blame Him or accuse Him of injustice, for you feel that His indifference and rejection of you are, because of your unworthiness, fully deserved. Although you think it is yourself you are doubting, you are really doubting the Lord and are indulging in as hard and wrong thoughts of Him as ever you did of a human enemy. For He declares that He came to save, not the righteous, but sinners; and your very sinfulness and unworthiness, instead of being a reason why He should not love you and care for you, are really your chief claim upon His love and His care.

He says, "What man of you, having an hundred sheep, if he lose one of them, doth not leave the ninety and nine in the wilderness, and go after that which is lost, until he find it?" Any thoughts of Him, therefore, that are different from this that He Himself has said, are hard thoughts; and to indulge in them is far worse than to indulge in hard thoughts of any earthly friend or foe. From beginning to end of your Christian life it is always sinful to indulge in doubts. Doubts and discouragements are all from an evil source and are always untrue. A direct and emphatic denial is the only way to meet them.

Deliverance from the bondage of doubting must be by the same means as the deliverance from any other sin. It is found in Christ, and in Him alone. Hand your doubting over to Him as you have learned to hand your other temptations. I believe the only effectual remedy is to take a pledge against it, as you would urge a drunkard to do against drink, trusting in the Lord alone to keep you steadfast.

Like any other sin, the stronghold is in the will, and the will or purpose to doubt must be surrendered exactly as you surrender the will or purpose to yield to any other temptation. God always takes possession of a surrendered will. And if we come to the point of saying that we will not doubt and surrender this central fortress of our nature to Him, His blessed Spirit will begin at once to "work in us all the good pleasure of His will," and we shall find ourselves kept from doubting by His mighty and overcoming power.

The liberty to doubt must be given up forever; and we must consent to a continuous life of inevitable trust. Make a definite transaction of this surrender of doubting and come to a point about it. It will not do to give it up by degrees. The total-abstinence principle is the only effectual one here.

Then, the surrender once made, rest absolutely upon the Lord for deliverance in each time of temptation. The moment the assault comes, lift up the shield of faith against it. Hand the very first suggestion of doubt over to the Lord and let Him manage it. Refuse to entertain the doubt a single moment. Do not stop to argue out the matter with yourself or with your doubts. Pay no attention to them whatever, but treat them with the utmost contempt. Shut your door in their very face, and emphatically deny every word they say to you. Then let the doubts clamor as they may. They cannot hurt you if you will not let them in.

Often it has happened to me to find, on awaking in the morning, a perfect army of doubts clamoring at my door for admittance. I have been compelled to lift up the "shield of faith" the moment I have become conscious of these suggestions of doubt, and handing the whole army over to the Lord to conquer, I have begun to assert, over and over, my faith in Him, in the simple words "God *is* my Father; I *am* His forgiven child; He *does* love me; Jesus saves me; Jesus saves me now!" The victory is always complete. The enemy has come in like a flood, but the "Spirit of the Lord has lifted up a standard against him," and my doubts have been put to flight. Dear doubting souls, go and do likewise, and a similar victory shall be yours. No earthly father has ever declared or shown his fatherhood a fraction as unmistakably or as lovingly as your heavenly Father has declared and shown His. If you would not "make God a liar," therefore, make your believing as inevitable and necessary a thing as your obedience. You would obey God, I believe, even though you should die in the act. Believe Him, also, even though the effort to believe should cost you your life. The conflict may be very severe; it may seem at times unendurable. But let your unchanging declaration be from this point on "Though He slay me, yet will I trust in Him." When doubts come, meet them, not with arguments, but with affirmations of faith. All doubts are an attack of the enemy. The Holy Spirit never suggests them, never. He is the comforter, not the accuser; and He never shows us our need without at the same time revealing the divine supply.

Turn from them with horror, as you would from blasphemy, for they *are* blasphemy. You cannot, perhaps, hinder the suggestions of doubt from coming to you, any more than you can hinder the boys in the street from swearing as you go by. Just as you can refuse to listen to the boys or join in their oaths, so you can also refuse to listen to the doubts or join in with them. Write out your determination never to doubt again. Make it a real transaction between your soul and the Lord. Give up your liberty to doubt forever. Put your will in this matter over on the Lord's side, and trust Him to keep you from falling. Tell Him all about your utter weakness and your long-encouraged habits of doubt, and how helpless you are before it, and commit the whole battle to Him. Tell Him you *will* not doubt again, putting forth all your willpower on

His side, and against His enemy and yours. Then, from now on, keep your face steadfastly "looking unto Jesus," away from yourself and away from your doubts, holding fast the profession of your faith without wavering, because "He is faithful that hath promised." Rely on *His* faithfulness, not on your own. You have committed the keeping of your soul to Him as unto a "faithful creator," and never again admit the possibility of His being unfaithful. Sooner or later you will come to *know* that it is true, and all doubts will vanish in the blaze of the glory of the absolute faithfulness of God!

Doubts and discouragements are, I believe, inlets by which evil enters, while faith is an impregnable wall against all evil.

Deliverance lies at your door. Try my plan, I beseech you, and see if it will not be true, that "according to your faith" it shall inevitably be unto you.

CHAPTER 10

Difficulties Concerning Temptations

Certain great mistakes are made concerning this matter of temptation in the practical working out of the life of faith.

First of all, people seem to expect that after the soul has entered into salvation through Christ, temptations will cease; and they think that the promised deliverance is to be not only from yielding to temptation but even also from being tempted. Next, they make the mistake of looking upon temptation as sin and of blaming themselves for suggestions of evil, even while they abhor them. This brings them into condemnation and discouragement. And continued discouragement always ends at last in actual sin. Sin makes an easy prey of a discouraged soul, so that we fall often from the very fear of having fallen.

To meet the first of these difficulties, it is only necessary to refer to the scripture declarations that state that the Christian life is to be throughout a warfare. It is to be especially so when we are "seated in heavenly places in Christ Jesus" and are called to wrestle against spiritual enemies, whose power and skill to tempt us must doubtless be far superior to any we have ever encountered before. When the children of Israel first left Egypt, the Lord did not lead them through the country of the Philistines, although that was the nearest way. "For God said, 'Lest peradventure the people repent when they see war, and they return to Egypt.' " But afterward, when they had learned how to trust Him better, He permitted their enemies to attack them. Moreover, even in their wilderness journey they met with but few enemies and fought but few battles compared to those they encountered in the land of Canaan, where they found seven great nations and thirty-one kings to conquer, besides taking walled cities and overcoming giants.

They could not fight until they went into the land where these enemies were. The very power of your temptations may perhaps be one of the strongest proofs that you really are in the land of promise you have been seeking to enter because they are temptations peculiar to that land. Consequently, never allow them to cause you to question the fact of your having entered it.

The second mistake is not quite so easy to deal with. It seems hardly worthwhile to say that temptation is not sin, and yet much distress arises from not understanding this fact. It is the enemy's grand ruse for entrapping us. He comes and whispers suggestions of evil to us—doubts, blasphemies,

61

jealousies, envyings, and pride—and then turns round and says, "Oh, how wicked you must be to think such things! It is very plain that you are not trusting the Lord, for if you had been, it would be impossible for these things to have entered your heart."

This reasoning sounds so very plausible that we often accept it as true and so come under condemnation and are filled with discouragement. Then it is easy for temptation to develop into actual sin. One of the most fatal things in the life of faith is discouragement. One of the most helpful is confidence. A very wise man once said that in overcoming temptations confidence was the first thing, confidence the second, and confidence the third. We must *expect* to conquer. That is why the Lord said so often to Joshua, "Be strong and of good courage." "Be not afraid, neither be thou dismayed." "Only be thou strong and very courageous." And it is also the reason He says to us, "Let not your heart be troubled, neither let it be afraid." The power of temptation is in the fainting of our own hearts. The enemy knows this well, and he always begins his assaults by discouraging us, if he can in any way accomplish it.

This discouragement arises sometimes from what we think is a righteous grief and disgust at ourselves that such things *could* be any temptation to us but which is really mortification coming from the fact that we have been indulging in a secret self-congratulation that our tastes were too pure or our separation from the world was too complete for such things to tempt us. This mortification and discouragement, though they present an appearance of true humility, are really a far worse condition than the temptation itself, for they are nothing but the results of wounded self-love. True humility can bear to see its own utter weakness and foolishness revealed because it never expected anything from itself and knows that its only hope and expectation must be in God. Therefore, instead of discouraging the humble soul from trusting, such revelations drive it to a deeper and more complete trust. But the counterfeit humility that self-love produces plunges the soul into the depths of a faithless discouragement and drives it into the very sin with which it is so distressed.

An allegory illustrates this wonderfully. Satan called together a council of his servants to consult how they might make a good man sin.

One evil spirit started up and said, "I will make him sin."

"How will you do it?" asked Satan.

"I will set before him the pleasures of sin," was the reply. "I will tell him of its delights and the rich rewards it brings."

"Ah," said Satan, "that will not do. He has tried it and knows better than that."

Then another imp started up and said, "I will make him sin."

"What will you do?" asked Satan.

"I will tell him of the pains and sorrows of virtue. I will show him that virtue has no delights and brings no rewards."

"Ah no!" exclaimed Satan. "That will not do at all, for he has tried it and knows that 'Wisdom's ways *are* ways of pleasantness, and all her paths are peace.'"

"Well," said another imp, starting up, "I will undertake to make him sin."

"And what will you do?" asked Satan, again.

"I will discourage his soul," was the short reply.

"Ah, that will do!" cried Satan. "That will do! We shall conquer him now."

But if we fail to recognize the truth about temptation, fleeing from discouragement is impossible. If the temptations are our own fault, we cannot help being discouraged. But they are not. The Bible says, "Blessed is the man that endureth temptation," and we are exhorted to "count it all joy when we fall into divers temptations." Temptation, therefore, cannot be sin. The truth is, it is no more a sin to hear these whispers and suggestions of evil in our souls than it is for us to hear the wicked talk of bad men as we pass along the street. The sin comes, in either case, only by our stopping and joining in with them.

A dear lady once came to me under great darkness, simply from not understanding this. She had been living very happily in the life of faith for some time and had been so free from temptation as almost to begin to think she would never be tempted again. She had lived a very sheltered, innocent life, and these thoughts seemed so awful to her that she felt she must be one of the most wicked of sinners to be capable of having them. She began by thinking that she could not possibly have entered into the rest of faith and ended by concluding that she had never been born again. I told her that these dreadful thoughts were purely and simply temptations, and that she herself was not to blame for them at all. She could not help them any more than she could help hearing if a wicked man should pour out his blasphemies in her presence. And I urged her to recognize and treat them as temptations only and not to blame herself or be discouraged but rather to turn at once to the Lord and commit them to Him. She grasped the truth, and the next time these blasphemous thoughts came, she said inwardly to the enemy, "I have found you out now. It is you who are suggesting these dreadful thoughts to me, and I hate them and will have nothing to do with them. The Lord is my helper. Take them to Him and settle them in His presence." Immediately the baffled enemy, finding himself discovered, fled in confusion, and her soul was perfectly delivered.

Another great mistake about temptations is in thinking that all time spent in combating them is lost. Hours pass, and we seem to have made no progress because we have been so beset with temptations. But it often happens that we have been serving God far more truly during these hours than in our times of comparative freedom from temptation. For we are fighting our Lord's battles when we are fighting temptation, and hours are often worth days to us under these circumstances. We read, "Blessed is the man that *endureth* temptation." Nothing so cultivates the grace of patience as the endurance of temptation, and nothing so drives the soul to an utter dependence upon the Lord Jesus as its continuance. And finally, nothing brings more praise and honor and glory to our Lord Himself than the trial of our faith that comes through manifold temptations. We cannot wonder, therefore, any longer at the exhortation with which the Holy Spirit opens the book of James: "Count it all joy when ye fall into divers temptations; knowing this, that the trying of your faith worketh patience. But let patience have her perfect work, that ye may be perfect and entire, wanting nothing."

The way of victory over temptation is by faith. We have discovered our own utter helplessness and know that we cannot do anything for ourselves. And we have learned that our only way, therefore, is to hand the temptation over to our Lord and trust Him to conquer it for us. But when we put it into His hands, we must *leave* it there. It seems impossible to believe that the Lord can or will manage our temptations without our help. To go on patiently "enduring" the continuance of a temptation without yielding to it and also without snatching ourselves out of the Lord's hands in regard to it is a wonderful victory for our impatient natures, but it is a victory we must gain if we would do what will please God.

We must then commit ourselves to the Lord for victory over our temptations, as we committed ourselves at first for forgiveness. And we must leave ourselves just as utterly in His hands for one as for the other.

Thousands of God's children have done this and can testify today that marvelous victories have been gained for them over numberless temptations, and that they have in very truth been made "more than conquerors" through Him who loves them.

CHAPTER 11

Difficulties Concerning Failures

The very title of this chapter may perhaps startle some. "Failures. . . ," they will say. "We thought there were no failures in this life of faith!"

There ought not to be and need not be; but, as a fact, there sometimes are, and we must deal with the facts and not with theories. No safe teacher of this interior life ever says that it becomes impossible to sin; they only insist that sin ceases to be a necessity, and that a possibility of continual victory is opened before us. And there are very few, if any, who do not confess that, as to their own actual experience, they have at times been overcome by at least a momentary temptation.

In speaking of sin here, I mean conscious, known sin, not sins of ignorance or what is called the inevitable sin of our nature, which are all met by the provisions of Christ and do not disturb our fellowship with God. A little baby girl was playing about the library one warm summer afternoon, while her father was resting on the lounge. A pretty inkstand on the table took the child's fancy, and unnoticed by anyone, she climbed on a chair and secured it. Then, walking over to her father with an air of childish triumph, she turned it upside down on the white expanse of his shirt bosom and laughed with glee as she saw the black streams trickling down on every side.

This was a very wrong thing for the child to do, but it could not be called sin, for she knew no better. When a believer enters upon the highway of holiness, he finds himself surprised into sin. He is tempted either to be utterly discouraged and to give everything up as lost, or else in order to preserve the doctrines untouched, he feels it necessary to cover up his sin, calling it an infirmity and refusing to be candid and aboveboard about it. Either of these courses is equally fatal to any real growth and progress in the life of holiness. The only way is to face the sad fact at once, call the thing by its right name, and discover, if possible, the reason and the remedy. This life of union with God requires the utmost honesty with Him and with ourselves.

A sudden failure is no reason for being discouraged and giving up all as lost. Neither is the integrity of our doctrine touched by it. We are not preaching a *state*, but a *walk*. The highway of holiness is not a *place*, but a *way*. Sanctification is not a thing to be picked up at a certain stage of our experience and forever after possessed, but it is a life to be lived day by day and hour by hour. We may for a moment turn aside from a path, but the path is not obliterated by our wandering and can be instantly regained. The great point is an instant return to God. Our sin is no reason for ceasing to trust but only an unanswerable argument why we must trust more fully than ever. From whatever cause we have been betrayed into failure, it is very certain that there is no remedy to be found in discouragement. A child who is learning to walk may lie down in despair when he has fallen and refuse to take another step; a believer who is seeking to learn how to live and walk by faith may give up in despair because of having fallen into sin. The only way in both cases is to get right up and try again. When the children of Israel had met with that disastrous defeat, soon after their entrance into the land, before the little city of Ai, they were all so utterly discouraged that we read: "Wherefore the hearts of the people melted, and became as water. And Joshua rent his clothes, and fell to the earth upon his face before the ark of the LORD until the eventide, he and the elders of Israel, and put dust upon their heads. And Joshua said, Alas, O, Lord GOD, wherefore hast thou at all brought this people over Jordan, to deliver us into the hand of the Amorites, to destroy us? would to God we had been content, and dwelt on the other side Jordan! O LORD, what shall I say, when Israel turneth their backs before their enemies!"

What a wail of despair this was! And how exactly it is repeated by many a child of God in the present day, whose heart, because of a defeat, melts and becomes as water. He cries out, " 'Would to God we had been content, and dwelt on the other side Jordan!' " and predicts for itself further failures and even utter discomfiture before its enemies. No doubt Joshua thought then, as we are apt to think now, that discouragement and despair were the only proper and safe condition after such a failure. But God thought otherwise. "And the LORD said unto Joshua, Get thee up; wherefore liest thou thus upon thy face?"

A little girl once expressed this feeling to me with a child's outspoken candor. She asked whether the Lord Jesus always forgave us for our sins as soon as we asked Him, and I had said, "Yes, of course He does."

"*Just* as soon?" she repeated doubtingly.

"Yes," I replied, "the very minute we ask, He forgives us."

"Well," she said deliberately, "I cannot believe that. I should think He would make us feel sorry for two or three days first. And then I should think He would make us ask Him a great many times and in a very pretty way, too, not just in common talk. And I believe that *is* the way He does, and you need not try to make me think He forgives me right at once, no matter what the Bible says."

She only *said* what most Christians *think*, and what is worse, what most

Christians act on, making their discouragement and their very remorse separate them infinitely further off from God than their sin would have done. Yet it is so totally contrary to the way we like our children to act toward us that I wonder how we ever could have conceived such an idea of God. How a mother grieves when a naughty child goes off alone in despairing remorse and doubts her willingness to forgive; and how, on the other hand, her whole heart goes out in welcoming love to the repentant little one who runs to her at once and begs her forgiveness! The fact is that the same moment that brings the consciousness of sin ought to bring also the confession and the consciousness of forgiveness. We can only walk this path by "looking continually unto Jesus," moment by moment. And if our eyes are turned away from Him to look upon our own sin and our own weakness, we shall leave the path at once. The believer who has entered upon this highway must flee with it instantly to the Lord, if he finds himself overcome by sin. But he must do as the children of Israel did, rise up *early* in the morning," and "*run*" to the place where the evil thing is hidden and take it out of its hiding place, and lay it "out before the LORD." He must confess his sin. And then he must stone it with stones and burn it with fire and utterly put it away from him and raise over it a great heap of stones that it may be forever hidden from his sight. He must claim by faith an immediate forgiveness and an immediate cleansing and must go on trusting harder and more absolutely than ever.

As soon as Israel's sin had been brought to light and put away, God's word came again in a message of glorious encouragement: "Fear not, neither be thou dismayed. . .see, I have given into thy hand the king of Ai, and his people, and his city, and his land." Our courage must rise higher than ever, and we must abandon ourselves more completely to the Lord that His mighty power may the more perfectly work in us "all the good pleasure of His will." We must forget our sin as soon as it is thus confessed and forgiven. We must not dwell on it and examine it and indulge in a luxury of distress and remorse. An earnest Christian man, an active worker in the church, had been living for several months in an experience of great peace and joy. He was suddenly overcome by a temptation to treat a brother unkindly. He spent three years of utter misery going further and further away from God and being gradually drawn off into one sin after another until his life was a curse to himself and to all around him. His health failed under the terrible burden, and his reason threatened to fail him. Later a Christian lady who understood this truth about sin that I have been trying to explain found out his trouble in a few minutes' conversation. At once she said, "You sinned in that act. There is no doubt about it, and I do not want you to try to excuse it. But have you never confessed it to the Lord and asked Him to forgive you?"

"Confessed it!" he exclaimed. "Why, it seems to me I have done nothing but confess it and beg God to forgive me, night and day, for all these three dreadful years."

"And you have never believed He did forgive you?" asked the lady.

"No," said the poor man, "how could I, for I never *felt* as if He did."

"But suppose He had said He forgave you—would not that have done as well as for you to feel it?"

"Oh yes," replied the man. "If God said it, of course I would believe it."

"Very well, He does say so," was the lady's answer. She turned to the verse we have taken above (1 John 1:9) and read it aloud. "Now," she continued, "you have been all these three years confessing and confessing your sin, and all the while God's record has been declaring that He was faithful and just to forgive it and to cleanse you, and yet you have never once believed it. You have been 'making God a liar' all this while by refusing to believe His record."

The poor man saw the whole thing and was dumb with amazement and consternation. When the lady proposed that they should kneel down and he should confess his past unbelief and sin and should claim, then and there, a present forgiveness and a present cleansing, he obeyed like one in a maze. But the result was glorious. The light broke in, his darkness vanished, and he began aloud to praise God for the wonderful deliverance. In a few minutes his soul was enabled to traverse back by faith the whole long weary journey that he had been three years in making, and he found himself once more resting in the Lord and rejoicing in the fullness of His salvation.

The truth is, the only remedy, after all, is to trust in the Lord. And if this is all we ought to do and all we can do, is it not better to do it at once? It is a life and walk of *faith* we have entered upon; and if we fail in it, our only recovery must lie in an increase of faith, not in a lessening of it.

Let every failure then, if any occur, drive you instantly to the Lord with a more complete abandonment and a more perfect trust. If you do this, you will find that, sad as it is, your failure has not taken you out of the land of rest nor broken for long your sweet communion with Him.

Having shown the way of deliverance from failure, I would now say a little as to the causes of failure in this life of full salvation. The causes do not lie in the strength of the temptation, nor in our own weakness, nor above all in any lack in the power or willingness of our Savior to save us. The promise to Israel was positive: "There shall not any man be able to stand before thee all the days of thy life." And the promise to us is equally positive: "God is faithful, who will not suffer you to be tempted above that ye are able; but will with the temptation also make a way to escape, that ye may be able to bear it." Anything cherished in the heart which is contrary to the will of God, let it seem ever so insignificant or be ever so deeply hidden, will cause us to fall before our enemies. The moment, therefore, that a believer who is walking in this interior life meets with a defeat, he must at once seek for the cause, not in the strength of that particular enemy, but in something behind—some hidden want of consecration lying at the very center of his being. I believe our blessed guide, the indwelling Holy Spirit, is always secretly discovering these things to us by continual little checks and pangs of conscience so that we are left without excuse. But it is very easy to disregard His gentle voice and insist upon it to ourselves that all is right while the fatal evil continues hidden in our midst, causing defeat in most unexpected quarters.

We had moved into a new house, and in looking over it to see if it was all ready for occupancy, I noticed in the cellar a very clean-looking cider cask headed up at both ends. I debated with myself whether I should have it taken out of the cellar and opened to see what was in it but decided to leave it undisturbed. I did not feel quite easy but reasoned away my scruples and left it. Every spring and fall, when housecleaning time came on, I would remember that cask with a little twinge of my housewifely conscience, feeling I could not quite rest in the thought of a perfectly clean house while it remained unopened. For two or three years the innocent-looking cask stood quietly in our cellar. Then, most unaccountably, moths began to fill our house. I used every possible precaution against them and made every effort to eradicate them but in vain. They increased rapidly and threatened to ruin everything we had. I suspected our carpets as being the cause and subjected them to a thorough cleaning. I suspected our furniture and had it newly upholstered. I suspected all sorts of impossible things. At last the thought of the cask flashed on me. At once I had it brought up out of the cellar and the head knocked in, and I think it safe to say that thousands of moths poured out. In the same way, some innocent-looking habit or indulgence, some apparently unimportant and safe thing, about which, however, we have now and then little twinges of conscience—something which is not brought out fairly into the light and investigated under the searching eye of God—lies at the root of most of the failure in this interior life. *All* is not given up. Some secret corner is kept locked against the entrance of the Lord. Some evil thing is hidden in the recesses of our hearts, and therefore we cannot stand before our enemies but find ourselves smitten down in their presence.

In order to prevent failure or to discover its cause if we find we have failed, it is necessary to keep continually before us this prayer: "Search me, O

God, and know my heart; try me, and know my thoughts: and see if there be any wicked way in me, and lead me in the way everlasting."

Let me beg of you, however, dear Christians, do not think because I have said all this about failure that I believe in it. There is no necessity for it whatever. The Lord Jesus *is* able, according to the declaration concerning Him, to deliver us out of the hands of our enemies that we may "serve him without fear, in holiness and righteousness before him, all the days of our life."

CHAPTER 12

Is God in Everything?

One of the greatest obstacles to an unwavering experience in the interior life is the difficulty of seeing God in everything. People say, "I can easily submit to things that come from God, but I cannot submit to man, and most of my trials and crosses come through human instrumentality." Or they say, "It is all well enough to talk of trusting, but when I commit a matter to God, man is sure to come in and disarrange it all. And while I have no difficulty in trusting God, I do see serious difficulties in the way of trusting men."

Nearly everything in life comes to us through human instrumentalities, and most of our trials are the result of somebody's failure or ignorance or carelessness or sin. We know God cannot be the author of these things, and yet, unless He is the agent in the matter, how can we say to Him about it, "Thy will be done"?

Moreover, things in which we can see God's hand always have a sweetness in them that comforts while it wounds. But the trials inflicted by man are full of nothing but bitterness.

What is needed, then, is to see God in everything and to receive everything directly from His hands with no intervention of second causes. And it is to this that we must be brought before we can know an abiding experience of entire abandonment and perfect trust. Our abandonment must be to God, not to man. And our trust must be in Him, not in any arm of flesh, or we shall fail at the first trial.

The question here confronts us at once, "But is God in everything, and have we any warrant from the scripture for receiving everything from His hands without regarding the second causes that may have been instrumental in bringing them about?" I answer to this, unhesitatingly, "Yes." To the children of God, everything comes directly from their Father's hand, no matter who or what may have been the apparent agents. There are no "second causes" for them.

The whole teaching of scripture asserts and implies this. Not a sparrow falls to the ground without our Father. The very hairs of our head are all numbered. We are not to be careful about anything, because our Father cares for us. We are not to avenge ourselves, because our Father has charged Himself with our defense. We are not to fear, for the Lord is on our side. No one can be against us, because He is for us. We shall not want, for He is our Shepherd.

When we pass through the rivers, they shall not overflow us, and when we walk through the fire, we shall not be burned, because He will be with us. He shuts the mouths of lions that they cannot hurt us. "He hath said, 'I will never leave thee, nor forsake thee.' So that we may boldly say, The Lord is my helper, and I will not fear what man shall do unto me."

To my own mind, these scriptures, and many others like them, settle forever the question as to the power of "second causes" in the life of the children of God. Second causes must all be under the control of our Father, and not one of them can touch us except with His knowledge and by His permission. It may be the sin of man that originates the action, and therefore the thing itself cannot be said to be the will of God; but by the time it reaches us, it has become God's will for us and must be accepted as directly from His hands. No man or company of men, no power in earth or heaven can touch that soul that is abiding in Christ without first passing through His encircling presence and receiving the seal of His permission. If God be for us, it matters not who may be against us; nothing can disturb or harm us except He shall see that it is best for us and shall stand aside to let it pass.

If the child is in his father's arms, nothing can touch him without the father's consent unless he is too weak to prevent it. And even if this should be the case, he suffers the harm first in his own person before he allows it to reach his child. How much more will our heavenly Father, whose love is infinitely greater and whose strength and wisdom can never be baffled, care for us! I am afraid there are some, even of God's own children, who scarcely think that He is equal to themselves in tenderness and love and thoughtful care, and who, in their secret thoughts, charge Him with a neglect and indifference of which they would feel themselves incapable. The truth really is that His care is infinitely superior to any possibilities of human care and that He, who counts the very hairs of our heads and suffers not a sparrow to fall without Him, takes note of the minutest matters that can affect the lives of His children and regulates them all according to His own perfect will, let their origin be what they may.

The instances of this are numberless. Take Joseph. What could have seemed more apparently on the face of it the result of sin and utterly contrary to the will of God than the action of his brothers in selling him into slavery? And yet Joseph, in speaking of it, said, "As for you, ye thought evil against me; but God meant it unto good." It was undoubtedly sin in Joseph's brothers, but by the time it had reached Joseph, it had become God's will for him and was, in truth, though he did not see it then, the greatest blessing of his whole life. I learned this lesson practically and through experience long years before

I knew the scriptural truth concerning it. I was attending a prayer meeting held in the interests of the life of faith when a strange lady rose to speak. I looked at her, wondering who she could be, little thinking she was to bring a message to my soul that would teach me a grand practical lesson. She said she had great difficulty in living the life of faith on account of the second causes that seemed to her to control nearly everything that concerned her. Her perplexity became so great that at last she began to ask God to teach her the truth about it, whether He really was in everything or not. After praying this for a few days, she had what she described as a vision. She thought she was in a perfectly dark place, and there advanced toward her, from a distance, a body of light that gradually surrounded and enveloped her and everything around her. As it approached, a voice seemed to say, "This is the presence of God! This is the presence of God!" While surrounded with this presence, all the great and awful things in life seemed to pass before her—fighting armies, wicked men, raging beasts, storms and pestilences, sin and suffering of every kind. She shrank back at first in terror. But she soon saw that the presence of God so surrounded and enveloped herself and each one of these things, that not a lion could reach out its paw, nor a bullet fly through the air, except as the presence of God moved out of the way to permit it. And she saw that if there were ever so thin a film, as it were, of this glorious presence between herself and the most terrible violence, not a hair of her head could be ruffled, nor anything touch her, except as the presence divided to let the evil through. Then all the small and annoying things of life passed before her; and equally she saw that there also she was so enveloped in this presence of God that not a cross look, nor harsh word, nor petty trial of any kind could affect her, unless God's encircling presence moved out of the way to let it.

Her difficulty vanished. Her question was answered forever. God *was* in everything. Would that it were only possible to make every Christian see this truth as plainly as I see it! For I am convinced it is the only clue to a completely restful life.

I once heard of a poor woman who earned a precarious living by daily labor but was a joyous, triumphant Christian.

"Ah, Nancy," said a gloomy Christian lady to her one day, who almost disapproved of her constant cheerfulness and yet envied it. "Ah, Nancy, it is all well enough to be happy now, but I should think the thoughts of your future would sober you. Only suppose, for instance, that you should have a spell of sickness and be unable to work. Or suppose your present employers should move away and no one else should give you anything to do; or suppose—"

"Stop!" cried Nancy. "I never supposes. De Lord is my shepherd, and I knows I shall not want. And, honey," she added to her gloomy friend, "it's all dem *supposes* as is makin' you so mis'able. You'd better give dem all up and just trust de Lord."

Nothing else but this: seeing God in everything will make us loving and patient with those who annoy and trouble us.

Nothing else will completely put an end to all murmuring or rebelling thoughts. If our Father permits a trial to come, it must be because the trial is the sweetest and best thing that could happen to us, and we must accept it with thanks from His dear hand. This does not mean, however, that we must like or enjoy the trial itself, but that we must like God's will in the trial. A good illustration of this may be found in the familiar fact of a mother giving medicine to her dearly loved child. The bottle *holds* the medicine, but the mother *gives* it; so the bottle is not responsible, but the mother.

The human beings around us are often the bottles that hold our medicine, but it is our Father's hand of love that pours out the medicine and compels us to drink it.

Shall we rebel against the human bottles then? Shall we not rather take thankfully from our Father's hand the medicine they contain?

If He always has His way, then we always have our way also, and we reign in a perpetual kingdom. He who sides with God cannot fail to win in every encounter; and whether the result is joy or sorrow, failure or success, death or life, we may under all circumstances join in the apostle's shout of victory, "Thanks be unto God, which always causeth us to triumph in Christ!"

PART III
Results

CHAPTER 13

Bondage or Liberty

There are two kinds of Christian experience, one of which is an experience of bondage and the other an experience of liberty.

In the first case, the soul is controlled by a stern sense of duty and obeys the laws of God, either from fear of punishment or from expectation of wages. In the other case, the controlling power is an inward life principle that works out, by the force of its own motions or instincts, the will of the divine Life Giver without fear of punishment or hope of reward. In the first, the Christian is a servant and works for hire; in the second, he is a son and works for love.

There ought not to be this contrast in the experience of Christians, for to "walk at liberty" is plainly their only right and normal condition. But as we have to deal with what is, rather than with what ought to be, we cannot shut our eyes to the sad condition of bondage in which so many of God's children pass a large part of their Christian lives. The reason is legality, and the remedy is Christ.

In the epistle to the Galatians, some Jewish brothers had come among the churches in Galatia and, by representing that certain forms and ceremonies were necessary to their salvation, had tried to draw them away from the liberty of the Gospel. And with these teachers Peter had allowed himself to unite. Therefore Paul reproves, not only the Galatians, but also Peter himself.

Neither Peter nor the Galatians had committed any moral sin, but they had committed a spiritual sin. They had gotten into a wrong attitude of soul toward God—a legalistic attitude. They began in the right attitude. But when it came to a question of how they were to live in this life, they had changed their ground. They had sought to substitute works for faith. We are, however, continually tempted to forget that it is not what men *do* that is the vital matter, but rather what they *are*. God is a great deal more concerned about our really *being* "new creatures" than about anything else, because He knows that if we *are* right as to our inward being, we shall certainly *do* right as to our outward actions.

Paul was grieved with the Galatian Christians because they seemed to have lost sight of this vital truth—that the inward life, the "new creature," was the only thing that availed. This passage is the only one in which the expression "fallen from grace" is used in the New Testament, and it means that the Galatians had made the mistake of thinking that something else besides Christ was necessary for their right Christian living. The Jewish brothers who had come among them had taught them that Christ alone was not enough, but that obedience to the ceremonial law must be added.

They added the ceremonial law; *we* add resolutions, or agonizings, or Christian work, or churchgoing, or religious ceremonies of one sort or another. It does not make much difference what you add; the wrong thing is to add anything at all.

The following contrasts may help some to understand the difference between these two kinds of religion and may also enable them to discover where the secret of their own experience of legal bondage lies:

The law says, This do, *and you shall live.*
The Gospel says, Live, *and then you shall do.*

The law says, Pay *me what you owe.*
The Gospel says, I frankly forgive *you all.*

The law says, Make *you a new heart and a new spirit.*
The Gospel says, A new heart will I give *you, and a new spirit will I put within you.*

The law says, Thou shalt love the LORD *thy God with all thine heart, and with all thy soul, and with all thy might.*
The Gospel says, Herein is love, not that we loved God, but that he loved us, and sent his Son to be the propitiation for our sins.

The law says, Cursed *is every one who continues not in all things written in the book of the law to do them.*
The Gospel says, Blessed is the man whose iniquities are forgiven, and whose sins are covered.

The law says, The wages *of sin is death.*
The Gospel says, The gift *of God is eternal life through Jesus Christ our Lord.*

The law demands *holiness.*
The Gospel gives *holiness.*

The law says, Do.
The Gospel says, Done.

The law extorts *the unwilling service of a bondman.*
The Gospel wins *the loving service of a son and freeman.*

The law makes blessings the result of obedience.
The Gospel makes obedience the result of blessings.

The law places the day of rest at the end *of the week's work.*
The Gospel places it at its beginning.

The law says, If.
The Gospel says, Therefore.

The law was given for the restraint *of the old man.*
The Gospel was given to bring liberty *to the new man.*

Under the law, salvation was wages.
Under the Gospel, salvation is a gift.

Paul tells us that the law "is our schoolmaster," not our savior, bringing us to Christ. After faith in Christ is come, he declares, we are no longer to be under a schoolmaster. He uses the contrast between a servant and a son as an illustration of his meaning. "Wherefore," he says, "thou art no more a servant, but a son." It is as if a woman had been a servant in a house, paid for her work in weekly wages, and under the law of her master, whom she had tried to please, but toward whom her service had been one of duty only. Finally, however, the master offers her his love and lifts her up from the place of a servant to be his bride and to share his fortunes. At once the whole spirit of her service is changed. She may perhaps continue to do the same things that she did before, but she does them now altogether from a different motive. The old sense of duty is lost in the new sense of love. The cold word *master* is transformed into the loving word *husband*. Imagine this bride feeling unworthy of union with her husband and to lose consequently the inward sense of this union. Who can doubt that very soon the old sense of working for wages would drive out the new sense of working for love? What happens to many Christians now? The servitude of duty takes the place of the service of love; and God is looked upon as the stern taskmaster who demands our obedience instead of as the loving Father who wins it.

Nothing so destroys the sweetness of any relation as the creeping in of this legalistic spirit. The moment a husband and wife cease to perform their services to each other out of a heart of love and union and begin to perform them from a sense of duty alone, that moment the sweetness of the union is lost, and the marriage tie becomes a bondage, and things that were a joy before are turned into crosses. Legalistic Christians do not deny Christ, they only seek to add something to Christ. Their idea is, Christ—and something besides. But to add anything to Christ, no matter how good it may be, as the procuring cause of salvation, is to deny His completeness and to exalt self. People will undergo many painful self-sacrifices rather than take the place of utter helplessness and worthlessness. A man will gladly be a Saint Simeon Stylites or even a fakir if only it is self that does it so that self may share the glory. And a religion of bondage always exalts self. It is what *I* do—*my* efforts, *my* wrestlings, *my* faithfulness. But a religion of liberty leaves self nothing to glory in. It is all Christ, and what He does, and what He is, and how wonderfully He saves.

I once had a friend whose Christian life was a life of bondage. She worked for her salvation harder than any slave ever worked to purchase his freedom. "What would you think," I asked, "of children who had to wrestle and agonize with their parents every morning for their necessary food and clothing, or of sheep that had to wrestle with their shepherd before they could secure the necessary care?"

"Of course I see that would be all wrong," she said, "but then why do I have such good times after I have gone through these conflicts?"

This puzzled me for a moment, but then I asked, "What brings about those good times finally?"

"Why, finally," she replied, "I come to the point of trusting the Lord."

"Suppose you should come to that point to begin with?" I asked.

"Oh," she replied, with a sudden illumination, "I never until this minute thought that I might!"

Christ says that except we "become as little children" we cannot enter into the kingdom of heaven. But it is impossible to get the child spirit until the servant spirit has disappeared. Notice, I do not say the spirit of service, but the servant spirit. Every good child is filled with the spirit of service but ought not to have anything of the servant spirit. The child serves from love; the servant works for wages.

One servant of whom we read in the Bible thought his lord was a "hard master," and the spirit of bondage makes us think the same now. Whenever any of the children of God find themselves "walking at liberty," they at once begin to think there must be something wrong in their experience because they no longer find anything to be a "cross" to them. Sometimes I think that the whole secret of the Christian life that I have been trying to describe is revealed in the child relationship. Nothing more is needed than just to believe that God is as good a Father as the best ideal earthly father. Children do not need to carry about in their own pockets the money for their support. It is not necessary for Christians to have all their spiritual possessions in their own keeping. It is far better that their riches should be stored up for them in Christ, and that when they want anything they should receive it directly from His hands.

Sometimes a great mystery is made out of the life hidden with Christ in God. This contrast between bondage and liberty makes it very plain. It is only to find out that we really are "no more servants, but sons," and practically to enter into the blessed privileges of this relationship. All can understand what it is to be a little child; there is no mystery about that. They are their Father's heirs and may enter now into possession of all that is necessary for their present needs.

It is because legalistic Christians do not know the truth of their relationship to God, as children to a father, and do not recognize His fatherly heart toward them, that they are in bondage. When they do recognize it, the spirit of bondage becomes impossible to them.

Our liberty must come, therefore, from an understanding of the mind and thoughts of God toward us.

"Against such there is no law" is the divine sentence concerning all who live and walk in the Spirit; and you shall find it most blessedly true in your own experience if you will but lay aside all self-effort and self-dependence of every kind and will consent to let Christ live in you and work in you and be your indwelling life.

The man who lives by the power of an inward righteous nature fulfills the law in his soul and is therefore free. The other rebels against the law in his soul and is therefore bound.

Abandon yourselves so utterly to the Lord Jesus Christ that He may be able to "work in you all the good pleasure of His will," and may, by the law of the Spirit of life in Himself, deliver you from every other law that could possibly enslave you.

CHAPTER 14

Growth

One great objection made against those who advocate this life of faith is that they do not teach a growth in grace. They are supposed to teach that the soul arrives in one moment at a state of perfection, beyond which there is no advance, and that all the exhortations in the scriptures that point toward growth and development are rendered void by this teaching.

Since exactly the opposite of this is true, I will try, if possible, to answer these objections and to show what seems to me the scriptural way of growing and in what place the soul must be in order to grow.

The text that is most frequently quoted is 2 Peter 3:18: "But grow in grace, and in the knowledge of our Lord and Savior Jesus Christ." Now, this text expresses exactly what we who teach this life of faith believe to be God's will for us, and what we also believe He has made it possible for us to experience. We believe in a growing that does really produce continually progressing maturity and in a development that, as a fact, does bring forth ripe fruit. We expect to reach the aim set before us. No parent would be satisfied with the growth of his child if day after day and year after year he remained the same helpless babe he was in the first months of his life. And no farmer would feel comfortable under such growing of his grain as should stop short at the blade and never produce the ear or the full corn in the ear. Growth, to be real, must be progressive, "Ah! But, Mrs. Smith, I believe in *growing* in grace." "How long have *you* been growing?" I asked. "About twenty-five years," was her answer. "And how much more unworldly and devoted to the Lord are you now than when your Christian life began?" I continued. "Alas!" was the answer. "I fear I am not nearly so much so." The trouble with her, and with every other such case, is simply this: they are trying to grow *into* grace, instead of *in* it. They are like a rosebush, planted by a gardener in the hard, stony path, with a view to its growing *into* the flower bed and which has of course dwindled and withered in consequence instead of flourishing and maturing. When the children of Israel started on their wanderings at Kadesh Barnea, they were at the borders of the land, and a few steps would have taken them into it. When they ended their wanderings in the plains of Moab, they were also at its borders, only with this difference: that now there was a river to cross, which at first there would not have been. To get possession of this land, it was necessary first to be in it; and to grow in grace, it is necessary first to be

83

planted in grace. When once in the land, however, their conquest was rapid; and when once planted in grace, the growth of the spiritual life becomes vigorous and rapid beyond all conceiving. For grace is a most fruitful soil, and the plants that grow therein are plants of a marvelous growth. They are tended by the divine Husbandman and are warmed by the Sun of Righteousness and watered by the dew from heaven. Surely it is no wonder that they bring forth fruit, "some an hundredfold, some sixtyfold, some thirtyfold."

Grace is the unhindered, wondrous, boundless love of God, poured out upon us in an infinite variety of ways, without stint or measure, not according to our deserving but according to His measureless heart of love. Put together all the tenderest love you know of—the deepest you have ever felt and the strongest that has ever been poured out upon you—and heap upon it all the love of all the loving human hearts in the world, and then multiply it by infinity, and you will begin perhaps to have some faint glimpses of the love and grace of God!

To "grow in grace," therefore, the soul must be planted in the very heart of this divine love, enveloped by it, steeped in it. It must let itself out to the joy of it and must refuse to know anything else. It must grow in the apprehensions of it, day by day; it must entrust everything to its care and must have no shadow of doubt but that it will surely order all things well.

To grow in grace is to put our growing, as well as everything else, into the hands of the Lord and leave it with Him. It is to grow as the lilies grow, or as the babies grow, without care and without anxiety; to grow because He who has planted us has planted a growing thing and has made us on purpose to grow.

Surely this is what our Lord meant when He said, "Consider the lilies of the field, how they grow; they toil not, neither do they spin: and yet I say unto you, that even Solomon in all his glory was not arrayed like one of these." Or when He says again, "Which of you by taking thought can add one cubit unto his stature?" There is no effort in the growing of a babe or of a lily. The lily does not toil or spin; it does not stretch or strain; it does not make any effort of any kind to grow; it is not conscious even that it is growing. The result of this sort of growing in the Christian life is sure. Even Solomon in all his glory, our Lord says, was not arrayed like one of God's lilies. Solomon's array cost much toiling and spinning, and gold and silver in abundance, but the lily's array costs none of these. And though we may toil and spin to make for ourselves beautiful spiritual garments and may strain and stretch in our efforts after spiritual growth, we shall accomplish nothing. For no man by taking thought *can* add one cubit to his stature, and no array of ours can ever equal the beautiful dress with which the great Husbandman clothes the plants that grow in His garden of grace and under His fostering care.

What we all need is to "consider the flowers of the field" and learn their secret. Grow, grow in God's way, which is the only effectual way. See to it that you are planted in grace, and then let the divine Husbandman cultivate you in His own way and by His own means. Put yourselves out in the sunshine of His presence and let the dew of heaven come down upon you and see what will be the result. Leaves and flowers and fruit must surely come in their season; for your Husbandman is skillful, and He never fails in His harvesting. Only see to it that you oppose no hindrance to the shining of the Sun of Righteousness or the falling of the dew from heaven. The thinnest covering may serve to keep off the sunshine and the dew, and the plant may wither, even where these are most abundant. And so also the slightest barrier between your soul and Christ may cause you to dwindle and fade as a plant in a cellar or under a bushel. Bask in the sunshine of His love. Drink of the waters of His goodness. Keep your face upturned to Him as the flowers do to the sun. Look, and your soul shall live and grow.

We are not inanimate flowers but intelligent human beings with personal powers and personal responsibilities. What the flower is by nature, we must be by an intelligent and free surrender. To be one of God's lilies means an interior abandonment of the rarest kind. It means that we are to be infinitely passive and yet infinitely active also: passive as regards self and its workings, active as regards attention and response to God. Self must step aside to let God work.

You need make no efforts to grow, therefore; but let your efforts instead be all concentrated on this, that you abide in the Vine. The divine Husbandman who has the care of the Vine will care also for you who are His branches and will so prune and purge and water and tend you that you will grow and bring forth fruit. Put yourselves absolutely into the hands of the good Husbandman, and He will at once begin to make the very desert blossom as the rose and will cause springs and fountains of water to start up out of its sandy wastes. Our divine Husbandman is able to turn any soil, whatever it may be like, into the soil of grace the moment we put our growing into His hands. He does not need to transplant us into a different field; but right where we are, with just the circumstances that surround us, He makes His sun to shine and His dew to fall upon us and transforms the very things that were before our greatest hindrances into the chief and most blessed means of growth.

Let yourselves grow. No difficulties in your case can baffle Him. If you will only put yourselves absolutely into His hands and let Him have His own way with you, no dwarfing of your growth in the years that are past, no apparent dryness of your inward springs of life, no crookedness or deformity in your development can in the least mar the perfect work that He will accomplish. "Consider the lilies of the field, *how they grow*; they toil not, neither do they spin." These words give us the picture of a life and growth far different from the ordinary life and growth of Christians—a life of rest and a growth without effort; and yet a life and a growth crowned with glorious results. We may rest assured that all the resources of God's infinite grace will be brought to bear on the growing of the tiniest flower in His spiritual garden as certainly as they are in His earthly creation. As the violet abides peacefully in its little place, content to receive its daily portion without concerning itself about the wandering of the winds or the falling of the rain, so must we repose in the present moment as it comes to us from God. This is the kind of "growth in grace" in which we who have entered into the life of full trust believe; a growth without care or anxiety on our part, but a growth that does actually grow. We rejoice to know that there are many such plants growing up now in the Lord's heritage. They are like the lilies. As the lilies behold the face of the sun and grow thereby, they are, by "beholding as in a glass the glory of the Lord," being changed into the same image from glory to glory, even as by the Spirit of the Lord.

They grow so rapidly and with such success, their answer would be that they are not concerned about their growing and are hardly conscious that they do grow. Their Lord has told them to abide in Him and has promised that, if they do thus abide, they shall certainly bring forth much fruit. They are content to leave the cultivating and the growing and the training and the pruning to their good Husbandman. Let us look at the subject practically. We all know that growing is not a thing of effort but is the result of an inward life principle of growth. All the stretching and pulling in the world could not make a dead oak grow, but a live oak grows without stretching. It is plain, therefore, that the essential thing is to get within you the growing life, and then you cannot help but grow. And this life is the "life hid with Christ in God," the wonderful divine life of an indwelling Holy Spirit. Be filled with this, dear believer, and whether you are conscious of it or not, you cannot help growing. Say a continual yes to your Father's will. And finally, in this, as in all the other cares of your life, "Be careful for nothing; but in every thing by prayer and supplication with thanksgiving, let your requests be made known unto God. And the peace of God, which passeth all understanding, shall keep your hearts and minds through Christ Jesus."

CHAPTER 15

Service

There is, perhaps, no part of Christian experience where a greater change is known upon entering into this life hid with Christ in God than in the matter of service.

In all the ordinary forms of Christian life, service is apt to have more or less of bondage in it. That is, it is done purely as a matter of duty and often as a trial and a cross. Certain things, which at the first may have been a joy and a delight, become after a while weary tasks, performed faithfully, perhaps, but with much secret disinclination and many confessed or unconfessed wishes that they need not be done at all, or at least that they need not be done so often. The soul finds itself asking, instead of the "May I?" of love, the "Must I?" of duty. The yoke, which was at first easy, begins to gall, and the burden feels heavy instead of light.

One dear Christian expressed it once to me in this way: "When I was first converted," she said, "I was so full of joy and love that I was only too glad and thankful to be allowed to do anything for my Lord, and I eagerly entered every open door. But after a while, as my early joy faded away, and my love burned less fervently, I began to wish I had not been quite so eager; for I found myself involved in lines of service that were gradually becoming very distasteful and burdensome to me. Since I had begun them, I could not very well give them up without provoking much talk, and yet I longed to do so increasingly. I was expected to visit the sick and pray beside their beds. I was expected to attend prayer meetings and speak at them. I was expected, in short, to be always ready for every effort in Christian work, and the sense of these expectations bowed me down continually. At last it became so unspeakably burdensome to me to live the sort of Christian life I had entered upon, and was expected by all around me to live, that I felt as if any kind of manual labor would have been easier. And I would have infinitely preferred scrubbing all day on my hands and knees to being compelled to go through the treadmill of my daily Christian work." Does this give a vivid picture of some of your own experiences, dear Christian? Have you never gone to your work as a slave to his daily task, believing it to be your duty and that therefore you must do it, but rebounding like an India rubber ball back into your real interests and pleasures the moment your work was over?

Or, if this does not describe your case, perhaps another picture will. You do love your work in the abstract, but in the doing of it you find so many cares and responsibilities connected with it and feel so many misgivings and doubts as to your own capacity or fitness that it becomes a very heavy burden, and you go to it bowed down and weary before the labor has even begun. Then also you are continually distressing yourself about the results of your work. Now, from all these forms of bondage the soul that enters fully into the blessed life of faith is entirely delivered. Service of any sort becomes delightful to it because, having surrendered its will into the keeping of the Lord, He works in it to will and to do of His good pleasure, and the soul finds itself really *wanting* to do the things God wants it to do. It is always very pleasant to do the things we *want* to do, let them be ever so difficult of accomplishment or involve ever so much of bodily weariness. If a man's *will* is really set on a thing, he regards with a sublime indifference the obstacles that lie in the way of his reaching it and laughs to himself at the idea of any opposition or difficulties hindering him. Many men have scorned the thought of any "cross" connected with it! It is all in the way we look at things. What we need in the Christian life is to get believers to *want* to do God's will as much as other people want to do their own will. It is what God intended for us, what He has promised. In describing the new covenant in Hebrews 8:6–13, He says, "I will put my laws into their mind, and write them in their hearts." This can mean nothing but that we shall *love* His law, for anything written in our hearts we must love. "And putting it into our mind" is surely the same as God working in us to "will and to do of his good pleasure," and means that we shall will what God wills and shall obey His sweet commands, not because it is our duty to do so, but because we ourselves want to do what He wants us to do.

And we, who are by nature a stiff-necked people, always rebel more or less against a law from outside of us while we joyfully embrace the same law springing up within.

God's way of working, therefore, is to get possession of the inside of a man, to take the control and management of his will, and to work it for him. If you are in bondage in the matter of service, you need to put your will over completely into the hands of your Lord, surrendering to Him the entire control of it. In one case, a lady had been for years rebelling fearfully against a little act of service that she knew was right but which she hated. I saw her, out of the depths of despair, and without any feeling whatever, give her will in that matter up into the hands of her Lord and begin to say to Him, "Thy will be done; *Thy will be done!*" And in one short hour, that very thing began to look sweet and precious to her.

It is wonderful what miracles God works in wills that are utterly surrendered to Him. Also there is deliverance in the wonderful life of faith. For in this life no burdens are carried, no anxieties felt. The Lord is our burden-bearer, and upon Him we must lay off every care. He says, in effect, "Be careful for nothing, but make your requests known to Me, and I will attend to them all." Be careful for *nothing*, He says, not even your service. Above all, I should think, our service, because we know ourselves to be so utterly helpless in regard to it, that, even if we were careful, it would not amount to anything. What have we to do with thinking whether we are fit or not? The Master Workman surely has a right to use any tool He pleases for His own work, and it is plainly not the business of the tool to decide whether it is the right one to be used or not. He knows, and if He chooses to use us, of course we must be fit. And in truth, if we only knew it, our chief fitness is in our utter helplessness. His strength is made perfect, not in our strength, but in our weakness. Our strength is only a hindrance.

It is no wonder that Paul could say, "Most gladly therefore will I rather *glory* in my infirmities, that the power of Christ may rest upon me." If the work is His, the responsibility is His also, and we have no room left for worrying about results. The most effectual workers I know are those who do not feel the least care or anxiety about their work, but who commit it all to their dear Master, and, asking Him to guide them moment by moment in reference to it, trust Him implicitly for each moment's needed supplies of wisdom and of strength.

There are one or two other bonds in service from which this life of trust delivers us. We find out that no one individual is responsible for all the work in the world, but only for a small share. Our duty ceases to be universal and becomes personal and individual. The Master does not say to us, "Go and do everything," but He marks out a special path for each of us and gives to each one of us a special duty. There are "diversities of gifts" in the kingdom of God, and these gifts are divided to "every man according to his several ability." I may have five talents or two or only one. I may be called to do twenty things or only one. My responsibility is simply to do that which I am called to do and nothing more. "The *steps* of a good man are ordered of the LORD," not his way only, but each separate step in that way.

Once a young Christian who, because she had been sent to speak a message to one soul whom she met while on a walk, supposed it was a perpetual obligation and thought she must speak to everyone she met on her walks about their souls. This was of course impossible, and as a consequence she was soon in hopeless bondage about it. She became absolutely afraid to go outside of her own door and lived in perpetual condemnation. At last this friend told her just to put herself under the Lord's personal guidance as to her work and trust Him to point out to her each particular person to whom He would have her speak, assuring her that He never puts forth His own sheep without going before them and making a way for them Himself. She followed this advice and laid the burden of her work on the Lord, and the result was a happy pathway of daily guidance in which she was led into much blessed work for her Master and was able to do it all without a care or a burden because He led her out and prepared the way before her.

Years ago I came across this sentence in an old book: "Never indulge, at the close of an action, in any self-reflective acts of any kind, whether of self-congratulation or of self-despair. Forget the things that are behind the moment they are past, leaving them with God." When the temptation comes, as it mostly does to every worker after the performance of any service, to indulge in these reflections, either of one sort or the other, I turn from them at once and positively refuse to think about my work at all, leaving it with the Lord to overrule the mistakes and to bless it as He chooses. To sum it all up, then, what is needed for happy and effectual service is simply to put your work into the Lord's hands and leave it there. Even in the midst of a life of ceaseless activity, you shall "find rest to your soul."

Be also yielded unto Him as "instruments of righteousness," to be used by Him as He pleases!

CHAPTER 16

Practical Results in the Daily Walk and Conversation

If all that has been written in the foregoing chapters on the life hid with Christ be true, its results in the practical daily walk and conversation ought to be very marked, and the people who have entered into the enjoyment of it ought to be, in very truth, a peculiar people, zealous of good works.

My son, now with God, once wrote to a friend something to this effect: that we are God's witnesses necessarily, because the world will not read the Bible, but they will read our lives; and that upon the report these give will very much depend their belief in the divine nature of the religion we possess. If, therefore, our faith is to make any headway in the present time, it must be proved to be more than a theory; and we must present to the investigation of the critical minds of our age the realities of lives transformed by the mighty power of God, "working in them all the good pleasure of His will."

I desire, therefore, to speak very solemnly for what I conceive to be the necessary fruit of a life of faith such as I have been describing and to press home to the hearts of every one of my readers their personal responsibility to "walk worthy of the high calling" with which they have been called.

The standard of practical holy living has been so low among Christians that the least degree of real devotedness of life and walk is looked upon with surprise and often even with disapproval by a large portion of the Church. And for the most part, the followers of the Lord Jesus Christ are satisfied with a life so conformed to the world and so like it in almost every respect that to a casual observer, no difference is discernible.

We who have heard the call of our God to a life of entire consecration and perfect trust must do differently. We must come out from the world and be separate. We must set our affections on heavenly things, not on earthly ones, and we must seek first the kingdom of God and His righteousness, surrendering everything that would interfere with this. We must walk through the world as Christ walked. We must have the mind that was in Him. As pilgrims and strangers, we must abstain from fleshly lusts that war against the soul. As good soldiers of Jesus Christ, we must disentangle ourselves inwardly from the affairs of this life that we may please Him who has chosen us to be soldiers. We must abstain from all appearance of evil. We must be kind to one another, tenderhearted, forgiving one another, even as God, for Christ's sake, has forgiven us. We must not resent injuries or unkindness but must return good for evil and turn the other cheek to the hand that smites us. We must take always the lowest place among our fellowmen and seek not our own honor, but the honor of others. We must be gentle and meek and yielding, not standing up for our own rights, but for the rights of others. We must do everything, not for our own glory, but for the glory of God. And, to sum it all up, since He who has called us is holy, so we must be holy in all manner of conversation.

Some Christians seem to think that all the requirements of a holy life are met when there is very active and successful Christian work. Because they do so much for the Lord in public, they feel a liberty to be cross and ugly and un-Christlike in private. We must be just as Christlike to our servants as we are to our minister. In daily home life, indeed, that practical piety can best show itself, and we may well question any "professions" that fail under this test of daily life.

A cross Christian or an anxious Christian; a discouraged, gloomy Christian; a doubting Christian; a complaining Christian; an exacting Christian, a selfish Christian; a cruel, hard-hearted Christian; a self-indulgent Christian; a Christian with a sharp tongue or bitter spirit—all these may be very earnest in their work and may have honorable places in the church, but they are *not* Christlike Christians. The life hid with Christ in God is a hidden life, as to its source, but it must not be hidden as to its practical results. We must prove that we "possess" that which we "profess." We must really and absolutely turn our backs on everything that is contrary to the perfect will of God. It means that we are to be a "peculiar people," not only in the eyes of God, but in the eyes of the world around us; and that wherever we go, it will be known from our habits, our tempers, our conversation, and our pursuits that we are followers of the Lord Jesus Christ and are not of the world, even as He was not of the world. We must no longer look upon our money as our own, but as belonging to the Lord, to be used in His service. We must not feel at liberty to use our energies exclusively in the pursuit of worldly means but must recognize that, if we seek first the kingdom of God and His righteousness, all needful things shall be added unto us. Our days will have to be spent, not in serving ourselves, but in serving the Lord, and we shall find ourselves called upon to bear one another's burdens and so fulfill the law of Christ. Whatever we do will be done "not with eyeservice, as menpleasers, but as the servants of Christ, doing the will of God from the heart."

Into all this we shall undoubtedly be led by the Spirit of God if we give ourselves up to His guidance. I have noticed that wherever there has been a faithful following of the Lord in a consecrated soul, several things have, sooner or later, inevitably followed.

Meekness and quietness of spirit become in time the characteristics of the daily life. A submissive acceptance of the will of God, as it comes in the hourly events of each day, is shown; pliability in the hands of God to do or to suffer all the good pleasure of His will; sweetness under provocation; calmness in the midst of turmoil and bustle; a yielding to the wishes of others, and an insensibility to slights and affronts; absence of worry or anxiety; deliverance from care and fear. God's glory and the welfare of His creatures, become the absorbing delight of the soul. Year after year such Christians are seen to grow more unworldly, more serene, more heavenly minded, more transformed, more like Christ until even their very faces express so much of the beautiful inward divine life that all who look at them cannot but take knowledge of them that they live with Jesus and are abiding in Him.

Have you not begun to feel dimly conscious of the voice of God speaking to you, in the depths of your soul, about these things? Has it not been a pain and a distress to you of late to discover how full life is are of self? Has not your soul been plunged into inward trouble and doubt about certain dispositions or pursuits in which you have been formerly accustomed to indulge? Have you not begun to feel uneasy with some of your habits of life and to wish that you could do differently in certain respects? Have not paths of devotedness and of service begun to open out before you with the longing thought, *Oh, that I could walk them!* All these questions and doubts and this inward yearning are the voice of the Good Shepherd in your heart, seeking to call you out of that which is contrary to His will. Let me entreat of you not to turn away from His gentle pleadings! The heights of Christian perfection can only be reached by each moment faithfully following the Guide who is to lead you there. He reveals the way to us one step at a time, in the little things of our daily lives, asking only on our part that we yield ourselves up to His guidance. Obey Him perfectly the moment you are sure of His will.

I knew a soul thus given up to follow the Lord wherever He might lead her, who in a very little while traveled from the depths of darkness and despair into the realization and actual experience of a most blessed union with the Lord Jesus Christ. Out of the midst of her darkness, she consecrated herself to the Lord, surrendering her will up altogether to Him that He might work in her to will and to do of His own good pleasure. Immediately He began to speak to her by His Spirit in her heart, suggesting to her some little acts of service for Him and troubling her about certain things in her habits and her life, showing her where she was selfish and un-Christlike and how she could be transformed. She recognized His voice and yielded to Him each thing He asked for the moment she was sure of His will. Her swift obedience was rewarded by a rapid progress, and day by day she was conformed more and more to the image of Christ until very soon her life became such a testimony to those around her that some even who had begun by opposing and disbelieving were forced to acknowledge that it was of God and were won to a similar surrender. If you would know a like blessing, abandon yourself, like her, to the guidance of your divine Master and shrink from no surrender for which He may call.

Things small to you may be in His eyes the key and the clue to the deepest springs of your being. No life can be complete that fails in its little things. A look, a word, a tone of voice even, however small they may seem to human judgment, are often of vital importance in the eyes of God. Whether you knew it or not, this, and nothing less than this, is what your consecration meant. It meant inevitable obedience. It meant that the will of your God was henceforth to be your will. You surrendered your liberty of choice. It meant an hourly following of Him, wherever He might lead you, without any turning back.

Let everything else go that you may live out, in a practical daily walk and conversation, the Christ-life you have dwelling within you. Day by day you will find Him bringing you more and more into conformity with His will in all things, molding you and fashioning you, as you are able to bear it, into a "vessel unto His honor, sanctified and meet for His use, and fitted to every good work." So shall be given to you the sweet joy of being an "epistle of Christ, known and read of all men"; and your light shall shine so brightly that men seeing not you but your good works shall glorify not you but your Father which is in heaven.

CHAPTER 17

The Joy of Obedience

Having spoken of some of the difficulties in this life of faith, let me now speak of some of its joys. And foremost among these stands the joy of obedience.

Long ago I came across this sentence somewhere: "Perfect obedience would be perfect happiness, if only we had perfect confidence in the power we were obeying." The rest has been revealed to me, not as a vision but as a reality. I have seen in the Lord Jesus the Master to whom we may yield up our implicit obedience and, taking His yoke upon us, may find our perfect rest.

You little know, dear hesitating soul, of the joy you are missing. The Master has revealed Himself to you and is calling for your complete surrender, and you shrink and hesitate. A measure of surrender you are willing to make and think indeed it is fit and proper that you should. But a *total* abandonment, without any reserves, seems to you too much to be asked for. You are afraid of it. It involves too much, you think, and is too great a risk. To be measurably obedient you desire; to be perfectly obedient appalls you.

You see other souls who seem able to walk with easy consciences in a far wider path than that which appears to be marked out for you. It seems strange, and perhaps hard to you, that you must do what they need not and must leave undone what they have liberty to do.

Your Lord says, "He that *hath* my commandments, and keepeth them, he it is that loveth me: and he that loveth me shall be loved of my father, and I will love him, and will manifest myself to him." You *have* His commandments; those you envy have them not. *You* know the mind of your Lord about many things, in which, as yet, *they* are walking in darkness. Is it a cause for regret that your soul is brought into such near and intimate relations with your Master that He is able to tell you things that those who are farther off may not know? Do you not realize what a tender degree of intimacy is implied in this?

Many relations in life require from the different parties only very moderate degrees of devotion. We may have really pleasant friendships with one another and yet spend a large part of our lives in separate interests and widely differing pursuits. When together, we may greatly enjoy one another's society and find many congenial points, but separation is not any especial distress to us, and other and more intimate friendships do not interfere. There is not enough love between us to give us either the right or the desire to enter into and share one another's most private affairs. Other relationships in life are different. The friendship becomes love. The two hearts give themselves to a union of the soul. Separate interests and separate paths in life are no longer possible. The deepest desire of each heart is that it may know every secret wish or longing of the other in order that it may fly on the wings of the wind to gratify it.

Do they not rather glory in these very obligations and inwardly pity, with a tender yet exulting joy, the poor far-off ones who dare not come so near? If you have ever loved any of your fellow human beings enough to find sacrifice and service on their behalf a joy; if a wholehearted abandonment of your will to the will of another has ever gleamed across you as a blessed and longed-for privilege or as a sweet and precious reality, then, by all the tender, longing love of your heavenly lover, I would entreat you to let it be so toward Christ!

He loves you with more than the love of friendship. As a bridegroom rejoices over his bride, so does He rejoice over you, and nothing but the bride's surrender will satisfy Him. He has given you all, and He asks for all in return. The slightest reserve will grieve him to the heart. He spared not Himself, and how can you spare yourself? For your sake He poured out in a lavish abandonment all that He had, and for His sake you must pour out all that you have, without stint or measure.

If, then, you are hearing the loving voices of your Lord calling you out into a place of nearness to Himself that will require a separation from all else and that will make an enthusiasm of devotedness not only possible, but necessary, will you shrink or hesitate? Will you think it hard that He reveals to you more of His mind than He does to others, and that He will not allow you to be happy in anything that separates you from Himself? Do you *want* to go where He cannot go with you or to have pursuits that He cannot share?

No! You will spring out to meet His lovely will with an eager joy. You will glory in the very narrowness of the path He marks out for you. The perfect happiness of perfect obedience will dawn upon your soul, and you will begin to know something of what Jesus meant when He said, "I *delight* to do thy will, O my God."

Do you think the joy in this will be all on your side? My friends, we are not able to understand this—the delight, the satisfaction, the joy our Lord has in us. That *we* should need Him is easy to comprehend; that *He* should need us seems incomprehensible. Continually at every heart He is knocking, asking to be taken in as the supreme object of love. "Will you have Me," He says to the believer, "to be your beloved? Will you follow

Me into suffering and loneliness and endure hardness for My sake and ask for no reward but My smile of approval and My word of praise? Will you throw yourself, with a passion of abandonment, into My will? Will you give up to Me the absolute control of yourself and of all that you have? Will you be content with pleasing Me, and Me only? May I have My way with you in all things? Will you come into so close a union with Me as to make a separation from the world necessary? Will you accept Me for your heavenly Bridegroom, and leave all others to cleave only to Me?"

In a thousand ways He makes this offer of union with Himself to every believer. But all do not say yes to Him. Other loves and other interests seem to them too precious to be cast aside. They do not miss the joy of heaven because of this. But they miss an unspeakable present joy.

You, however, are not one of these. From the very first your soul has cried out eagerly and gladly to all His offers, "Yes, Lord, yes!" The life of love upon which you have entered gives you the right to a lavish outpouring of *all* of you upon your beloved One. An intimacy and friendship, which more distant souls cannot enter upon, become now, not only your privilege, but also your duty. Your Lord can make known His secrets, and to you He looks for an instant response to every requirement of His love.

What a wonderful, glorious, unspeakable privilege upon which you have entered! How little it will matter to you if men shall hate you and shall separate you from their company and shall reproach you and cast out your name as evil for His dear sake! You may well "rejoice in that day, and leap for joy," for behold, your reward is great in heaven; for if you are a partaker of His suffering, you shall also be of His glory.

He sees in you the "travail of His soul" and is satisfied. Your love and devotedness are His precious reward for all He has done for you. It is unspeakably sweet to Him. Do not be afraid, then, to let yourself go in a heartwhole devotedness to your Lord that can brook *no* reserves. Others may not approve, but He will, and that is enough. Do not stint or measure your obedience or your service. Let your heart and your hand be as free to serve Him as His heart and hand were to serve you. Let Him have all there is of you—body, soul, mind, spirit, time, talents, voice, everything. Lay your whole life open before Him that He may control it. Do not let there be a day nor an hour in which you are not consciously doing His will and following Him wholly.

Christ Himself, when He was on earth, declared the truth that there was no blessedness equal to the blessedness of obedience. It is more blessed to hear and obey His will than to have been the earthly mother of our Lord or to have carried Him in our arms and nourished Him at our breasts!

May our surrendered hearts reach out with an eager delight to discover and embrace the lovely will of our loving God!

CHAPTER 18

Divine Union

All the dealings of God with the soul of the believer are in order to bring them into oneness with Himself. "That they all may be one; as thou, Father, art in me, and I in thee, that they also may be one in us."

This divine union was the glorious purpose in the heart of God for His people before the foundation of the world. It was accomplished in the death of Christ. God has not hidden it or made it hard, but the eyes of many are too dim, and their hearts too unbelieving for them to grasp it. It is therefore for the purpose of bringing His people into the personal and actual realization of this that the Lord calls upon them so earnestly and so repeatedly to abandon themselves to Him.

The usual course of Christian experience is pictured in the history of the disciples. First they were awakened to see their condition and their need, and they came to Christ and gave their allegiance to Him. Then they followed Him, worked for Him, believed in Him; and yet how unlike Him they were! Seeking to be set up one above the other running away from the cross, misunderstanding His mission and His words, forsaking their Lord in time of danger, they were still sent out to preach, recognized by Him as His disciples, and they possessed power to work for Him. They knew Christ only "after the flesh," as outside of them, their Lord and Master, but not yet their life.

Then came Pentecost, and these same disciples came to know Him as He revealed Himself inwardly. From then on He was to them Christ within, working in them to will and to do of His good pleasure, delivering them, by the law of the Spirit of His life, from the bondage to the law of sin and death under which they had been held. No longer was it, between themselves and Him, a war of wills and a clashing of interests. One will alone animated them, and that was His will. One interest alone was dear to them, and that was His. They were made *one* with Him.

Perhaps as yet the final stage of it has not been fully reached. You may have left much to follow Christ. You may have believed on Him, worked for Him, and loved Him, yet may not be like Him. Allegiance you know and confidence you know, but not yet union. There are two wills, two interests, two lives. You have not yet lost your own life that you may live only in His. Once it was "I and not Christ." Next it was "I and Christ." Perhaps now it is even "Christ and I." But has it come yet to be Christ only and not I at all?

All you need, therefore, is to understand what the scriptures teach about this marvelous union, that you may be sure it is really intended for you.

If you read such passages as 1 Corinthians 3:16, "Know ye not that ye are the temple of God, and that the Spirit of God dwelleth in you?" and then look at the opening of the chapter, you will see that this soul-union of which I speak, this unspeakably glorious mystery of an indwelling of God, is the possession of even the weakest and most failing believer in Christ. Every believer in the "body is the temple of the Holy Ghost."

But although this is true, it is also equally true that unless the believer knows it and lives in the power of it, it is to him as though it were not. This union with Christ is not a matter of emotions, but of character. It is not something we are to *feel*, but something we are to *be*. We may feel it very blessedly, and probably shall, but the vital thing is not the feeling, but the reality.

No one can be one with Christ who is not Christlike. This is entirely contrary to the scripture declaration that "he that *saith* he abideth in him ought himself also so to *walk*, even as he walked." There is no escape from this, for it is not only a divine declaration but is in the very nature of things as well.

Oneness with Christ means being made a "partaker of his nature," as well as of His life; for nature and life are, of course, one.

If we are really one with Christ, therefore, it will not be contrary to our nature to be Christlike and to walk as He walked, but it will be in accordance with our nature. Sweetness, gentleness, meekness, patience, long-suffering, charity, and kindness will all be natural to the Christian who is a partaker of the nature of Christ. It could not be otherwise.

But people who live in their emotions do not always see this. They *feel* so at one with Christ that they look no further than this feeling, and they often delude themselves with thinking they have come into the divine union, when all the while their nature and dispositions are still under the sway of self-love.

We all know that our emotions are most untrustworthy and are largely the result of our physical condition or our natural temperaments. It is a fatal mistake, therefore, to make them the test of our oneness with Christ. This mistake works both ways. If I have very joyous emotions, I may be deluded by thinking I have entered into the divine union when I have not; and if I have no emotions, I may grieve over my failure to enter when I really have entered.

Character is the only real test. God is holy, and those who are one with Him will be holy also. Our Lord Himself expressed His oneness with the Father in such words as these: "The Son can do nothing of himself, but what he seeth the Father do: for what things soever he doeth, these also doeth the Son likewise." The test Christ gave, then, by which the reality of His oneness with the Father was known, was the fact that He did the works of the Father. And I know no other test for us now.

It is forever true in the nature of things that a tree is known by its fruit. If we have entered into the divine union, we shall bear the divine fruit of a Christlike life and conversation. Pay no regard to your feelings, therefore, in this matter of oneness with Christ, but see to it that you have the really vital fruits of a oneness in character and walk and mind. Undeveloped Christians often have very powerful emotional experiences. I knew one who was kept awake often by the "waves of salvation," but who yet did not tell the truth in her interaction with others and was very far from honest in her business dealings. No one could possibly believe that she knew anything about a real divine union, in spite of all her fervent emotions in regard to it.

Your joy in the Lord is a far deeper thing than a mere emotion. It is the joy of knowledge, of perception, of actual existence. It is as though Christ were living in a house, shut up in a far-off closet, unknown and unnoticed by the dwellers in the house, longing to make Himself known to them and to be one with them in all their daily lives and share in all their interests, but unwilling to force Himself upon their notice, because nothing but a voluntary companionship could meet or satisfy the needs of His love. The days pass by over that favored household, and they remain in ignorance of their marvelous privilege. They come and go about all their daily affairs with no thought of their wonderful guest. Their plans are laid without reference to Him. His wisdom to guide and His strength to protect are all lost to them. Lonely days and weeks are spent in sadness, which might have been full of the sweetness of His presence.

Suddenly the announcement is made, "The Lord is in the house!" How will its owner receive the intelligence? Will he call out an eager thanksgiving and throw wide open every door for the entrance of his glorious guest? Or will he shrink and hesitate, afraid of His presence, and seek to reserve some private corner for a refuge from his all-seeing eye?

It is far more glorious to be brought into such a real and actual union with Him as to be one with Him—one will, one purpose, one interest, one life—than it would be to have Christ a dweller in the house or in the heart. And yet it ought to be expressed, and our souls ought to be made so unutterably hungry to realize it that day or night we shall not be able to rest without it. It seems too wonderful to be true that such poor, weak, foolish beings as we are should be created for such an end as this; and yet it is a blessed reality. We are even *commanded* to enter into it. We are exhorted to lay down our own lives that His life may be lived in us; we are asked to have no interests but His interests, to share His riches, to enter into His joys, to partake of His sorrows, to manifest His likeness, to have the same mind as He had, to think and feel and act and walk as He did.

Shall we consent to all this? The Lord will not force it on us, for He wants us as His companions and His friends, and a forced union would be incompatible with this. It must be voluntary on our part. The bride must say a willing yes to the bridegroom, or the joy of their union is wanting. It is a very simple transaction and yet very real. The steps are but three: first, be convinced that the scriptures teach this glorious indwelling of God; then surrender our whole selves to Him to be possessed by Him; and finally, we must believe that He *has* taken possession and *is* dwelling in us. We must begin to reckon ourselves dead and to reckon Christ as our only life. It will help us to say, "I am crucified with Christ: nevertheless I live, yet not I, but Christ liveth in me," over and over, day and night, until it becomes the habitual breathing of our souls. We must put off our self-life by faith continually and put on the life of Christ; and we must do this, not only by faith, but practically as well. We must continually put self to death in all the details of daily life and must let Christ instead live and work in us. I mean, we must never do the selfish thing, but always the Christlike thing. We must let this become, by its constant repetition, the attitude of our whole being. As surely as we do, we shall come at last to understand something of what it means to be made one with Christ as He and the Father are one. Christ left all to be joined to us; shall we not also leave all to be joined to Him?

CHAPTER 19

The Chariots of God

It has been well said that "earthly cares are a heavenly discipline," but they are even something better than discipline—they are God's chariots, sent to take the soul to its high places of triumph.

They do not look like chariots. They look instead like enemies, sufferings, trials, defeats, misunderstandings, disappointments, unkindnesses. Could we see them as they really are, we should recognize them as chariots of triumph in which we may ride to those very heights of victory for which our souls have been longing and praying. The chariot of God is the invisible.

The king of Syria came up against the man of God with horses and chariots that could be seen by every eye, but God had chariots that could be seen by none save the eye of faith. The servant of the prophet could only see the outward and visible; and he cried, as so many have done since, "Alas, my master! how shall we do?" but the prophet himself sat calmly within his house without fear, because his eyes were opened to see the invisible; and all he asked for his servant was, "LORD, I pray thee open his eyes, that he may see."

This is the prayer we need to pray for ourselves and for one another, for the world all around us, as well as around the prophet, is full of God's horses and chariots, waiting to carry us to places of glorious victory. And when our eyes are thus opened, we shall see in all the events of life, whether great or small, whether joyful or sad, a "chariot" for our souls.

Everything that comes to us becomes a chariot the moment we treat it as such. If we climb up into them, as into a car of victory, and make them carry us triumphantly onward and upward, they become the chariots of God.

Whenever we mount into God's chariots, the same thing happens to us spiritually that happened to Elijah. We shall have a translation. We shall be carried away from the low, earthly, groveling plane of life, where everything hurts and everything is unhappy, up into the "heavenly places in Christ Jesus," where we can ride in triumph over all below.

These are interior, and the road that leads to them is interior. But the chariot is generally some outward loss or trial or disappointment that afterward "yieldeth the peaceable fruit of righteousness."

In the Song of Solomon we are told of "chariots paved with love." We cannot always see the love-lining to our own particular chariot. It often looks very unlovely. It may be a cross-grained relative or friend; it may be the result of human malice or cruelty or neglect; but every chariot sent by God must necessarily be paved with love since God is love, and God's love is the sweetest, softest, tenderest thing to rest one's self upon that was ever found by any soul anywhere. It is His love, indeed, that sends the chariot.

Look upon your chastenings then, no matter how grievous they may be for the present, as God's chariots sent to carry your souls into the "high places" of spiritual achievement and uplifting, and you will find that they are, after all, "paved with love."

The Bible tells us that when God went forth for the salvation of His people, then He did ride upon His horses and chariots of salvation; and it is the same now. The clouds and storms that darken our skies and seem to shut out the shining of the Sun of Righteousness are really only God's chariots. Have you made the clouds in your life your chariots? Are you "riding prosperously" with God on top of them all?

I knew a lady who had a very slow servant. She was an excellent girl in every other respect and very valuable in the household, but her slowness was a constant source of irritation to her mistress, who was naturally quick, and who always chafed at slowness. This lady would consequently get out of temper with the girl twenty times a day, and twenty times a day she would repent of her anger and resolve to conquer it, but in vain. Her life was made miserable by the conflict. One day it occurred to her that she had for a long while been praying for patience, and that perhaps this slow servant was the very chariot the Lord had sent to carry her soul over into patience. She immediately accepted it as such and from that time used the slowness of her servant as a chariot for her soul. The result was a victory of patience that no slowness of anybody was ever after able to disturb.

I knew another lady, at a crowded convention, who was put to sleep in a room with two others on account of the crowd. *She* wanted to sleep, but *they* wanted to talk; and the first night she was greatly disturbed and lay there fretting and fuming long after the others had hushed, and she might have slept. But the next day she heard something about God's chariots, and at night she accepted these talking friends as her chariots to carry her over into sweetness and patience and was kept in undisturbed calm. When, however, it grew very late, and she knew they all ought to be sleeping, she ventured to say slyly, "Friends, I am lying here riding in a chariot!" The effect was instantaneous, and perfect quiet reigned! Her chariot had carried her over to victory, not only inwardly, but at last outwardly as well.

If we would ride in God's chariots instead of our own, we should find this to be the case continually.

Our constant temptation is to trust in the "chariots of Egypt" or, in other words, in earthly resources. We can *see* them; they are tangible and real and look substantial; while God's chariots are invisible and intangible, and it is hard to believe they are there.

We try to reach high spiritual places with the "multitude of our chariots." We depend first on one thing and then on another to advance our spiritual condition and to gain our spiritual victories. We "go down to Egypt for help." And God is obliged often to destroy all our own earthly chariots before He can bring us to the point of mounting into His.

We lean too much upon a dear friend to help us onward in the spiritual life, and the Lord is obliged to separate us from that friend. We feel that all our spiritual prosperity depends on our continuance under the ministry of a favorite preacher, and he is mysteriously removed. We look upon our prayer meeting or our Bible class as the chief source of our spiritual strength, and we are kept from attending them. And the "chariot of God" which alone can carry us to the place where we hoped to be taken by the instrumentalities upon which we have been depending is to be found in the very deprivations we have so mourned over. With the fire of His love, God must burn up every chariot of our own that stands in the way of our mounting into His.

We have to be brought to the place where all other refuges fail us before we can say, "He only." We say, "He *and*—something else." As long as visible chariots are at hand, the soul will not mount into the invisible ones.

Let us be thankful, then, for every trial that will help to destroy our earthly chariots and that will compel us to take refuge in the chariot of God that stands ready and waiting beside us in every event and circumstance of life. When we mount into God's chariot, our goings are "established," for no obstacles can hinder His triumphal course. All losses, therefore, are gains that bring us to this. Paul understood this, and he glorified in the losses that brought him such unspeakable rewards. "But what things were gain to me, those I counted loss for Christ. Yea doubtless, and I count all things but loss for the excellency of the knowledge of Christ Jesus my Lord: for whom I have suffered the loss of all things, and do count them but dung, that I may win Christ, and be found in him."

Even the "thorn in the flesh," the messenger of Satan sent to buffet him, became a "chariot of God" to his willing soul and carried him to the heights of triumph, which he could have reached in no other way. To "take pleasure" in one's trials—what is this but to turn them into the grandest chariots?

Joseph had a revelation of his future triumphs and reigning, but the chariots that carried him there looked to the eye of sense like dreadful cars of failure and defeat. Slavery and imprisonment are strange chariots to take one to a kingdom, and yet by no other way could Joseph have reached his exaltation. And our exaltation to the spiritual throne that awaits us is often reached by similar chariots.

The great point, then, is to recognize each thing that comes to us as being really God's chariot for us and accept it as from Him. He does not command or originate the thing, perhaps; but the moment we put it into His hands, it becomes His, and He at once turns it into a chariot for us. He makes all things, even bad things, work together for good to all those who trust Him. All He needs is to have it entirely committed to Him.

When your trial comes, then, put it right into the will of God and climb into that will as a little child climbs into her mother's arms. Get into your chariot, then. Take each thing that is wrong in your lives as God's chariot for you. No matter who the builder of the wrong may be, whether men or devils, by the time it reaches your side, it is God's chariot for you and is meant to carry you to a heavenly place of triumph. No doubt the enemy will try to turn your chariot into a juggernaut car by taunting you with the suggestions that God is not in your trouble, and that there is no help for you in Him. But you must utterly disregard all such suggestions and must overcome them with the assertion of a confident faith. "God *is* my refuge and strength, a very present help in trouble" must be your continual declaration, no matter what the "seemings" may be.

You must not be halfhearted about it. You must climb wholly into your chariot, not with one foot dragging on the ground. There must be no "ifs" or "buts" or "supposings" or "questionings." Accept God's will fully and hide yourself in the arms of His love, which are always underneath to receive you in every circumstance and at every moment. Say, "Thy will be done, Thy will be done," over and over. Shut out every other thought but the one thought of submission to His will and of trust in His love. There can be no trials in which God's will has not a place somewhere. The soul has only to mount into His will as in a chariot, and it will find itself "riding upon the heavens" with God in a way it had never dreamed could be.

The soul that thus rides with God "on the sky" has views and sights of things that the soul that grovels on the earth can never have. One dear Christian said to me at the close of a meeting where I had been speaking about these chariots: "I am a poor woman and have all my life long grieved that I could not drive in a carriage like some of my rich neighbors. But I have been looking over my life while you have been talking, and I find that it is so full of chariots on every side that I am sure I shall never need to walk again."

There is no need for any one of us to walk for lack of chariots. That misunderstanding, that mortification, that unkindness, that disappointment, that loss, that defeat—all these are chariots waiting to carry you to the very heights of victory you have so longed to reach.

Mount into them then, with thankful hearts, and lose sight of all second causes in the shining of His love, who will "carry you in His arms" safely and triumphantly over it all.

CHAPTER 20

The Life on Wings

This life hid with Christ in God has one aspect that has been a great help and inspiration to me, and I think may be also to some other longing and hungry souls. It is what I call the life on wings.

This cry for "wings" is as old as humanity. Our souls were made to "mount up with wings," and they can never be satisfied with anything short of flying. Like the captive-born eagle that feels within it the instinct to flight and chafes and frets at its imprisonment, hardly knowing what it longs for, so do our souls chafe and fret and cry out for freedom. We can never rest on earth, and we long to "fly away" from all that so holds and hampers and imprisons us here.

This restlessness and discontent develop themselves generally in seeking an outward escape from our circumstances or from our miseries. We do not at first recognize the fact that our only way of escape is to "mount up with wings," and we try to "flee on horses," as the Israelites did, when oppressed by their trials (see Isaiah 30:16).

Our "horses" are the outward things upon which we depend for relief, some change of circumstances or some help from man; and we mount on these and run east or west, or north or south, anywhere to get away from our trouble, thinking in our ignorance that a change of our environment is all that is necessary to give deliverance to our souls. But all such efforts to escape are unavailing as we have each one proved hundreds of times. For the soul is not so made that it can "flee upon horses" but must make its flight always upon wings.

Moreover, these "horses" generally carry us, as they did the Israelites, out of one trouble, only to land us in another. How often have we also run from some "lion" in our pathway only to be met by a "bear," or have hidden ourselves in a place of supposed safety, only to be bitten by a "serpent"! No, it is useless for the soul to hope to escape by running away from its troubles to any earthly refuge, for there is not one that can give it deliverance.

There is a glorious way of escape for every one of us if we will but mount up on wings and fly away from it all to God. It is not a way east or west, or north or south, but it is a way upward. "They that wait upon the LORD shall renew their strength; they shall mount up with wings as eagles; they shall run, and not be weary; and they shall walk, and not faint."

All creatures that have wings can escape from every snare that is set for them if only they will fly high enough, and the soul that uses its wings can always find a sure "way to escape" from all that can hurt or trouble it.

Their secret is contained in the words, "They that wait upon the LORD." The soul that waits upon the Lord is the soul that is entirely surrendered to Him and that trusts Him perfectly. Therefore we must name our wings the wings of Surrender and of Trust. I mean by this that if we will only surrender ourselves utterly to the Lord and trust Him perfectly, we shall find our souls "mounting up with wings as eagles" to the "heavenly places" in Christ Jesus, where earthly annoyance or sorrows have no power to disturb us.

The wings of the soul carry it up into a spiritual plane of life, into the "life hid with Christ in God," which is a life utterly independent of circumstances, one that no cage can imprison and no shackles bind.

Things look very different according to the standpoint from which we view them. The caterpillar, as it creeps along the ground, must have a widely different "view" of the world around it from that which the same caterpillar will have when its wings are developed, and it soars in the air above the very places where once it crawled. And, similarly, the crawling soul must necessarily see things in a very different aspect from the soul that has "mounted up with wings." I was at one time spending a winter in London, and during three long months we did not once see any genuine sunshine because of the dense clouds of smoke that hung over the city like a pall. But many a time I have seen that above the smoke the sun was shining, and once or twice through a rift I have had a glimpse of a bird, with sunshine on its wings, sailing above the fog in the clear blue of the sunlit sky. Not all the brushes in London could sweep away the fog, but if we could only mount high enough, we should reach a region above it all.

And this is what the soul on wings does. It overcomes the world through faith. To overcome means to "come over," not to be crushed under; and the soul on wings flies over the world and the things of it. These lose their power to hold or bind the spirit that is made in very truth "more than a conqueror."

Birds overcome the lower law of gravitation by the higher law of flight; and the soul on wings overcomes the lower law of sin and misery and bondage by the higher law of spiritual flying. The "law of the spirit of life in Christ Jesus" must necessarily be a higher and more dominant law than the law of sin and death; therefore the soul that has mounted into this upper region of the life in Christ cannot fail to conquer and triumph.

But it may be asked how it is, then, that all Christians do not always triumph. A great many Christians do not "mount up with wings" but live on the same low level with their circumstances. On this plane the soul is powerless; it has no weapons with which to conquer there; and instead of overcoming, or coming over, the trials and sorrows of the earthly life, it is overcome by them and crushed under them.

A friend once illustrated to me the difference between three of her friends in the following way. She said, if they should all three come to a spiritual mountain that had to be crossed, the first one would tunnel through it with hard and wearisome labor; the second would meander around it in an indefinite fashion, hardly knowing where she was going, and yet, because her aim was right, getting around it at last; but the third, she said, would just flap her wings and fly right over. If any of us in the past have tried to tunnel our way through the mountains that have stood across our pathway or have been meandering around them, we must resolve to spread our wings and "mount up" into the clear atmosphere of God's presence, where it will be easy to overcome. The largest wings ever known cannot lift a bird one inch upward unless they are used. We must *use* our wings or they avail us nothing.

It is not worthwhile to cry out, "Oh that I had wings, and then I would flee," for we *have* the wings already, and what is needed is not more wings, but only that we should use those we have. The power to surrender and trust exists in every human soul and only needs to be brought into exercise. With these two wings we *can* "flee" to God at any moment, but in order really to reach Him, we must actively use them. We must not merely want to use them, but we must *do* it definitely and actively. We shall not "mount up" very high if we only surrender and trust in theory or in our especially religious moments. We must do it definitely and practically, about each detail of daily life as it comes to us. We must meet our disappointments, our thwartings, our persecutions, our malicious enemies, our provoking friends, our trials and temptations of every sort, with an active and experimental attitude of surrender and trust. We must spread our wings and "mount up" to the "heavenly places in Christ" above them all, where they will lose their power to harm or distress us. Instead of stirring up strife and bitterness by trying, metaphorically, to knock down and walk over our offending brothers and sisters, we should escape all strife by simply spreading our wings and mounting up to the heavenly region where our eyes would see all things covered with a mantle of Christian love and pity.

The mother eagle teaches her little ones to fly by making their nest so uncomfortable that they are forced to leave it and commit themselves to the unknown world of air outside. So does our God to us. He stirs up our comfortable nests and pushes us over the edge of them, and we are forced to use our wings to save ourselves from fatal falling.

With this end in view, we can surely accept with thankfulness every trial that compels us to use our wings, only so they can grow strong and large and fit for the highest flying. Unused wings gradually wither and shrink and lose their flying power; and if we had nothing in our lives that made flying necessary, we might perhaps at last lose all capacity to fly.

A bird may be imprisoned in a cage, or it may be tethered to the ground with a cord, or it may be loaded with a weight that drags it down, or it may be entrapped in the "snare of the fowler." Hindrances that answer to all these in the spiritual realm may make it impossible for the soul to fly until it has been set free from them by the mighty power of God.

One "snare of the fowler" that entraps many souls is the snare of doubt. The doubts look so plausible and often so humble that Christians walk into their "snare" without dreaming for a moment that it is a snare at all until they find themselves caught and unable to fly; for there is no more possibility of flying for the soul that doubts than there is for the bird caught in the fowler's snare.

The reason of this is evident. One of our wings, namely, the wing of trust, is entirely disabled by the slightest doubt; and just as it requires two wings to lift a bird in the air, so does it require two wings to lift the soul. A great many people do everything but trust. They spread the wing of surrender and use it vigorously and wonder why it is that they do not mount up, never dreaming that it is because all the while the wing of trust is hanging idle by their sides. It is because Christians use one wing only that their efforts to fly are often so irregular and fruitless.

It may be that for some the "snare of the fowler" is some subtle form of sin, some hidden want of consecration. Where this is the case, the wing of trust may seem to be all right, but the wing of surrender hangs idly down; and it is just as hopeless to try to fly with the wing of trust alone as with the wing of surrender alone. Both wings must be used, or no flying is possible.

If we find ourselves imprisoned, then, we may be sure of this, that it is not our earthly environment that constitutes our prison-house, for the soul's wings scorn all paltry bars and walls of earth's making. The only thing that can really imprison the soul is something that hinders its upward flight. The prophet tells us that it is our iniquities that have separated God and ourselves, and it is our sins that have hid His face from us. Therefore, if our soul is imprisoned, it must be because some indulged sin has built a barrier between us and the Lord, and we cannot fly until this sin is given up and put out of the way.

But often, where there is no conscious sin the soul is still unconsciously tethered to something of earth and so struggles in vain to fly. Our souls are often not unmoored from earthly things. We must cut ourselves loose. As well might an eagle try to fly with a hundred-ton weight tied fast to its feet as the soul try to "mount up with wings" while a weight of earthly cares and anxieties is holding it down to earth.

We are commanded to have our hearts filled with songs of rejoicing and to make inward melody to the Lord. But unless we mount up with wings, this is impossible, for the only creature that can sing is the creature that flies. When the prophet declared that though all the world should be desolate, yet he would rejoice in God and joy in the God of his salvation, his soul was surely on wings. Paul knew what it was to use his wings when he found himself to be "sorrowful, yet always rejoicing." On the earthly plane all was dark to both Paul and the prophet, but on the heavenly plane all was brightest sunshine.

Do you think that by flying I mean necessarily any very joyous emotions or feelings of exhilaration? There is a great deal of emotional flying that is not real flying at all. It is such flying as a feather accomplishes that is driven upward by a strong puff of wind but flutters down again as soon as the wind ceases to blow. The flying I mean is a matter of *principle*, not a matter of *emotion*. It may be accompanied by very joyous emotions, but it does not depend on them. It depends only upon the facts of an entire surrender and an absolute trust. Every one who will honestly use these two wings and will faithfully persist in using them, will find that they *have* mounted up with wings as an eagle, no matter how empty of all emotion they may have felt themselves to be before.

For the promise is sure: "They that wait upon the LORD. . .*shall* mount up with wings as eagles." Not "may perhaps mount up," but "*shall.*" It is the inevitable result. May we each one prove it for ourselves!

FOXE'S
CHRISTIAN
MARTYRS

John Foxe was born in 1516 in Boston, Lincolnshire, England. At the age of sixteen, he went to Oxford, where he received his bachelor's degree in 1537, became a professor, and completed his master's in 1543. While teaching at Oxford, he became friends with Hugh Latimer and William Tyndale, embracing Protestantism.

After leaving the university and marrying in 1545, Foxe was ordained a deacon of the Church of England and worked for the Reformation, writing tracts and beginning work on his account of Christian martyrs. But he was forced to leave the country in 1553 when the Catholic queen Mary took the throne.

The first portion of Foxe's "book of martyrs" was published in France in 1554. Foxe then moved to Basel, Switzerland, where he worked as a printer's proofreader and received manuscripts and eyewitness accounts of Queen Mary's persecution of Protestants in England. After Elizabeth I became queen, Foxe returned to England and published his entire book under the title *Acts and Monuments of These Latter and Perilous Days* in 1563.

Becoming popularly known as *The Book of Martyrs,* the text was widely read by English Puritans, shaping public opinion about Catholicism for at least a century.

Ordained an Anglican priest in 1560, Foxe refused all church offices due to his Puritan beliefs. He continued to preach and minister, though, serving victims of the plague of 1563 and urging Queen Elizabeth against the execution of Anabaptists in 1575 and Jesuits in 1581.

John Foxe died in 1587.

PERSECUTION OF THE EARLY CHRISTIANS

In the Gospel of Matthew, we read that Simon Peter was the first person to openly acknowledge Jesus as the Son of God and that Jesus, seeing God's hand in this acknowledgment, called Peter a rock on which He would build His church—a church that even the gates of hell would not be able to defeat.

This indicates three things. First, that Christ will have a church in this world. Second, that the church would be persecuted, not only by the world, but also by all the powers of hell. Third, despite its persecutions, the church would survive.

The whole history of the church to this day verifies this prophecy of Christ. Princes, kings, and other rulers of this world have used all their strength in plotting against the church, yet it continues to endure and hold its own. The storms that it has overcome are remarkable. I have written this history so the wonderful works of God within the church will be visible to all who might profit from them.

Of all the people who heard Jesus speak, the Pharisees and scribes should have been the first to accept Him, since they were so familiar with God's law. Yet they persecuted and rejected Him, choosing to remain subject to Caesar, and it was Caesar who eventually destroyed them.

God's punishment also fell heavily on the Romans. Hearing of Christ's works, death, and resurrection, Emperor Tiberius proposed to the Roman senate that He be adored as God, but the senators refused, preferring the emperor to the King of heaven. In reply, God stirred their own emperors against them, causing most of the senate to be destroyed and the city of Rome to be afflicted for nearly three hundred years.

Tiberius became a tyrant, killing his own mother, his nephews, the princesof the city, and his own counselors. Seutonius reported him to be so stern that one day alone he saw twenty people executed. Pilate, under whom Christ was crucified, was sent to Rome and banished to the town of Vienne in Dauphiny, where he eventually committed suicide. Agrippa the elder was even imprisoned by Tiberius for some time.

After Tiberius's death came Caligula, who demanded to be worshipped as a god. He banished Herod Antipas, the murderer of John the

Baptist and condemner of Christ, and was assassinated in the fourth year of his reign.

Following thirteen cruel years under Claudius, the people of Rome fell under the power of Nero, who reigned for fourteen years, killing most of the Roman senate and destroying the whole Roman order of knighthood. He was so cruel and inhumane that he put to death his own mother, his brother-in-law, his sister, his wife, and his instructors Seneca and Lucan. Then he ordered Rome set on fire in twelve places while he sang the verses of Homer. To avoid the blame for this, he accused the Christians of setting the fires and caused them to be persecuted.

In the year AD 70, Titus and his father, Vespasian, destroyed Jerusalem and all of Galilee, killing over 1,100,000 Jews and selling the rest into slavery. So we see that those who refused Jesus were made to suffer for their actions.

THE APOSTLES

The first apostle to suffer after the martyrdom of Stephen was James, the brother of John. Clement tells us, "When this James was brought to the tribunal seat, he that brought him and was the cause of his trouble, seeing him to be condemned and that he should suffer death, was in such sort moved within heart and conscience that, as he went to the execution, he confessed himself also, of his own accord, to be a Christian. And so they were led forth together, where in the way he desired of James to forgive him what he had done. After James had a little pause with himself upon the matter, turning to him he said, 'Peace be to thee brother,' and kissed him. And both were beheaded together, AD 36."

Thomas preached to the Parthians, Medes, Persians, Carmanians, Hyrcanians, Bactrians, and Magians. He was killed in Calamina, India.

Simon, brother of Jude and James the younger, who were all the sons of Mary Cleophas and Alpheus, was bishop of Jerusalem after James. He was crucified in Egypt during the reign of the Roman emperor Trajan.

Simon the Apostle, called Cananeus and Zelotes, preached in Mauritania, Africa, and Britain. He was also crucified.

Mark, the first bishop of Alexandria, preached the Gospel in Egypt. He was burned and buried in a place named Bucolus during Trajan's reign.

Bartholomew is said to have preached in India and translated the Gospel of Matthew into their tongue. He was beaten, crucified, and beheaded in Albinopolis, Armenia.

Andrew, Peter's brother, preached to the Scythians, Sogdians, and the Sacae in Sebastopolis, Ethiopia, in the year AD 80. He was crucified by Aegeas, the governor of the Edessenes, and was buried in Patrae, in Archaia. Bernard and St. Cyprian mentioned the confession and martyrdom of this blessed apostle. Partly from them and partly from other reliable writers, we gather the following material.

When Andrew, through his diligent preaching, had brought many to the faith of Christ, Aegeas the governor asked permission of the Roman senate to force all Christians to sacrifice to and honor the Roman idols. Andrew thought he should resist Aegeas and went to him, telling him that a judge of men should first know and worship his Judge in heaven. While worshipping the true God, Andrew said, he should banish all false gods and blind idols from his mind.

Furious at Andrew, Aegeas demanded to know if he was the man who had recently overthrown the temple of the gods and persuaded men to become Christians—a "superstitious sect" that had recently been declared illegal by the Romans.

Andrew replied that the rulers of Rome didn't understand the truth. The Son of God, who came into the world for man's sake, taught that the Roman gods were devils, enemies of mankind, teaching men to offend God and causing Him to turn away from them. By serving the devil, men fall into all kinds of wickedness, Andrew said, and after they die, nothing but their evil deeds are remembered.

The proconsul ordered Andrew not to preach these things anymore or he would face a speedy crucifixion, whereupon Andrew replied, "I would not have preached the honor and glory of the cross if I feared the death of the cross." He was condemned to be crucified for teaching a new sect and taking away the religion of the Roman gods.

Andrew, going toward the place of execution and seeing the cross waiting for him, never changed his expression. Neither did he fail in his speech. His body fainted not, nor did his reason fail him, as often happens to men about to die. He said, "Oh cross, most welcome and longed for! With a willing mind, joyfully and desirously, I come to you, being the scholar of Him which did hang on you, because I have always been your lover and yearn to embrace you."

Matthew wrote his Gospel to the Jews in the Hebrew tongue. After he had converted Ethiopia and all Egypt, Hircanus the king sent someone to kill him with a spear.

After years of preaching to the barbarous nations, Philip was stoned and crucified in Hierapolis, Phrygia, and buried there with his daughter.

Of James, the brother of the Lord, we read the following. James, being considered a just and perfect man, governed the church with the apostles. He drank no wine or any strong drink, ate no meat, and never shaved his head. He was the only man allowed to enter into the holy place, for he never wore wool, just linen. He would enter into the temple alone, fall on his knees, and ask remission for the people, doing this so often that his knees lost their sense of feeling and became hardened, like the knees of a camel. Because of his holy life, James was called "The Just" and "the safeguard of the people."

When many of their chief men had been converted, the Jews, scribes, and Pharisees began to fear that soon all the people would decide to follow Jesus. They met with James, saying, "We beg you to restrain the people, for they believe Jesus as though He were Christ. Persuade those who come to the Passover to think correctly about Christ, because they will all listen to you. Stand on top of the temple so you can be heard by everyone."

During Passover, the scribes and Pharisees put James on top of the temple, calling out to him, "You just man, whom we all ought to obey, this people is going astray after Jesus, who was crucified."

And James answered, "Why do you ask me of Jesus the Son of Man? He sits on the right hand of the Most High and shall come in the clouds of heaven."

Hearing this, many in the crowd were persuaded and glorified God, crying, "Hosanna to the Son of David!"

Then the scribes and Pharisees realized they had done the wrong thing by allowing James to testify of Christ. They cried out, "Oh, this just man is seduced, too!" Then they went up and threw James off the temple.

But James wasn't killed by the fall. He turned, fell on his knees, and called, "O Lord God, Father, I beg You to forgive them for they know not what they do."

They decided to stone James, but a priest said to them, "Wait! What are you doing? The just man is praying for you!" But one of the men there—a fuller—took the instrument he used to beat cloth and hit James on the head, killing him, and they buried him where he fell. James was a true witness for Christ to the Jews and the Gentiles.

THE FIRST PERSECUTION

The first of the ten persecutions was stirred up by Nero about AD 64. His rage against the Christians was so fierce that Eusebius records, "A man might then see cities full of men's bodies, the old lying together with the young, and the dead bodies of women cast out naked, without reverence of that sex, in the open streets." Many Christians in those days thought that Nero was the Antichrist because of his cruelty and abominations.

The apostle Peter was condemned to death during this persecution, although some say he escaped. It is known that many Christians encouraged him to leave the city, and the story goes that as he came to the city's gate, Peter saw Jesus coming to meet him. "Lord, where are You going?" Peter asked.

"I am come again to be crucified," was the answer.

Seeing that his suffering was understood, Peter returned to the city, where Jerome tells us he was crucified head down at his own request, saying that he was not worthy to be crucified the same way his Lord was.

Paul also suffered under this persecution when Nero sent two of his esquires, Ferega and Parthemius, to bring him to his execution. They found Paul instructing the people and asked him to pray for them so they might believe. Receiving Paul's assurance that they would soon be baptized, the two men led him out of the city to the place of execution, where Paul was beheaded. This persecution ended under Vespasian's reign, giving the Christians a little peace.

THE SECOND PERSECUTION

The second persecution began during the reign of Domitian, the brother of Titus. Domitian exiled John to the island of Patmos, but on Domitian's death, John was allowed to return to Ephesus in the year AD 97. He remained there until the reign of Trajan, governing the churches in Asia and writing his Gospel until he died at about the age of one hundred.

Why did the Roman emperors and senate persecute the Christians so? First of all, they didn't understand that Christ's kingdom is not a temporal kingdom, and they feared for their powerful leadership roles if too many citizens followed Christ. Second, Christians despised the false Roman gods, preferring to worship only the true, living God. Whatever happened in Rome—famine, disease, earthquake, wars, bad weather—was blamed on the Christians, who defied the Roman gods.

Death was not considered enough punishment for the Christians, who were subjected to the cruelest treatment possible. They were whipped, disemboweled, torn apart, and stoned. Plates of hot iron were laid on them; they were strangled, eaten by wild animals, hung, and tossed on the horns of bulls. After they were dead, their bodies were piled in heaps and left to rot without burial. Nevertheless, the church continued to grow, deeply rooted in the doctrine of the apostles and watered with the blood of the saints.

THE THIRD PERSECUTION

During the third persecution, Pliny the Second wrote to the emperor Trajan, complaining that thousands of Christians were being killed daily, although none of them had done anything worthy of persecution.

During this persecution, Ignatius was condemned to death because he professed Christ. At the time, he was living in Antioch, next in line as bishop after Peter. As he made the trip from Syria to Rome, he preached under heavy guard; he preached to the churches he passed and asked the church in Rome not to try to save him. Condemned to be thrown to the lions, Ignatius replied, "I am the wheat of Christ: I am going to be ground with the teeth of wild beasts, that I may be found pure bread."

THE FOURTH PERSECUTION

After a respite, the Christians again came under persecution, this time from Marcus Aurelius, in AD 161.

One of those who suffered this time was Polycarp, the venerable bishop of Smyrna. Three days before he was captured, Polycarp dreamed that a pillow under his head caught fire, and when he awoke, he told those around him that he would burn alive for Christ's sake.

Hearing his captors had arrived one evening, Polycarp left his bed to welcome them, ordered a meal prepared for them, and then asked for an hour alone to pray. The soldiers were so impressed by Polycarp's advanced age and composure that they began to wonder why they had been sent to take him; but as soon as he had finished his prayers, they put him on a donkey and brought him to the city.

As he entered the stadium with his guards, a voice from heaven was heard to say, "Be strong, Polycarp, and play the man." No one nearby saw anyone speaking, but many people heard the voice.

Brought before the tribunal and the crowd, Polycarp refused to deny Christ, although the proconsul begged him: "Consider yourself and have pity on your great age. Reproach Christ and I will release you."

Polycarp replied, "Eighty-six years I have served Him, and He never once wronged me. How can I blaspheme my King who saved me?"

Threatened with wild beasts and fire, Polycarp stood his ground. "What are you waiting for? Do whatever you please." The crowd demanded Polycarp's death, gathering wood for the fire and preparing to tie him to the stake.

"Leave me," he said. "He who will give me strength to sustain the fire will help me not to flinch from the pile." So they bound him but didn't nail him to the stake. As soon as Polycarp finished his prayer, the fire was lit, but it leaped up around him, leaving him unburned, until the people convinced a soldier to plunge a sword into him. When he did, so much blood gushed out that the fire was immediately extinguished. The soldiers then placed his body into a fire and burned it to ashes, which some Christians later gathered up and buried properly.

In this same persecution, the Christians of Lyons and Vienne, two cities in France, also suffered, including Sanctus of Vienne, Maturus, Attalus of Pergamos, and the woman Blandina, all of whom endured extreme torture and death with fortitude and grace.

THE FIFTH PERSECUTION, AD 200

During the reign of Severus, the Christians had several years of rest and could worship God without fear of punishment. But after a time, the hatred of the ignorant mob again prevailed, and the old laws were remembered and put in force against them. Fire, sword, wild beasts, and imprisonment were resorted to again, and even the dead bodies of Christians were stolen from their graves and mutilated. Yet the faithful continued to multiply. Tertullian, who lived at this time, said that if the Christians had all gone away from the Roman territories, the empire would have been greatly weakened.

By now, the persecutions had extended to northern Africa, which was a Roman province, and many were murdered in that area. One of these was Perpetua, a married lady twenty-six years old with a baby at her breast. On being taken before the proconsul Minutius, Perpetua was commanded to sacrifice to the idols. Refusing to do so, she was put in a dark dungeon and deprived of her child; but two of her keepers, Tertius and Pomponius, allowed her out in the fresh air several hours a day, during which time she was permitted to nurse her child.

Finally the Christians were summoned to appear before the judge and urged to deny their Lord, but all remained firm. When Perpetua's turn came, her father suddenly appeared, carrying her infant in his arms, and begged her to save her own life for the sake of her child. Even the judge seemed to be moved. "Spare the gray hairs of your father," he said. "Spare your child. Offer sacrifice for the welfare of the emperor."

Perpetua answered, "I will not sacrifice."

"Are you a Christian?" demanded Hilarianus, the judge.

"I am a Christian" was her answer.

Perpetua and all the other Christians tried with her that day were ordered killed by wild beasts as a show for the crowd on the next holiday. They entered the place of execution clad in the simplest of robes, Perpetua singing a hymn of triumph. The men were to be torn to pieces by leopards and bears. Perpetua and a young woman named Felicitas were hung up in nets, at first naked, but the crowd demanded that they should be allowed their clothing.

When they were again returned to the arena, a bull was let loose on them. Felicitas fell, seriously wounded. Perpetua was tossed, her loose robe torn and her hair falling loose, but she hastened to the side of the dying Felicitas and gently raised her from the ground. When the bull refused to attack them again, they were dragged out of the arena, to the disappointment of the crowd, which wanted to see their deaths. Finally brought back in to be killed by gladiators, Perpetua was assigned to a trembling young man who stabbed her weakly several times, not being used to such scenes of violence. When she saw how upset the young man was, Perpetua guided his sword to a vital area and died.

THE SIXTH PERSECUTION, AD 235

This persecution was begun by the emperor Maximinus, who ordered all the Christians hunted down and killed. A Roman soldier who refused to wear a laurel crown bestowed on him by the emperor and confessed he was a Christian was scourged, imprisoned, and put to death.

Pontianus, bishop of Rome, was banished to Sardinia for preaching against idolatry and murdered. Anteros, a Grecian who succeeded Pontianus as bishop of Rome, collected a history of the martyrs and suffered martyrdom himself after only forty days in office.

Pammachius, a Roman senator, and forty-two other Christians were all beheaded in one day and their heads set out on the city gates. Calepodius, a Christian minister, after being dragged through the streets, was thrown into the Tiber River with a millstone fastened around his neck. Quiritus, a Roman nobleman, and his family and servants were barbarously tortured and put to death. Martina, a noble young lady, was beheaded; and Hippolitus, a Christian prelate, was tied to a wild horse and dragged through fields until he died.

Maximinus was succeeded by Gordian, during whose reign and that of his successor, Philip, the church was free from persecution for more than six years. But in 249, a violent persecution broke out in Alexandria without the emperor's knowledge.

Metrus, an old Christian of Alexandria, refused to worship idols. He was beaten with clubs, pricked with sharp reeds, and stoned to death. Quinta, a Christian woman, was dragged by her feet over sharp flint stones, scourged with whips, and finally stoned to death. Apollonia, an old woman nearly seventy, confessed that she was a Christian, and the mob fastened her to a stake, preparing to burn her. She begged to be let loose, and the mob untied her, thinking she was ready to recant, but to their astonishment, she immediately threw herself back into the flames and died.

THE SEVENTH PERSECUTION, AD 249

By now, the heathen temples of Rome were almost forsaken, and the Christian churches were crowded with converts. The emperor Decius decided it was time to crush the Christians once and for all.

Fabian, the bishop of Rome, was the first person of authority to feel the severity of this persecution. The former emperor, Philip, had put his treasure into the care of Fabian. When Decius examined the treasure, there was far less than he had expected, so he had Fabian arrested and beheaded.

Decius, having built a pagan temple at Ephesus, commanded everyone in the city to sacrifice to its idols. This order was refused by seven of his own soldiers: Maximianus, Martianus, Joannes, Malchus, Dionysius, Constantinus, and Seraion. The emperor, willing to try a little persuasion, gave them time to consider until he returned from a journey, but in his absence, they escaped and hid in a cave. Decius was told of this on his return, and the mouth of the cave was closed up so all seven soldiers starved to death.

Theodora, a beautiful young lady of Antioch, refused to sacrifice to the Roman idols and was condemned to prison. Didymus, her Christian lover, disguised himself as a Roman soldier and went to Theodora's cell, where he convinced her to put on his armor and escape. When he was discovered, Didymus was taken to the governor and condemned to death. When she heard Didymus's sentence, Theodora threw herself at the judge's feet and begged that she be the one to suffer, not Didymus. The judge ordered them both beheaded and their bodies burned.

Origen, the celebrated author and teacher of Alexandria, was arrested at the age of sixty-four and thrown into prison in chains, his feet placed in the stocks, which held his legs stretched widely apart. Even though Origen was rich and famous, he received no mercy. He was threatened by fire and tormented by every means available, but his fortitude carried him through it all, even when his judge ordered the torturers to prolong his suffering. During the torture, Decius died and his successor began a war with the Goths, which turned the empire's attention away from the Christians. Origen was freed; he lived in Tyre until he died at the age of sixty-nine.

THE EIGHTH PERSECUTION, AD 257

When Valerian was first made emperor, he was moderate and kind to the Christians, but then he fell under the influence of an Egyptian magician named Macrianus and ordered the persecutions to continue, which they did for the next three years and six months.

Stephen, the bishop of Rome, was beheaded; and Saturnius, bishop of Toulouse, was attacked and seized by the crowd there for preventing the oracles from speaking. On refusing to sacrifice to the idols, he was fastened by the feet to the tail of a bull, which was then driven down the steps of the temple, dragging Saturnius until his head opened and his brains fell out. None of the Christians in Toulouse had the courage to carry away his dead body until two women took it and buried it in a ditch.

In Rome, Lawrence was brought before the authorities, who knew he was not only a minister of the sacraments but also a distributor of the church's riches. When they demanded he hand over all the church possessed, Lawrence asked for three days to collect it. On the third day, when the persecutor demanded the wealth of the church, Lawrence stretched his arms out over a group of poor Christians he'd gathered together. "These are the precious treasures of the church," he told his judge. "What more precious jewels can Christ have than those in whom He promised to dwell?"

Furious at being tricked and out of his mind with anger, Lawrence's persecutor ordered him whipped, beaten, tied to burning-hot plates of iron, then laid out on a bed of iron over a fire and roasted alive.

The first English martyr was a man named Alban, who was converted by a poor clerk who took shelter in his house. When the authorities eventually came for the clerk, Alban dressed in his clothes and went in his place. The judge recognized Alban and demanded he sacrifice to his heathen gods or die. When Alban refused, he was tortured and beheaded.

THE NINTH PERSECUTION, AD 270

This persecution began under the emperor Aurelian. Among those who suffered at this time was Felix, bishop of Rome, who was beheaded. Agapetas, a young Roman who sold his estate and gave the money to the poor, was seized as a Christian, tortured, and then brought to Praeneste, a city near Rome, where he was beheaded. These are the only martyrs whose names were recorded during this reign.

THE TENTH PERSECUTION, AD 303

In the beginning of the tenth persecution, which was in the nineteenth year of his reign, the emperor Diocletian appointed Maximian to share his throne with him; and the two of them chose Galerius and Constatius to serve under them. Under these rulers, the Christians were again persecuted furiously, a state that would continue until AD 313, even though Diocletian and Maximian gave up their offices in the year AD 305.

Constatius and Galerius divided the empire between them, Galerius taking the eastern countries and Constatius ruling France, Spain, and Britain. Meanwhile, the Roman soldiers set up Maxentius as their caesar in Rome. While Galerius and Maxentius continued the persecution for seven or eight years, Constatius became a supporter of the Christians in his empire, being an enlightened, intelligent ruler who was always concerned for the welfare of his subjects, never waging unjust wars or aiding those who did. Churches were terribly persecuted in other parts of the empire, but Constatius gave Christians the freedom to live and worship as they chose, even appointing them as his closest protectors and advisers.

Constatius died in AD 306 and was buried at York, England. His son Constantine, an English-born Christian, succeeded him—a ruler every bit as compassionate and dedicated as his father.

In Rome, Maxentius was ruling as a tyrant, killing his own noblemen, confiscating their goods for himself, and practicing magic—the only thing he seemed to do well. In the beginning of his reign, he pretended to be a friend of the Christians, but only to win popular support while he secretly continued the persecution.

The citizens and senators of Rome soon grew weary of Maxentius's tyranny and wickedness and petitioned Constantine to come and free them. At first Constantine tried to convince Maxentius to mend his ways; but when it had no effect, he gathered an army in Britain and France and began marching toward Italy in AD 313.

Knowing he didn't have the support of his people, Maxentius had to rely on his magic arts and occasional ambushes of Constantine's advancing army, neither of which slowed Constantine's advance toward Rome.

But as he neared Rome, Constantine began to feel nervous about the coming battle. He'd seen Maxentius defeat others by the use of his magic, and he wished he had a force to use against it. One day at sunset, Constantine looked to the south to see the bright form of the cross and the words "In this overcome." He and the men with him were astonished at the sign, although no one was too sure what it actually meant. But one night as Constantine slept, Christ appeared to him with the same cross, telling him to make a cross to carry before him into battle.

This sign and its message weren't given to induce superstitious worship of the cross, as though the cross had any power in itself, but as an admonition to seek Jesus and set forth the glory of His name.

The next day Constantine had a cross made of gold and precious stones, which he had carried before the army in place of his flag.

With added confidence that God had blessed his cause, he hurried toward Rome and the showdown with Maxentius.

Maxentius was now forced out of the city to meet Constantine on the far side of the Tiber River. After he crossed the bridge named Pons Milvius, Maxentius destroyed it, replacing it with an unstable bridge made of boats and planks, thinking to trap Constantine. The two armies clashed. Constantine drove Maxentius backward farther and farther until, in his haste to safety, he tried to retreat over the new bridge and fell into his own trap. His horse tumbled off the unstable planking, taking Maxentius and his armor to the bottom of the Tiber, where he drowned.

Maxentius was the last Roman persecutor of the Christians, whom Constantine set free after three hundred years of oppression and death. Constantine so firmly established the rights of Christians to worship God that it would be a thousand years before they would again suffer for their faith.

For three hundred years, the strongest and richest rulers in the world had tried to snuff out Christianity, using force, politics, torture, and death—everything at their disposal. Now all those emperors were gone, while Christ and His church still stood.

PERSECUTIONS UNDER JULIAN, AD 361

Julian became emperor at the death of his brother Constantius, the son of Constantine the Great. Although Julian had been educated by his father in the Christian faith, he was at heart a pagan; no sooner was he seated on the throne than he made a public avowal of his belief and trust in the ancient gods of the heathen, earning himself the title Julian the Apostate.

Julian restored idolatrous worship by opening the temples and ordering the magistrates and people to follow his example, but he did not make any laws against Christianity. He allowed every religious sect its freedom, although he exerted all the influence he could to restore the old faith. Although no violent deaths of Christians are recorded as resulting from any orders from Julian, several executions did take place around the empire on orders of heathen governors and officers.

SEVERUS

Venus, the goddess of love, was revered by the Romans, and April was considered the appropriate month to celebrate the triumphs of this goddess. During the month, her temples were thronged with worshippers and her marble statues were decked with flowers. Severus, a Christian centurion in the Roman army, dared to raise his voice against this popular custom, not only refusing to take part in the heathen ceremony but denouncing Venus herself. Enraged by his words, the crowd seized Severus and dragged him before the judge. He repeated his beliefs firmly in the judge's presence and was condemned to be taken before the temple of Venus to be insulted, stripped, and scourged with a whip called the *plumbetae*, which had lead balls tied at the end of each of its thongs. Severus was beaten by two strong men, delivered over to the public executioners, and beheaded.

CASSIAN

Cassian was a schoolmaster in a town not far from Rome. When he was arrested for refusing to sacrifice to the idols, his judge decided that his punishment should be entrusted to his students, who didn't like their schoolmaster at all. He was bound and delivered to his students, who fell on him with their styles (the sharp-pointed pieces of iron used to write on wax-covered tablets) and stabbed him to death.

THEODORUS

Theodorus, a Christian, was seized and tortured. After being taken from the rack, he was asked how he could endure the pain so patiently. "At first I felt some pain," he replied, "but afterward there appeared to be a young man beside me who wiped the sweat from my face and refreshed me with cold water. I enjoyed it so much that I was sorry to be released."

MARCUS

Marcus, the bishop of Arethusa, a town in Thrace, destroyed a heathen temple and had a Christian church built in its place. This so enraged the heathens of the town that they waited until he was alone and captured him one day. After they had beaten him with sticks, they asked whether he would rebuild the temple he'd torn down. Marcus not only refused to rebuild it but threatened to destroy it again if anyone else rebuilt it. His persecutors looked around for some way of punishing him, finally deciding on a plan that was as cruel as it was unusual. They tied Marcus with ropes and placed him in a large basket, which they hung in a tree after smearing the poor man's body with honey. After being hung up in the tree, Marcus was asked once more to restore the temple; he refused, and his tormentors left him to die from the stings of the wasps he attracted.

PERSECUTIONS BY THE GOTHS

During the reign of Constantine the Great, the light of the Gospel penetrated into the land of the barbarians. In northeastern Europe, which was then called Scythia, some of the Goths were converted, but most of them continued as pagans.

Fritegern, king of the Western Goths, was a friend of the Romans; but Athanaric, king of the Eastern Goths, was at war with them. The Christians living in Fritegern's area lived in peace; but Athanaric, being defeated by the Romans, took out his anger on the Christians in his land.

Sabas was the first to feel the king's anger. He was a humble, modest man, eager to see the church expand. Athanaric sent out orders that everyone in his land had to sacrifice to the heathen gods and eat the meat that had been offered to the idols. If they refused, they would be put to death. Some of the heathens who had Christian relatives provided them with meat that hadn't been sacrificed to the idols, but Sabas refused to take this way out. He not only refused to comply with the new laws but publicly said that those who ate the substitute meat were not true Christians.

Sabas was soon arrested and taken before a judge who, seeing he was a poor, unimportant man, had him released. Soon Sabas went to visit Sansala, a Christian missionary; on the third night after his arrival, they were both arrested by a party of soldiers. Sansala was allowed to dress himself and ride, but Sabas was forced to leave his clothing behind and walk. All during the long journey, they drove him through thorns and briars, beating him all the way. In the evenings, they stretched him between two beams, fastening his legs to the one and his arms to the other, and left him that way for the night. Even when he was released by a woman who pitied him, Sabas refused to run away.

In the morning, the soldiers tried to persuade both men to renounce their religion and eat the meat that had been consecrated to the idols. They refused, and although Sansala was finally set free, Sabas was drowned.

Nicetas, a Goth living near the Danube with his parents, was a Christian, too. One day Athanaric commanded that an idol should be drawn around on a chariot in all the Christian towns; everyone was ordered to worship the idol when it stopped in front of their house. Nicetas refused to come out when the idol arrived at his house, so the house was set on fire and everyone in it burned to death.

PERSECUTION BY THE VANDALS, AD 429

The Vandals crossed over from Spain to the north coast of Africa and defeated the Roman army there, conquering the whole country under their leader, Genseric. Since the Vandals were of the Arian sect, they abused the Christians wherever they found them, laying waste to all their cities and ruining every beautiful or valuable object they found. They even burned the fields of grain so anyone escaping their swords would die from famine. They plundered the churches and murdered the bishops and ministers in many cruel ways. Often they poured rancid, filthy oil down the throats of those they captured, drowning them. Others they martyred by stretching their limbs with cords until the veins and sinews burst. Old men found no mercy from them, and even innocent babies felt the rage of their barbarity.

When a town held out against them, the Vandals brought great numbers of Christians to the town walls and killed them, leaving their bodies to rot under the walls until the town had to surrender to escape the plague.

After they took Carthage, the Vandals put the city's bishop and many other Christians into a leaky ship and committed it to the waves, thinking everyone on it would soon die, but the vessel arrived safely at another port. Several Christians were beaten, scourged, and banished to the desert, where God used them to convert many of the Moors to Christianity. Once Genseric discovered this, he sent orders that they and their converts should be tied by the feet to chariots and dragged until they were beaten to pieces.

The bishop of Urice was burned, and the bishop of Habensa was banished for refusing to turn over the sacred books. Archinimus, a devout Christian, was brought before Genseric himself for trial. Finding the man firm in his faith, Genseric ordered him beheaded but privately told the executioner, "If the prisoner is courageous and willing to die, don't kill him. I don't want him to have the honor of being a martyr." When the executioner found Archinimus quite willing to die, he returned him to the prison, from which he soon disappeared, probably murdered in secret at the king's order.

Cyrilla, the Arian bishop of Carthage, was a great enemy to those Christians who professed the pure faith. He persuaded Genseric that he could not allow so many of his subjects to practice their Christianity and enjoy any peace. Genseric first attempted to bribe the Christians away from their faith with promises of worldly gains, but they stood firm, saying, "We acknowledge but one Lord and one faith. You may do whatever you please with our bodies, for it is better we suffer a few temporary pains than endure everlasting misery." Looking for an efficient way to kill so many people at once, the governor finally ordered them all put on a ship filled with wood and straw. The ship was then set on fire, and everyone aboard was either drowned or burned to death. The names of the chief Christians on board the ship were Rusticus, Liberatus, Rogatus, Servus, Septimus, and Boniface.

TELEMACHUS

Rome was celebrating its temporary victory over Alaric the Goth in its usual manner, by watching its gladiators fight to the death in the arena, when suddenly there was an interruption. A rudely clad, robed figure boldly leaped down into the arena. Telemachus was one of the hermits who devoted themselves to a holy life of prayer and self-denial and kept themselves apart from the wicked life of Rome. Although few of the Roman citizens followed their example, most of them had great respect for these hermits, and the few who recognized Telemachus knew he had come from the wilds of Asia on a pilgrimage to visit the churches and celebrate Christmas in Rome.

Without hesitating an instant, Telemachus advanced upon two gladiators who were engaged in their life-and-death struggle. Laying a hand on one of them, he sternly reproved him for shedding innocent blood and then, turning toward the thousands of angry faces around him, called to them: "Do not repay God's mercy in turning away the swords of your enemies by murdering each other!"

Angry shouts drowned out his voice. "This is no place for preaching! On with the combat!" Pushing Telemachus aside, the two gladiators prepared to continue their combat, but Telemachus stepped between them. Enraged at the interference of an outsider of their chosen vocation, the gladiators turned on Telemachus and stabbed him to death.

The crowd fell silent, shocked by the death of this holy man; but his death had not been in vain, for from that day on, no more gladiators ever went into combat in the Colosseum.

THE SPANISH INQUISITION

The Inquisition of the Church of Rome was, in its days, one of the most terrible engines of tyranny ever created by man. It may be said to date from about the year 1200, when Pope Innocent III sent his inquisitors among the Waldenses and other sects differing from the church, and continued until 1808. In its course, it totally crushed any Protestants living in Spain: its final count numbered 31,912 people burned alive and 291,450 imprisoned. In the eighteen years that the Dominican monk Thomas of Torquemada led the Inquisition, 10,220 people were burned and 97,322 punished with the loss of property or imprisonment. Although its main victims were citizens of Spain, there were others who became its victims, too.

The Inquisition continued until the invasion of Spain by Napoleon Bonaparte in 1808 and the abdication of the throne by Charles IV in favor of his son, Ferdinand VII. On February 22, 1813, the Cortes General of the kingdom assembled in Madrid and decreed that the existence of the Inquisition was no longer in accord with the political constitution that had been adopted by the nation. The bishops and civil courts were returned to their ancient powers, and the oppression of the people of Spain finally ended.

WILLIAM LITHGOW

William Lithgow was an Englishman born about 1580. Being fond of travel, he was on his way to Alexandria, Egypt, when he was suddenly attacked by nine men, who threw a black cloak over his head and dragged him to the governor's house in Malaga, Spain. There he was accused of being an English spy. Nothing Lithgow could say would convince the local authorities that he was only a tourist passing through the city, so it was decided to torture him until he made his confession. Lithgow was tortured on the rack and then asked if he acknowledged the pope's supremacy, to which he answered, "You almost murdered me for pretended treason without any grounds. Now you intend to make me a martyr for my religion?"

"You have been arrested as a spy and accused of treachery," his inquisitor replied. "Perhaps you are not a spy, but we have found by your books and writings that you surely are a heretic and therefore deserve even worse punishment than you have received."

They gave Lithgow eight days to consider whether he would convert or not. During this time the inquisitor and others argued frequently with him to no avail. At last, finding their arguments had no effect and that their threats of torment couldn't shake him, they left Lithgow alone. The eight days were soon over. Lithgow was asked one more time to convert and save his life. "I fear neither death nor fire," he replied. "I am prepared for both, so do your worst!"

That night Lithgow was sentenced to eleven different tortures, and if he did not die from them, he was to be taken to Granada and burned after Easter. The first part of the sentence was carried out with cold-blooded cruelty, but it pleased God to give the poor victim strength of body and mind, and he survived. Then Lithgow waited with resignation for the day that would end his torments.

All of this had been carried out in the strictest of secrecy, since Lithgow was an English subject and not a citizen of Spain; but a servant boy happened to hear the city's mayor discuss Lithgow's case at dinner one night, and he secretly told the story to an English merchant in town named Mr. Wild. Wild told the story to other English merchants living in the town and to the English ambassador at Madrid, Sir Walter Aston, who quickly appealed to the king and council of Spain, obtained an order for Lithgow's immediate release, and put him on board an English warship visiting the city. Two months later, Lithgow arrived safely at Deptford, England, although his left arm remained useless to him for the rest of his life.

JOHN WYCLIFFE

John Wycliffe, who lived during the reign of Edward III in 1371, was the public reader of divinity at the University of Oxford. In a time when few people were educated, he was well known for his scholarship in the fields of philosophy and religion.

At this time Christianity was in a sad state. Although everyone knew the name of Christ, few if any understood His doctrine. Faith, consolation, the use of the law, the works of Christ, our human weakness, the Holy Ghost, the strength of sin, the works of grace, justification by faith, and Christian liberty were never mentioned in the church.

Instead, the church was solely concerned with outward ceremony and human traditions. People spent their entire lives heaping up one ceremony after another in hopes of salvation, not knowing it was theirs for the asking. Simple, uneducated people who had no knowledge of scripture were content to know only what their pastors told them, and these pastors took care to only teach what came from Rome—most of which was for the profit of their own orders, not for the glory of Christ.

Wycliffe, seeing Christ's Gospel defiled by the errors and inventions of these bishops and monks, decided to do whatever he could to remedy the situation and teach people the truth. He took great pains to publicly declare that his only intention was to relieve the church of its idolatry, especially that concerning the sacrament of Communion.

This, of course, aroused the anger of the country's monks and friars, whose orders had grown wealthy through the sale of their ceremonies and from being paid for doing their duties. Soon their priests and bishops took up the outcry, followed by the archbishop, Simon Sudbury, who took away Wycliffe's salary at Oxford and ordered him to stop preaching against the church. When even that failed, he appealed to the pope.

Nevertheless, Wycliffe continued speaking his mind to the people in his sermons. King Edward was sympathetic to his preaching, and he also had the support of others of high rank including John of Gaunt, the Duke of Lancaster, the king's son, and Lord Henry Percy.

The following points, taken from Wycliffe's sermons, summarize his teachings:

The holy eucharist, after consecration, is not the actual body of Christ.
The Church of Rome is no more important than any other church, and
  Peter had no more power given to him by Christ than any other apostle.
The pope has no more power than any other priest.
The Gospel is enough for any man, without the rules of men,
  which add nothing to the Gospel.
Neither the pope nor any other church official has the power
  or right to punish transgressors.

In 1377, Wycliffe was ordered to appear before his bishops and answer to their charges, since he had continued to preach on these matters after having been told to stop. He appeared before them on Thursday, February 19, 1377, accompanied by four learned friars. The Duke of Lancaster and Lord Percy became involved in a heated argument with the bishop over whether Wycliffe should be allowed to sit or must remain standing. Soon arguments gave way to threats, the whole assembly joined in taking sides, and the council had to be dissolved before it was even 9:00 a.m. Wycliffe had escaped punishment for his beliefs.

Soon King Edward III died, and his grandson, Richard II, took the throne. The Duke of Lancaster and Lord Percy gave up their government positions and retired to private life, but Wycliffe still enjoyed the support of many noblemen. In 1377, Pope Gregory sent a message to the University of Oxford, rebuking it for allowing Wycliffe's doctrine to take root and demanding he be silenced. This encouraged the archbishop of Canterbury and other bishops, who decided to meet and agree on what should be done to punish Wycliffe.

On the day Wycliffe was to be examined, a man named Lewis Clifford, who was a member of the prince's court but not a particularly powerful man, strode up to the bishops and sternly warned them not to pass any sentence on Wycliffe. The bishops were so taken aback by his demand that they took no action against Wycliffe that day.

Wycliffe's sect continued to grow despite church opposition. Some authorities at Oxford attempted to silence him; others gave him whatever support they could. The church considered him a heretic and threatened his followers with excommunication. For some time Wycliffe was either banished or in hiding, but he returned to his parish of Lutterworth to die in 1384.

In 1415, the Synod of Constance declared John Wycliffe a notorious heretic who died in his heresy and ordered his bones removed from consecrated ground. In 1425, Wycliffe was disinterred, his bones burned and thrown into the river. But there is no denying truth, which will even spring up from dust and ashes. Although they burned his bones and drowned his ashes, the Word of God and the truth of John Wycliffe's doctrine would never be destroyed.

Although King Richard allowed himself to be influenced by popes Urban and Boniface IX and published several decrees against the new Protestant doctrines, there is no record of anyone being put to death for holding them during his reign.

SIR WILLIAM SAUTRE

Richard II was deposed in 1399 and succeeded by Henry IV. In 1400, during a meeting of Parliament at Westminster, Sir William Sautre, a good man and faithful priest, asked permission to speak for the good of the kingdom. The bishop present, suspecting that he wanted to address the subject of religion, convinced Parliament that the matter should be referred to the church convocation; so on February 12, 1400, Thomas Arundel, archbishop of Canterbury, and his provincial council held a hearing with Sautre.

They charged that he had previously renounced several heretical opinions but continued to teach and preach them. The charges against Sautre, the parish priest of St. Scithe the Virgin in London, were as follows:

> *He would not worship the cross on which Christ suffered.*
> *He would rather worship a temporal king, the bodies of the*
> *saints, or a contrite man than the cross.*
> *He thought it was more important for a priest to teach the*
> *Word of God than say the canonical hours.*
> *He believed that the consecrated bread of Communion*
> *remains bread and is not physically the body of Christ.*

Sautre was given time to prepare an answer to these charges, reappearing before the convocation the following Friday, February 18. He refused to abandon his beliefs and was given one more day to consider his position. Still adamant on the nineteenth, Sautre was ordered stripped of all his church offices: priest, deacon, subdeacon, acolyte, exorcist, reader, sexton, and even doorkeeper. Reduced to the state of layman, Sautre was then handed over to the secular legal authorities, and the church petitioned the king to execute him—something it could not do itself. King Henry readily agreed, becoming the first English king to ever put a heretic to death; Sir William Sautre became the first Englishman to suffer martyrdom in Henry's reign.

After Sautre's death, others who believed as he did took pains to conceal themselves while the unpopular king gathered what support he could by doing the will of the church, legally condemning the books of Protestantism, and making the burning of anyone convicted of heresy legal in England.

JOHN BADBY

On March 1, 1409, John Badby, a layman, was examined before Thomas Arundel, the archbishop of Canterbury, and a number of other lords. The principal charge against him was that he believed the bread was not turned into the actual physical body of Christ upon consecration.

When the examination was finished and all the conclusions were read in English, the archbishop asked Badby if he would renounce his beliefs and adhere to the doctrine of the Catholic faith. He answered that he would stay with his own beliefs. Badby was locked in the friars' mansion, with the archbishop holding the key, until he appeared again on March 15, was declared a heretic, and was turned over to the secular authorities for punishment.

That afternoon, John Badby was brought to Smithfield and put in an empty barrel, bound with chains to the stake, and surrounded by dry wood. As he stood there, the king's eldest son happened by and encouraged Badby to save himself while there was still time, but Badby refused to change his opinions. The barrel was put over him and the fire lit.

When Badby felt the fire, he cried, "Mercy, Lord!" and the prince immediately ordered the fire extinguished. Then he promised Badby a yearly stipend from the king if he would return to the faith of the church. Even then, Badby held his ground to the death.

After Badby's death, the bishops, seeking to suppress the doctrine forever and knowing they had a king willing to act on their wishes, drafted a law that condemned the books of heretics and ordered all diocesans to proceed against any heretic with zeal. Death by fire was declared the fate of any heretic who would not recant. After this, the archbishop of Canterbury issued similarly harsh laws against the Protestants.

With all these laws against them, you would think the Protestants would have been utterly destroyed, and yet such are the works of the Lord that these men multiplied daily instead of being defeated. Their numbers especially increased in London, Lincolnshire, Norfolk, Herefordshire, Shrewsbury, and Calais. Some, however, did recant, among whom were John Purvey, who recanted at Paul's Cross; John Edward, priest of the diocese of Lincoln; Richard Herbert and Emmot Willy, of London; John Becket, of London; and John Seynons, of Lincolnshire.

WILLIAM THORPE

William Thorpe was a valiant warrior under the banner of Christ. He was examined before the archbishop of Canterbury in 1407, accused of traveling through England for over twenty years, preaching his reformed beliefs to the people.

The archbishop not only demanded that Thorpe deny his beliefs and return to the Catholic Church, but that he turn in anyone he found holding similar beliefs in the future. He was also forbidden to preach until the archbishop was sure he was truly converted.

"Sir," Thorpe replied, "if I agree to this, I would have to be a spy for every bishop in England." Thorpe refused to pledge unconditional submission to the church. "I will willingly obey God and His law," he said, "and every member of the holy church that agrees with Christ."

What happened to Thorpe after he was committed to prison isn't known. There is no record of his being burned, so he may have died in prison or secretly escaped.

Poor Christians were being oppressed everywhere, but especially in England at this time, where the king supported the Catholic Church. The church was so strong there that no one could stand against it; whatever it decreed was obeyed by all men.

JOHN HUSS

Richard II had married a native of Bohemia, and through her servants, the works of Wycliffe were carried to that country, where they were effectively preached to the people by John Huss of Prague.

Pope John XXIII, seeking to suppress the Bohemians, appointed Cardinal de Columna to look into Huss's preaching and deal with any heresy he might find, so Columna set a date for Huss to appear before him in Rome.

Huss never appeared on the designated date, but King Wenceslaus of Bohemia sent ambassadors to assure Columna that any false doctrine being preached in his country would be taken care of by him, at his expense. At the same time, Huss sent his own ambassadors to assure the cardinal he was innocent of heresy. Columna refused all their pleas and excommunicated Huss for failing to appear in person.

The Bohemians couldn't have cared less about the proclamation of excommunication. The more they grew in knowledge of the Lord through Huss, the less they cared for the pope and his rules, especially since the church was divided at that time, with three men arguing over the office of pope. Although the Bohemian church officials succeeded in having Huss banned from Prague, he carried on his work, spreading Wycliffe's message among the people and causing a great uproar over the church's riches and abuses.

Wenceslaus took advantage of his subjects' states of mind to levy heavy taxes on the clergy, silencing them in Bohemia and filling his treasury at the same time.

In 1414, a general church conference was held in Constance to resolve the problem of the three popes and also deal with the Bohemians. Assured of safe conduct by both Emperor Sigismund and one of the popes, Huss traveled to the conference, arriving in Constance on November 3. Twenty-six days later, he appeared before the bishops to defend himself but was not allowed to speak. In violation of the promises made to him, he was imprisoned for "safe keeping" and charged with eight articles of heresy.

On June 7, 1415, Huss was brought before a council and condemned as a heretic when he refused to recant his support of Wycliffe's theology. He was stripped of all his church offices, made to wear a paper hat with the words ARCH HERETIC on it, and led past a fire consuming his books.

On July 6, 1415, the hangman stripped Huss of his clothes, tied his hands behind him, then chained his neck to the stake. At that point, Huss told the hangman that he was glad to accept the chain for the Lord's sake. Straw and wood were piled around him to his chin, and the fire was lit. As the flames rose around him, Huss was heard to say over and over, "Jesus Christ, the Son of the living God, have mercy upon me," until the flames choked him. When all the wood was burned, the upper part of his body was still hanging in the chain, so they threw it down, made a new fire, and burned it after cutting his head into small pieces. When he was totally burned, Huss's ashes were carefully collected and thrown into the Rhône River.

JEROME OF PRAGUE

Upset by the unjust treatment of John Huss, Jerome of Prague arrived in Constance on April 4, 1415, volunteering to appear before the council if promised safe conduct. This was denied him, so Jerome wrote out his thoughts on the council's treatment of Huss and had them hung on the gates and porches of Constance's churches and public buildings. Then he returned to Bohemia, where he was captured and brought back to face the council.

Jerome denied that he had done anything against the church, answering his accusers firmly and calmly, and was imprisoned for eleven days, hung by his heels with chains the whole time. Brought back before the council, he eventually gave in to their threats to save his life and agreed that John Huss had been fairly condemned as a heretic. Even then, he wasn't freed but returned to prison under slightly better conditions. It soon became obvious that Jerome had given in to save his life, not because he had truly changed his mind about the council, and new articles of heresy were drawn up against him.

On May 25, 1416, after 340 days of imprisonment, Jerome was brought before the Council of Constance and charged with 107 offenses, all of which he denied or disproved in short order, silencing his interrogators with his strength and knowledge of God's law. However, the outcome of the hearing was never really in doubt, no matter what Jerome said.

The Saturday before Ascension Day, Jerome was brought to hear judgment passed on him. He was given one more chance to take back his support of John Wycliffe and John Huss but refused. The council condemned him as a heretic, excommunicated him, and turned him over to the secular authorities.

Jerome went to his death bravely, singing hymns, canticles, and the doxology, then embracing a drawing of John Huss that he was bound to. Before the fire was lit, he said to the assembled crowd, "What I have just sung, I believe. This creed is my whole faith, but I'm dying today because I refuse to deny that John Huss was a true preacher of the Gospel of Jesus Christ."

As the fire flared up around him, Jerome continued his singing; and even when no more sound could be heard from him, his lips continued to move and his head to shake for fifteen minutes. Finally dead in the fire, all his possessions from prison were burned, and his ashes were thrown into the Rhône River.

❧

Henry Chicesley succeeded Thomas Arundel as archbishop of Canterbury, continuing the persecutions. Under him, King Henry VI commissioned John Exeter and Jacolet Germain, the keeper of Colchester Castle, to apprehend William White and others suspected of heresies. Soon after, John Exeter attacked six people in the town of Burgay, Norwich, and sent them to the castle of Norwich.

The old records also show that a great number of people from the towns of Beccles, Ersham, and Ludney were thrown into prison and openly shamed after they recanted. From 1428–1431, about 120 men and women were taken, some only for eating meat on vigil days. Others were handled more cruelly, and some were burned; 78 were forced to recant. Many of the charges against these people were untrue or reported incorrectly by the notaries. Often the simple, uneducated people did not understand the charges brought against them or know how to answer them. Most of them seemed to have been instructed in their faith by William White, a follower of John Wycliffe.

WILLIAM WHITE

William White, a well-educated, upright, and well-spoken priest, also became a follower of John Wycliffe. He surrendered his priesthood and its salary to marry a godly young woman but continued to read, write, and preach the doctrines of Wycliffe throughout the Norfolk area, drawing many people to God and developing a reputation as a good, honest man.

His main points of doctrine were:

> *That men should seek forgiveness of sins only from God,*
> *not priests.*
> *That the pope's wicked living made him an enemy of Christ.*
> *That men should not worship images, other idolatrous*
> *paintings, or the saints.*
> *That the Roman Church brought forth no true doctrine.*
> *That all monks, friars, and priests were the soldiers of*
> *Lucifer and damned.*

Brought before Archbishop Henry Chicesley in 1424, White held his ground for some time before being forced to recant. He returned to Norfolk, where he continued to teach and convert the people to the true doctrine of Christ. Captured and tried before William, the bishop of Norwich, he was condemned under thirty articles and burned in September 1424. After his death, his wife continued his work, bringing even more people to God, until she, too, was captured and punished at the hands of the same bishop.

JEROME SAVONAROLA

Savonarola was an Italian monk, very well educated, who began to preach to the people against the evil living he witnessed within his own order, demanding reforms. As Savonarola's popularity grew, Pope Alexander VI ordered his vicar to proceed with the needed reforms in an attempt to silence the monk, but Savonarola wouldn't be silenced.

When the pope denounced Savonarola's testimony and ordered him to be silent, the monk finally realized the danger he was in and temporarily stopped preaching. But he took it up again in Florence in 1496 at the request of the people longing for God's Word. Cursed as a heretic, Savonarola told the people that such curses were against true doctrine and should be ignored.

Savonarola was taken from his cloister in 1498, along with two other friars who supported him, and burned as a heretic on May 24, 1499.

THE STATE OF RELIGION

By reading this history, a person should be able to see that the religion of Christ, meant to be spirit and truth, had been turned into nothing but outward observances, ceremonies, and idolatry. We had so many saints, so many gods, so many monasteries, so many pilgrimages. We had too many churches, too many relics (true and fake), too many untruthful miracles. Instead of worshipping the only living Lord, we worshipped dead bones; in place of immortal Christ, we worshipped mortal bread.

No care was taken about how the people were led as long as the priests were fed. Instead of God's Word, man's word was obeyed; instead of Christ's testament, the pope's canon. The law of God was seldom read and never understood, so Christ's saving work and the effect on man's faith were not examined. Because of this ignorance, errors and sects crept into the church, for there was no foundation for the truth that Christ willingly died to free us from our sins—not bargaining with us but giving *to* us.

Although God allowed His Church to wander for a long time, at last it pleased Him to restore it to its original foundation. And here we must admire God's wisdom, for just as the church fell into ruin because of the ignorance of its teachers, shortly after the burning of John Huss and Jerome, God gave man the art of printing, which restored knowledge to the church.

Through the grace of God, men of wisdom were now able to communicate their thoughts accurately and widely so others could distinguish light from darkness, truth from error, religion from superstition. Knowledge grew in science and in languages, opening a window of light for the world and clearing the way for the Reformation of the church. Still, many were left to suffer before that reform would be complete.

THOMAS CHASE

One of those persecuted for the Gospel and Word of Christ was Thomas Chase of Amersham, a good man who often spoke against idolatry and superstition. Chase was brought before the blind bishop at Woburn and examined, and although we have no record of his examination, he must have professed Christ's true Gospel against idolatry, for he was locked in the bishop's house in Woburn. There he remained in chains, manacles, and irons, all of which he took quietly and faithfully, until they lost patience with him and secretly strangled him one day.

There would have been a public uproar if the truth came out about how Thomas Chase had died, so the church let out a rumor that the good man had hung himself. This would have been impossible, since Chase was chained in such a small area that he could neither sit nor stand, as a woman who saw him dead testified. To be sure no one would be able to examine the body, the authorities buried Chase secretly somewhere near the road between Woburn and Little Marlow.

A GODLY WOMAN

Of all the people who suffered for Christ and His truth, I know of none so admirable as the godly woman put to death in Chipping Sodbury about this time. Her constancy was glorious to behold, especially when contrasted to the character of the chancellor who condemned her, one Dr. Whittenham.

When she was condemned for heresy and brought to the place of execution, a great crowd of people gathered, including Dr. Whittenham. This faithful woman persisted in her truthful testimony to the end, committing her cause to the Lord and refusing no pain, to keep her conscience clear. Her suffering finally over, the people began to disperse to their homes.

Meanwhile, as the church was slaughtering this innocent lamb just outside the town, a butcher in town was preparing to slay a bull. Having tied him with ropes, the butcher attempted to hit the bull on the head and kill him, but he missed his killing blow—not being as skilled at killing as the church's persecutors. The bull, somewhat put out at being hit, broke loose as the people returned from the execution, scattering the townspeople but harming no one until he came to Dr. Whittenham, whom he immediately gored through and killed to everyone's wonder.

1520–1521

As the light of the Gospel began to appear and its number of supporters grew, the bishops became more vehement in their persecutions, causing much suffering in the land. Especially affected were the areas of Buckinghamshire, Amersham, Uxbridge, Henley, and Newbury in the diocese of London, as well as areas in Essex, Coulcester, Suffolk, and Norfolk.

It must be understood that this move toward reformation began before the name of Luther was even known. England had always had godly people who were dedicated to the Word of God, sitting up all night reading and hearing and going to great expense to purchase the few books that were available in their tongue. Some would pay as much as a load of hay for a few translated chapters of St. James or St. Paul. Considering the scarcity of books and teachers, it's amazing how the Word of Truth spread as far as it did, neighbor teaching neighbor, sharing books and truth and so passing on the knowledge of God.

There were four main areas in which these early reformers disagreed with the church of Rome:

They denied the value of pilgrimages.

They refused to worship the saints.

They insisted on reading scripture for themselves.

*They did not believe the physical body of Christ was present
in the sacramental bread.*

These were simple, honest people who studied and spoke openly of their beliefs, so it was easy for church examiners to trap them into heretical statements they barely understood and make them implicate others who studied God's Word with them.

In the diocese of Lincoln, Bishop John Longland renewed the old persecution by bringing in one or two men who had previously recanted and reexamining them. These implicated others, until a great number of people were brought before the bishop for the crime of assembling together to read the scriptures. Those who were found to have relapsed were burned; the rest were so burdened with penance that they either died from grief or survived in shame.

King Henry VIII made the bishop of Lincoln's task even easier by ordering all his secular legal authorities to give the bishop any aid and assistance he needed. Now both the law of the land and law of the church were against any who studied the scriptures and upheld their truth.

MARTIN LUTHER

Martin Luther, born in Eisleben, Saxony, in 1483, was sent to the University of Erfurt. There he entered the monastery of the Augustinians and met an old man of his order with whom he discussed many things, especially the remission of sins.

Here he learned the full meaning of Paul's statement, "We are justified by faith." Through his readings of the prophets and apostles and the exercise of faith in prayer, Luther came to believe the truth of Paul's statement and realized the error of what was being taught by the church's schoolmen. In his four years at Erfurt, Luther also read Augustine, Gabriel, Cameracensis, Oceam, Aquinas, Scotus, and Gerson, preferring Augustine above the others.

In 1508, at the age of twenty-six, Luther began teaching and preaching at the University of Wittenberg, impressing many educated men with his scholarship. Three years later he traveled to Rome about a disagreement among the monks and was granted his doctorate at the expense of the Duke of Saxony on his return. Luther soon began to compare the Epistle to the Romans and the Psalms, showing people the difference between the law and the Gospel. He also argued against the error that said men could earn remission of their sins through works, leading his listeners and readers to God's remission of sins, through love of Jesus, not through indulgences or pilgrimages.

All this time, Luther changed nothing in the ceremonies, carefully observing the rules of his order. The only way he differed from other priests was in stressing the role of faith in the remission of sins.

In 1516, Pope Leo X began selling pardons, by which he gained a large amount of money from people who were eager to save the souls of their loved ones. His collectors assured the people that for every ten shillings they gave, one specified soul would be delivered from the pains of purgatory. The pope's collector in Germany was a Dominican friar named Tetzel.

On September 30, 1517, Luther put his objections to this practice on the temple adjoining the castle of Wittenberg. Tetzel immediately called him a heretic, burning his objections and his sermons on indulgences. Luther replied that he was not totally against indulgences but preferred they be used in moderation. Soon Maximilian (the German emperor), Charles (the king of Spain), and the pope contacted Duke Frederick of Saxony and asked him to silence Luther. The duke conferred with many educated men on the problem, including Erasmus, who supported Luther but urged a little more moderation in his writing and preaching. Duke Frederick communicated his concern to Luther but took no action to silence him. The argument continued, but in

1518, Luther wrote to the pope, totally submitting himself to his authority.

On August 7, 1518, Luther was ordered to appear before the pope in Rome. The University of Wittenberg and Duke Frederick immediately sent letters back to the pope requesting that Cardinal Cajetan in Augsburg hear Luther. The pope told Cajetan to call Luther before him in Augsburg and bring him to Rome by force, if necessary.

Early in October, Luther traveled to Augsburg at the request of the cardinal, waiting there three days to receive a promise of safe conduct from the emperor. When Luther came before him, Cajetan rather gently demanded three things of him:

That he repent and revoke his errors.
That he promise not to revert back to them.
That he not do anything that would trouble the church.

When Luther asked exactly where he had erred, the cardinal showed him Clement's papal bull on indulgences and maintained that faith isn't necessary to someone who receives the sacrament.

In his written reply to the cardinal, Luther stated that the pope was to be obeyed as long as what he says agrees with the scriptures, but that the pope may make mistakes, and any faithful Christian has the right to disagree with him if he is using better reason or better authority for his opinions. He also stated that no one is righteous and that a person receiving the sacrament must believe.

The cardinal told Luther to go away until he was ready to repent. Luther waited for three days in Augsburg then sent a message to the cardinal that he would keep silent on the pardons if his enemies would do the same. He asked that every other point of conflict be referred to the pope for his decision. After three more days of waiting, Luther left Augsburg; but before he went, he sent a letter of explanation to the cardinal, along with an appeal to the pope, which he had published before leaving town.

In January 1519, Emperor Maximilian died. In October 1520, he was succeeded by Charles, king of Spain, who received the crown through the efforts of Duke Frederick. In November of that year, two cardinals arrived from Pope Leo to see Frederick and make two demands of him: that all Luther's books be burned and that Luther either be killed or sent to Rome. Frederick refused, asking for permission to carry on an investigation by educated men, which would determine if Luther was actually in error. If he was proved wrong and refused to recant, Frederick would no longer protect

Luther; until then, he would.

In 1521, Luther attended the Diet of Worms at the request of the emperor and with his assurance of safe conduct. The fourth day after he arrived, he was ordered to appear before the emperor and other nobles of the German state, which he did. Told to keep silent until he was asked to speak, Luther was presented with two questions:

Were the books gathered there his?
Would he recant them or stand on what he'd written?

Luther replied that the books were his work but asked for time to answer the second question. Brought back the next day, he said it was impossible to categorically defend what he'd written, since he knew he was a fallible man, but he would be willing to be shown where he had made any errors. Asked for a simple *yes* or *no* answer to the two questions, Luther said he would stand on what he'd written until proven wrong by the scriptures.

Unable to move him, the council sent Luther home under his safe-conduct pass. He was kept in hiding for a while but eventually returned to Wittenberg, where he died at the age of sixty-three after continuing to write and preach for an additional twenty-nine years.

ULRIC ZWINGLE

Ulricus Zuinglius moved to Zurich in about 1519, living with the priests near the abbey, observing all their rites and ceremonies for two to three years, and instructing the people in scripture.

The same year, Pope Leo renewed his pardons throughout the world, but Zwingle opposed them, finding proof in the scriptures that they were wrong; he also opposed the other corruptions that were currently reigning in the church. Finally Hugo, the bishop of Constance, wrote to the senate of Zurich and the college of canons where Zwingle was living, complaining about him and warning everyone to beware of his teachings. Zwingle explained his faith before the senate of Zurich, which wrote back to the bishop in 1522, saying he should restrain the filthy and infamous lives of the priests and do nothing to hinder the liberty of the Gospel.

Zwingle himself wrote to the whole Swiss nation. In his letter, he urged them not to oppose the advance of pure doctrine or bring trouble to any priests who had married. Since the Swiss custom was to allow priests their concubines, Zwingle urged them to allow them lawful marriages instead.

Zwingle continued teaching the Word of the Lord for several more years, the Dominican friars preaching against him, until Zwingle offered to debate with them. At this, the judges and senate of Zurich called all the priests in Zurich to a meeting on January 29, 1523, where everyone would be free to speak their minds. The bishop of Constance sent John Faber as his spokesman. At the close of the meeting, the senate of Zurich declared that the Gospel of Christ should be taught out of the Bible and the traditions of man should be abandoned.

Soon the bishop of Constance wrote to defend the Catholic Church; about June 13, the senate rejected his doctrine and ordered all Catholic images in the city burned. The following April, the city of Zurich suppressed the Catholic Mass, replacing it with the Lord's Supper, the reading of the prophets, prayer, and preaching.

Only Zurich took part in this reformation, not the other twelve cities of Switzerland, who remained with the Catholic Church. In December 1527, a meeting was called in the town of Berne, where the two schools of religion were permitted to debate the issues freely. On the Protestant side were Zwingle, Oecolampadius, Bucer, Capito, and Blaurerus. The chief speaker for the Catholics was Conrad Tregerus, an Augustinian friar who tried to prove his points by sources other than the Bible, which was not allowed. Forced to stay within the Bible, Tregerus left the assembly. The arguments continued for nineteen days, with the end result that the city of Berne and those adjoining it abolished the Mass, altars, and images of the Catholic Church.

In 1531, the cantons of Zurich and Berne, the only two that had reformed their religion, were insulted by the other five cantons, which led to a war between them. When the five cantons refused to agree to a truce that would allow freedom of religion, Zurich and Berne cut off their roads, starving the cities and forcing them to attach Zurich. Zwingle died in an attempt to reinforce a cut-off garrison of soldiers. His body was mutilated and burned by the Catholic troops. He died at the age of forty-four.

WENDELMUTA

In the year 1527, a virtuous widow named Wendelmuta was martyred in Holland. Arrested for her Protestant beliefs, she was imprisoned in Werden Castle until she appeared before the general session of Holland. Several monks were appointed to convince her to recant, but she refused. She also refused the appeals of her family and friends, including a noble lady who was fond of her.

"Wendelmuta," the lady said, "why don't you be quiet and just believe in your heart?"

"You don't know what you're saying," Wendelmuta replied. "It is written, 'With the heart man believeth unto righteousness; and with the mouth confession is made unto salvation.'"

On November 20, she was condemned as a heretic and ordered burned. Coming to the stake, Wendelmuta refused to kiss the cross a monk brought to her. She put a packet of gunpowder to her chest, gave her neck to be bound, and commended herself into God's hands. Wendelmuta closed her eyes and meekly bowed her head. The fire was then set, and she was burned to ashes.

THE WALDENSES

About 1160, Peter Waldo, a citizen of Lyons, suddenly changed his lifestyle, giving away large amounts of money, studying God's Word, and teaching others how to live virtuous lives. In time, people flocked to him, eager to receive the scriptures he translated into French and passed out to those who wanted to learn.

Soon the churchmen in the area, who would not explain the scripture to the people, ordered Waldo to stop his work or face excommunication. Although Waldo ignored their orders, they persecuted his followers so badly that they were all forced to leave the city. The exiled Waldenses dispersed to many places, including Bohemia, Lombardy, and other French provinces. So perfect were they in their knowledge of scripture that unlettered countrymen were able to recite the entire book of Job by heart. Others knew the whole New Testament. One of their fiercest persecutors admitted, "This sect of the Lyonists has a great show of holiness. They live justly before men, believe all good things come from God, and hold all the articles in the creed. Only they blaspheme the Roman Church and hate it."

Everywhere they lived for the next four hundred years, the Waldenses were subject to terrible persecution, especially in the year 1545. Finally, about 1559, the Waldenses living under the Duke of Savoy in the Piedmont area were given freedom to practice their religion without persecution—after generations of patient suffering.

THOMAS BILNEY

Thomas Bilney was brought up in the University of Cambridge, even as a child studying the liberal sciences and laws. But at last, having found a better teacher in the Holy Spirit, he gave up his study of man's laws to learn the Word of God.

Excited by his love of true religion and godliness, Bilney felt a need to spread the Gospel to others. He was quite successful in this, converting, among others, Thomas Arthur and Hugh Latimer. Soon Bilney left the university to travel widely, teach, and preach, accompanied by Thomas Arthur.

Bilney's attacks on the insolence, pomp, and pride of the clergy soon drew the attention of Thomas Wolsey, the cardinal of York, who ordered both Bilney and Arthur imprisoned. On November 29, 1527, Bilney and Arthur were brought before Wolsey and a group of bishops, priests, and lawyers at Westminster.

Asked if he had privately or publicly taught the opinions of Martin Luther or anyone else against the church, Bilney said that he hadn't. He was then asked if he hadn't previously sworn to actively oppose this type of teaching wherever it was found. Bilney admitted he had sworn to do that but only under pressure, not legally. Told to recant his errors, Bilney refused, saying he would stand on his conscience; he was declared a heretic.

From December 5–7, Bilney continued to take the position that he had done nothing against the church doctrine and asked permission to call witnesses to that effect. No witnesses were allowed, since he had already been declared a heretic, and on December 7 he was given his last chance to recant before being sentenced. On the advice of his friends, Bilney gave in and was absolved by the bishop. He was sentenced to prison for some time and forced to do penance by going before the procession at St. Paul's, bare-headed and carrying a bundle of wood on his shoulder, then standing before the preacher during the sermon.

Returning to Cambridge in 1528, Bilney fell into a deep depression that nothing could lift. His friends stayed with him day and night, afraid that he might kill himself if left alone. This depression stayed with him until 1531, at which time Bilney decided he could no longer deny God's truth, said good-bye to his friends, and left to resume preaching in Norfolk. He urged everyone there to learn from his example and never trust their friends' advice when it came to matters of religion and conscience. He had denied God's truth once to save his life but never would again.

Bilney was soon arrested and given to the city's sheriffs for execution, one of whom, Thomas Necton, was a close friend. Although Necton was powerless to stop Bilney's execution, he was able to make his waiting more comfortable than normal, even allowing friends to visit him the night before he died.

Bilney approached the stake in a layman's gown, his arms hanging out, his hair mangled by the church's ritual divestiture of office. He was given permission to speak to the crowd and told them not to blame the friars present for his death and then said his private prayers.

The officers put reeds and wood around him and lit the fire, which flared up rapidly, deforming Bilney's face as he held up his hands and called out, "Jesus," and "I believe."

Bilney's travel, teaching, and example were very influential at Cambridge, drawing many there to Christ. Among those affected were Hugh Latimer, Dr. Barnes, Dr. Thistel, Master Fooke, Dr. Warner, and Master Soude.

JOHN FRITH

Among all evils of the persecution, none seemed worse to us than the cruel treatment and death of John Frith, a young man who stood far above his companions in knowledge and godliness. Even though his brilliance could have brought him honor and dignity in the secular world, Frith chose to dedicate himself to the church, believing that the truly good man should live for others, not for himself.

After studying at Cambridge and becoming a very well-educated man, Frith became acquainted with William Tyndale, who planted the seed of the Gospel and sincere godliness in his heart.

At that time Thomas Wolsey, cardinal of York, built a college in Oxford named Frideswide, now known as Christ's Church—not so much because of his love of learning but to leave himself a perpetual monument. He gathered together the best vestments, vessels, and ornaments in the land and gave them to the college, also appointing the best professors he could find, one of whom was John Frith. When these professors conferred together about the abuses of the church, they were all accused of heresy and thrown in prison.

Frith was eventually released on the condition that he stay within ten miles of Oxford, a condition he immediately violated by going abroad for two years. He secretly returned to visit the prior of Reading and was arrested there as a vagabond. Frith was an honest man who found it very difficult to lie convincingly, so the authorities were fairly sure he wasn't a tramp, despite his disguise, but they failed to make him reveal his identity. Until he could be identified, he was locked in the stocks at Reading without food. When he began to suffer badly from hunger, he asked that the local schoolmaster be brought to him.

As soon as Leonard Cox arrived, Frith began to complain of his captivity—in Latin. They talked of many things in both Latin and Greek, then Cox hurried to the town judges and complained of the treatment being given such an excellent, well-educated young man. Frith was freed from the stocks without further punishment.

But he had no time to enjoy his freedom because Sir Thomas More, then the chancellor of England, was looking for him all over the country and offering rewards for his capture. Even though he moved from place to place and disguised himself, Frith was eventually captured and imprisoned in the Tower of London.

While there, he and More wrote back and forth to each other, arguing about the sacrament of Communion and purgatory. Frith's letters were always moderate, calm, and learned. Where he was not forced to argue, he tended to give in for the sake of peace.

Eventually Frith was taken before the archbishop of Canterbury, then before the bishop of Winchester, to plead his case. Last of all, he appeared before the assembled bishops in London. His examinations revolved around two points: purgatory and the substance of the sacrament. As Frith wrote to his friends, "I cannot agree with the divines and other head prelates that it is an article of faith that we must believe—under pain of damnation—that the bread and wine are changed into the body and blood of our Savior Jesus Christ while their form and shape stay the same. Even if this were true, it should not be an article of faith."

On June 20, 1533, John Frith was brought before the bishops of London, Winchester, and Lincoln and condemned to death. On July 4, he was led to the stake, where he willingly embraced the wood and fire, giving a perfect testimony with his own life. The wind blew the fire away from him, toward Andrew Hewet, who was burning with him, so Frith's death took longer than usual, but he seemed to be happy for his companion and not to care about his own prolonged suffering.

THOMAS BENNET

Thomas Bennet was born in Cambridge and made a master of arts there. The more he grew in the knowledge of God and His holy Word, the more he came to abhor the time's corrupt state of religion until, hoping to live with more freedom of conscience, he left the university and moved to Exeter in 1524, where he became a teacher.

Bennet was a quiet man whose greatest pleasure was attending sermons. In his spare time, he studied the scripture privately, not sharing his views with anyone until he was sure they felt as he did. But every tree and herb has its due time for bringing forth fruit, so did Bennet. Seeing the glory of God blasphemed, idolatrous religion maintained, and the power of the pope extolled, he finally decided he had to speak out, even though he knew he would be punished. In October, he fastened to the doors of the cathedral a scroll that said, "The pope is Antichrist, and we ought to worship God only, not saints."

As soon as the message was found, the authorities attempted to find the heretic who had posted it. Bennet quietly went about his life, attending services and teaching his students while church and secular authorities looked for the culprit. But Bennet was such a quiet, faithful man that no one would ever suspect him of doing such a bold, dangerous thing.

After a while, when it had no success finding the heretic, the church decided to publicly curse him or her with book, bell, and candle—considered in those days to be the most terrible curse of all. Bennet sat in the congregation and heard himself excommunicated, given over to the devil, and deprived of the benefits of the church's pardon for his sins. All the powers of the corrupted church were invoked against him: the saints, the pope, the monks and friars—everything that Bennet considered worthless, anyway.

The congregation was sitting silently, awed by this display of the church's wrath and hoping none of it fell on them by mistake, when Bennet, suddenly seeing the irony of the situation, began to laugh. Once started, he couldn't seem to stop, and he was apprehended as the heretic the church was damning so theatrically. When his friends later asked him why he'd betrayed himself by laughing in church, Bennet replied, "Who could keep from laughing at their little conceits and interludes?" At his trial he confessed, "It was I who put up those bills, and I would do it again, for what I wrote is true."

At his execution, Bennet exhorted the people to worship and know the true God, forsaking the devices, fantasies, and imagination of the church. Most of the people there, including the scribe who wrote his death sentence, were convinced that Bennet was a good man and a servant of God.

WILLIAM TYNDALE

William Tyndale was born near the border of Wales and brought up in the University of Oxford, where he studied languages, the liberal arts, and the scriptures. After further study at Cambridge, he became the tutor of the children of Lord Welch, a nobleman of Gloucestershire.

Abbots, deans, archdeacons, and other well-educated men often visited Lord Welch to discuss the works of Luther and Erasmus, as well as questions of scripture. Whenever he disagreed with their positions—which was often— Tyndale never hesitated to defend his opinion with scripture. One evening Lord and Lady Welch returned from a dinner and told Tyndale about the discussion that had taken place there. Tyndale began to explain that what they'd heard was wrong but was cut short by Lady Welch. "There was a doctor there who could afford to spend a hundred pounds. Another could easily spend two hundred, and the third, three hundred. Why should we believe you instead of them?"

At the time, Tyndale was translating Erasmus's *Manual of a Christian Soldier*. When it was done, he gave a copy to Lord and Lady Welch. Once they read the book, they entertained the churchmen far less frequently.

Soon the area priests began to complain about Tyndale in the pubs and other places, saying his works were heresy and adding to what he said to make their accusations appear true. Tyndale was called before the bishop's chancellor, threatened, and charged with many things, but he was allowed to leave unharmed.

After this, Tyndale decided he'd better leave the area, so he traveled to London, hoping to secure a place with Cuthbert Tonstal, the bishop of London. When he was unable to do that, he left for Germany.

Tyndale, partly through the influence of John Frith, had decided that the people needed to be able to read scripture for themselves instead of trusting the church to explain it to them honestly and fully. He believed that the corruption of the church was tolerated only because people didn't know any better—and the church wasn't about to teach them any better, or its excesses and privileges would be in danger.

In 1526, Tyndale published his English translation of the New Testament and began on the Old Testament, adding prologues to each book. In addition, he published *The Wicked Mammon* and *The Practise of Prelates*, sending copies to England.

After traveling to Germany and Saxony, where he met with Luther and other learned men, he finally settled in Antwerp, The Netherlands.

When his books—especially the New Testament—began to be widely read in England, the bishops and prelates of the church did everything in their power to condemn them and point out their "errors." In 1527, they convinced the king to ban all Tyndale's works in England.

Meanwhile, Cuthbert Tonstal, the bishop of London, worked with Sir Thomas More to find a way to keep the translations out of the public's hands. He became acquainted with Augustine Packington, an English merchant who secretly supported Tyndale, and Packington promised the bishop that he would deliver every copy of the translation's next edition, if the bishop supplied the funds for the purchase. When the bishop agreed, Packington explained the deal to Tyndale. Soon the bishop of London had his books, Packington his praise, and Tyndale all the money, part of which he promptly used to print a new edition that he shipped into the country. The rest of the money supported Tyndale for a while.

Tonstal publicly burned all the copies he had bought, an act that offended the people so much that the church promised that it would provide its own error-free translation. Nothing was done to fulfill this promise. In fact, in May 1530, the church declared that such a translation was unnecessary, which immediately increased the sale of Tyndale's work.

Tyndale was eventually captured by the emperor in Antwerp, his books were all seized, and he was imprisoned for a year and a half before being condemned under the emperor's decree of Augsburg. He was tied to the stake, strangled, and burned in Vilvorden in 1536, dying with these words: "Lord, open the king of England's eyes!"

JOHN LAMBERT

John Lambert, who was converted by Bilney, fled the persecution of the time by going abroad, where he joined Tyndale and Frith and served as chaplain for the British living in Antwerp. After a little over a year, he was captured in 1532 and brought to London to answer forty-five charges before Warham, the archbishop of Canterbury; but the archbishop died in August 1532, and Lambert was set free.

This was during the reign of Henry VIII, shortly after the destruction of England's monasteries and Henry's divorce from Queen Catherine and remarriage, a time when supporters of the Gospel were generally safe in their beliefs.

On his release, Lambert returned to London as an instructor of Greek and Latin. In 1538, he was present at a sermon preached at St. Peter's Church by Dr. Taylor, a Protestant who would later become the bishop of London and die under Queen Mary. When the sermon was over, Lambert approached Taylor to disagree with him on the matter of the sacrament.

In an effort to satisfy Lambert, Taylor discussed the matter with Dr. Barnes. Now Dr. Barnes was in favor of preaching the Gospel, but he thought bringing this issue up would only hinder the spread of the Gospel at that time, so he suggested Taylor talk to Archbishop Cranmer.

What had started as a private conversation was rapidly becoming a public matter. Cranmer hadn't yet changed his mind on the sacrament—although he would later—so he called Lambert into open court to defend his case. Although we don't know what went on in the meeting, rumors about their disagreement spread throughout the whole court.

The bishop of Winchester was one Stephen Gardiner, counselor to the king—a cruel, crafty man who was always looking for a way to hinder the Gospel. He went to King Henry and told him he was hated by the people for several reasons: for destroying the monasteries, abolishing the pope's authority, and divorcing his wife. But if the king showed the people that heretics would still be punished, Gardiner said, Henry would regain his popularity with the people. The king immediately agreed, saying he would personally judge every heretic in the land.

Lambert was brought from prison under guard to be judged by Henry, with all the nobles and bishops in attendance. Given permission to speak, Lambert said that he was glad the king was willing to hear religious controversies, especially since he was a king with such judgment and knowledge.

"I didn't come here," Henry interrupted brusquely, "to hear my own praises! Go straight to the matter."

Taken aback by the king's harsh words, Lambert was silent.

"Why are you just standing there?" Henry demanded. "In the sacrament of the altar, do you say it's Christ's body or not?"

"I agree with Saint Augustine. It is the body of Christ in certain ways," Lambert answered.

"Don't answer me from Saint Augustine or anyone else. What do *you* say?" Henry was addressing Lambert in Latin.

"Then I deny it's the body of Christ."

Henry then turned the interrogation over to Cranmer, who, along with the bishop of Winchester and Tonstal, the bishop of Durham, attempted to change Lambert's mind.

Lambert was overwhelmed. Besieged by taunts and threats from men of power, amazed at the majesty of the place and the king's presence, and exhausted from standing for five hours, he lapsed into silence.

Finally the day was over. King Henry turned to Lambert once more. "What do you say now, after all the instruction of these learned men? Are you satisfied? Will you live or die? What do you say? Take your choice."

Lambert answered, "I yield and submit myself wholly into your hands."

"Commit yourself into God's hands, not mine," was the reply.

"I commend my soul into God's hands, but my body I yield to your clemency."

"If you commit yourself to my judgment, you will die," Henry replied. "I will not be a patron to heretics." The king turned to Cromwell, the chief friend of the Protestants. "Cromwell, read the sentence of condemnation against him."

Through the advice of the bishop of Winchester, Satan had Lambert condemned by his fellow Protestants—Taylor, Barnes, Cranmer, and Cromwell—all of whom would later suffer for the Gospel's sake. Of all the people burned at Smithfield, none was handled as cruelly as Lambert; yet in the midst of his torments, lifting up his mangled burned hands, he cried to the people, "None but Christ. None but Christ!"

ROBERT BARNES

On his graduation from the University of Louvain, Robert Barnes was made prior and master of the Augustines at Cambridge. At that time little literature was taught at Cambridge, but Barnes introduced its study and produced many educated young men who were familiar with the works of Terence, Plautus, Cicero, and others. Once literature was established, Barnes began teaching Paul's epistles, producing many good men for the church.

Through his reading, discussions, and preaching, Barnes became famous for his knowledge of scripture, always preaching against bishops and hypocrites, yet he continued to support the church's idolatry until he was converted to Christ by Bilney.

Barnes preached his first sermon as a Protestant at St. Edward's Church in Cambridge and was immediately accused of heresy. Brought before Cardinal Wolsey, his friends convinced Barnes to abjure, and he did public penance at St. Paul's before being imprisoned for a year and a half. On his release from prison, Barnes was sent as a freed prisoner to the Austin friars in London, but they soon brought more charges on him, and he was forced to flee to Luther at Antwerp.

While in Antwerp, Barnes became friends with Luther, Melancthon, the Duke of Saxony, and the king of Denmark, who sent him with the Lubecks as an ambassador to Henry VIII. Sir Thomas More wanted to capture Barnes while he was in the country, but the king wouldn't allow him to, since Cromwell, his friend and advisor, had become the protector of the Protestants. Barnes was allowed to dispute with the bishops and leave the county at will. He returned to Luther at Wittenberg to publish his books then went back to England at the beginning of Queen Anne Boleyn's reign, becoming a well-respected preacher.

Once Stephen Gardiner arrived from France, trouble fell on the Protestants again. From then on, religion suffered, as did Queen Anne and Cromwell; and Barnes was imprisoned in the Tower of London, until he was burned on July 30, two days after Cromwell's death. Two other Protestants were burned with him—Gerrand and Jerome—plus three Catholics—Powel, Featherstone, and Abel. Seeing both Protestant and Catholic being punished for their faith at the same time confused the whole nation, although it was the political result of a division of the king's council, half of whom were Catholic, half Protestant.

THE LAW OF THE SIX ARTICLES

In 1539, at the instigation of Henry VIII, Parliament passed the Six Articles upholding the Catholic doctrines of priestly celibacy and transubstantiation. The punishment for breaking this law was death, with no provision for recantation, although this was softened a bit by Parliament in 1544, which made provision for recantation and penance for the first two convictions and required death for the third offense.

At the same time, Parliament banned all of Tyndale's books and all songs, plays, and books in English that violated the Six Articles. The text of the Bible was forbidden to all women, craftsmen, apprentices, journeymen, servants, yeomen, farmers, and laborers. Noblemen and their wives were allowed to read the Bible if they did so quietly and didn't expound upon it.

Another provision of the law of the Six Articles allowed a person accused of heresy to bring forward witnesses on his behalf in equal or greater number of witnesses being called against him. This had never been allowed before in heresy trials.

THE DEATH OF HENRY VIII

After a long illness, toward the end of January 1547, it became obvious to King Henry's doctors that he was dying. Although they felt he should know the state of his health, no one was willing to risk telling him. The task fell on one Master Denny, who boldly told Henry that he was dying and urged him to prepare for it by calling on God in Christ for grace and mercy.

The king listened to Denny and considered his sins, which he regretted, yet concluded that "the mercy of Christ is able to pardon me all my sins, even if they were worse than they are."

Glad to hear Henry thinking this way, Denny asked if he would like to speak to anyone. Henry replied that he would like to see Dr. Cranmer, but by the time Cranmer arrived, Henry was unable to speak and barely conscious. He was able to reach out and grasp Cranmer's hand, however. Cranmer urged the king to put his trust in Christ and call on His mercy, and Henry pressed Cranmer's hand as a sign that he was doing so and then died. Henry had ruled for thirty-seven years and nine months, leaving behind three children—Edward, Mary, and Elizabeth.

PATRICK HAMILTON

The first Scottish martyr was Patrick Hamilton, abbot of Ferne, the son of Sir Patrick Hamilton of Kincavil and Catherine Stewart, a daughter of the Duke of Albany. Young Hamilton was educated at St. Andrews in the liberal philosophy of John Mair then read Luther for himself. He was always noted for having a liberal mind and adopted Protestant theology wholeheartedly, but he fled to Wittenberg when he was called to appear before an ecclesiastical council.

There Hamilton became friendly with Luther and Melancthon, who recommended him to Lambert, the head of the University of Marburg. Lambert instructed Hamilton even more fully in Protestantism, which produced a great change in him. Where before he had been skeptical and timid, he now became courageous, almost rash, and decided to return to Scotland and preach the faith there.

He arrived back in Scotland in 1527 and publicly addressed the people for a time before being arrested and imprisoned. His youth—he was only twenty-eight—his talent, and his pleasant, gentle disposition made many churchmen try to change Hamilton's mind or at least convince him to stop preaching his beliefs and disturbing the church. Hamilton held so firm that he converted a Catholic priest named Aless who visited his cell. In time, Aless suffered persecution for his new faith and was burned.

On the scaffold, Hamilton gave his servant all his clothing, comforting him by saying, "What I am about to suffer, dear friend, appears fearful and bitter to the flesh. But remember, it is entrance to everlasting life, which none shall possess who deny their Lord." Even though his executioner's lack of skill prolonged Hamilton's suffering, he never ceased preaching to those standing near him. "How long, oh God," he exclaimed, "shall darkness cover this kingdom? How long will You allow this tyranny of men?" He died with the words "Lord Jesus, receive my spirit" on his lips.

JAMES HAMILTON, CATHERINE HAMILTON, STRAITON, GOURLAY

In 1534, James Hamilton, Catherine Hamilton, David Straiton, and Norman Gourlay were called before King James V in Edinburgh. James Hamilton had been accused by the church of holding the opinions of his brother Patrick. King James warned Hamilton not to appear at his trial, where he wouldn't be able to help him, but to leave the country and forfeit his lands and property to save his life.

Catherine Hamilton, James's sister and King James's aunt, was charged with not believing she could be saved by works. After a long discussion with a lawyer named John Spens, she concluded, "Work here, work there! What kind of working is all this? I know perfectly that no kind of work can save me except the works of Christ, my Lord and Savior!"

The king turned aside and laughed at her reply then called her up to him and convinced her to recant for the sake of her family. She was set free.

Straiton was a gentleman from a good family, but he quarreled with the bishop of Moray over his tithes. One day when he was challenged by the church collectors, Straiton ordered his servants to throw every tenth fish they caught back into the sea and told the collector to go look for his tax there. After this, he calmed down and became a sincere convert of the Reformation. Accused of heresy, Straiton refused to recant and was burned with Gourlay on August 27, 1534.

DEAN THOMAS FORRET

Every Sunday, Dean Thomas Forret preached from the Gospel, something that was normally only done by the friars. In retaliation, the friars accused him of showing the mysteries of scripture to the common people, reading the Bible in the common tongue, and making clergy detestable in the sight of the people.

The bishop of Dunkeld called in Dean Forret and advised him not to preach to the people every Sunday. If he wanted to do that, he should become a friar.

Dean Forret replied that preaching the Gospel once a week was barely enough, but the bishop maintained that they were not ordained to preach, admitting that even he didn't know the Old and New Testaments himself, being content to know his Mass book and pontifical. At this time, nothing was done to Dean Forret, even though he stood his ground and refused to stop preaching the Bible.

Shortly afterward, Dean Forret was arrested, along with two friars named Keillor and Beveridge, a priest named Duncan Simpson, a gentleman named Robert Forrester, and three or four others from the town of Stirling. Accused of being chief heretics and teachers of heresy, none of them was given the opportunity to recant. The main charges against them were that they were present at the marriage of a priest and ate meat at the wedding, which was held during Lent. In February 1538 or 1539, they were all burned in Edinburgh.

GEORGE WISHART

In 1543, George Wishart was teaching at the University of Cambridge. He was a tall man, slightly sad-looking, with black hair and a long beard. A pleasant man, this native of Scotland was polite and humble, a man who loved to travel, learn, and teach. He dressed simply in black and regularly gave his used clothing to the poor.

Wishart was noted for his Christian charity and spartan style of living, eating only two meals a day and fasting one day out of four. He slept on a straw mattress under canvas sheets that he gave away whenever he changed his bed.

Wishart had been arrested and imprisoned in the castle of St. Andrew, locked in chains for his doctrine. On the day he was summoned to appear before the cardinal at St. Andrews, he was escorted to the church by one hundred armed men. Pausing momentarily to hand his purse to a poor man lying by the door, he was then escorted to the cardinal. Dean John Winryme stood in the pulpit to deliver a sermon on heresy; then Wishart stood by the pulpit and heard John Lauder read the charges against him.

When this well-fed priest had read them all, his face running with sweat and frothing at the mouth like a boar, he spit in Master George's face and demanded, "What do you say to these accusations, you traitor and thief?"

Master George briefly knelt down in the pulpit to pray then answered calmly and politely, requesting that they allow him to explain his doctrine for three reasons.

"The first is because through preaching the Word of God, His glory is made manifest. It is reasonable, therefore, for the advancing of the glory of God, that you hear me teaching the pure Word of God.

"Second, since your salvation comes from the Word of God, it would be unrighteous of you not to hear me teach the Word of God.

"Third, your doctrine is full of blasphemous and abominable words coming from the devil. You should know my doctrine so I don't die unjustly to the peril of your own souls.

"Since I came to this country, I taught nothing but the commandments of God, the twelve articles of the Creed, and the Lord's Prayer in the mother tongue. In Dundee, I taught the Epistle of Paul to the Romans. And I will show you how I taught. . . ."

His accuser suddenly shouted, "You heretic, traitor, and thief! It wasn't legal for you to preach! You took that power into your own hands without the authority from the church."

The assembled prelates exclaimed, "If we allow him to preach here, he is so crafty and knowledgeable of the scripture that he'll turn the people against us."

Master George, seeing what they were planning, asked to appeal his case to the lord governor, since he was arrested by him in the first place and should be judged by his legal authorities, not the church.

Despite his appeal, eighteen articles of heresy were read against Wishart, each of which he answered with scripture that soundly supported his doctrine. When the bishops were through, they condemned Wishart to burn as a heretic, ignoring all his replies, and told the congregation to leave.

Returned to prison in the castle, Wishart refused to make his confession to the two friars who arrived, demanding instead Dean John Winryme, who had preached at his hearing.

The fire was made ready and the gallows erected. The cardinal, afraid Wishart would be freed by his friends, ordered all the castle's arms aimed at the gallows. Wishart's hands were tied behind him, and he was led to the fire with a rope around his neck and a chain of iron around his waist.

He told the assembled crowd not to let his death turn them from the Word of God. "I exhort you to love the Word of God and suffer patiently, with a comfortable heart, for the sake of the Word, which is your salvation and everlasting comfort." Then he asked the crowd to help his followers remain firm in his teaching. "I don't fear this grim fire. If any persecution comes to you for the Word's sake, don't fear those who kill the body but cannot kill the soul. Tonight I will dine with the Lord."

After Wishart asked God to forgive those who condemned him, the hangman kneeled before him. "Sir, please forgive me. I am not guilty of your death."

"Come here," Wishart replied. When the hangman went to him, Wishart kissed his cheek and said, "There's a token of my forgiveness. Do your job." As Wishart was hung and burned, the crowd mourned and complained that an innocent lamb had been slaughtered.

WALTER MILNE

Among the martyrs of Scotland, Walter Milne was pivotal, for out of his ashes sprang thousands of others holding the same opinions, which forced the Church of Scotland to debate true religion with the French and the Catholic Church.

Milne was a parish priest of Lunan who embraced the doctrines of the Reformation and was condemned in the time of Beaton. He was able to escape safely from prison and hid in the country of Scotland until the leniency of the queen dowager allowed him to resume his preaching. Forced into hiding a second time, he was captured and tried for heresy at St. Andrews at the age of eighty-two.

The following dialogue took place between Milne and Andrew Oliphant, one of the bishop's priests, at his April 1551 trial.

"What do you think of priests marrying?" Oliphant asked Milne.

"I hold it a blessed bond; for Christ Himself maintained it, approved of it, and made it available for all men. But you don't think it's available for you. You abhor it while taking other men's wives and daughters, not respecting the bond God made. You vow chastity and break it. St. Paul would rather marry than burn, which I have done, for God never forbade marriage to any man."

"You say there are not seven sacraments."

"Give me the Lord's Supper and Baptism, and you can divide the rest among yourselves. If there are seven, why have you omitted one of them—marriage—and given yourself to immorality?"

"You are against the sacrament of the altar. You say the Mass is idolatry."

"A lord or a king calls many to a dinner; then when the hall is ready, he rings a bell to summon the crowd, turns his back on his guests, eats alone, and mocks them. This is what you do, too."

"You deny the sacrament of the altar is the actual body of Christ."

"The scripture of God is not to be taken carnally, but spiritually, and stands in faith only. As far as the Mass, it is wrong. Christ was offered once on the cross for man's sins and will never be offered again. He ended all sacrifice."

"You deny the office of bishop."

"Those you call bishops don't do a bishop's work as defined by Paul's letter to Timothy. They live for sensual pleasure and don't care for their flock. They don't honor the Word of God but seek honor for themselves."

"You speak against pilgrimages."

"They are not commanded in scripture. There is no greater immorality committed in any place than at your pilgrimages."

"You preach secretly in houses and openly in the fields."

"Yes. And on the sea, too, in a ship."

"Will you recant? If not, I will sentence you."

"I am accused of my life. I know I must die once and therefore, as Christ said to Judas, what thou doest, do quickly. I will not recant the truth. I am corn, not chaff; I will not be blown away with the wind or burst by the flail. I will survive both."

Andrew Oliphant ordered Milne given to a secular judge to be burned as a heretic, but the provost of the town, Patrick Learmont, refused to be Milne's secular judge, as did the bishop's chamberlain. The whole town was so offended at the sentence that they wouldn't even sell the bishop's servants a rope for tying Milne to the stake or a tar barrel. Finally Alexander Summer-wail, more ignorant and cruel than the rest, acted as a secular judge and sent Milne to the stake.

When Milne was brought to be executed, Oliphant ordered him to climb up to the stake. "No," Milne replied. "You put me up there and take part in my death. I am forbidden by God's law from killing myself. But I go up gladly."

Oliphant put the old man up himself.

Then Milne addressed the crowd. "Dear friends, I suffer today for the defense of the faith of Jesus Christ, set forth in the Old and New Testaments. I praise God that He has called me to seal up His truth with my life, which, as I have received it from Him, I willingly offer to His glory. If you would escape eternal death, do not be seduced by the lies of priests, monks, friars, priors, abbots, bishops, and the rest of the sect of Antichrist. Depend only on Jesus Christ and His mercy to save you."

There was great mourning and crying among the crowd as Milne died, and their hearts were so inflamed by his death that he was the last religious martyr to die in Scotland.

JOHN ROGERS

John Rogers was educated at the University of Cambridge then served as chaplain to the English merchants living in Antwerp, The Netherlands. There he met William Tyndale and Miles Coverdale, both of whom had previously fled England. Converted to Protestantism, Rogers aided the two in translating the Bible into English, married, and moved to Wittenberg, where he was given a congregation of his own.

Rogers served his congregation for many years before returning to England during the reign of King Edward VI, who had banished Catholicism and made Protestantism the state religion. He served in St. Paul's until Queen Mary took the throne, banished the Gospel, and brought Catholicism back to England.

Even then, Rogers continued to preach against the queen's proclamation until the council ordered him to remain under house arrest in his own home, which he did, even though he could easily have left the country. Protestantism was not going to flourish under Queen Mary. Rogers knew he could find work in Germany; and he did have a large family to think of, but he refused to abandon his cause to save his life. He remained a prisoner in his own house for a long time, but eventually Bonner, bishop of London, had Rogers imprisoned in Newgate with thieves and murderers, and Stephen Gardiner, bishop of Winchester, condemned him to death.

Early on the morning of Monday, February 4, 1555, the jailer's wife woke Rogers and told him to hurry and dress; this was the day he was to burn. His wife and children met him on the way to Smithfield, but Rogers still refused to recant. Arriving at Smithfield, he was given one more chance by Sheriff Woodroofe.

"That which I have preached I will seal with my blood," Rogers replied.

"Then," said Woodroofe, "you are a heretic."

"That will be known on the Day of Judgment."

"Well, I'll never pray for you!"

"But I will pray for you."

A little before the burning, a pardon arrived, but Rogers refused to recant and accept it, becoming the first martyr to suffer death during the reign of Queen Mary.

LAWRENCE SANDERS

After Queen Mary prohibited Protestant preaching in the first year of her reign, several ministers continued to preach the Gospel as private pastors. One of these was Lawrence Sanders.

Sanders, from a prosperous noble family, studied at Eton and King's College, Cambridge. His widowed mother wanted him to become a merchant, so he apprenticed himself to a merchant named Sir William Chester. But soon Sanders realized that he really wanted to be a preacher, and his master, who was a good man, set him free from his contract so Sanders could return to Cambridge as a divinity student.

Sanders began to preach during the reign of King Edward, when Protestantism became the official religion of England. After holding several positions, he became a preacher in the countryside of Leicestershire, where he taught diligently until being offered a church in London named Allhallows. Just as he was about to give up his position in the country to concentrate on his London parish, Queen Mary made her bid for the throne. Seeing that Mary would bring hard times on all Protestants, Sanders kept both positions. If he had given one of them up, he would certainly have been replaced by a Catholic.

So he traveled back and forth to serve both parishes until it became illegal to preach from the Gospel. Sanders continued to preach to his rural congregation until he was forcibly prevented from doing so. Since he couldn't work there, he traveled back to London.

As he entered the city on Saturday, October 14, Sanders was met by Sir John Mordant, an advisor of Queen Mary, who warned him against preaching the next day. Sanders ignored his advice and gave his morning sermon; then, as he was preparing for the afternoon one, he was taken from his church and brought before the bishop, Sir John Mordant, and some chaplains. The bishop asked Sanders to write out his beliefs concerning transubstantiation and sent him to see the Lord Chancellor, who put him in prison.

After being imprisoned for fifteen months, during which he stayed loyal to his conscience, Sanders was brought to trial before the lord chancellor on charges of treason, heresy, and sedition. Presented with the paper he'd written earlier on transubstantiation, Sanders replied, "What I have written, I have written. I won't accuse myself of anything else. There's nothing you can bring against me."

After he was excommunicated and turned over to the legal authorities, the bishop of London came to prison to strip Sanders of his offices on February 4. When he was done, Sanders told him, "I thank God I'm not of your church."

On February 8, Sanders embraced the stake and kissed it, saying, "Welcome to the cross of Christ. Welcome everlasting life."

JOHN HOOPER

During the reign of King Edward, John Hooper served as bishop of two dioceses, always acting as Paul instructed bishops to act in his Epistle to Timothy. He never looked for personal gain, only for the care and salvation of his flocks, giving away any money that came his way. Twice I [Foxe] saw Hooper's house filled with beggars and poor people who were eating at a table filled with meat, an event a servant told me took place every evening before Hooper sat down to eat his own dinner.

Hooper served as bishop for more than two years under Edward. When Edward died and Mary was crowned queen, Hooper was one of the first ordered to report to London and imprisoned. He remained there for eighteen months, gravely ill most of the time, forced to spend his own money to obtain food. On March 19, 1554, Hooper was called before the bishops of Winchester, London, Durham, Llandaff, and Chichester and deprived of his bishoprics. On January 22, 1555, the bishop of Winchester called him in to demand he forsake his Protestant beliefs and accept the pope as the head of the Church of England. If he did so, he would be pardoned—as many other English churchmen had been. Hooper refused.

On January 28, 1555, Hooper appeared before the bishop of Winchester and others and was given another chance to accept the Catholic Church. This was the same day that Rogers was appearing, and they met outside as they left the church with their guards.

"Brother Rogers!" Hooper exclaimed. "Should we take this matter in hand and begin to fry these bundles of wood?"

"Yes, sir," Rogers replied, "by God's grace."

"Be sure, God will give strength."

Hooper was returned to Newgate Prison for six days on January 29; on February 4 the bishop of London stripped him of all church offices, and Hooper was transported to Gloucester to be burned.

On February 5, Hooper was brought to the stake. He had been given packages of gunpowder by the guard to hasten his death and lessen his suffering. These he put under his arms and between his legs. Three irons were brought to fasten him to the stake—one for his neck, one for his waist, one for his legs—but Hooper said they weren't necessary. Just the one around his waist was used.

After Hooper forgave the men who made the fire, it was lit, but the fire builder had used green wood, and even when it finally caught, the wind blew the flames away from Hooper. A second fire was lit, but it only burned low, not flaring up as it should have. When the fire was lit the third time, the gunpowder on Hooper went off, but even that didn't do much good because of the wind.

Even when Hooper's mouth was black and his tongue swollen, his lips continued to move until they shrank to the gums. He knocked on his breast with his hands until one of his arms fell off. Then he knocked with the other—fat, water, and blood dropping off the ends of his fingers—until his hand stuck to the iron around his waist.

Hooper was in the fire for over forty-five minutes, suffering patiently even when the lower part of his body burned off and his intestines spilled out. Now he reigns as a blessed martyr in the joys of heaven that are prepared for the faithful in Christ.

ROWLAND TAYLOR

The town of Hadleigh, in Suffolk, was one of the first towns in England to hear the Word of God from Thomas Bilney. Through his work, a great number of men and women in that parish became educated in the scriptures, many of them having read the entire Bible. Some could have recited most of Paul's epistles by heart, and most were qualified to give a godly judgment in any matter of controversy. The town's children and servants were also brought up and trained in God's Word, so Hadleigh seemed more like a university town of educated people than a town of laborers. Even more importantly, those in the town were faithful followers of God's Word in their daily lives.

Hadleigh's pastor was Dr. Rowland Taylor, a doctor of both civil and church law. At that time most pastors received a house and land to support themselves, but most rented the land out to farmers and appointed an un-educated priest to serve the town, living elsewhere and not really helping with their congregations, nor fulfilling Jesus' charge to Peter: "[Peter], lovest thou me? Feed my sheep." Taylor took every opportunity to gather his people together and teach them the doctrine of salvation.

Taylor's whole life was a blessing to the town. He was a humble man, easily approachable by the poor who came to him for help. He never hesi-tated to correct the rich, either, as a good pastor should. He was always a gentle man, without rancor or ill will, ready to do good to all men, forgiving his enemies, and never trying to do evil to anyone. Anyone who was poor, blind, lame, sick, or had many children to support found Taylor to be a faith-ful provider, much like a father. He saw that his parish contributed gener-ously to the poor among them and made a generous contribution to the alms box himself every year.

Taylor served the town of Hadleigh all the days of Edward VI. But after Edward's death, the Catholics openly ignored the reformations made under Henry VIII and Edward, overthrew the doctrine of the Gospel, and perse-cuted everyone who refused to abandon the Reformation's gains and accept the pope as the head of the Church of England.

Soon a lawyer named Foster—an unskilled court steward—conspired with John Clerk to return Catholicism to Hadleigh. They hired John Averth, a money-grabbing, immoral man, to come to Hadleigh and reinstitute the Mass, hastily constructing an altar in the town's church that was torn down the next day. They rebuilt the altar, this time setting guards to protect it overnight. The next day Foster, Clerk, and Averth brought in all the necessary implements and garments for the Mass, setting out armed guards to prevent anyone from interfering.

Hearing the church bells ringing, Dr. Taylor assumed he was needed at his office but found the church doors tightly locked. Gaining entrance through the chancel door, he saw Averth celebrating the Mass, surrounded by guards with drawn swords.

"You devil!" Taylor shouted. "How do you dare enter this church of Christ and profane and defile it with this abominable idolatry?"

Foster stood up. "You traitor! Why are you disturbing the queen's proceedings?"

"I'm no traitor," Taylor called back. "I'm the shepherd of this flock, with every right to be here. I order you—you popish wolf—in the name of God, leave! Don't poison Christ's flock with your idolatry."

"Are you going to make a commotion and violently resist the queen's proceedings?" Foster demanded.

"I'm not making a commotion. You papists do that. I only resist your idolatries, which are against God's Word and the queen's honor and subvert the country. Furthermore, you're breaking the law that says no Mass may be said at an unconsecrated altar."

When Averth heard that, he began to move away from the altar. John Clerk commanded him to continue the Mass while Foster's guards forcibly led Taylor out of his church.

Mrs. Taylor saw her husband being pushed out, fell to her knees, and said loudly, "I beg God, the righteous judge, to avenge the injury this popish idolater does to the blood of Christ!" They threw her out, too, and locked the doors against the people who were gathering outside.

A day or two later, Foster and Clerk complained about Taylor to Stephen Gardiner, bishop of Winchester. When he was summoned to appear before the bishop, the townspeople begged Taylor to run away, knowing he was doomed if he went to London; but Taylor took his servant and obediently appeared before Gardiner.

Gardiner greeted Taylor in his usual manner, calling him a "knave, traitor, heretic" and other names.

"My lord," Taylor replied, "I am not a traitor or heretic, but a true subject and Christian. I came here at your command. Why did you send for me?"

"Are you come, villain? How do you dare look me in the face? Don't you know who I am?"

"Yes," answered Taylor, "I know who you are. You're Dr. Stephen Gardiner, bishop of Winchester, lord chancellor—but still a mortal man. If I should fear your lordly looks, why don't you fear God? How can you look any Christian in the face? You have forsaken the truth, denied our Savior Jesus Christ and His Word, and gone against your oaths. How will you look when you appear before the judgment seat of Christ and answer to the oaths you made to King Henry VIII and King Edward VI?"

"I did well in breaking those oaths and coming home again to our mother, the Catholic Church of Rome. I want you to do the same."

Taylor spent the next two years in prison, reading, preaching, and exhorting the great number of godly ministers that filled the country's prisons at that time, one of whom was Master Bradford. So many of them were locked up together that the jails began to resemble universities.

About the end of January 1555, Taylor, Bradford, and Sanders were called before the bishops of Winchester, Norwich, London, Salisbury, and Durham and charged with heresy. Given the opportunity to submit to the pope and confess their errors, all three refused. On February 4, 1555, Edmund Bonner, bishop of London, came to the prison to strip Taylor of his church offices. Told to put on his vestments, Taylor refused.

"You won't?" Bonner sneered. "Then I'll *make* you!"

"You won't, by the grace of God."

Taylor was dressed by force so the ceremony could continue.

The next night, Taylor's wife and son were allowed to eat dinner with him since the king's jailers tried to be as kind as possible, unlike the bishop's. His wife suspected that he would be taken away that night, so she watched the prison until he and his guards appeared at 2:00 a.m. The sheriffs allowed them a few minutes together to say good-bye, and Taylor encouraged them all to stay firm in their faith. That night he was taken to an inn named the Woolpack, where he stayed until the sheriff of Essex arrived at eleven the next morning. Taylor was put on a horse and led out of the inn's courtyard, where his servant, John Hull, and Taylor's son met them. Taylor was allowed to hold the boy, bless him, and say good-bye to his servant before being led off.

All the way, Taylor was joyful and happy, busily preaching to his guards and trying to convert them. In a few days, they arrived in Hadleigh, where Taylor was to be burned. The streets of the town were lined with townspeople crying and lamenting their pastor's fate, but Taylor's head was hooded until they reached the common, and he wasn't sure where he was until a guard told him.

"Thanks be to God!" he exclaimed. "I'm home!" He was taken off his horse and unhooded.

When the people saw his ancient face and long white beard, they began calling out encouragement, but Taylor had promised not to speak—probably under the threat of having his tongue cut out. After he gave away his clothing, he looked up and said two sentences: "Good people, I have taught you nothing but God's holy Word, and those lessons I took out of the Holy Bible. Today I come to seal it with my blood." He was promptly hit in the head by one of the guards.

After saying his prayers, Taylor stepped into the pitch barrel, folded his hands in prayer, and stood against the stake as the fire was lit. A man in the crowd hurled a piece of wood at him, hitting him in the head and bloodying his face. "Friend," Taylor said, "I have enough problems. Why was that necessary?" Then he recited the Fifty-first Psalm until Sir John Shelton hit him in the mouth. "Speak in Latin!" he demanded.

Taylor lifted up his hands. "Merciful Father of heaven, for Jesus Christ my Savior's sake, receive my soul into Your hands." He stood still without moving or crying until Soyce struck him on the head with a halberd, spilling out his brains, and his corpse fell into the fire.

WILLIAM HUNTER

On March 26, 1555, William Hunter—a godly man only nineteen years old—was martyred. His story should be an example to all Christian parents who find their emotions at odds with their convictions, for William's parents allowed their son to follow his beliefs, even though it led to his death.

William was apprenticed to a silk weaver in London. In the first year of Queen Mary's reign, his parish priest ordered him to receive Communion at the Easter Mass, which he refused to do. His master, afraid he himself would be in danger if William remained in his house, asked the boy to move back to his father's house in Brentwood for several weeks, which he did.

Five or six weeks later, William picked up a Bible he found in the chapel at Brentwood and began to read it aloud to himself. He was interrupted when Father Atwell came into the chapel. "Are you meddling with the Bible?" Atwell demanded. "Do you know what you're reading? Can you expound the scriptures?"

"I don't take it upon myself to expound the scriptures," William explained. "I found it here and was reading it to comfort myself."

Father Atwell commented, "It hasn't been a happy world since the Bible was published in English."

"Oh, don't say that! It's God's book, from which we learn to know what pleases and displeases God."

"Didn't we know that before?"

"Not as well as we do now with the Bible available," William replied. "I pray we always have it with us."

Father Atwell fumed. "I know you! You're one of those who dislike the queen's laws. That's why you left London. If you don't mend your ways, you and many other heretics will broil!"

"God give me grace to believe His Word and confess His name, no matter what happens," William retorted.

Atwell rushed out of the chapel, calling back, "I can't reason with you, but I'll find someone who can, you heretic!"

William stayed in the chapel and continued to read until Atwell returned with the vicar of Southwell. "Who gave you permission to read and expound on the Bible?" the vicar demanded.

"I don't expound on it, sir," William answered. "I only read it for comfort."

"Why do you need to read it at all?"

"I'll read it as long as I live. You shouldn't discourage people from doing so. You should encourage them."

"Oh, so you want to tell me what I should do?" the vicar muttered. "You're a heretic!"

"I'm not a heretic just because I speak the truth."

More words passed between them concerning the sacrament of Communion, on which William explained his point of view. Accused of being a heretic, he replied, "I wish you and I were both tied to the stake, to prove which of us would defend his faith the longest. I think you'd recant first."

"We'll see about that!" the vicar replied, leaving to report the boy.

The vicar went directly to Master Brown, who called in William's father and the local policeman and demanded that Mr. Hunter go find his son, since William had wisely left town after his argument with the vicar. Mr. Hunter rode for two or three days to satisfy Brown, intending to go back and say he couldn't find the boy, when suddenly they met. Mr. Hunter told his son to hide; he would go back and say he couldn't find him.

"No, Father," William said, "I'll go home with you so you don't get in trouble." As soon as they arrived in town, William was arrested and taken before Brown, who argued with him about transubstantiation. William was so firm in his beliefs that he enraged Brown, who sent him to Bishop Bonner in London.

William was put in the stocks in London for two days, fed only a crust of brown bread and a cup of water before he defended himself to the bishop. Getting nowhere with the boy, Bonner ordered him locked up in jail with as many claims against him as he could bear. "How old are you?" he asked William.

"Nineteen."

"Well, you'll be burned before you're twenty if you don't do better than you did today!"

William spent nine months in jail, appearing before the bishop six times, including the time he was condemned on February 9. That day the bishop made William his final offer: "If you recant, I'll make you a freeman and give you forty pounds to set up a business. Or I'll make you the steward of my house. I like you. You're smart, and I'll take care of you if you recant."

William replied, "Thank you, but if you can't change my mind through scripture, I can't turn from God for love of the world. I count all worldly things but loss and dung, compared to the love of Christ."

"If you die believing this way," the bishop continued, "you will be condemned forever."

"God judges righteously, justifying those whom man condemns unjustly," William maintained.

William was sent back to Newgate Prison for a month then taken home to Brentwood for burning. When his parents visited him there, they encouraged him to remain faithful, saying they were proud to have a son willing to die for Christ's sake.

At the stake, William asked the people to pray for him. Master Brown sneered, "Pray for you? I wouldn't pray for you any more than I would for a dog!"

"I forgive you."

"I'm not asking for your forgiveness!" yelled Brown.

Seeing a priest approaching with a Bible, William called out, "Get away, you false prophet! Beware of them, people. Don't take part in their plagues."

The priest replied, "As you burn here, so you will burn in hell."

"You lie, you false prophet!" William cried. "Get out of here!"

A man in the crowd spoke up. "I pray God will have mercy on his soul."

"Amen, amen," answered the crowd.

As the fire was lit, William tossed his psalter to his brother. "William," his brother called, "think of the holy passion of Christ. Don't be afraid of death."

"I'm not." William lifted his hands to heaven and said, "Lord, Lord, Lord, receive my spirit." Dropping his head into the smoke, William Hunter gave up his life for the truth, sealing it with his blood to the praise of God.

RAWLINS WHITE

Rawlins White fished for many years in the town of Cardiff, a man who was well liked by his neighbors. During the reign of King Henry VIII, he was a good Catholic, but when Edward came into power, White became a great searcher of the truth. He was a totally uneducated man, unable to read, so he sent his young son to school; and when the boy had learned to read, his father had him read the Bible and other books to him every evening.

White enjoyed studying the scriptures so much that he soon gave up his fishing to travel from place to place and instruct others, taking his son everywhere with him. Although he never learned to read, White did have a remarkable memory and was able to cite the scripture more accurately than many educated men of the day. He soon became a well-known, successful professor of the truth.

Five years after White began his work, Queen Mary took the throne. White gave up preaching openly but continued to do so privately, bringing a great number of people to Christ. As the persecutions increased, his friends urged him to sell his goods, give the money to his wife and children, and go into hiding, but White refused to deny Christ.

The town's officers soon captured White, taking him to the bishop of Llandoff, who sent him to prison after having many arguments with him about theology. He was imprisoned in the castle of Cardiff for a whole year. Even though White knew he was doomed and his family would suffer terribly when he was gone, he continued to pray for and preach to the friends who regularly visited him this year.

At the end of this time, White was tried before the bishop of Llandoff. The bishop made a long speech explaining why White was being tried, to which he replied, "My lord, I thank God I am a Christian, and I hold no opinions against the Word of God. If I do, I want to be corrected by the Word of God, as a Christian should be."

After discussing the charges back and forth for some time, the bishop suggested they take time to pray that God would change White's mind. "Ah, now you're doing the right thing!" White exclaimed. "If your request is godly and lawful and you pray as you should, God will hear you. So go ahead. You pray to your god, and I'll pray to mine. I know my prayer will be answered."

When they were done, the bishop said, "How do you stand? Will you revoke your opinions or not?"

"Surely, my lord," White replied, "Rawlins you left me, and Rawlins you find me. By God's grace, Rawlins I will continue to be. Certainly, if your prayers had been just and lawful, God would have heard them; but you honor a false god and pray incorrectly, so God didn't answer your prayers. I'm only one poor, simple man, but God has heard my prayer and will strengthen me in His cause."

As the furious bishop was about to condemn White, someone suggested they have a Mass, to see if that worked a miracle in the man. Rawlins White left to pray in private while they went about their Mass, returning when he heard the elevation bell ring—the principle point in the Mass's idolatry.

"Good people," he cried to the congregation, "bear witness on the Day of Judgment that I did not bow to this idol [the host]."

White was condemned and returned to prison in the castle of Cardiff—a dark, horrible place. He was brought to his execution wearing his wedding shirt, an old russet coat, and an old pair of leather pants. On the way to the stake, he met his weeping wife and children, the sight of them making him cry, too, until he hit his chest with his hand and said, "Flesh, you're in my way! You want to live? Well, I tell you, do what you can, you won't win."

White went cheerfully to the stake, leaning against it for a while, then motioning to a friend in the crowd. "I feel my body fighting against my spirit and am afraid it will win. If you see me tempted, hold a finger up to me so I'll remember myself." As the smith chained him to the stake, White told him to tighten it well in case his body struggled with his soul.

They began to pile the straw and wood around White, who reached down and helped them pile it up the best he could. When a priest stood next to him to preach to the crowd, he listened respectfully until the man reached the sacrament of the altar, then called out, "Don't listen to this false prophet!"

The fire was lit. White held out his hands in the flames until his sinews shrunk and the fat dropped away, only taking them out once to wipe his face with the fire. All the while he was suffering—which was longer than usual—he cried loudly, "O Lord, receive my soul. O Lord, receive my spirit!" until he could no longer open his mouth. At last the fire consumed his legs, and his whole body fell over into the flames. Rawlins White died for testifying of God's truth and was rewarded the crown of everlasting life.

GEORGE MARSH

George Marsh lived quietly for many years with his wife and children on a farm in the countryside. When his wife died, he attended the University of Cambridge to become a minister, serving for a while as Lawrence Sander's curate. Marsh preached for some time before being arrested and imprisoned for four months by the bishop of Chester, who did not allow him any visitors and had the names of any who asked for Marsh reported to him.

He was brought before Dr. Cotes several times but maintained the theology he had been taught during Edward's reign and would not be moved, although he did admit, "I want to live as much as you do. But I cannot deny my master, Christ, or He will deny me before His Father in heaven." Marsh was condemned as a heretic and turned over to the sheriffs.

Since he wasn't allowed any visitors in prison, Marsh's friends would stand by a hole in the outer prison wall and call out, asking how he was. He always replied that he was fine, anxious to die as a witness of God's truth and trusting Him to help him bear it bravely. On the day of his execution, Marsh was brought out in irons. Some people tried to hand him money, which criminals being executed would accept to bribe a priest to say Masses for them, but Marsh told them to give their money to prisoners or the poor, not him.

Outside the city near Spittle-Boughton, by the stake, the deputy chamberlain of Chester showed Marsh the pardon he would receive from the queen if he recanted. Marsh said he would love to accept it, that he even loved the queen, but he could not recant.

The fire was poorly made, so Marsh suffered terribly, bearing it with patience. He had been in the fire for a long time—his flesh broiled and puffed up so much that the chain around him couldn't be seen—when he suddenly spread his arms and called, "Father of heaven, have mercy on me," and died. Many people who witnessed Marsh's death said he was a martyr who died with patience and godliness, which caused the bishop to preach a sermon saying that Marsh was a heretic, burned like a heretic, and was now a firebrand in hell.

WILLIAM FLOWER

William Flower, sometimes called Branch, was born at Snow Hill, Cambridge. He entered the Abbey of Ely and was made a monk at the age of seventeen, observing all the rules of the order, becoming a priest, and celebrating Mass. But at the age of twenty-one, Flower left the order, abandoned his habit, became a secular priest, and returned to Snow Hill. There he celebrated Mass and taught children for about six months.

He moved to several other places before he settled in Tewkesbury for a while and married; then he moved to London. One Easter morning, Flower saw a priest giving Communion to the people in St. Margaret's Church in Westminster. Suddenly offended at the ceremony and the priest, he drew his knife and slashed the priest on the head, arm, and hand, causing the chalice, with its consecrated host, to fall to the floor, where it mingled with the priest's blood.

When he was brought before Bishop Bonner, Flower admitted he had acted in an unchristian manner by striking the priest and should be punished for that. But as far as his beliefs about Communion went, he refused to submit. He told the bishop that he could do as he chose with his body, but he had no power over his soul, which belonged to God.

Given a few hours to think about it, Flower returned to the bishop, who asked him to reconsider his views of Communion. "I'll stand by what I've said," Flower stated. "Let the law punish me." Every time he was seen by the bishop, his answer was the same: "I have nothing to say. I've already said all I have to say, and I won't change that."

On April 24, Flower was brought to St. Margaret's churchyard to be burned. First his left hand was held behind him while his right hand was cut off, then the fire was lit. As he burned, he cried aloud three times, "O Son of God, have mercy upon me!" Then he spoke no more, holding the stump of his arm up as long as he could with his other hand.

JOHN CARDMAKER AND JOHN WARNE

John Cardmaker was an observant friar before the dissolution of abbeys. After that, he served as a married minister then was appointed a reader at St. Paul's under Edward's reign. The papists in that church were so upset by Cardmaker's doctrine that they cut and mangled his gown with their knives.

At the beginning of Queen Mary's reign, Cardmaker was brought to London and jailed with Barlow, the bishop of Bath. After the chancellor examined both men, he declared them faithful Catholics—probably so he could use them as an example to encourage others to recant, although they might have weakened, too. It is known that in every examination that followed, the chancellor held Barlow and Cardmaker up as examples of discreet, educated men. Whatever really happened, Barlow was freed and continued to bear witness to the truth of Christ's Gospel during the rest of his life. Cardmaker was returned to jail while the bishop of London announced to the public that he would shortly be freed after accepting transubstantiation and some other articles of faith. However, he was never set free.

John Warne, an upholsterer, was charged with not believing in transubstantiation and refusing to accept Communion, charges he willingly pled guilty to. No matter what the bishop said or threatened, Warne refused to budge from his beliefs.

On May 30, John Cardmaker and John Warne were led to the stake together. Warne said his prayers and was bound to the stake, and the wood and reeds were piled around him; all that was needed was the torch. Meanwhile, the sheriffs had taken Cardmaker aside and were talking to him privately, until the crowd became convinced that he was about to recant. Cardmaker left the sheriffs, approached the stake, and knelt down to pray, still in his clothes. By now the people were sure he would be freed. When he finished his prayers, Cardmaker took off his clothing and kissed the stake, comforting Warne as they bound Cardmaker, too.

Realizing that Cardmaker had refused to save himself, the crowd called out blessings to him as the fire was lit under both men.

THOMAS HAWKES

On February 8, 1555, six men were brought before Bishop Bonner: Stephen Knight, William Pigot, Thomas Tompkins, John Lawrence, William Hunter, and Thomas Hawkes. All of them were condemned the following day.

Thomas Hawkes, a tall, good-looking man with excellent qualities, was born in Essex and raised as a gentleman. He was known for his gentle behavior toward others and his dedication to true religion and godliness. Hawkes entered into the service of the Lord of Oxford, staying there as long as Edward VI lived, enjoying a good reputation and being well loved by everyone in the household. But when Edward died, everything suffered: religion decayed, the godly fell into danger, and the houses of good men came on hard times. Rather than change his religious beliefs to fit those of Queen Mary's court and the Lord of Oxford's house, Hawkes left the nobleman's service and returned home, hoping to worship in peace there.

Soon after, Hawkes had a son. Since he refused to have the baby baptized in the Catholic Church, he put the sacrament off for three weeks and was reported to the Earl of Oxford for contempt of the sacraments. The earl was either unable or unwilling to argue matters of religion with Hawkes; he sent him to Bishop Bonner of London.

Hawkes told Bonner that he had nothing against baptism itself, just against its Catholic embellishments.

"Would you agree to have your child christened by the book that was set out by King Edward?" the bishop asked.

"Yes. That's exactly what I want," Hawkes replied.

When Bonner could not convince Hawkes that the Catholic service was as effective as the Protestant one, he called in Mr. Harpsfield, the archdeacon of London.

"Christ used ceremonies," Harpsfield began. "Didn't He take clay from the ground, spit on it, and make the blind man see?"

"I know that," Hawkes replied. "But He never used it in baptism. If you want to use it, use it as Christ did."

"Suppose your child should die unchristened?"

"So?"

"Why, then both you and your child would be damned."

"Don't judge further than you may by the scriptures," Hawkes retorted.

"Don't you know your child is born in original sin?"

"Yes, I do."

"How is original sin washed away?"

"By true faith and belief in Christ Jesus," Hawkes replied.

"How can your baby believe?"

"His deliverance from sin is grounded in the faith of his parents."

"How can you prove that?"

"Saint Paul, in First Corinthians seven, verse fourteen, says: 'For the unbelieving husband is sanctified by the wife, and the unbelieving wife is sanctified by the husband: else were your children unclean; but now are they holy.'"

"Recant, recant! Don't you know that Christ said, 'Except a man be born of water and of the Spirit he cannot enter into the kingdom of God.'"

"Does Christianity depend on outward ceremonies?" Hawkes asked.

"Partly, yes. What do you think about the Mass?"

Hawkes replied, "I say it's detestable, abominable, and useful for nothing!"

"Useful for nothing? What about the epistle and Gospel?"

"That's good, if it's used as Christ left it to be used."

"How about the confessional?"

"That's abominable and detestable. It's blasphemy to call upon, trust, or pray to anyone but Christ Jesus."

"We don't ask you to trust anyone, just call on them and pray to them. You know that you can't speak with a king or queen without first speaking to someone else."

"You mean I should call on those I don't trust? Saint Paul said, 'How [then] shall they call on him in whom they have not believed?'"

"Don't you want someone to pray for you when you're dead?"

"No," Hawkes replied. "Once you're dead, no man's prayers can help you. Unless you can prove otherwise by scripture."

"Don't the prayers of the righteous prevail?"

"Only for the living. David said, 'None of them can by any means redeem his brother, nor give to God a ransom for [them].'"

"What books do you have?"

"The New Testament, Solomon's books, and the psalter."

"Will you read other books?"

"Certainly. If you give me the ones I want."

"What do you want?"

"Latimer's books, my lord of Canterbury's books, Bradford's sermons, and Ridley's books."

"Take him away! The books he wants all support his heresies."

The next day Fecknam came to talk to Hawkes. "Are you the one who won't have his child christened unless it's done in English and will have no ceremonies?"

"Whatever scripture commands done, I will do," Hawkes replied.

They continued for a while, Hawkes standing his ground and quoting scripture to prove each point they debated. The following day Dr. Chedsay and Bishop Bonner talked with Hawkes, asking him what he thought of the Catholic Church.

"It's a church of vicious cardinals, priests, monks, and friars, which I will never give credit or believe," he replied.

Bonner explained to Chedsay, "He won't come to my chapel or hear Mass. His services have to be in English."

"Christ never spoke English," Chedsay replied.

"Neither did He speak Latin," Hawkes retorted. "What good does it do me to hear a language I don't understand?" Hawkes went on to say that the Catholic Church engaged in the worship of idols, praying to saints, holy bread, and holy wine, none of which are found in or commanded by scripture. On February 9, 1555, he was condemned as a heretic. He remained in prison until June 10.

A little before his death, some of Hawkes's friends asked him a favor. They were afraid for their own lives and wondered how long faith could stand in the midst of the fire. Hawkes agreed to lift his hand over his head if the pain was tolerable and his mind was still at peace. When he had been in the fire so long that he could no longer speak, his skin had shrunk, his fingers had been burned off, and everyone thought he was dead, Hawkes suddenly raised his burning hands over his head and clapped them together three times! The people there—especially those who understood his gesture—broke into shouts of praise and applause as Thomas Hawkes sank down into the fire and gave up his spirit.

THOMAS WATTS

Thomas Watts of Billericay, Essex, was a linen draper. Knowing he would soon be arrested, he sold all the cloth in his shop, gave almost everything he owned to his wife and children, donated the rest to the poor, and waited. On April 26, 1555, Watts was arrested and brought before Lord Rich and others in Chelmsford on charges of not going to Mass.

Anthony Brown, the judge, asked Watts where he'd learned his religion, to which he replied, "From you, sir. In King Edward's day, you spoke against this religion. No preacher could say more than you did then. You said the Mass was abominable and exhorted us not to believe them, saying we should only believe Christ. You said that anyone bringing a foreign religion in here was a traitor."

Brown turned to Lord Rich. "He's slandering me, my lord! What kind of criminal is he? If he talks like this to my face, imagine what he says to my back!"

Finally growing weary of Watts, the commissioners sent him to the bishop of London, who brought the following charges against him.

Thomas Watts lived in Billericay, within the jurisdiction of the bishop of London.

Watts replied this was true.

He did not believe in the sacraments or take part in them.

Watts replied that he believed in all the sacraments according to Christ's institution but not according to the Catholic Church. Once he had believed as a Catholic, but the church deceived the people.

He believed—and taught others—that Communion was only a remembrance of Christ's body and blood, nothing else.

Watts said he believed Christ's body was in heaven, nowhere else. He would never believe His body is in the host.

He believed that the true presence of Christ's body and blood was not in the host but in heaven.

Watts agreed that that was exactly what he believed.

He believed that the Mass is full of idolatry, abomination, and wickedness, that Christ did not institute it, ordain it, or believe it was good.

Watts said he still believed that and would never change his mind.

He believed confession to a priest was unnecessary and that all a man needed to do was believe and confess to God.

Watts replied that no priest could absolve him of his sins, but he said it was a good thing to ask a priest for advice.

He believed that Luther, Wycliffe, Barnes, and all others put to death for their beliefs about Communion were good men, faithful servants, and martyrs of Christ.

Watts said that he didn't know the theology of men they'd listed, but if they didn't believe the body and blood of Christ were physically in the sacrament, they were good Christian men.

He believed fasting, praying, and giving alms were useless. If a man was saved, he didn't need to do them; if he wasn't, doing them wouldn't save him.

Watts denied he'd said that, saying he believed fasting, prayers, and giving alms were works of a lively faith.

He openly admitted that he refused to go to church and receive Communion because that service was abominable. He also said other erroneous and arrogant things, serving as a bad example to the people present.

Watts replied that was true, and he would die believing the same.

He was an open heretic, to be cursed by the church and turned over to the secular authorities for punishment.

Watts said he would submit to the law, trusting God would bless him even if he was cursed by men.

He said the Church of Rome was the synagogue of Satan.

Watts said he believed the pope was a mortal enemy of Christ and His church.

All of the above charges are common knowledge in the area of Billericay.

Watts replied that everything he'd said before was true.

From May 10–17, Watts saw one churchman after another, none of whom could make him move an inch from what he'd maintained all along. He was turned over to the sheriffs of London and imprisoned in Newgate until May 22 or June 9 before being transferred to Chelmsford, where he had dinner with Hawkes and others who'd been brought down for burning. Given the opportunity to speak to his wife and six children, he encouraged them to be faithful to their beliefs, no matter what; two of his children promptly offered to go to the stake with their father.

Watts kissed the stake before he turned to Lord Rich and warned him, "My lord, beware! You act against your conscience in this, and unless you repent, the Lord will revenge it, for you are the cause of my death."

PROCLAMATION AGAINST BOOKS

About this time a book was brought into England that warned Englishmen of the Spaniards and disclosed some secret plans for the church's recovery of abbey lands that had previously been confiscated. The book was titled *A Warning for England*.

On June 13, 1555, the king and queen banned all books that disagreed with Catholicism, specifically naming all books by the following authors: Martin Luther, Oecolampadius, Zwingle, John Calvin, Pomerane, John Alasco, Bullinger, Bucer, Melancthon, Bernardinus, Ochinus, Erasmus, Sarcerius, Peter Martyr, Hugh Latimer, Robert Barnes (Friar Barnes), John Bale (Friar Bale), Justus, Jonas John Hooper, Miles Coverdale, William Tyndale, Thomas Cranmer, William Turner, Theodore Basil (Thomas Beacon), John Frith, and Roy. In addition, *The Book of Common Prayer in English* that was used during King Edward's reign was banned.

Anyone owning any of these books was ordered to turn them in within fifteen days, and all civil authorities were given permission to search homes and arrest anyone possessing them.

Books supporting the Catholic Church were acceptable, including the *Primer in English*, which taught children to pray to Mary and the saints, and *Our Lady's Psalter*, which substituted Mary's name for God's in the psalms.

The apostles taught us that we are fully complete in Christ and need no one's intercession for our sins. And if idolatry is making an idol to be worshipped as a god, isn't it idolatry to worship Mary? If God hadn't explained His will to us in plain words, telling us exactly what to believe, how to worship, and how to be saved, perhaps Catholicism's use of mediators for reconciliation might have made sense, but God's Word plainly tells us that salvation and justification only come through Christ. Not believing what He promised is infidelity; following any other belief is idolatry. Yet the Church of Rome refuses to accept what God has freely given and will not seek salvation through Christ but through its saints and superstitions.

JOHN BRADFORD

John Bradford was born in Manchester and educated until he was able to earn a living in the secular world, which he did successfully for several years before giving up his business affairs to study the Gospel. Bradford left his study of secular law in London to enroll as a divinity student at Cambridge, working so diligently that he was awarded his Master of Arts degree within a year.

Immediately after, he was given a fellowship at Pembroke Hall, where Martin Bucer encouraged him to become a preacher. Bradford believed he wasn't educated enough to preach, to which Bucer replied, "If you don't have fine white bread, give the poor people barley bread or whatever else the Lord has given you."

Finally convinced to preach during King Edward's reign, Bradford accepted the degree of Deacon from Bishop Ridley, was licensed to preach, and given a position at St. Paul's.

For the next three years, Bradford preached the Gospel faithfully. He sharply reproved sin, sweetly preached Christ crucified, pithily spoke against heresies and errors, and earnestly persuaded his people to live godly lives. When Queen Mary took the throne, Bradford continued his work.

On August 13, 1553, Mr. Bourne, the bishop of Bath, gave a sermon at St. Paul's Cross in London supporting the return of Catholicism under Mary. His words so angered the congregation that they threatened to pull him out of the pulpit. The more Bishop Bonner and the mayor of London tried to calm the crowd, the angrier everyone became, until Bourne actually began to fear for his life and asked Bradford to speak to the people.

As soon as Bradford moved to the pulpit, the crowd shouted, "Bradford! Bradford! God save your life, Bradford!" Bradford calmed the crowd, and soon they all left peacefully for their homes.

Even though the mayor and sheriffs were there to see Bourne safely home, he refused to leave the church until Bradford agreed to accompany him, so Bradford walked closely behind Bourne, protecting him from harm with his own body.

Three days later, Bradford was summoned by the council and charged with sedition—for saving Bourne's life!—and with illegal preaching—although he had been asked to speak. He was imprisoned for nearly a year and a half, until his hearing before the lord chancellor in January 1555. There he was offered a pardon if he would recant his Protestant beliefs and rejoin the Catholic Church, as many preachers had already done. On July 29, the offer was repeated. Bradford urged the council not to condemn the innocent. If they believed he was guilty, they should pass sentence on him; if not, they should set him free.

In reply, the chancellor told Bradford that his actions at St. Paul's Cross had been presumptuous and arrogant in that he took it upon himself to lead the people. He was also charged with writing seditious letters.

The following day Thomas Hussey and Dr. Seton visited Bradford in prison. Both men urged him to request time to discuss his religious beliefs with learned men, saying this would remove him from immediate danger and look good to the council. Bradford refused. "That would make the people think I doubt the doctrine I confess. I don't doubt it at all."

Brought back before the council, which asked him to rejoin the Catholic Church, Bradford replied, "Yesterday I said I would never consent to work for the pope. I say the same today." He was condemned and returned to prison.

All the time Bradford spent in prison, he continued his work, preaching twice a day to the many people allowed to visit him and administering the sacrament. Preaching, reading, and praying occupied his whole life; he only ate one small meal a day, and even then he meditated as he ate. Bradford's keepers thought so highly of him that he was often allowed to leave the prison unescorted to visit sick parishioners on his word that he would return by a certain hour. He was so precise in obeying the terms that he usually arrived back well before his curfew.

Bradford was a tall, slender man with an auburn beard. He rarely slept more than four hours a night, preferring to spend his time in writing, preaching, or reading. Once or twice a week he would visit the common criminals in the prison and give them money to buy food or other comforts.

One of his friends once asked Bradford what he would do if he were freed. Bradford said he would marry and hide in England while he continued to preach and teach the people.

One day in July 1555, the keeper's wife warned Bradford that he was to be burned the following day.

"Thank God," he replied. "I've looked forward to this for a long time. The Lord make me worthy."

Bradford was transferred to Newgate Prison about eleven or twelve that night, the authorities hoping no one would be up to see him then; but a crowd of people watched him as he passed, prayed for him, and told him good-bye.

His execution was announced for four o'clock the next morning. No one was sure why such an unusual hour was chosen, but if the authorities hoped the hour would discourage a crowd, they were disappointed. The people waited faithfully at Smithfield until Bradford was brought there at nine in the morning, led by an unusually large number of armed guards. Bradford fell to the ground to say his prayers then went cheerfully to the stake with John Leaf, a young man of twenty.

JOHN LEAF

John Leaf, who was burned with Bradford, was born in Kirby Moreside, York, and became a candlemaker's apprentice, living in the parish of Christ's Church, London.

Brought before Bishop Bonner, Leaf admitted he did not believe the bread and wine were Christ's actual body and blood but were a remembrance of them. He also stated that Catholic confession wasn't necessary and that a priest had no power to absolve sins.

Leaf was returned to prison until June 10, when Bonner saw him again and tried—by persuasion, threats, and promises—to convince the young man to change his mind. Getting nowhere, the bishop asked Leaf if he was one of Rogers's scholars. Leaf replied he was, that he believed the doctrine of Rogers, Hooper, Cardmaker, and others who had recently been killed for their testimony, and he would die for the same doctrine. "My lord," he said, "you call my opinion heresy. It is the true light of the Word of God." Unable to move the boy, Bonner condemned him and sent him back to prison.

It's said that shortly after this, two letters were brought to Leaf: one containing a recantation, the other a confession. When the recantation was read to him, he refused to sign it. When the confession was read, he took a pin, pricked his hand, and sprinkled his blood on the paper to show the bishop he was ready to seal his beliefs with his blood.

Bradford and Leaf went to the stake together, Bradford lying on one side of it to pray and Leaf on the other. After they had prayed silently for an hour, one of the sheriffs said to Bradford, "Get up and end this. The press of the crowd is great." They both got up. Bradford kissed a piece of firewood then the stake itself before addressing the crowd.

"England," he cried, "repent of your sins! Beware of idolatry. Beware of false antichrists. See they don't deceive you!" Then he forgave his persecutors and asked the crowd to pray for him. Turning his head to Leaf, Bradford told him, "Be at peace, brother. We will have a happy supper with the Lord tonight." Both men ended their lives without fear, hoping to obtain the prize for which they had long run.

JOHN BLAND

John Bland was a teacher before becoming the vicar of a congregation in Relvendon, Kent. Thrown into Canterbury Prison for preaching the Gospel during Queen Mary's reign, he was freed once or twice by his friends' petitions, yet as soon as he was freed, he always returned to his Protestant preaching. Arrested a third time, Bland refused to promise his friends that he wouldn't preach his beliefs again, and they were no longer able to help him.

On November 26, two of Bland's parishioners, Richard and Thomas Austen, approached him after the service. "Parson," Richard Austen said, "you took down the tabernacle where the rood hung and other things. The queen has ordered that they be put up again, and we think you should pay for that. You go against the queen's laws when you say these are abominations."

"Mr. Austen," Bland replied, "if that's what I said, I'll say it again."

Thomas Austen replied, "Tell us what's devilish in the Mass, then!"

"I often preached it to you. You didn't believe me then, and you won't now."

"You pulled down the altar. Will you rebuild it?"

"No. Not unless I'm ordered to, because I was ordered to take it down," Bland insisted.

On December 28, the priest of Stodmarsh was invited to say Mass by the Austens. He was well into matins when Bland arrived, and when he finished, he said to Bland, "Your neighbor asked me to say matins and Mass. I trust you won't disobey the queen's law?"

"No," Bland replied, "I won't disobey the queen's laws, God willing."

Pretending he couldn't hear Bland's reply, the priest asked the question twice more, until Bland raised his voice so the whole congregation could hear his answer. The priest then sat down while Bland stood in the chancel door to give his address to the congregation. Bland explained his beliefs about the bread and wine, how Christ instituted the sacrament, and how it had been perverted by the Catholic Church. In a few minutes, he was stopped by the church warden and constable and locked in a side chapel until the Mass was over.

On February 23 or 24, Bland was locked in Canterbury Castle for ten weeks before being allowed to post bail. On May 18, he appeared before the archdeacon of Canterbury, who demanded to know what Bland preached on Communion. Bland refused to answer, saying they were trying to gather material to use against him and that English law said he did not have to speak against himself. He was called again on May 21, again refusing to state his beliefs and requesting a lawyer.

On June 28, Bland reported to the secular authorities as ordered. They said they had nothing against him and ordered him to reappear seven weeks later, but when the date came, Bland was before the church authorities and missed his court date. He was locked in Maidstone Prison for that until February 18 or 19. After he would not promise to reform and be a good Catholic, Bland was sent to Canterbury Castle until March 2.

Bland continued to be tossed to and fro, from prison to prison, session to session, until on June 13 he was brought before Richard Thornton, the bishop of Dover; Robert Collins, the commissary; and Nicholas Harpsfield, archdeacon of Canterbury. Under these three men, a great number of Protestants were cruelly treated and killed at Canterbury, John Bland being one of the first. With him that day the following men were also tried: John Frankesh, Nicholas Sheterden, Thomas Thacker, Humphrey Middleton, and William Cocker.

Bland pleaded guilty to the following charges:

He believed the physical body of Christ was in heaven not in the bread and wine.

He believed it was against God's Word to have the sacraments administered in Latin, and no one should accept any sacrament he could not understand.

On June 25, Bland appeared before the authorities for the last time and refused to accept the pope's authority. He was condemned as a heretic and turned over to the secular authorities for burning.

CARVER AND LAUNDER

On July 22, 1555, Dirick Carver was burned at Lewes, Sussex; the following day John Launder suffered at Stening. These two men were arrested about the end of October 1554, along with other men who were praying at Carver's house. After examination they were sent to Newgate Prison to wait for a hearing before Bonner, the bishop of London, which occurred on June 8, 1555.

There they were examined on many points of religion, writing and signing their own confessions of faith. After the bishop spoke with them for some time, trying to convince them to recant and accept the Catholic Church, they were dismissed and returned to Newgate until June 10.

Dirick Carver confessed to the following points:

He did not believe Christ's physical body was present in the sacrament.

He did not believe there was any sacrifice in the Mass and no salvation in a Mass said in Latin.

He believed in seeing a good priest for advice but not for confession, which did nothing to save a man.

He did not believe the Catholic doctrine agreed with God's Word. He believed that Bishop Hooper, Cardmaker, Rogers, and others recently burned were good Christians, martyrs who preached the true doctrine of Christ.

Since the queen's coronation, he had kept his Bible and psalter in English and read them. He had also had English prayers and services said in his home. Thomas Iveson, John Launder, and William Vesie, his fellow prisoners in Newgate, were arrested with him while hearing the Gospel read in English.

John Launder confessed to the following:

He was present in Carver's house with twelve others to hear the English service and prayers, being in town on business and hearing of the service.

He believed that all the services, sacrifices, and ceremonies of the Catholic Church are full of errors, worth nothing, and against God's Word.

He believed that the bread and wine were only a remembrance of Christ, not His actual body and blood.

He believed the Mass was directly against God's Word and church.

He believed confession to a priest was useless and no man could absolve another from his sins. A sinful man who regrets his sins before God and sins no more is forgiven.

On June 10, 1555, Carver, Launder, and others were brought before the bishop again. Carver was asked if he would recant or stand by his confession. "Your doctrine," he replied, "is poison and sorcery. If Christ were here, you would put Him to a worse death than He was put to before. You say that you can make a god. You can make a pudding, too. Your ceremonies in the church are beggary and poison, and confession is contrary to God's Word. It's poison."

John Launder also remained firm in his confession, and both men were condemned.

When Dirick was brought to the stake, his book was thrown into the pitch barrel to burn with him, but he reached down, picked it up, and tossed it into the crowd. The sheriff ordered the book returned on pain of death, but Dirick immediately began to speak to the crowd.

"Dear brothers and sisters, I am here to seal Christ's Gospel with my blood because I know it is true. You know the Gospel—it's been preached to you here and all over England, even though it's not preached now. Because I will not deny God's Gospel to obey man's laws, I am condemned to die. Dear brothers and sisters, if you believe in the Father, the Son, and the Holy Ghost, do the works of your belief and you will have everlasting life. If you believe in the pope and his laws, you are condemned. Unless God has mercy on you, you will burn in hell forever."

The sheriff scoffed, "If you don't believe in the pope, you are damned, body and soul! Speak to your God. Ask Him to deliver you now or strike me down as an example!"

"The Lord forgive you for your words," Dirick replied. "Dear brethren, if I have offended anyone by word or deed, I ask you to forgive me. And I forgive all you who have offended me in thought, word, or deed.

"O Lord, my God, You have written, 'He that loveth father or mother more than me is not worthy of me: and he that loveth son or daughter more than me is not worthy of me. And he that taketh not his cross, and followeth after me, is not worthy of me' (Matthew 10:37–38). But You know I have forsaken all to come to You. Lord, have mercy upon me, for unto You do I commend my spirit, and my soul rejoices in You."

WARNE, TANKERVIL, AND OTHERS

After this came the persecution of ten other true servants and saints of the Lord. Not saints that the pope made or those mentioned in *The Legend of the Saints* or in *The Lives of the Fathers*, but those spoken of in Revelation: These be they that follow the Lamb withersoever he goeth, and who have washed their robes and made them white in the blood of the Lamb. In a way, the pope did make these people saints, for if he had not killed them, they would not be martyrs.

The ten were Elizabeth Warne, George Tankervil, Robert Smith, Stephen Harwood, Thomas Fust, William Hall, Thomas Leyes, George King, John Wade, and Joan Lashford.

Now that the prisons of London were full and more prisoners were still arriving, the council and commissioners sent these ten people to Bonner at once, to make room for others.

Elizabeth Warne was the wife of John Warne, who had been burned earlier as a heretic. She was captured with others on January 1 in a house in Bow Churchyard, London, as they gathered for prayers, then was imprisoned until June 11 before being transferred to Newgate, where she stayed until July 2. On July 6, Elizabeth appeared before Bishop Bonner, along with the nine others listed above.

The chief charge against them all was not believing that the physical body and blood of Christ were present in the bread and wine, although there were other charges, such as not going to church, speaking against the Mass, and hating the Catholic ceremonies and sacraments.

After being brought before Bonner several times, Elizabeth Warne told him, "Do whatever you want. If Christ was in error, then so am I." On July 12 she was condemned as a heretic and burned at Stratford-le-Bow in August.

George Tankervil, born in the city of York, lived in London. He was a Catholic in King Edward's days, but when the persecutions began under Queen Mary, Tankervil was disgusted by them and began to doubt the church. He asked God to show him the truth about transubstantiation—something he'd always had doubts about—and came to believe as the Protestants did on the subject. Moved to read the New Testament for himself, Tankervil soon turned from the Catholic Church entirely and began to try to convert his friends, work that soon brought him before the bishop of London, who condemned him.

Tankervil was brought to St. Albans to die on August 26 and was locked in an inn there while the sheriffs attended a local wedding. Since he was forbidden Communion, he asked for and received a pint of malmsey and a loaf of bread, knelt down to make his confession to God, and read the institution of the Last Supper from the Gospel. "Lord," he prayed, "You know I don't do this to usurp anyone's authority or in contempt of Your ministers, but only because I cannot have it administered according to Your Word." When he had finished, he received the bread and wine with thanksgiving.

Then Tankervil asked his host to build him a good fire. He took off his shoes and stockings and stretched his leg into the flame, pulling it back when the flames hit it, showing how his flesh wanted one thing and his spirit another.

About two o'clock the sheriffs returned to take Tankervil to Romeland, a green near the west end of the abbey church. A priest approached while the wood was being arranged around him, and Tankervil called out, "I defy the whore of Babylon! Fie on that abominable idol! Good people, do not believe him!" Embracing the fire, he bathed himself in it, and, calling on the name of the Lord Jesus, was quickly out of pain.

෴

Robert Smith was brought to Newgate on November 5. He was a tall, slender man, active in many things, especially painting, which he found relaxing. Once he was converted by the preaching and reading of Mr. Turner and others, he was very fervent in his religion. When Queen Mary came to the throne, Smith was fired from his clerkship in Windsor College, arrested, and brought before Bishop Bonner. Smith saw Bonner four times, answering all his questions boldly, arguing theology without fear—perhaps even a little rashly—until Bonner realized he would get nowhere and condemned him on July 12.

While he was in prison, Smith had been used by God to comfort those suffering with him. At the stake on August 8, he determined to do the same, telling everyone present he was sure his body would rise again. "And," he added, "I'm sure God will show you some sign of that." By the time he was nearly half burned and black from the fire, everyone thought Smith was dead, but he suddenly rose upright, lifted the stumps of his arms, and clapped them together joyfully before sinking back into the flames.

෴

Stephen Harwood and Thomas Fust died about the same time as Robert Smith and George Tankervil, being tried and condemned with them. One was burned at Stratford and the other at Ware. William Hall died at Barnet.

Of the ten people sent to Bonner at once, six were executed at various places. Three others—George King, Thomas Leyes, and John Wade—became so sick in prison that they were moved to houses in London, where they all died. Their bodies were thrown out into the fields and secretly buried at night by the faithful. The last of the ten was Joan Laysh or Layshford. She was reprieved for a while but was eventually martyred, too.

WILLIAM WOLSEY AND ROBERT PYGOT

On October 9, 1555, William Wolsey and Robert Pygot of Wisbeach were condemned at Ely by John Fuller, the bishop's chancellor; Dr. Shaxton, his suffragan; Robert Stewart, the dean of Ely; and John Christopherson, the dean of Norwich.

William Wolsey was a policeman in the town of Wells who was accused by Richard Everard, a justice, and put in jail.

Before he was condemned, Dr. Fuller and others visited Wolsey and urged him to return to the church but got nowhere. Before he left the prison, Fuller gave Wolsey a book by Dr. Watson, the bishop of Lincoln, hoping that might show Wolsey where his theology was wrong and convince him to recant his current beliefs. As Wolsey suspected, he found the book full of opinions that were contrary to scripture, so he returned it to the chancellor on his next visit.

That night when Dr. Fuller looked at his book, he found Wolsey had written notes in it—in ink. "This obstinate heretic has ruined my book!" he complained. Still, as the time approached for Wolsey to appear in court, Fuller went back to visit him again. "You bother my conscience," he admitted. "Leave, but watch what you say, so no one complains to me again. Come to church when you want to, and if someone complains about you, I'll send them away."

"Doctor," Wolsey replied, "I was brought here by the law, and I will be freed by the law." Brought to trial, Wolsey was imprisoned in the castle at Wisbeach for some time.

About the same time, Robert Pygot, a painter, was accused of not going to church. Appearing before the judge at Wisbeach, he was asked why he had left the church.

"Sir," he replied, "I am not out of the church. I trust in God."

"But this isn't a church. This is a hall."

"True, but he that is in the true faith of Jesus Christ is always in the church."

"Ah! You know too much for me to talk to. I'll send you to those with more learning."

Pygot joined Wolsey in jail until the court session was over and they were transferred to Ely. On October 9, 1555, they were both examined by Dr. Fuller on their beliefs, especially those on transubstantiation. After their sentence was read and a sermon preached, they were bound to the stake with a chain. Asked once more to recant his errors, Wolsey replied, "I ask God to witness that I am not wrong in any point of the Holy Bible. I hold it to be sound doctrine for my salvation and for others until the end of the world. Whatever my enemies say, I ask God to forgive them."

Just before the fire was lit, someone brought a pile of English New Testaments to be burned with them. "Oh!" said Wolsey. "Give me one of them." Pygot asked for one, too, and they died together, singing Psalm 106 and clasping the testaments to their hearts.

BISHOP RIDLEY

The same day that Wolsey and Pygot died in Ely—October 16, 1555—two other outstanding leaders of the church died at Oxford: Bishop Ridley of London and Bishop Hugh Latimer of Worcester.

Among those martyred for the true Gospel of Christ in Queen Mary's time, Dr. Ridley serves as an excellent example of spiritual inspiration and godly education. Born in Northumberland, Ridley learned his grammar as a child in Newcastle and attended Cambridge, where he soon became well known for his intelligence and advanced rapidly, becoming a doctor of divinity and the head of Pembroke Hall. After that, he traveled to Paris, was made Henry VIII's chaplain on his return, and appointed bishop of Rochester by the king. In King Edward's days, he served as the bishop of London.

Ridley worked so diligently at preaching and teaching his flock the true doctrine of Christ that his parishioners loved him the way a child loves his father. People swarmed to his sermons like bees to honey, knowing their bishop not only preached Christ but lived a pure, holy life. He was well educated, with a remarkable memory, and even his enemies admired his writing, pithy sermons, and lectures.

Besides all this, Ridley gave excellent advice, being very judicious in all his doings. He was merciful and careful when dealing with Catholics during Edward's reign, winning many of them over through his gentle teaching.

Ridley was an attractive man who never held a grudge and always forgave any injury done to him. He was kind and affectionate to his relatives but expected as much from them in their daily lives as he did from any other parishioner. Any family member doing evil could expect no special treatment from Ridley; those who lived honest, godly lives were his brothers and sisters, no matter who they were.

Ridley lived a well-regulated, strict life. As soon as he was dressed in the morning, he prayed on his knees for half an hour in his room. Then he would go to his study, where he worked until the ten o'clock prayers for his household. After prayers, he would go to dinner, where he talked very little, then return to his study until afternoon prayers at five. He would have his dinner, go back to his study until eleven, then retire for the night.

At his manor in Fulham, he would give a lecture to his family every day, beginning at Acts and going through all Paul's epistles. He gave every member of his household who could read a copy of the New Testament. He was extremely careful to see that his family served as good examples of virtue and honesty. In short, he was so godly and virtuous himself that those qualities reigned in his whole household.

When Bishop Ridley was at home in Fulham, he always had his next-door neighbor, Mrs. Bonner, and her sister over for supper and dinner, giving her the honored seat at the end of the table, even if someone else of importance was present. "By your lordship's favor," he would tell his guest, "this place is for my mother Bonner." Mrs. Bonner was the mother of the man who would later become Bishop Bonner during Queen Mary's time—the man responsible for the deaths of many Protestants, including Ridley.

Dr. Ridley was first brought to the Gospel through Bertram's *Book of the Sacraments* and discussion with Bishop Cranmer and Peter Martyr. When Queen Mary came to the throne, he was arrested. First imprisoned in the Tower of London, he was then sent to jail in Oxford with the archbishop of Canterbury and Hugh Latimer. After being condemned, he was kept in the house of Mayor Irish from 1554 until his death in 1555.

BISHOP LATIMER

Bishop Latimer was the son of Hugh Latimer of Thurcaston Leicester, a farmer with a good reputation. At the age of four, he was sent to school and trained in literature; at fourteen, he entered the University of Cambridge to study divinity, becoming a scrupulously observant Catholic priest. At first Latimer was a bitter enemy of the Protestants, opposing the works of Philip Melancthon and Master Stafford. But Thomas Bilney felt pity for Latimer and decided to try to win him to the true knowledge of Christ. Bilney asked Latimer to hear his confession of faith, and Latimer was so moved by what he heard that he left his study of the Catholic doctors to learn true divinity. Where before he was an enemy of Christ, he now became a zealous seeker of Him, even asking Stafford's forgiveness before that man died.

In 1529, a great number of friars and doctors of divinity from all schools at Cambridge began to preach against Latimer and his new beliefs. Dr. West, bishop of Ely, forbade him to preach within the churches of that university, but Dr. Barnes, the prior of the Augustine friars, licensed Latimer to preach in his church. Like a true disciple, Latimer spent the next three years working to convert his brothers of the university and the parishioners of his church, speaking Latin to the educated and English to the common people.

Latimer and Bilney stayed at Cambridge for some time, having many conversations together; the place they walked soon became known as Heretics' Hill. Both of them set a good Christian example by visiting prisoners, helping the needy, and feeding the hungry.

After preaching and teaching at Cambridge for three years, Latimer was called before the cardinal for heresy. At this time he bent to the will of the church and was allowed to return to the university, where he met Dr. Buts, Henry VIII's doctor and supporter. Latimer joined Buts in Henry's court for some time, preaching in London, but became tired of court life and accepted a position in West Kingston that was offered him by the king. There he diligently instructed his parish and everyone in the nearby countryside. It didn't take Latimer long to infuriate a good number of country priests and higher church doctors with his beliefs on reform. Latimer was called before William Warham, archbishop of Canterbury, and John Stokesley, bishop of London, on January 29, 1531. He was kept in London for some time, being called for examination three times a week, until he wrote to the archbishop and said he was too ill to see him anymore. In the same letter, Latimer complained that he was being kept from his parish without just cause, for preaching the truth about certain abuses within the church. Eventually Latimer seems to have accepted the charges against him (although there is no proof of this), and he was freed through the efforts of Buts, Cromwell, and the king.

In time, Henry VIII made Latimer the bishop of Worcester, where he served faithfully, although the dangerous times prevented him from doing everything he wanted to. He wasn't able to rid his diocese of superstitions but did what he could within the Catholic Church, helping his parishioners exclude as much superstition as possible from their lives and worship. Even then, he continued to be harassed by other members of the clergy.

When the Six Articles were passed, Latimer voluntarily resigned his post, as did Shaxton, the bishop of Salisbury. Latimer went to London, where he was harassed by the bishops and imprisoned in the Tower of London until King Edward took the throne. On his release, Latimer went back to work, preaching twice every Sunday and once every weekday, unlike many clergymen who ignored their duties during Edward's reign. He was now sixty-seven years old and suffering from an injury received by the fall of a tree.

Not long after King Edward's death, Latimer was arrested on Queen Mary's command and thrown back into the Tower of London, where he suffered greatly. He was transferred to Oxford with Cranmer, the archbishop of Canterbury, and Ridley, bishop of London, to answer charges made by Gardiner, the bishop of Winchester.

Because of his age, Latimer wrote less than Ridley and Cranmer while in prison, devoting himself more to prayer. He prayed about three main concerns:

Since God had appointed him a preacher, Latimer asked Him for the grace to stand to His doctrine until his death.

He asked God to restore His gospel to England once again.

He prayed for the accession of Elizabeth, asking God to make her a comfort to the comfortless realm of England.

In time, all three of Latimer's prayers would be answered.

RIDLEY AND LATIMER

On September 30, 1555, Ridley and Latimer appeared together in Oxford before a panel of bishops to answer the charges of heresy that had been brought against them. Ridley was examined first.

The bishop of London began by urging Ridley to recant and submit himself to the pope. "If you will renounce your errors, recant your heretical and seditious opinions, consent to yield yourself to the undoubted faith and truth of the Gospel. . .authority is given to us to receive you, to reconcile you, and upon due penance to join you into Christ's church." The bishop stressed three points:

> *That the pope was descended from Peter, who was the foundation of the church.*
> *That the early church fathers confessed the pope's supremacy in their writings.*
> *That Ridley once believed this himself.*

Ridley replied to the three points. First, he said, it was not Peter who was the church's foundation, but Peter's confession that Christ was the Son of God. This belief is the foundation of the church, not a mere man.

Second, the bishop of Rome was supreme in the early church because the city of Rome was supreme in the world of the day, not because he had any more religious power than other bishops. As long as the diocese of Rome was true to the Gospel, its bishop deserved respect from everyone in the church; but as soon as they began setting themselves above kings and emperors for their own honor, the bishops of Rome became anti-Christian.

To the last point, Ridley admitted he did once believe as they did, just as Paul was once a persecutor of Christ.

The bishop of Lincoln cut Ridley short, reminding him of the panel's power to either accept him back into the church or excommunicate him. Anything they did would receive the support of the queen, who was a faithful member of the church. The following articles were then put forward against him (and Latimer):

> *He maintained that the true body of Christ was not present in the bread and wine.*
> *He taught that the bread and wine remained bread and wine after consecration.*

*He believed that the Mass is not a propitiatory sacrifice for the living and
   the dead.*
That Dr. Weston and others declared these beliefs heretical.
That all of the above is true and well known.

Ridley was asked to reply to the charges with simple *yes* or *no* answers
and was promised that he could amend his answers the next day, when he'd
had more time to think about them. Before he answered, Ridley protested
that whatever he said, he would be saying it unwillingly and his answering
would not indicate that he accepted either the panel's or the pope's authority
over him.

To the first charge, he said that Christ's body and blood were present
spiritually in the bread and wine but not physically. To the second, he replied
that the bread and wine remain bread and wine after consecration. To the
third, he said that Christ made one perfect sacrifice for the sins of the whole
world. Communion was an acceptable sacrifice of praise and thanksgiving,
but saying it removed man's sins implied that Christ's work was not enough.
To the fourth, Ridley replied that his beliefs had been declared heretical by
Dr. Watson, but unjustly. To the fifth, that he believed exactly what he said,
although he didn't know what everyone thought of his beliefs.

Ridley was dismissed until the following day, and Latimer was brought
in. As with Ridley, the bishop urged Latimer to give up his beliefs and rejoin the Catholic Church, which was again universally accepted. He was then
asked to reply to the same charges as Ridley.

"I do not deny," he said in answer to the first charge, "that in the sacrament, by spirit and grace, is the very body and blood of Christ. Every man
receiving the bread or wine spiritually receives the body and blood of Christ.
But I deny that the body and blood of Christ is in the sacrament the way you
say it is."

To the second, he replied, "There is a change in the bread and wine, and
yet the bread is still bread and the wine is still wine."

On whether the Mass is a sacrifice for sins, Latimer replied, "No. Christ
made one perfect sacrifice. No one can offer Him up again. Neither can the
priest offer Him for the sins of man, which He took away by offering Himself
once for all upon the cross. There is no propitiation for our sins except the
cross."

When Latimer was asked about his beliefs being called heresy, he replied,
"Yes, I think they were condemned. But He that will judge us all knows they
were condemned unjustly." Latimer was also dismissed until eight o'clock the
next morning.

Ridley arrived on October 1 with his answers to the charges written out, asking permission to read them to the crowd that filled St. Mary's Church. But he was forced to turn his papers over to the bishops first, and they declared them heretical, refusing to read them aloud. In return, Ridley refused to answer their questions, saying all his answers were contained in his written replies. He was condemned as a heretic and turned over to the secular authorities for punishment.

Latimer was brought in. He agreed to answer the panel's charges again, but his answers were the same as the day before, and he refused to recant. He was also condemned and turned over to the authorities.

The morning of October 15, the bishop of Gloucester (Dr. Brooks) and the vice chancellor of Oxford (Dr. Marshall), along with others from the university, arrived at Mayor Irish's house, where Ridley was being held a prisoner. Ridley was given the opportunity to rejoin the church. When he refused, they forced him to go through the ceremony expelling him from the priesthood. The ceremony over, Ridley read a petition to the queen asking that she help Ridley's sister and brother-in-law and others who had depended on him for their support. Dr. Brooks promised to forward the petition to the queen but doubted she would honor it.

That night Ridley's beard and legs were washed. At supper, he invited everyone in the mayor's house to his burning, as well as his sister and brother. When the mayor's wife began to cry, he comforted her by saying, "Quiet yourself. Though my breakfast will be somewhat sharp and painful, I'm sure my supper will be pleasant and sweet."

Ridley and Latimer were to be burned on the north side of Oxford, in a ditch by Baliol College, well guarded by the queen's orders. When everything was ready, they were brought out by the mayor and bailiffs. Ridley wore a furred black gown, velvet nightcap, and slippers. Latimer wore a worn frock, a buttoned cap, and a new long shroud hanging down to his feet.

Looking back, Ridley saw Latimer following him. "Oh. Are you here?" he called.

"Yes. As fast as I can follow," Latimer answered.

Ridley reached the stake first. Holding up his hands, he first looked toward heaven. When Latimer arrived, Ridley ran to him cheerfully, held him, and kissed him, saying, "Be of good cheer, brother, for God will either assuage the fury of the flame or else strengthen us to bear it." After they said their prayers, the two men talked quietly together for a little while, but no one knows what they said.

The officers prevented Ridley and Latimer from answering the sermon that was given by Dr. Smith. They would be allowed to speak only if it were to recant.

"Well, then," said Ridley, "I commit our cause to Almighty God, who shall impartially judge all."

Latimer added, "Well, there is nothing hid but it shall be made manifest."

Ridley cheerfully gave away his clothing and other items he possessed then asked Lord Williams to do what he could to help those who depended on him for their living. The chain was fastened around the two men. "Good fellow, tie it tight, for the flesh will have its way," Ridley commented. Then his brother brought him a bag of gunpowder to hang around his neck. "I will take it to be sent by God, therefore I will receive it as sent of Him. And do you have some for my brother?" Told he did, Ridley sent his brother to Latimer before it was too late. Then they brought a torch and laid it at Ridley's feet.

"Be of good comfort, brother Ridley, and play the man," Latimer called. "We shall this day light such a candle by God's grace in England, as I trust shall never be put out."

When Ridley saw the flames leap up, he cried with a loud voice, "Lord, into Thy hands I commend my spirit? Lord, receive my spirit!"

Latimer cried as vehemently on the other side, "O Father of heaven, receive my soul!" He received the flame as if embracing it. After he stroked his face with his hands and bathed them a little in the fire, Latimer died with little visible pain.

But Ridley suffered longer because the fire did not flare up on his side of the stake, and he called out to them, asking them to let the fire come to him. His brother-in-law, misunderstanding the problem, covered Ridley with even more wood, which made the fire burn stronger on the bottom but kept it from flaring up as it should have. It burned all Ridley's lower parts before ever touching his upper body, which made him leap up and down under the wood piled around him as he cried, "I cannot burn!" Even after his legs were consumed, his shirt was still untouched by the flames. He suffered in terrible pain until one of the onlookers pulled off the wood that was smothering the flames. When Ridley saw the fire flame up, he leaned toward it until the gunpowder exploded. He moved no more after that, falling down at Latimer's feet.

The sight of Ridley and Latimer's struggle moved hundreds in the crowd to tears, seeing years of study and knowledge, all the godly virtues, so much dignity and honor—all consumed in one moment. Well, they are gone, and the rewards of this world they already have. What a reward remains for them in heaven on the day of the Lord's glory, when He comes with His saints!

RIDLEY'S FAREWELL

Dr. Ridley wrote the following letter to all his friends in Christ before his death:

As a man about to take a long journey naturally wants to say good-bye to his friends, so I, expecting to leave you any day now, want to bid all my sisters and brothers here on earth good-bye.

Farewell, my dear brother George Shipside, who has always been faithful, trustworthy, and loving. Now in the time of my cross, you have been my most friendly, steadfast supporter, always serving God's cause.

Farewell, my sister Alice [Shipside's wife]. I'm glad to hear that you have accepted Christ's cross, which is now lain on your back as well as mine. Thank God for giving you a godly, loving husband; honor and obey him, according to God's law. Honor your mother-in-law and love everyone in his family, doing them as much good as you can. As for your children, I have no doubt that your husband will treat them as though they were his own.

Farewell, my dearly beloved brother, John Ridley, and you, my gentle and loving sister, Elizabeth. The tender love you were said to have for me above the rest of your family binds me to you in love. I wish I could repay you with deeds instead of words. I say good-bye to your daughter Elizabeth, whom I love for her meek, gentle spirit. This is a precious thing in the sight of God.

Farewell, my beloved sister of Unthank, with all your children, nephews, and nieces. Since the death of my brother Hugh, I wanted to treat them as my own children, but the Lord God must and will be their Father, if they love and fear Him and live according to His law.

Farewell, my beloved cousins, Nicholas Ridley of Willi-mountswicke and your wife. I thank you for all the kindness you showed me and the rest of our families. Since God has made you a leader of our family and given you His gifts of grace above others, continue in truth, honesty, righteousness, and godliness and resist falsehood, unrighteousness, and ungodliness, which are condemned by the Word of God.

Farewell, my young cousin, Ralph Whitfield. Oh, your time was very short with me! I wanted to do good for you, but all you received was loss. I trust God will make that up to you.

Farewell, my family and countrymen; farewell in Christ to you all.

The Lord knows I wanted to bring Christ's blessed Gospel to you all; it was my duty as a minister.

I warn you all: Do not be ashamed by my death. I think it is the greatest honor of my life and thank God for calling me to give my life for His sake and in His cause. He gave the same honor to the holy prophets, His dearly beloved apostles, and His blessed chosen martyrs. I have no doubt that I am dying for God's cause and the cause of truth. Having a heart willing to stand for Christ to the death is an inestimable and honorable gift from God, given only to the true elect and dearly beloved children of God and inheritors of the kingdom of heaven. All of you that love me should rejoice that I, a sinful and vile wretch, was called to give up this temporal life in defense of His eternal, everlasting truth.

You, my family and countrymen, know you will always have reason to rejoice and thank God, and I know you will find favor and grace in my cause, for the Lord said He will be full of mercy to those who love Him.

Through the goodness and grace of Almighty God, the Church of England has recently enjoyed great substance, great riches of heavenly treasure, great plenty of God's true Word, the correct administration of Christ's holy sacraments—the whole profession of Christ's religion. It also observed the Lord's Supper correctly, observing Christ's commands. Thanks was given for the bread and wine, and the Lord's death was commemorated. The bread was broken in remembrance of Christ's body being torn upon the cross, the cup was shared in remembrance of Christ's shed blood, and everyone received both.

All this was done in English, so everyone would understand and give God the glory. Recently, all the services of this church were performed in English according to the command of the Lord and Paul's doctrine, so people could understand and profit from them.

The Church of England also had holy, wholesome sermons urging people to lead godly lives, as well as those condemning the vices that used to reign in England. It had articles of belief grounded in scripture that could have expelled the errors and heresies almost overgrowing the church.

But alas, lately thieves have come in and stolen all this treasure. These

232

*robbers have robbed the Church of England of all its holy treasure,
carried it away, and overthrown it. Instead of God's Holy Word
and true sacraments, they added their foolish fantasies and ungodly
traditions.*

*Instead of the Lord's Holy Table, they give the people their Mass—
a mockery of the true supper of the Lord. They have bewitched the
minds of simple people, brought them from true worship into
idolatry, making the bread and wine into Christ our Lord and
Savior, even though Christ said, "Do [this] in remembrance of me."*

*Instead of prayers in English, these thieves give the people prayers in
a language they cannot understand, preventing them from praying
together with the priest. Paul called praying in a strange tongue
barbarous, childish, unprofitable folly, and plain madness.*

*Instead of godly articles of unity in religion and wholesome sermons,
these thieves provide the pope's laws and decrees, lying legends,
feigned fables and miracles.*

*I cannot consent to this robbery, because it is blasphemy against God,
high treason against Christ. It is plainly against God's Word and
Christ's Gospel, against my salvation and that of my brothers and
sisters, which Christ so dearly bought for us all. This is why I am
being put to death, which I willingly accept, sure that I will receive
everlasting life in return.*

*These thieves are worse than a thief who robs and kills the body, for these
kill both body and soul. These church robbers so disguise their
spiritual robbery that they can make people believe that lies are
truth and truth is a lie; light is darkness, and darkness light; evil
good and good evil; superstition true religion and idolatry true worship.*

*These robbers cannot be fought as common robbers are, with spears and
lances. Our weapons must be spiritual and heavenly. We must
fight them with the armor of God, not intending to kill their bodies
but their errors, their heresies, idolatries, superstitions, and
hypocrisy, in an attempt to save both their bodies and their souls.
Our weapons are faith, hope, charity, righteousness, truth, patience,
and prayer; our sword is the Word of God. With these weapons, we
will win by never yielding to the enemy, even though we are
murdered like sheep. The crueler and more painful our deaths, the
more glorious they are in God and the more blessed our martyrdom.*

*I tell you this so you won't be ashamed by my death. If you love me, you
will rejoice that God has called me to this honor, which is greater*

than any earthly honor I could ever attain. Who wouldn't be happy to die for this cause? I trust in my Lord God, who put His mind, will, and affection in my heart, and choose to lose all my worldly substance and my life, too, rather than deny His known truth. He will comfort me, aid me, and strengthen me forever, even to the yielding of my spirit and soul into His hands. I most heartily beg His infinite goodness and mercy, through Christ our Lord. Amen.

ARCHBISHOP CRANMER

Thomas Cranmer came from an ancient family dating back to the conquest. He was born in Arselacton, Nottinghamshire, brought up in schools from the time he was an infant, and attended the University of Cambridge, where he received his master of arts and was made a professor of Jesus College. When he married a gentleman's daughter, he gave up his fellowship at Cambridge and became the reader at Buckingham College.

Cranmer's wife died in childbirth, and he returned to Cambridge, where, as a doctor of divinity, he became one of those who examined students before they were granted their bachelors or doctorates. Since he strongly believed that students of divinity should know scripture, that knowledge became one of the prerequisites for graduation. This meant that some friars and monks who were educated in the study of church authors and knew little scripture were denied degrees and disliked Cranmer, although some took the time to study the Bible and were successful.

Because of his reputation as a scholar, Cranmer was offered a position in Cardinal Wolsey's new college at Oxford, which he turned down. About this time Cardinal Campegio and Cardinal Wolsey had been appointed by the pope to decide the case between Henry VIII and his wife. They delayed the proceedings all that summer and adjourned in August, saying it was against the law to decide ecclesiastical matters during the harvest, since this was a decision no one really wanted to be responsible for. Furious at the delay, Henry ordered Campegio to return to Rome.

Two of the king's advisors happened to spend a night in the same house in Waltham where Cranmer was staying to avoid the plague that was sweeping through Cambridge, and the three of them met at supper, where Cranmer was asked for his opinion on the king's divorce and remarriage.

Cranmer replied that he hadn't studied the matter but thought they were spending too much time prosecuting the ecclesiastical law. He thought the question should be decided according to the Bible. This would satisfy Henry, instead of dragging the decision out from year to year, since the learned men of England could easily find the answer in the Bible.

The two men thought that was a good idea and said they would mention it to the king, which they did the next day.

"Where is this Dr. Cranmer?" the king asked. "Is he still at Waltham?"

They said he was there when they left that morning.

"I want to speak with him. Send for him. I think that man has the sow by the right ear. If I'd known about this two years ago, it could have saved me a great deal of money and eased my mind."

Cranmer didn't want to go to the king, saying he hadn't studied the matter thoroughly enough, but eventually he had no choice but to appear at the king's court.

"I think you have the right idea," the king told Cranmer. "You must understand that my conscience has bothered me for a long time, and this could relieve it one way or another. I command you to see my cause furthered as much as you can. I don't want to be divorced from the queen if our marriage is not against God's laws. No prince ever had a more gentle, obedient, and loving companion than my wife. If this doubt hadn't arisen, I would be content to stay with her, as long as it is in the will and pleasure of Almighty God."

Cranmer said it would be a good idea to have the matter examined by the best men of Cambridge and Oxford, according to the Bible.

"That's fine. But I also want you to write your opinion," the king agreed, ordering the Earl of Wiltshire to put Cranmer up in his house at Durham Place while he studied the matter. Cranmer's decision was that the pope had no authority to dispense with the Word of God and the scriptures.

"Will you stand by this before the bishop of Rome?" Henry asked him.

"I will, by God's grace, if your majesty sends me there," Cranmer replied.

Through Cranmer, learned men were sent to most of the universities in Christendom to discuss the question, as well as at Oxford and Cambridge. The decision was that Henry's marriage to his brother's wife was unlawful according to God's Word and they should be divorced. A delegation was sent to Rome to meet with the pope: the Earl of Wiltshire, Dr. Cranmer, Dr. Stokesley, Dr. Carne, Dr. Bennet, and others.

When the time came for them to see the pope, he sat in his rich apparel with sandals on his feet, which he offered to be kissed by the ambassadors. The Earl of Wiltshire made no move to kiss the pope's feet, so no one else did, either. They offered to defend their belief that no man could legally marry his brother's wife and that the pope could not provide a dispensation for this infraction of God's law. Although the delegation was promised time to discuss the matter with the pope, they were dismissed without ever seeing him again.

Everyone but Cranmer returned to England, while he went to the emperor's council to support the divorce, receiving no argument on the point from them.

At the time of the passing of the Six Articles, Cranmer stood against the whole Parliament for three days, arguing against their passage, until Henry ordered him to leave the chamber so the act could be passed.

When Lord Cromwell was arrested and the Catholics thought everything was going their way, they appointed ten or twelve bishops to go to Cranmer and convince him to support several new laws about religion. Even those he trusted—Bishop Heath and Bishop Skip—urged him to yield to what they thought was Henry's will on these matters, but Cranmer refused. Instead, he went to the king, argued against the proposed regulations, won him over, and the laws were not passed.

Not long after, the bishop of Winchester and others told Henry that Cranmer was stirring the people up with his ideas and should be examined for heresy. Henry reluctantly agreed, telling Cranmer the news himself.

When he heard that he was to be tried for heresy, Cranmer replied, "I most humbly thank Your Highness, for there are those who have slandered me, and I hope to prove myself innocent."

"Don't you know how many enemies you have?" Henry asked. "Think how easy it would be to find three or four liars to witness against you. Do you think you'll have any better luck than your master, Christ, did? You would run headlong to your death, if I let you!

"Tomorrow, when the council sends for you, go to them. If they commit you to the Tower, ask to have your accusers brought before you without being imprisoned. You're a member of the council, and that's your right. If they insist on imprisoning you, give them my ring and appeal to me. As soon as they see my ring, they'll know I have agreed to take over the matter and have dismissed them."

The following day Cranmer answered as the king had instructed him. Deciding that no persuasion of his would keep him out of prison, he appealed to the king and delivered the ring to them. Somewhat amazed, the whole council immediately rose and took the king his ring, surrendering the matter into his hands.

The king addressed the council. "Ah, my lords, I thought I had wiser men in my council. I was content that you try him as a councillor, not as a common subject, but now I see you would have treated him harshly. If a prince can be beholden to a subject, I am most beholden to my lord Canterbury."

Cranmer's enemies decided they had to ruin his good reputation with the king before proceeding against him. They arranged to have him accused of preaching erroneous doctrine by the clerics of his own cathedral and the most famous justices of the peace in the county; then they delivered the charges to the king.

Henry read the charges, put them in his shirt, and then went for a ride on the Thames to calm down. Seeing Cranmer on the shore at Lambeth Bridge, he asked him to come aboard for a talk. "I have news from Kent for you," the king began.

"Good, I hope," Cranmer replied.

"So good that I now know the greatest heretic in Kent." Henry pulled out the charges against Cranmer, giving them to him for reading.

Cranmer was deeply hurt to see those he thought were his friends accusing him but asked the king to appoint a commission to look into the charges.

"I intend to," the king said. "And you will be the chief commissioner, along with the two or three others you appoint."

"People will say the commission isn't impartial if I judge myself," Cranmer protested.

Within three weeks it was obvious that the charges were a Catholic plot against Cranmer. The king told him to appoint twelve or sixteen men to search the houses and persons of those in the plot and bring anything they found to him. In less than four hours of searching, the conspiracy was brought to light by the seizure of letters from the bishop of Winchester and others.

Two of the men involved were especially good friends of Cranmer: the suffragan bishop of Dover and Dr. Barber, a layman. One day Cranmer called them both into his study. "I need some good advice from you," he began. "One or two men whom I trusted have disclosed my secrets and accused me of heresy. How should I behave toward them? You're both my friends, and I have always talked to you when I needed advice. What do you think?"

"Such villains should be hung!" Dr. Barber replied.

"Hanging's too good for them! I would hang them myself!" said the suffragan.

Cranmer threw his hands up toward heaven. "O Lord, most merciful God," he called, "who can a man trust these days?" Pulling the letters out, he asked, "Do you know these letters?"

The two men fell on their knees, begging forgiveness, saying they had been tempted to write the letters by others.

"Well," said Cranmer, "God make you both good men. I never deserved this at your hands, but you should ask God's forgiveness. If I can't trust you, what should I do? I see now that there is no trust among men. I even fear my left hand will accuse my right hand. This shouldn't surprise me, for our Savior Jesus Christ warned that such a world would come in the last days. I beseech Him of His great mercy to finish that time shortly."

This was the last attempt made against Cranmer during the days of Henry VIII. Under Edward VI, Cranmer's influence was even greater (he was the young king's godfather). It was during Edward's reign that Cranmer had discussions with Bishop Ridley that confirmed his views of theology. He took on the defense of the entire Protestant doctrine regarding the idolatry of the Mass, writing five books for the Church of England on the subject.

At sixteen, King Edward fell sick and bequeathed the throne to Lady Jane Grey, King Henry's niece, not wanting his sister Mary, who was a Catholic, to have the throne. All the nobles agreed then sent for Cranmer and asked if he would join them in supporting Lady Jane, but Cranmer refused. He had taken an oath to abide by Henry's will, which specified Mary, not Lady Jane Grey. Cranmer talked to Edward about the matter and was assured that Lady Jane could legally have the throne. Once he discussed it with some lawyers, Cranmer, too, agreed.

On Edward's death, the lords commanded that Lady Jane should take the throne, even though she was unwilling to be queen. This was opposed by the House of Commons—not because it favored Mary but because it hated some of Lady Jane's supporters. With their support, Mary took the throne, came to London, and beheaded Lady Jane when she refused to worship as a Catholic.

The nobles who had supported Lady Jane were required to pay a fine and were forgiven, except for the dukes of Northumberland and Suffolk and Archbishop Cranmer. He desired a pardon, but Mary refused to see him because of the role he had played in Henry's divorce from her mother. She also held Cranmer responsible for Protestantism being accepted in Edward's reign.

Soon rumor was spread around that Cranmer had offered to say a Mass at Edward's funeral, hoping to find favor with Mary. He immediately denied the rumor, stating his feelings about the Mass in a letter that someone made public. Cranmer was ordered to appear before the commissioners. Although he was allowed to leave the hearing at that time, he was soon arrested, imprisoned in the Tower, and condemned for treason.

The queen realized that she had pardoned everyone else from Edward's time and that Cranmer had supported her longer than anyone else when Edward wanted to give the throne to Lady Jane, so she pardoned him from treason but let the charges of heresy stand.

In time Cranmer was transferred to Oxford to dispute his theology with the doctors and divines there. Now the queen and her bishops had already decided what would happen to Cranmer, but the dispute would serve to cover his murder.

On September 12, 1555, Cranmer appeared before Bishop Brooks, Dr. Martin, Dr. Story, the queen's commissioners, and a number of other officials at St. Mary's. Brought before the panel, Cranmer took off his cap and bowed to the queen's commissioners one at a time. Then, looking the pope's representative in the eye, he put his cap back on and stood straight, refusing to accept his authority.

"This I do profess concerning my faith," Cranmer began. "I want you to note that I will never agree that the bishop of Rome has any jurisdiction in this country. I made an oath to the king, and no foreign person is above him. The pope is contrary to the crown, and I cannot serve both.

"The bishop of Rome is also against God's laws, which set aside one day a week for church, so all people should hear God's laws in their own tongue and understand them. But the pope commands the service to be said in Latin, which no one understands. God would have it otherwise.

"Concerning the sacrament, I have taught no false doctrine. If it can be proved by any doctor that Christ's body is really present there, I will submit.

"Christ commands all to drink of the cup; the pope takes it away from the laymen. Christ tells us to obey the king; the pope tells us to obey him. If I obey him, I cannot obey Christ.

"Christ said the Antichrist will appear. Who shall he be? One that advances himself above all other creatures. Until someone advances himself more than the pope does, let him be the Antichrist."

After Cranmer's speech, he answered the charges against him.

Before he entered holy orders, he had married Joan Black or Brown, from Cambridge.

Cranmer said he had married Joan but wasn't sure if her name was Black or Brown.

After her death he took holy orders and was made an archbishop by the pope.

Cranmer said he'd received a letter from the pope that he delivered to the king, and the king made him an archbishop.

Being in holy orders, he married a woman named Anne.

That was true, Cranmer said.

During Henry VIII's reign, he kept his wife secretly and had children.

Cranmer said that was true. It was better to have his own wife than do as the other priests did and steal other men's wives.

During Edward's time, he lived openly with his wife.

Cranmer said he did because the laws of England said he could.

That he was not ashamed of his wife.

He had no reason to be ashamed of her, he said.

That he refused the authority of the church, held the heresy concerning the sacrament of the altar, and published his beliefs.

Cranmer agreed he had written the books the panel named.

That he compelled others, against their wills, to agree with him.

He exhorted those who agreed but compelled no one to agree.

Since he would not stop perpetuating such enormous crimes, he was locked in the Tower.

Cranmer replied that he knew of no enormous crimes he'd committed.

That he was convicted of heresy in Oxford.

Cranmer admitted he was denounced but maintained he was not heretic.

He left the Catholic Church and moved the king and his subjects to do the same.

Cranmer admitted he had left the pope but said there was no schism in it.

That he had twice been sworn to the pope.

He replied that he had obeyed the laws of the country when he did so.

That he usurped the power of the pope by consecrating bishops and priests.

Cranmer said he did consecrate bishops and priests, but the laws of the land had given him that power.

That although the whole country submitted to the authority of the pope, he would not.

Cranmer agreed that he would not submit to the pope but said he was correct in not doing so.

On February 14, 1555, Cranmer was recalled before a new commission, condemned, stripped of his church offices, and turned over to the secular authorities.

By now Cranmer had been in prison for almost three years. The doctors and divines of Oxford all tried to make him recant, even allowing him to stay in the dean's house while they argued with him, and eventually Cranmer gave in to their requests and signed a recantation accepting the pope's authority in all things. The queen was delighted with his recantation but still determined that Cranmer would die. He remained in prison.

Cranmer was miserable, not being able to die honestly or live dishonestly. In the meantime, Queen Mary secretly told Dr. Cole to prepare a funeral sermon for Cranmer's burning on March 21. On March 20, Cole went to Cranmer to see if he was standing by his recantation. Assured that he was, Cole returned early on March 21 to give Cranmer some money for the poor. Cranmer realized what was about to happen to him. A Spanish friar came in to ask him to write his recantation out twice with his own hand and sign it, which he did, then Cranmer wrote a prayer and sermon that he secretly tucked into his shirt and waited.

Since it was a cold, rainy day, Cranmer was brought into St. Mary's Church with all the nobles, justices, and the crowd that had gathered. Dr. Cole gave his sermon, saying that although Cranmer had repented of his errors, the queen had other reasons for sending him to his death. He commended Cranmer for his works, saying he was unworthy of death but that Masses would be said for his soul in all the churches of Oxford. Then Cole asked Cranmer to read his profession of faith, so everyone would see he was a good Catholic.

Cranmer's prayers and confession of faith were well within the doctrine of the Catholic Church until the very end, when he said, "And now I come to the great thing that troubles my conscience more than anything I ever did or said in my whole life, and that is the publishing of a writing contrary to the truth, which now here I renounce and refuse, as things written by my hand contrary to the truth I believed with my whole heart, written because I feared death. Since my hand offended, it will be punished: when I come to the fire, it first will be burned. As for the pope, I refuse him, as Christ's enemy and Antichrist, with all his false doctrine. And as for the sacrament, I believe as I have taught in my book. . . ."

The congregation was amazed at Cranmer's words, and the Catholic churchmen there raged, fretted, and fumed because they had nothing left to threaten him with. He could only die once, after all.

When he came to the place where Hugh Latimer and Ridley had been burned before him, Cranmer knelt down briefly to pray then undressed to his shirt, which hung down to his bare feet. His head, once he took off his caps, was so bare there wasn't a hair on it. His beard was long and thick, covering his face, which was so grave it moved both his friends and enemies.

As the fire approached him, Cranmer put his right hand into the flames, keeping it there until everyone could see it burned before his body was touched. "This unworthy right hand!" he called out often before he gave up the ghost.

GERTRUDE CROKHAY

Gertrude Crokhay lived with her second husband in St. Katherine's parish, near the Tower of London. In 1558, a child portraying St. Nicholas made his way around the parish, but Gertrude refused to let him into her house. The next day Dr. Mallet and twenty others appeared at her door to ask why she wouldn't let St. Nicholas in and receive his blessing.

"Sir," she answered, "I didn't know St. Nicholas came here."

"Yes," said the doctor. "Here's the boy who played him."

"My neighbor's child was here, but not St. Nicholas, for St. Nicholas is in heaven. I was afraid he would steal from me, because I'd heard of men robbed by St. Nicholas's clerks." Dr. Mallet left Gertrude, not able to trap her into saying anything that could be construed as heresy.

In 1559, Gertrude served as godmother for a child being baptized with the Protestant service. When her enemies heard of this, they began looking for her, but she had gone across the sea to Guelderland to see some land that had been left to her children by her first husband. After three months, she started home by way of Antwerp. She was seen there by John Johnson, a Dutchman who was fighting with her husband over a bill. He accused her of being an Anabaptist and had her imprisoned to get even with her husband.

Gertrude remained in prison for two weeks, during which she saw some prisoners secretly drowned in wine vats and cast into the river. She expected the same would eventually be done to her, and in her fear she came down with the sickness that later killed her.

Finally called to be tried as an Anabaptist, Gertrude declared her faith so boldly in Dutch that she was released from prison and allowed to return to England.

THE SPURGES, CAVILL, AMBROSE, DRAKE, AND TIMS

These six men lived in the county of Essex. Being accused of heresy, they were all arrested and sent up to Bishop Gardiner of London, who sent the first four to Marshalsea Prison and the last two to the King's Bench.

After having been confined for a year, they were all brought into the court at St. Paul's Church to be examined by Bishop Bonner. Bonner began his examination with Tims, whom he called the ringleader, telling him he had taught the others heresies and made them as guilty as himself. After talking this way for a while, the bishop asked Tims to submit himself to the church.

In answer to this, Tims reminded the bishop that he himself had formally given up the church he had now professed such a love for during the reign of Henry VIII. "My lord, that which you have written against the supremacy of the pope can be proved true by scripture. What you are doing now is contrary to the Word of God, as I can show." At this, Bonner called Tims an obstinate heretic and condemned him.

Drake's trial came next. He frankly declared that he denied the authority of the pope, and no persuasion would change his mind. No time was wasted in condemning Drake and turning him over to the secular authorities for punishment. The four remaining prisoners, Thomas and Richard Spurge, George Ambrose, and John Cavill, were then asked if they would forsake their heresies and return to the church. They all refused to acknowledge any wrongdoing and declined to change their beliefs.

On April 14, 1556, the six men were taken to Smithfield, where they were chained to the same stake and burned in one fire. They patiently submitted themselves to the flames and quietly resigned their souls to that Redeemer for whose sake they had given their bodies to be burned.

JULIUS PALMER

Julius Palmer was the son of a merchant living in the city of Coventry. He received his early education at the public school there and was sent to Oxford, where he was graduated and elected a fellow of Magdalene College.

Palmer had been brought up as a Catholic, and he refused to conform to the religious changes made during Edward VI's time, so he was expelled from the college and served as a schoolteacher in the town of Oxford. When Queen Mary came to power, Palmer was returned to his post at the college. But while he had been away from the college, Palmer had made the acquaintance of several leaders of the reform party and began to doubt whether it was necessary to obey the pope in order to be a good Christian. When the persecution began, he began to look into the cases of those arrested and how they behaved themselves through the whole process of condemnation and burning, even sending one of his pupils to report back to him on the burning of Bishop Hooper.

Before this, Palmer was inclined to think that very few men would brave the fire for the sake of their religion, but when he heard of Hooper's heroism and attended the examination of Ridley and Latimer, he totally changed his mind. From then on, he studied the scriptures thoroughly and became a zealous reformer.

Palmer began to miss Mass and other church ceremonies, which brought enough suspicion on him that he felt he should leave the college. He accepted a post as a grammar-school teacher in Reading, Berkshire, until driven out of there by enemies who threatened to turn him in for his Protestant beliefs.

Entirely destitute, Palmer went to his mother, hoping to obtain the legacy his father had left him four years before. But his mother was a heartless, bigoted woman who hated the reformers and was afraid of being accused of harboring a heretic. As soon as she saw him standing at her door, she motioned him away: "Get thee gone, heretic! Get thee gone!" she exclaimed.

"Mother, I don't deserve this!" Palmer replied.

"You have been banished from Oxford and Reading as a heretic."

Nothing Palmer could say would change his mother's mind, so he decided to travel to Reading in hopes of getting his back pay there but was arrested and thrown into prison with Thomas Askine and John Gwin. After standing firm at their trials, all three were condemned as heretics.

While in prison awaiting their execution, Palmer comforted his two fellow-sufferers and urged them to hold on to the faith they professed. When the fire was kindled and began to take hold on the bodies of the three martyrs, they lifted up their hands toward heaven and cried out, "Lord, strengthen us! Lord, receive our souls!" And so they continued without any struggle, holding up their hands and calling on the Lord until they died.

RICHARD WOODMAN

Woodman's parish priest, a man named Fairbank, had tried without success to convince Woodman to attend church services. Annoyed by his failure, Fairbank preferred charges of heresy against Woodman and had him brought before the justices of the peace for the county of Sussex, who committed him to the King's Bench Prison for a considerable amount of time.

At length Woodman and four others were brought to be examined by Bishop Bonner of London, who advised them that they should become members of the true church. They answered that they considered themselves members of the church, and Bonner, satisfied with their replies, set all five men free.

Not long after Woodman returned home, the rumor was spread that he had joined the Catholic Church. He denied this so often and so publicly that a warrant was issued for his arrest. Three men approached Woodman one day as he worked in his father's warehouse, telling him he had to go with them before the Lord Chamberlain. Surprised and alarmed at this sudden attack, Woodman begged to be allowed to go home to tell his wife of the arrest and dress properly for court. The officers agreed to this and accompanied Woodman to his home. Once there, Woodman asked to see their warrant.

"It's not here," one of them replied. "It's at my house. The most you can do is make me go get it."

"If you have a warrant, fetch it," Woodman demanded. "Until you do have it, leave my house." He then shut the door in their faces. Knowing they would soon return, Woodman ran to a window in the rear of the house and escaped to a nearby forest, where he hid himself. The officers soon came back with the warrant and searched the house from top to bottom, but Woodman was safe in the woods.

Woodman knew they would search the whole country for him, including the seacoast, and it would be impossible for him to leave the country, so he decided the best thing to do would be to stay close to home, which no one would even think of. Bringing out his Bible, pen, ink, and other necessities, Woodman hid under a tree in the nearby woods for six or seven weeks. His wife brought him food every day. At last there was a report that he had been seen in Flanders, and the local search was given up. Woodman took the opportunity to escape to Flanders and France, but he missed his home and family too much to stay and sneaked back into the country. Within three weeks, another warrant was issued for his arrest, and his house was searched as often as twice a week for the next two months.

In the end, Woodman was betrayed by his own brother, who told the authorities that he left his hiding place in the evening to sleep at home. When the authorities came to his house, Woodman hid in a secret loft that had never been discovered in all of the previous searches. Although they knew he had to be somewhere in the house, the officers couldn't find him anywhere. Woodman's brother knew the loft existed, but he didn't know exactly where it was, so the search was renewed until one of them finally spotted the loft, forcing Woodman to make a run for it.

"As soon as I found myself on the ground, I started and ran down a lane that was full of sharp cinders, and the men came running after me," Woodman said. "I turned about hastily to go on, when I stepped on a sharp stone with one foot, and in trying to save it, I slipped into a great miry hole and fell down, and before I could arise and get away, they were upon me. Then they bound me and took me away."

Woodman was taken to London and examined by several church officials but refused to yield to anything that was not founded on the Bible's authority. About two weeks after being sentenced, Woodman was taken to the town of Lewes, in Sussex, with nine other prisoners. On July 22, 1557, the ten men were led to the place of execution. There they were chained to several stakes and consumed in one great fire. It is recorded that they all went to their deaths with wonderful courage and resignation, with their last words committing their souls to that blessed Redeemer who was to be their final judge.

SIMON MILLER AND ELIZABETH COOPER

Simon Miller was a prosperous merchant of the town of Lynn-Regis. He was an earnest supporter of the reformers' doctrines, and having occasion to go to Norwich on business, he inquired while there for a place of worship. This being reported to Chancellor Dunning, he ordered Miller to appear before him. When the chancellor asked him the usual questions, Miller answered without attempting to hide his thoughts on the subject of religion, so he was committed to the bishop's palace as a prisoner.

After spending some time in prison, Miller was allowed to go home to settle his affairs. On his return he was again examined by the chancellor, who warned him to recant and return to the Catholic Church, but Miller remained firm in his faith and was condemned as a heretic.

Elizabeth Cooper, who was burned with Simon Miller, was the wife of a tradesman in Norwich. She had formerly been persuaded to recant, but her conscience bothered her so that one day she went to St. Andrew's Church and withdrew her recantation in the presence of a large congregation. For this she was immediately arrested and sent to prison. The next day she was brought before the bishop and examined. This time she remained true to her faith and was condemned as a relapsed heretic.

On July 30, 1557, Simon Miller and Elizabeth Cooper were both led to the stake, which was set up in a field outside Norwich, near Bishopgate. When the fire was lit, Elizabeth Cooper was afraid and cried out. Miller put his hand out toward her, telling her to be strong and of good cheer, "For, good sister," he said, "we shall have a joyful meeting hereafter." Upon hearing Miller's words, the woman seemed reassured and stood still and quiet until they both committed their souls to Almighty God and ended their lives.

A WOMAN AT NORWICH

Cicely Ormes, of the city of Norwich, wife of Edmund Ormes, was arrested on the day that Simon Miller and Elizabeth Cooper were executed. She drew the attention of the officers to herself by speaking encouraging words to the two prisoners on the way to the stake. For this she was put in prison and soon after taken before the chancellor for examination.

The chancellor offered to release her "if she would go to church and keep her beliefs to herself" and told her "she could hold to any faith she would."

But she answered, "I will not enter your church."

Then the chancellor told her he had shown more favor to her than he ever did to any person, and he didn't want to condemn her because she was only a foolish young woman.

Cicely replied that if she was only a foolish young woman, he shouldn't be worried about her belief. Foolish or not, she was content to give up her life for a cause so good.

The chancellor then read the sentence of condemnation and delivered Cicely Ormes to the care of the sheriffs of the city. Cicely was a young woman in the prime of life, uneducated, but very earnest in her cause. She was born in East Dereham and was the daughter of Thomas Haund, a tailor. The first time she was brought before the magistrate, she recanted but was afterward so troubled by her conscience that she wrote a letter to the chancellor to let him know she repented of her action. But before the letter could be delivered, she was arrested, tried, and convicted.

Cicely Ormes was burned on September 23, 1557, between seven and eight in the morning. When she came to the stake, she kneeled down and made her prayers to God. That being done, she rose up and said, "Good people, I believe as I have been taught from the Bible. This I do, and I will never change my mind. My death is a witness of my faith to all present here. Good people, as many of you as believe the same as I do, pray for me." When she had said this, she laid her hand on the stake and saw it was black—she was burned at the same stake as Simon Miller and Elizabeth Cooper—and wiped it on her dress. After she had been bound and the fire was lit, she clasped her hands together against her heart, turning her face upward, and raised her hands little by little, until they fell helpless at her side when she died.

THOMAS HUDSON

Thomas Hudson was a glover by trade, living in the town of Ailesham in Norfolk. Although he had little schooling, he was a great student of the scriptures and preached on Sundays to any of his neighbors who were interested in hearing the Bible read and explained.

When Queen Mary began her reign, all unlicensed ministers who publicly preached to the people became marked men. Hudson would have been among the first to be arrested and thrown into prison if he had not fled from his home. He traveled to Suffolk and, by constantly changing his lodgings from one house to another, escaped arrest.

But after a time, Hudson's desire to see his wife and family became too strong to be resisted. In spite of the danger, he went home. Soon he heard that his enemies knew of his return, so he left his house and built a crude shelter beneath a pile of nearby firewood, only coming out in the darkness. This worked until the town's vicar threatened to burn Mrs. Hudson for hiding her husband. Hudson left his hiding place and openly walked into town, where he was arrested.

The bishop asked Hudson a great number of questions, all of which he answered honestly; and though he wasn't an educated man, Hudson's arguments were very strong. Finding he couldn't do anything with the man, the bishop finally condemned him and sent him to prison.

On May 19, 1558, Thomas Hudson was taken out of prison and led to a place called the Lollards' Pit, just outside the bishop's gate at Norwich, along with two other condemned men. Just before the chain around him was made fast, Hudson stopped, slipped out from under the chain, and stood a little to one side. This caused many to wonder if he was about to recant or if he was coming forward for his parents' blessing. But no one knew the real reason: Hudson had suddenly been afflicted with doubts and felt his faith growing weak. Therefore, not willing to die while feeling this way, he fell upon his knees and prayed to God, who sent him comfort. Then he rose with great joy as a reborn man and cried, "Now, thank God, I am strong and care not what man can do unto me." So going to the stake again, he put the chain around himself, and they were all burned together.

HISTORY OF BISHOP BONNER

Edmund Bonner, bishop of London, who took so prominent a part in the persecution of the Protestants during Queen Mary's reign, was born at Hanley in Worcestershire about the year 1500. He was educated at Oxford and, having been admitted to the priesthood, entered the household of Cardinal Wolsey.

All through Henry's reign, Bonner appeared to be very earnest in his opposition to the pope and strongly in favor of the Reformation. Upon Henry's death, however, he refused to take the Oath of Supremacy for Edward and was sent to prison until he agreed to be obedient to the new king, was released, and later imprisoned once again until Queen Mary took the throne.

Mary saw just what she needed in Bonner, who threw himself into the work of persecuting the Protestants with all his energy. It's said that two hundred of the martyrs of this time were personally tried and sentenced by him. Bonner was a harsh, persistent man, with no pity or compassion for the people brought before him. Nothing short of complete surrender would satisfy Bonner. So far did his rage against heresy carry him that he is said to have called for rods and beaten stubborn witnesses himself on several occasions.

When Elizabeth came to the throne, she singled Bonner out to mark with her disapproval, sending him to prison in her second year for refusing to accept her as the head of the Church of England. He remained there for ten years, dying in misery and wretchedness at the age of seventy. Although no one had seen Bonner for over ten years, his memory was so fresh and he was so hated by the people that he was buried at midnight to avoid a riot.

THE DEATH OF QUEEN MARY

After a long illness, Queen Mary died on November 17 at three or four in the morning, yielding her life to nature and her kingdom to her sister, Elizabeth.

Hearing her sighs before she died, her council asked if she was sad about the death of her husband. "Indeed, that may be one cause," the queen replied, "but that is not the greatest wound that pierces my oppressed mind."

No other king or queen of England spilled as much blood in a time of peace as Queen Mary did in four years through her hanging, beheading, burning, and imprisonment of good Christian Englishmen. When she first sought the crown and promised to retain the faith and religion of Edward, God went with her and brought her the throne through the efforts of the Protestants. But after she broke her promises to God and man, sided with Stephen Gardiner, and gave up her supremacy to the pope, God left her. Nothing she did after that thrived.

Instead, she married King Philip and made England subject to a stranger. With Philip came the pope and his Mass, monks, and the nuns, but still God prevented her from having her way.

No woman was ever more disappointed than Mary when she did not have children, even with the help of the Catholic Church's prayers. She seemed unable to win the favor of God, the hearts of her subjects, or the love of her husband.

At last, when nothing could sway her to stop the tyranny of her priests and spare her subjects who were being drawn daily as sheep to the slaughter, it pleased God to cut off her rule by death, giving her throne to another after she reigned for five years and five months.

I mentioned this unlucky reign of Queen Mary not to detract from her position, which she was called to by the Lord, but as a warning to men and women in authority who persecute Christ's Church and shed Christian blood, so they will not stumble on the same stone as the Jews who persecuted Christ and His Church to their own destruction.

QUEEN ELIZABETH

The death of Queen Mary seemed to dispel a black, gloomy cloud that for five years had hung like a pall over England. The crowning of Elizabeth was welcomed with joy by the Protestants, and their sufferings during the previous bloody reign were for a moment forgotten in the hope that better days had come.

But Elizabeth, Protestant and friend of the Reformation, loved power as much as her father, Henry VIII, and intended to be no less an absolute ruler of both church and state than he had been. Laws were speedily passed establishing Elizabeth as the supreme head of the church as well as the nation. She was empowered to create a high commission, or court, to try people accused of not taking part in the services of the established Church of England. The power of this court extended over the whole kingdom; the clergy as well as the people were subject to its rule. Any three members of this court could take measures to discover, by summoning witnesses or any other means, anyone who spoke against the queen's supremacy or refused to observe the forms of worship of the established church. They had the power to inquire into any heretical opinions that might be held, to look for seditious books or writings, to try all cases of willful absence from services, and to punish the offenders by fines.

As can be seen, religious liberty, as we know it today, was almost as far as ever from being realized. More than a century would pass before persecution entirely ceased and the passage of a Toleration Act finally established complete freedom of worship in England. But at least Elizabeth was not cruel; aversion to bloodshed was as marked a feature of her character as the reverse had been in that of Mary. The dreadful fires continued for a while longer in Spain and the counties within her grasp, but with the ending of the reign of Queen Mary, the history of the English martyrdom was brought to a close.

IN HIS STEPS

Born in Wellsville, New York, in 1857, Charles M. Sheldon served the Lord as a pastor, a magazine editor, and a prolific author. Although he wrote more than fifty books, his best-known work remains *In His Steps*, of which millions of copies have been sold.

His privileged education at Phillips Academy and Brown University most likely laid the groundwork for his well-known advocacy of religious involvement in the social milieu of his time. After graduating from Andover Theological Seminary in 1886, Sheldon went on to serve churches in Vermont and Kansas before becoming editor-in-chief of the *Christian Herald* from 1920 to 1925.

During the 1890s, Sheldon penned *In His Steps* in serial form, with first publication of the entire story occurring in 1896. Sheldon's novel introduced the "WWJD" question that would enjoy a revival among young Christians a hundred years later: in the story, a Midwestern pastor shakes up his congregation (and his entire community) by encouraging his parishioners to ask "What Would Jesus Do?" before make any decision, however large or small.

That penetrating question guided Sheldon's own life. He was an active participant in the equality and Prohibition movements of the early twentieth century. As part of the latter, he served on the "Flying Squad" that promoted anti-alcohol laws in 247 American churches over 243 days in 1914 and 1915.

Charles M. Sheldon died two days shy of his eighty-ninth birthday and was buried in Topeka, Kansas.

CHAPTER 1

One Friday morning the Reverend Henry Maxwell tried to finish his Sunday morning sermon. Interrupted several times, he grew nervous as the morning wore away.

"Mary," he called to his wife, as he went upstairs after the last interruption, "if anyone comes, I wish you would say I am very busy and cannot come down."

"But I am going over to visit the kindergarten. You will have the house all to yourself."

In a few minutes he heard his wife go out, and everything was quiet. He settled himself at his desk with a sigh of relief. His text was from 1 Peter 2:21: "For even hereunto were ye called: because Christ also suffered for us, leaving us an example, that ye should follow his steps."

In the first part of the sermon he emphasized the atonement as a personal sacrifice, calling attention to the fact of Jesus' suffering in His life as well as in His death. He then went on to emphasize the atonement from Jesus' life and teachings to show how faith in Christ helped to save human beings because of the pattern or character He displayed for their imitation. He was now on the third and last point, the necessity of following Jesus in His sacrifice and example.

He wrote, "Three steps. What are they?" and was about to enumerate them in logical order when the bell rang. Henry Maxwell frowned and made no movement to answer it. When the bell rang again, he rose and walked over to a window that commanded the view of the front door. A very shabbily dressed young man stood on the steps. "Looks like a tramp," said the minister. "I suppose I'll have to go down and—"

He went downstairs and opened the front door. After a moment's pause the young man said, "I'm out of a job, sir, and thought maybe you might help me."

"I don't know of anything. Jobs are scarce—," replied the minister, beginning to shut the door slowly.

"I thought you might be able to give me a reference to the city railway or the superintendent of the shops or something," continued the young man, shifting his faded hat from one hand to the other.

"It wouldn't help. You will have to excuse me. I am very busy this morning. I hope you find something."

Mr. Maxwell closed the door and heard the man walk down the steps. As he went up into his study, he saw from his hall window that the man moved slowly down the street, still holding his hat between his hands. Something in the figure so dejected, homeless, and forsaken caused the minister to hesitate a moment as he watched. Then he turned to his desk and with a sigh began writing where he had left off.

"A queer thing happened at the kindergarten this morning, Henry," said his wife while they were eating dinner. "Just after the games the door opened and a young man came in holding a dirty hat in both hands. He sat down near the door and never said a word. He was evidently a tramp, and Miss Wren and Miss Kyle were a little frightened at first, but he sat there very quietly, and after a few minutes he went out."

"The same man called here, I think. Did you say he looked like a tramp?"

"Yes, very dusty, shabby, and generally tramplike. Not more than thirty or thirty-three years old, I should say."

"The same man," said the minister thoughtfully.

"Did you finish your sermon, Henry?" his wife asked after a pause.

"Yes, all done. It has been a very busy week, and the two sermons have cost me a good deal of labor."

"They will be appreciated by a large audience Sunday," replied his wife, smiling. "I hope it won't rain Sunday."

Mr. Maxwell sighed as he thought of the careful, laborious effort he had made in preparing sermons for large audiences that failed to appear.

But when Sunday morning dawned on the town of Raymond, the air was clear and bracing, the sky free from all threatening signs. The service opened at eleven o'clock, and the large building was filled with an audience of the best-dressed, most comfortable-looking people of Raymond.

The First Church of Raymond was the first in the city, with a membership composed of the representatives of the wealth, society, and intelligence of Raymond. It believed in having the best music that money could buy, and its choir was a source of great pleasure to the congregation. The anthem was an elaborate adaptation of the words "Jesus, I my cross have taken, all to leave and follow Thee."

Just before the sermon the soprano sang a solo. There was a general rustle of expectation over the audience as Rachel Winslow stood up behind the screen of carved oak, and Mr. Maxwell settled himself contentedly behind the pulpit. Rachel's voice was even more beautiful than her face as she sang, "Where He leads me I will follow; I'll go with Him, with Him, all the way."

Henry Maxwell felt a glow of satisfaction as he rose to speak, and it was reflected in his delivery of the sermon. The pastor of the First Church loved to preach. The half hour he faced a church full of people exhilarated him. The sermon was interesting, spoken with the passion of a dramatic utterance that had the good taste never to offend with a suspicion of ranting or declamation.

The sermon came to a close, and Mr. Maxwell was about to sit down as the quartet rose to sing the closing selection, when a man's voice coming from the rear of the church startled the entire congregation. The next moment a man came out of the shadow there and walked down the middle aisle. Before the stunned congregation realized what was going on, the man reached the open space in front of the pulpit and turned around, facing the people. It was so unexpected that it offered no room for argument or resistance.

"I've been wondering since I came in here," he said, "if it would be okay to say a word at the close of the service. I'm not drunk and I'm not crazy. I am perfectly harmless, but if I die, as there is every likelihood I shall in a few days, I want the satisfaction of thinking that I said my say in a place like this and before this sort of a crowd."

Mr. Maxwell remained standing, leaning on his pulpit, looking down at the stranger. It was the same dusty, worn, shabby-looking young man who had come to his house the Friday before. He still held his faded hat in his two hands. There was nothing offensive in the man's manner or tone. He was not excited, and he spoke in a low but distinct voice.

The stranger went on as if he had no thought of the unusual element that he had introduced into the decorum of the First Church service. "I'm not an ordinary tramp, though I don't know of any teaching of Jesus that makes one kind of a tramp less worth saving than another. Do you?" He put the question as naturally as if the whole congregation had been a small Bible class. He paused just a moment and coughed painfully. "I am a printer by trade. The new linotype machines are beautiful specimens of invention, but I lost my job ten months ago on account of those machines. I never learned but the one trade, and that's all I can do. I've tramped all over the country trying to find work. I'm not complaining, am I? Just stating facts.

"I've tramped through this city for three days trying to find a job; and in all that time I've not had a word of sympathy or comfort except from your minister here, who said he was sorry for me and hoped I would find a job somewhere.

"Of course, I know you can't all go out of your way to hunt up jobs for other people like me. I'm not asking you to; but what I feel puzzled about is what you mean when you sing, 'I'll go with Him, with Him, all the way.' Do you mean that you are suffering and denying yourselves and trying to save lost, suffering humanity just as I understand Jesus did?

"What did He mean when He said, 'Follow me'? The minister said"—the man turned about and looked up at the pulpit—"that it is necessary for the disciple of Jesus to follow His steps, and he said the steps are 'obedience, faith, love, and imitation.' But I did not hear him tell you just what he meant, especially the last step.

"Somehow I get puzzled when I see so many Christians living in luxury and singing, 'Jesus, I my cross have taken, all to leave and follow Thee,' and remember how my wife died in a tenement in New York City four months ago, gasping for air and asking God to take my little girl, too.

"Of course I don't expect you people can prevent everyone from dying of starvation, lack of proper nourishment, and tenement air, but what does following Jesus mean? It seems to me there's an awful lot of trouble in the world that somehow wouldn't exist if all the people who sing such songs as "All for Jesus, all for Jesus, all my being's ransomed powers; all my thoughts, and all my doing, all my days, and all my hours" went and lived them out.

"What would Jesus do? Is that what you mean by following His steps? It seems to me the people in the big churches have good clothes and nice houses to live in and money to spend for luxuries and summer vacations and all that, while the people outside the churches, thousands of them, die in tenements and walk the streets for jobs and never have a piano or a picture in the house and grow up in misery and drunkenness and sin."

The man suddenly gave a queer lurch over in the direction of the communion table and laid one grimy hand on it. His hat fell upon the carpet at his feet. A stir went through the congregation. Dr. West half rose from his pew, but as yet the silence was unbroken by any voice or movement worth mentioning in the audience. The man passed his other hand across his eyes and then, without any warning, fell heavily forward on his face, full length up the aisle.

Henry Maxwell spoke: "We will consider the service closed."

He was down the pulpit stairs and kneeling by the prostrate form before anyone else.

CHAPTER 2

The man lay on the couch in the pastor's study and breathed heavily. When the question of what to do with him came up, the minister insisted on taking charge of the man, and with the entrance of that humanity into the minister's spare room, a new chapter in Henry Maxwell's life began.

The third day after the stranger entered the minister's house, there was a marked change in his condition. But Sunday morning, just before the clock struck one, he rallied and spoke with great difficulty. "You have been good to me. Somehow I feel as if it was what Jesus would do."

After a few minutes he turned his head slightly, and before Mr. Maxwell could realize the fact, the doctor said quietly, "He is gone."

That Sunday morning Mr. Maxwell entered his pulpit to face one of the largest congregations that had ever crowded the First Church. He was haggard and looked as if he had just risen from a long illness. His sermon this morning was neither striking nor impressive. He talked with considerable hesitation. It was evident that some great idea struggled in his thought for utterance, but it was not expressed in the theme he had chosen. Near the close of his sermon, he gathered a certain strength that had been painfully lacking at the beginning.

He closed the Bible, stepped to the side of the pulpit, and faced his people.

"Our brother passed away this morning. I have not yet had time to learn all his history. He had one sister living in Chicago. I have written her and have not yet received an answer."

He paused and looked over the house. He had never seen so many earnest faces during his entire pastorate. He was not able yet to tell his people his experiences, the crisis through which he was even now moving. But he didn't feel it was careless impulse that caused him to tell them something of the message he bore in his heart.

So he went on. "The stranger's appearance and words in church last Sunday made a very powerful impression on me. I am not able to conceal from you or myself the fact that what he said has compelled me to ask as I never asked before, 'What does following Jesus mean?' A good deal that was said here last Sunday was in the nature of a challenge to Christianity as it is seen and felt in our churches. And I do not know that any time is more appropriate than the present for me to propose a plan which has been forming in my mind as a satisfactory reply."

Again Henry Maxwell paused and looked into the faces of his people. There were some strong, earnest men and women in the First Church.

He saw Edward Norman, editor of the Raymond *Daily News*, who had been a member of the First Church for ten years. Alexander Powers was superintendent of the great railroad shops in Raymond. There sat Donald Marsh, president of Lincoln College, located in the suburbs of Raymond. Milton Wright, one of the great merchants of Raymond, had in his employ at least one hundred men in various shops. Dr. West, still comparatively young, was quoted as authority in special surgical cases. Young Jasper Chase, the author, had written one successful book and was said to be at work on a new novel. Miss Virginia Page had inherited at least a million dollars through the recent death of her father. And not least of all, Rachel Winslow, from her seat in the choir, glowed with her peculiar beauty of light.

"What I am going to propose now is something which ought not to appear unusual or at all impossible of execution. I want volunteers from the First Church who will pledge themselves, earnestly and honestly for an entire year, not to do anything without first asking the question, 'What would Jesus do?'

"At the close of the service, all those members who are willing to join such a group may stay, and we will talk over the details of the plan. I will of course include myself in this company of volunteers. Our aim will be to act just as He would if He were in our places, regardless of immediate results. In other words, we propose to follow Jesus' steps as closely and as literally as we believe He taught His disciples to do."

The people glanced at one another in astonishment. It was not like Henry Maxwell to define Christian discipleship in this way. His proposition was understood well enough, but there was a great difference of opinion as to the application of Jesus' teaching and example.

Mr. Maxwell calmly closed the service with a brief prayer, and the organist began his postlude immediately after the benediction. After several minutes the minister asked all who expected to remain to pass into the lecture room that joined the large room on the side. He was himself detained at the front of the church, and when he finally walked over to the lecture room entrance and went in, he was amazed to see the people who were there. He had hardly expected that so many were ready to enter into such a literal testing of their Christian discipleship. There were perhaps fifty present, among them Rachel Winslow and Virginia Page, Mr. Norman, President Marsh, Alexander Powers, Milton Wright, Dr. West, and Jasper Chase.

He closed the door of the lecture room and went and stood before the little group, his face pale and his lips trembling with genuine emotion. Henry Maxwell was conscious of a great upheaval in his definition of Christian discipleship, and he was moved with a depth of feeling he could not measure.

He asked them all to pray with him. And almost with the first syllable he uttered, there was a distinct presence of the Spirit felt by them all. The room filled with it as plainly as if it had been visible. When the prayer closed there was a silence that lasted several moments. All the heads were bowed. Henry Maxwell's face was wet with tears. He spoke very quietly. "The experience I have been through since last Sunday has left me so dissatisfied with my previous definition of Christian discipleship that I am compelled to take this action. I did not dare begin it alone. Do we understand fully what we have undertaken?"

"I want to ask a question," said Rachel Winslow. Her face glowed with a beauty that no physical loveliness could ever create. "I am a little in doubt as to the source of our knowledge concerning what Jesus would do. Who is to decide for me just what He would do in my case? There are many perplexing questions in our civilization that are not mentioned in the teachings of Jesus. How am I going to tell what He would do?"

"There is no way that I know of," replied the pastor, "except as we study Jesus through the medium of the Holy Spirit. You remember what Christ said speaking to His disciples about the Holy Spirit in John 16:13: 'Howbeit when he, the Spirit of truth, is come, he will guide you into all truth.' There is no other test that I know of. We shall all have to decide what Jesus would do after going to that source of knowledge."

"What if others say of us, when we do certain things, that Jesus would not do so?" asked the superintendent of railroads.

"We cannot prevent that. But we must be absolutely honest with ourselves. The standard of Christian action cannot vary in most of our acts. When it comes to a genuine, honest, enlightened following of Jesus' steps, I cannot believe there will be any confusion either in our own minds or in the judgment of others. But we need to remember this great fact. After we have asked the Spirit to tell us what Jesus would do and have received an answer to it, we are to act regardless of the results to ourselves. Is that understood?"

All the faces in the room were raised toward the minister in solemn assent.

They agreed to report to one another every week the result of their experiences in following Jesus this way. Henry Maxwell prayed again, and the Spirit's presence was again evident. Every head remained bowed a long time. They went away finally in silence.

CHAPTER 3

Edward Norman, editor of the Raymond *Daily News*, sat in his office room Monday morning and faced a new world of action. He had made his pledge in good faith to do everything after asking, "What would Jesus do?" and, as he supposed, with his eyes open to all the possible results. But as the regular life of the paper started on another week's rush and whirl of activity, he confronted it with a degree of hesitation and a feeling nearly akin to fear.

He had come down to the office very early and for a few minutes was by himself. He rose and shut his door, and then did what he had not done for years. He knelt down by his desk and prayed for the Divine Presence and wisdom to direct him.

He rose with the day before him and his promise distinct and clear in his mind. He opened his door and began the routine of the office work by writing an editorial. The *Daily News* was an evening paper, and Norman usually completed his leading editorial before nine o'clock.

Fifteen minutes later the managing editor called out from his desk in the adjoining room, "Here's this press report of yesterday's prizefight at the Resort. It will make up three and a half columns. I suppose it all goes in?"

"Yes—no. Let me see it."

Norman took the typewritten matter just as it came from the telegraph editor and ran over it carefully. Then he laid the sheets down on his desk and did some very hard thinking.

"We won't run this today," he said finally.

The managing editor stood in the doorway between the two rooms. "What did you say?"

"Leave it out. We won't use it."

"But—" The managing editor stared at Norman as if the man were out of his mind.

"I don't think, Clark, that it ought to be printed, and that's the end of it," said Norman, looking up from his desk.

Clark seldom had any words with the chief. The circumstances now, however, seemed to be so extraordinary that he could not help expressing himself.

"Do you mean that the paper is to go to press without a word of the prize fight in it?"

"Yes. That's what I mean."

"But it's unheard of. What will our subscribers say? Why, it is simply—" Clark paused, unable to find words to say what he thought.

Norman looked at Clark thoughtfully. The two men had never talked together on religious matters, although they had been associated on the paper for several years.

"Come in here a minute, Clark, and shut the door." Clark came in, and the two men faced each other alone.

Norman did not speak for a minute. Then he said abruptly, "Clark, if Christ were editor of a daily paper, do you honestly think He would print three and a half columns of prizefight in it?"

"No, I don't suppose He would."

"Well, that's my only reason for shutting this account out of the *News*. I have decided not to do a thing in connection with the paper for a whole year that I honestly believe Jesus would not do."

Clark could not have looked more amazed if the chief had suddenly gone crazy. "What effect will that have on the paper?" he finally managed to ask in a faint voice.

"What do you think?" asked Norman with a keen glance.

"I think it will ruin the paper," replied Clark promptly. "It's too ideal. You can't make it pay. If you shut out this prizefight report, you will lose hundreds of subscribers."

Norman spoke gently but firmly. "Clark, in your honest opinion, would you say that the highest, best law for a man to live by was contained in asking the question, 'What would Jesus do?' And then doing it regardless of results?"

Clark turned red and moved uneasily in his chair before he answered the editor's question. "Why—yes—I suppose if you put it on the ground of what men ought to do, there is no other standard of conduct. But to succeed in the newspaper business, we have got to conform to custom and the recognized methods of society."

"Do you mean that we can't run the paper strictly on Christian principles and make it succeed?"

"Yes, that's just what I mean. We'll go bankrupt in thirty days."

Norman did not reply at once. He was very thoughtful. "We shall have occasion to talk this over again, Clark. Meanwhile I think we ought to understand each other frankly. I shall continue to do as I have pledged in the belief that not only can we succeed, but we can succeed better than we ever did."

Clark rose. "The report does not go in?"

"It does not. There is plenty of good material to take its place, and you know what it is."

Clark hesitated. "Are you going to say anything about the absence of the report?"

"No, let the paper go to press as if there had been no such thing as a prizefight yesterday."

When the *Daily News* came out that evening, it carried to its subscribers a distinct sensation. The presence of the report of the prizefight could not have produced anything equal to the effect of its omission. Hundreds of men in the hotels and stores downtown, as well as regular subscribers, eagerly opened the paper and searched it through for the account of the great fight; not finding it, they rushed to the newsstands and bought other papers. That evening, as Mr. Norman walked out of the office and went home, he could not avoid that constant query, "Would Jesus have done it?" It was not so much with reference to this specific transaction as to the entire motive that had urged him on since he had made the promise.

He came to the conclusion that Jesus would have done either what he did or something similar in order to be free from any possible feeling of injustice.

CHAPTER 4

During the week Norman received numerous letters commenting on the absence of the account of the prizefight from the *News*.

> *Dear Sir—I want a journal that is up to the times, progressive, and enterprising, supplying the public demand at all points. The recent freak of your paper in refusing to print the account of the famous contest at the Resort has decided me finally to change my paper. Please discontinue it.*

From one of Norman's old friends, an editor of a daily in a nearby town:

> *Dear Ed.—What is this sensation you have given the people of your burg? What new policy have you taken up? Hope you don't intend to try the "Reform Business" through the avenue of the press. It's dangerous to experiment much along that line. Take my advice and stick to the enterprising modern methods you have made so successful for the News.*

> *My Dear Mr. Norman,*
> *I hasten to write you a note of appreciation for the evident carrying out of your promise. It is a splendid beginning, and no one feels the value of it more than I do. I know something of what it will cost you, but not all.*
> Your pastor,
Henry Maxwell.

One other letter he opened immediately after reading this:

> *Dear Sir—At the expiration of my advertising limit, you will do me the favor not to continue it as you have done heretofore. I enclose check for payment in full and shall consider my account with your paper closed after date.*

It was signed by one of the largest dealers in tobacco in the city. His usual ad was a column of conspicuous advertising, for a very large price.

After a moment he took up a copy of his paper and looked through the advertising columns. He had not considered this before. As he glanced over the columns, he could not escape the conviction that his Master could not permit some of them in his paper.

As a member of a church and a respected citizen, he had incurred no special censure because the saloon men advertised in his columns. No one thought anything about it. It was all legitimate business. He was simply doing what every other businessman in Raymond did. And it was one of the best-paying sources of revenue. What would the paper do if it cut these out? Could it live? That was the question. But—was that the question after all? "What would Jesus do?" That was the question he was answering, or trying to answer, this week. Edward Norman asked it honestly, and after a prayer for help and wisdom, he asked Clark to come into the office.

"Clark," said Norman, speaking slowly and carefully, "I've been looking at our advertising columns and have decided to dispense with some of the matter as soon as the contracts run out. I wish you would notify the advertising agent not to solicit or renew the ads that I have marked here."

He handed the paper with the marked places over to Clark, who took it and looked over the columns with a very serious air.

"This will mean a great loss to the *News*. How long do you think you can keep this sort of thing up?"

"Clark, do you think if Jesus were the editor and proprietor of a daily paper in Raymond, He would permit advertisements of whiskey and tobacco in it?"

"Well—no—I don't suppose He would. But newspapers can't be run on any such basis."

"Why not?" asked Norman quietly.

"Because they will lose more money than they make, that's all!" Clark spoke out with an irritation that he really felt.

"We shall certainly bankrupt the paper with this sort of business policy."

"Do you think so?" Norman asked the question not as if he expected an answer, but simply as if he were talking with himself. After a pause he said, "You may direct Marks to do as I have said. I cannot believe that by any kind of reasoning we could reach a conclusion justifying our Lord in the advertisement of whiskey and tobacco in a newspaper. I feel a conviction in regard to these that cannot be silenced."

Clark went back to his desk feeling as if he had been in the presence of a very peculiar person. What would become of business if this standard were adopted? It would upset every custom and introduce endless confusion. It was simply foolishness. It was downright idiocy.

❧

When Edward Norman came down to the office Friday morning, he was confronted with the usual program for the Sunday morning edition. The *News* was one of the few evening papers in Raymond to issue a Sunday edition, and it had always been remarkably successful financially. It had always been welcomed by all the subscribers, church members and all, as a Sunday morning necessity.

Edward Norman now put to himself the question, "What would Jesus do?" If He were editor of a paper, would He deliberately plan to put into the homes of all the church people and Christians of Raymond such a collection of reading matter on the one day in the week that ought to be given up to something better and holier? Taking everything into account, would Jesus edit a Sunday morning paper? No matter whether it paid. That was not the question. As a matter of fact, the Sunday *News* paid so well that it would be a direct loss of thousands of dollars to discontinue it.

He was honestly perplexed by the question. So much was involved in the discontinuance of the Sunday edition that for the first time he almost decided to refuse to be guided by the standard of Jesus' probable action. As he sat there surrounded by the usual quantity of material for the Sunday edition, he reached some definite conclusions. And among them was a determination to call in the force of the paper and frankly state his motive and purpose.

He sent word for all his employees to come into the mailing room. The men came in curiously and perched around on the tables and counters.

"I called you in here to let you know my further plans for the *News*. I understand very well that you consider some things I have already done as very strange. I wish to state my motive in doing what I have done."

Here he told the men what he had already told Clark, and they stared as Clark had done and looked as painfully conscious.

"Now, in acting on this standard of conduct, I have reached a conclusion which will, no doubt, cause some surprise.

"I have decided that the Sunday morning edition of the *News* shall be discontinued after next Sunday's issue. I shall state in that issue my reasons for discontinuing. In order to make up to the subscribers the amount of reading matter they may suppose themselves entitled to, we can issue a double number on Saturday, as is done by many evening papers that make no attempt at a Sunday edition. I am convinced that from a Christian point of view our Sunday morning paper has done more harm than good. I do not believe that Jesus would be responsible for it if He were in my place today. It will take some trouble to arrange the details caused by this change with the advertisers and subscribers. That is for me to look after. So far as I can see, the loss will fall on myself. Neither the reporters nor the pressmen need make any particular changes in their plans."

He looked around the room and no one spoke. He was struck for the first time in his life with the fact that in all the years of his newspaper life, he had never had the force of the paper together in this way. Would Jesus do that?

The vague picture that came up in the mailing room would not fade away when he had gone into his office and the men had gone back to their places with wonder in their looks and questions of all sorts on their tongues as they talked over the editor's remarkable actions.

Clark came in and had a long, serious talk with his chief, almost reaching the point of resigning his place. Norman guarded himself carefully. Every minute of the interview was painful to him, but he felt more than ever the necessity of doing the Christlike thing. Clark was a very valuable man. It would be difficult to fill his place.

"Mr. Norman, I don't understand you. You are not the same man this week that I always knew before."

"I don't know myself either, Clark. But I was never more convinced of final success and power for the paper. Will you stay with the *News*?"

Clark hesitated a moment and finally said yes.

CHAPTER 5

The next Sunday morning Henry Maxwell's church was again crowded.

Henry Maxwell faced it all with a calmness that indicated an unusual strength and purpose. While his prayers were very helpful, his sermon was not so easy to describe. He did not preach as he had done two Sundays before.

He agonized over his preparation for his sermon, and yet he knew he had not been able to fit his message into his ideal of the Christ. Nevertheless, no one in the First Church could remember ever hearing such a sermon before. There was in it rebuke for sin—things that First Church never heard rebuked this way before. And there was a love of his people that gathered new force as the sermon went on. When it was finished there were those who said in their hearts, "The Spirit moved that sermon." Then Rachel Winslow rose to sing, this time after the sermon, by Mr. Maxwell's request. Today there was no lack of power in her grand voice, but there was an added element of humility and purity that the audience noted.

Before the service closed, Mr. Maxwell asked those who had remained the week before to stay again for a few moments of consultation, and welcomed any others who were willing to make the pledge at that time. When he went into the lecture room, it was almost filled. As before, Maxwell asked them to pray with him, and again a distinct answer came from the presence of the divine Spirit. There was no doubt in the minds of any present that what they purposed to do was clearly in line with the divine will. There was a feeling of fellowship such as they had never known in their church membership. Jasper Chase said, "I have been puzzled several times during the week to know just what Jesus would do. It is not always an easy question to answer."

"I think perhaps I find it specially difficult to answer that question on account of my money," Virginia Page said. "Our Lord never owned any property, and there is nothing in His example to guide me in the use of mine." Virginia smiled slightly. "What I am trying to discover is a principle that will enable me to come to the nearest possible to His action as it ought to influence the entire course of my life so far as my wealth and its use are concerned."

"That will take time," said the minister slowly.

Milton Wright told how he was gradually working out a plan for his business relations with his employees, and it was opening up a new world to him and to them.

There was almost general consent over the fact that the application of the Christ spirit and practice to the everyday life required a knowledge of Him and an insight into His motives that most of them did not yet possess.

When they finally adjourned after a silent prayer that marked with growing power the Divine Presence, they went away discussing earnestly their difficulties and seeking light from one another.

After the others had gone, Alexander Powers spoke to his pastor. "I want you to come down to the shops tomorrow and see my plan and talk to the men. Somehow I feel as if you could get nearer to them than anyone else just now."

How was he fitted to stand before two or three hundred workingmen and give them a message? Yet in the moment of his weakness, he asked the question, "What would Jesus do?" That was an end to the discussion.

He went down the next day and found Mr. Powers in his office. The superintendent said, "Come upstairs, and I'll show you what I've been trying to do."

They went through the machine shop, climbed a long flight of stairs, and entered a very large, empty room that had once been used by the company for a storeroom.

"My plan is to provide a good place where the men can come up and eat their noon lunch, and give them, two or three times a week, the privilege of a fifteen-minute talk on some subject that will be a real help to them in their lives."

Maxwell asked if the men would come for any such purpose.

"Yes, they'll come. They are among the most intelligent workingmen in the country today. But they are, as a whole, entirely removed from church influence. I asked, 'What would Jesus do?' and it seemed to me He would begin to act in some way to add more physical and spiritual comfort to the lives of these men. I have asked them to come up at noon and see the place, and I'll tell them something about it. I want you to speak to them, too."

There were a dozen rude benches and tables in the room, and when the noon whistle sounded, about three hundred men poured upstairs from the machine shops below and, seating themselves at the tables, began to eat their lunch.

At about twenty minutes to one, Mr. Powers told the men what he had in mind. He spoke very simply, like one who understands thoroughly the character of his audience, and then introduced the Reverend Henry Maxwell of the First Church, his pastor, who had consented to speak a few minutes.

Maxwell would never forget the feeling with which, for the first time, he stood before the grimy-faced audience of workingmen. Like hundreds of other ministers, he had never spoken to any gatherings except those made up of people of his own class in the sense that they were familiar in their dress and education and habits. This was a new world to him, and nothing but his new rule of conduct could have made possible his message and its effect.

Alexander Powers went back to his desk that afternoon with a glow of satisfaction. After all, he wanted to do as Jesus would, he said to himself.

It was nearly four o'clock when he opened one of the company's long envelopes. He ran over the first page of typewritten matter in his usual quick, businesslike manner before he saw that what he was reading was not intended for his office but for the superintendent of the freight department.

He turned over a page mechanically. Before he knew it, he was in possession of evidence that conclusively proved that the company was engaged in a systematic violation of the Interstate Commerce Laws of the United States and the new state laws.

He dropped the papers on his desk as if they were poison, and instantly the question flashed across his mind, "What would Jesus do?"

He had known in a more or less definite way that this had been going on. But he was not in a position to prove anything directly, and he had regarded it as a matter that did not concern him at all. Now the papers before him revealed the entire affair.

If he came out against this lawlessness as a witness, it would drag him into courts, his motives would be misunderstood, and the whole thing would end in his disgrace and the loss of his position. Surely it was none of his business. He could easily get the papers back to the freight department and no one would be the wiser.

Let the iniquity go on. Let the law be defied. What was it to him? He would work out his plans for bettering the condition of his men. What more could a man do in this railroad business when there was so much going on anyway that made it impossible to live by the Christian standard? But what would Jesus do if He knew the facts? Day wore into evening as Alexander

Powers pondered the question. At six o'clock the whistle blew, the engine slowed, and the men dropped their tools and ran for the blockhouse.

Powers waited until he heard the last man clock out. Then he knelt and buried his face in his hands as he bowed his head upon the papers on his desk.

CHAPTER 6

After the Sunday meeting, Virginia Page asked Rachel Winslow to come and lunch with her at noon the next day. There they continued their conversation.

"The fact is," Rachel said, "I cannot reconcile this offer with my judgment of what Christ would do."

"What will you do, then?" asked Virginia with great interest.

"I don't know yet, but I have decided to refuse this offer."

Rachel picked up the letter lying in her lap and ran over its contents again. It was from the manager of a comic opera, offering her a place with a large traveling company. The salary was a very large figure, and the prospect was flattering.

"The concert offer is harder to decide," Rachel went on thoughtfully. "Here is a reputable company, and I would travel with people of good reputation. I'm asked to go as one of the company and sing leading soprano. The salary is guaranteed to be $200 a month for the season. But I don't feel satisfied that Jesus would go. What do you think?"

"You mustn't ask me to decide for you," replied Virginia with a sad smile. "Mr. Maxwell was right when he said we must each one of us decide according to the judgment we feel for ourselves to be Christlike."

Rachel rose and walked over to the window and looked out. Virginia came and stood by her. The street was crowded with life, and the two young women looked at it silently for a moment.

Suddenly Virginia broke out: "Rachel, I've been educated in one of the most expensive schools in America and launched into society as an heiress. I'm perfectly well; I can do as I please. I can gratify almost any want or desire; and yet when I honestly try to imagine Jesus living the life I have lived and am expected to live, and doing for the rest of my life what thousands of other rich people do, I am under condemnation for being one of the most wicked, selfish, useless creatures in all the world."

Virginia turned away and walked up and down the room. Rachel watched her and could not repress the rising tide of her own growing definition of discipleship. She, too, was in sound health, was conscious of her great powers as a singer, and knew that if she went out into public life, she could make a great

281

deal of money and become well known. When lunch was announced, they were joined by Virginia's grandmother, Madam Page, a handsome, stately woman of sixty-five, and Virginia's brother, Rollin, a young man who spent most of his time at one of the clubs and had no ambition for anything but a growing admiration for Rachel Winslow.

These three made up the Page family. Virginia's father had been a banker and grain speculator. Her mother had died ten years before, her father within the past year. The grandmother, a Southern woman in birth and training, had all the traditions and feelings that accompany the possession of wealth and social standing that have never been disturbed. She was a shrewd, careful businesswoman of more than average ability. The family property and wealth were invested, in large measure, under her personal care.

Rachel, who had known the family since she was a girl playmate of Virginia's, could not help thinking of what confronted Virginia in her own home when she once decided on the course she honestly believed Jesus would take.

"I understand that you are going on the stage, Miss Winslow. We shall all be delighted, I'm sure," said Rollin during the conversation.

Rachel answered quietly, "You're mistaken. I'm not going on the stage."

"It's a great pity. You'd make a hit. Everybody is talking about your singing."

Rachel flushed with genuine anger. Before she could say anything, Virginia broke in: "Whom do you mean by 'everybody'?"

"Whom? I mean all the people who hear Miss Winslow on Sundays. It's a great pity, I say, that the general public outside of Raymond cannot hear her voice."

"Let us talk about something else," said Rachel a little sharply.

Madam Page glanced at her and spoke with a gentle courtesy. "My dear, we are all curious to know something of your plans. We claim the right from old acquaintance, you know; and Virginia has already told us of your concert company offer."

"I understand that, Madam Page," Rachel replied hastily. "I have decided not to accept."

What Rollin Page had said and his manner in saying it had hastened her decision in the matter.

"Would you mind telling us your reasons for refusing the offer? It looks like a great opportunity for a young girl like you. A voice like yours belongs to a larger audience than Raymond and the First Church."

"I have no other reason than a conviction that Jesus Christ would do the same thing," she said, looking into Madam Page's eyes with a clear, earnest gaze.

Madam Page turned red and Rollin stared.

Before her grandmother could say anything, Virginia spoke. Her rising color showed how she was stirred. "Grandmother, you know we promised to make that the standard of our conduct for a year. We have not been able to arrive at our decisions very rapidly. The difficulty in knowing what Jesus would do has perplexed Rachel and me a good deal."

Madam Page looked sharply at Virginia before she said anything. "Mr. Maxwell's statement is visionary and absurd. I have nothing to say about Miss Winslow's affairs, but"—she paused and continued with a sharpness that was new to Rachel—"I hope you have no foolish notions in this matter, Virginia."

"I have a great many notions," replied Virginia quietly. "Whether they are foolish or not depends upon my right understanding of what He would do."

"What you have promised, in a spirit of false emotion, is impossible of performance."

"Do you mean, Grandmother, that we cannot possibly act as our Lord would? Or do you mean that, if we try to, we shall offend the customs and prejudices of society?" asked Virginia.

"It is not required! It is not necessary! Besides, how can you act with any—" Madam Page paused, broke off her sentence, and then turned to Rachel. "What will your mother say to your decision?"

"I don't know what Mother will say yet," Rachel answered, with a great shrinking from trying to give her mother's probable answer. If there was a woman in all Raymond with great ambitions for her daughter's success as a singer, Mrs. Winslow was that woman.

"Oh! You will see it in a different light after wiser thought of it. My dear," continued Madam Page, rising from the table, "you will live to regret it if you do not accept the concert company's offer or something like it."

CHAPTER 7

Rachel was glad to escape and be by herself to carefully think out a plan that was slowly forming in her mind. But before she had walked two blocks, she was annoyed to find Rollin Page walking beside her.

"Sorry to disturb your thoughts, Miss Winslow, but I happened to be going your way. In fact, I've been walking here for a whole block, and you haven't objected."

"I did not see you," said Rachel briefly.

She had known Rollin as a boy. She was used to his direct attempts at compliments and was sometimes amused by them. Today she honestly wished him anywhere else.

"Do you ever think of me, Miss Winslow?" asked Rollin after a pause.

"Oh yes, quite often!" said Rachel with a smile.

"Are you thinking of me now?"

"Do you want me to be absolutely truthful?"

"Of course."

"Then I was thinking that I wished you were not here."

Rollin bit his lip and looked gloomy. "Now look here, Rachel, you know how I feel. You used to like me a little, you know."

"Did I? Of course we used to get on very well as boy and girl. But we are older now."

Rachel spoke in a light, easy way, still somewhat preoccupied with her plan.

They walked along in silence a little way. The avenue was full of people. Among them was Jasper Chase, who bowed as Rachel and Rollin went by. Rachel colored in spite of herself.

"You know well enough, Rachel, how I feel toward you. I could make you happy. I've loved you a good many years—"

"Why, how old do you think I am?" broke in Rachel with a nervous laugh, shaken out of her usual poise of manner.

"You know what I mean," went on Rollin doggedly. "And you have no right to laugh at me just because I want you to marry me."

"I'm not! But it is useless for you to speak, Rollin," said Rachel after a little hesitation. "It is impossible."

"Would—that is—do you think—if you gave me time, I would—"

"No!" said Rachel. She spoke firmly.

They walked on for some time without a word. As they turned off the avenue into one of the quieter streets, Rollin spoke suddenly and with more manliness than he had yet shown. There was a distinct note of dignity in his voice that was new to Rachel.

"Miss Winslow, I ask you to be my wife. Is there any hope for me that you will ever consent?"

"None in the least." Rachel spoke decidedly.

"Will you tell me why?"

"Because I do not feel toward you as a woman ought to feel toward the man she marries."

"In other words, you do not love me?"

"I do not and I cannot."

"Why?" That was another question, and Rachel was a little surprised that he should ask it. "Tell me. You can't hurt me more than you have already."

"Well, I do not and I cannot love you because you have no purpose in life. What do you ever do to make the world better? You spend your time in club life, in amusements, in travel, in luxury. What is there in such a life to attract a woman?"

"Not much, I guess," said Rollin with a bitter laugh. "Still, I don't know that I'm any worse than the rest of the men around me."

He suddenly stopped, took off his hat, bowed gravely, and turned back. Rachel went on home and hurried into her room, disturbed in many ways.

When she had time to think it all over, she found herself condemned by the very judgment she had passed on Rollin Page. What purpose had she in life? There was a fortune in her voice. She knew it, not necessarily as a matter of personal pride or professional egotism, but simply as a fact. And she was obliged to acknowledge that until two weeks ago she had purposed to use her voice to make money and win admiration and applause. Was that a much higher purpose, after all, than Rollin Page lived for?

After much thought, she finally resolved to have a frank talk with her mother. Mrs. Winslow was a large, handsome woman, fond of much company, ambitious for distinction in society, and devoted to the success of her children. Rachel's father, like Virginia's, had died while the family was abroad. Like Virginia, she found herself, under her present rule of conduct, in complete antagonism with her own immediate home circle.

Rachel came at once to the point. "Mother, I have decided not to go out with the company."

Mrs. Winslow said nothing but waited for Rachel to go on.

"You know the promise I made two weeks ago?"

"Mr. Maxwell's promise?"

"No, mine."

"What has that to do with your decision in the concert company matter?"

"It has everything to do with it. After asking, 'What would Jesus do?' and going to the source of authority for wisdom, I'm obliged to say that I do not believe He would make that use of my voice."

"Why? Is there anything wrong about such a career?"

"No, I don't know that I can say there is. As I look at it, I have a conviction that Jesus would do something else."

"What else?"

"Something that will serve humanity where it most needs the service of song. Something that will satisfy me when I ask, 'What would Jesus do?' I have been unable, since I made my promise two weeks ago, to imagine Jesus joining a concert company to do what I should do and live the life I should have to live if I joined it."

Rachel spoke with a vigor and earnestness that surprised her mother. But Mrs. Winslow was angry now.

"It is simply absurd! Rachel, you are a fanatic!" Mrs. Winslow rose and then sat down again. With a great effort she composed herself. "What do you intend to do, then?"

"I shall continue to sing for the time being in the church. During the week I am going to sing at the White Cross meetings, down in the Rectangle."

"What? Rachel Winslow! Do you know what you are saying? Do you know what sort of people those are down there?"

For a moment Rachel shrank back and was silent. Then she spoke firmly. "I know very well. Mr. and Mrs. Gray have been working there several weeks. I learned only this morning that they want singers from the churches to help them in their meetings."

Rachel cried out with the first passionate utterance she had yet used. "What have we done all our lives for the suffering, sinning side of Raymond?

How much have we denied ourselves or given of our personal ease and plea-sure to bless the place in which we live or imitate the life of the Savior of the world? I want to do something that will cost me something in the way of sacrifice."

"Are you preaching at me?" asked Mrs. Winslow slowly.

Rachel rose. "No. I am preaching at myself," she replied gently. She paused a moment as if she thought her mother would say something more, and then went out of the room.

৵

About seven o'clock Virginia and her uncle, Dr. West, appeared, and together the three started for the scene of the White Cross meetings.

The Rectangle, close by the railroad shops and the packinghouses, was the most notorious district in Raymond. The great slum and tenement district was shut in by rows of saloons, gambling halls, and cheap, dirty boarding and lodging houses.

Into this heart of the coarse part of the sin of Raymond, the traveling evangelist and his brave little wife had pitched a good-sized tent and begun meetings.

It was after eight o'clock when Alexander Powers opened the door of his office and started for home. He was going to take a car at the corner of the Rectangle, but he was stirred by a voice coming from the tent.

How did Rachel Winslow happen to be down here? Her voice struck through his consciousness of struggle over his own question that had sent him into the Divine Presence for an answer, though he had not yet reached a conclusion.

Several windows nearby went up. Some men quarreling near a saloon stopped and listened. Other figures walked rapidly in the direction of the Rectangle and the tent.

Surely Rachel Winslow had never sung like that in the First Church. What was it she was singing?

"Where He leads me I will follow,
Where He leads me I will follow,
Where He leads me I will follow,
I'll go with Him, with Him
All the way!"

After a minute of indecision the superintendent went on to the corner and took the car for his home. But before he was out of the sound of Rachel's voice, he had settled for himself the question of what Jesus would do.

CHAPTER 8

Henry Maxwell paced his study back and forth, thinking out the subject of his Wednesday evening service. After a while he sat down at his desk and drew a large piece of paper toward him. Then he wrote in large letters the following:

Things Jesus Would Probably
Do in This Parish

1. Live in a simple, plain manner.
2. Preach fearlessly to the hypocrites in the church.
3. Show in some practical form His sympathy and love for all people.
4. Identify Himself with the great causes of humanity in some
   personal way that would call for self-denial and suffering.
5. Preach against the saloon in Raymond.
6. Become known as a friend and companion of the sinful people
   in the Rectangle.
7. Give up the summer trip to Europe this year.

He was conscious that his outline of Jesus' probable action painfully lacked depth and power, but he searched for concrete shapes into which he might cast his thought of Jesus' conduct. Nearly every point he'd put down meant a complete overturning of his custom and habit of years in the ministry. But still he searched deeper for sources of the Christlike spirit. A servant broke into his thoughts, announcing a caller, Mr. Gray. He immediately stated the reason for his call.

"You have heard what a wonderful meeting we had Monday night and last night. Miss Winslow has done more with her voice than I could do, and the tent won't hold the people."

Maxwell nodded.

"But I came to ask if you could come down tonight and preach. I am suffering from a severe cold. I know it is asking a good deal from such a busy man. But if you can't come, say so frankly, and I'll try somewhere else."

"It's my regular prayer meeting night," began Henry Maxwell. Then he flushed and added, "I shall be able to arrange it in some way so as to come down."

Gray thanked him earnestly and rose to go.

"Won't you stay a minute, Gray, and let us have a prayer together?"

So the two men knelt together in the study. Gray was touched to tears as Henry Maxwell begged for wisdom and strength to speak a message to the people in the Rectangle.

The night was mild and the sides of the tent were up and a great border of faces stretched around, looking in and forming part of the audience. After the singing and a prayer by one of the city pastors who was present, Gray stated the reason for his inability to speak and in his simple manner turned the service over to "Brother Maxwell, of the First Church."

Henry Maxwell stood up, and a great wave of actual terror went over him. This was not like preaching to the well-dressed, respectable, good-mannered people up on the boulevard. He began to speak, but the crowd was unruly. He turned to Rachel with a sad smile.

"Sing something, Miss Winslow. They will listen to you," he said, and then sat down and covered his face with his hands.

Before Rachel finished the verse, the Rectangle lay like some wild beast at her feet, and she sang it into harmlessness.

When the song was over, Maxwell rose again. This time he felt calmer. What would Jesus do? He spoke as he thought once he never could speak. Who were these people? They were immortal souls. What was Christianity? A calling of sinners, not the righteous, to repentance. How would Jesus speak? What would He say? He could not tell all that His message would include, but he felt sure of a part of it. And in that certainty he spoke on.

When the meeting closed, the people rapidly melted away from the tent, and the saloons, which had been experiencing a dull season while the meetings progressed, again drove a thriving trade. Maxwell and his little party, including Virginia, Rachel, and Jasper Chase, walked down past the row of saloons and dens until they reached the corner where the cars passed.

"This is a terrible spot," said the minister as he stood waiting for their car. "I never realized that Raymond had such a festering sore. It does not seem possible that this is a city full of Christian disciples."

"Do you think anyone can ever remove this great curse of drink?" asked Jasper.

"I have thought lately as never before of what Christian people might do to remove the curse of the saloon. Why don't we all act together against it? What would Jesus do? Would He keep silent? Would He vote to license these causes of crime and death?"

He talked to himself more than to the others. He remembered that he had always voted for license, and so had nearly all his church members. What would Jesus do? Would the Master preach and act against the saloon if He lived today? Suppose it was not popular to preach against license? Suppose the Christian people thought it was all that could be done to license the evil and so get revenue from the necessary sin? Or suppose the church members themselves owned the property where the saloons stood—what then?

He went up into his study the next morning with that question only partly answered. He was still thinking of it and reaching certain real conclusions when the *Evening News* came. His wife brought it up and sat down a few minutes while he read to her.

The *Evening News* was at present the most sensational paper in Raymond. It no longer printed accounts of crime with detailed descriptions or scandals in private life. The advertisements of liquor and tobacco were dropped, together with certain others of a questionable character. Now the character of the editorials was creating the greatest excitement. Monday's editorial was headed:

THE MORAL SIDE OF POLITICAL QUESTIONS

The editor of the News *has always advocated the principles of the great political party at present in power and has discussed all political questions from the standpoint of expedience, or of belief in the party as opposed to other political organizations. From now on, the first question asked in this office will be, "Is this measure in accordance with the spirit and teachings of Jesus as the author of the greatest standard of life known to men?" The moral side of every political question will be considered its most important side, and the ground will be distinctly taken that nations as well as individuals are under the same law to do all things to the glory of God as the first rule of action.*

The same principle will be applied toward candidates for places of responsibility and trust in the republic. The editor of the News *will do*

all in his power to bring the best men into power, and will not know-
ingly help to support for office any candidate who is unworthy, no mat-
ter how much he may be endorsed by the party. The first question asked
about the man and about the measures will be, "Is he the right man for
the place?" "Is he a good man with ability?" "Is the measure right?"

As Maxwell read to his wife, he could see in almost every column evidences of Norman's conscientious obedience to his promise. There was an absence of slangy, sensational scare heads. The reading matter under the headlines was in perfect keeping with them. He noticed in two columns that the reporters' names appeared signed at the bottom. And there was a distinct advance in the dignity and style of their contributions.

Maxwell suddenly paused. His wife looked up from some work she was doing. He was reading something with the utmost interest. "Listen to this, Mary," he said after a moment while his lip trembled:

This morning Alexander Powers, superintendent of the L&T RR shops
in this city, handed in his resignation to the road, and gave as his reason
the fact that certain proofs had fallen into his hands of the violation of the
Interstate Commerce Law and state law, which has recently been framed
to prevent and punish railroad pooling for the benefit of certain favored
shippers. Mr. Powers has placed his evidence against the company
in the hands of the Commission and it is now for them to take action.

The News wishes to express itself on this action of Mr. Powers. In
the first place, he has nothing to gain by it. He has lost a very valuable
place voluntarily, when by keeping silent he might have retained it. In
the second place, we believe his action ought to receive the approval of all
thoughtful, honest citizens who believe in seeing law obeyed and law-
breakers brought to justice. In our judgment, Mr. Powers did the only
thing that a Christian man could do. He has rendered brave and useful
service to the state and the general public. It is not always an easy matter
to determine the relations that exist between the individual citizen and
his fixed duty to the public. In this case, there is no doubt in our minds
that the step that Mr. Powers has taken commends itself to everyone who
believes in law and its enforcement. Mr. Powers has done all that a loyal,
patriotic citizen could do. It now remains for the Commission to act upon

his evidence, which, we understand, is overwhelming proof of the law-lessness of the L&T. Let the law be enforced, no matter who the persons may be who have been guilty.

CHAPTER 9

Henry Maxwell finished reading and dropped the paper. "I must go and see Powers. This is the result of his promise."

Maxwell walked over to the next block where Superintendent Powers lived. To his relief, Powers himself came to the door.

The two men shook hands silently. They instantly understood each other without words. "What are you going to do?" Henry Maxwell asked after they had talked over the facts in the case.

"I have no plans yet. I can go back to my old work as a telegraph operator. My family will not suffer, except in a social way."

Powers spoke calmly and sadly. "There is one matter I wish you would see to—the work begun at the shops. So far as I know, the company will not object to that going on. Will you see that my plan is carried out?"

"Yes," replied Henry Maxwell. Before he went away, he and the superintendent had a prayer together.

As Maxwell thought of Edward Norman and Rachel and Mr. Powers, and of the results that had already come from their actions, he could not help a feeling of intense interest in the probable effect if all the persons in the First Church who had made the pledge faithfully kept it. The next morning the president of the Endeavor Society of his church called to see him.

"I thought," said young Morris, coming at once to his errand, "that you might advise me a little. I've been doing reporter work on the morning *Sentinel* since I graduated last year. Well, last Saturday Mr. Burr asked me to go down the road Sunday morning and get the details of that train robbery at the Junction and write the thing up for the extra edition that came out Monday morning. I refused to go, and Burr gave me my dismissal."

"You kept your promise, Fred."

"Thank you, Mr. Maxwell."

Morris rose to go, and his pastor rose and laid a loving hand on the young man's shoulder.

"What are you going to do, Fred?"

"I don't know yet."

"Why don't you try the *News*?"

"They are all supplied."

Maxwell thought a moment. "Come down to the *News* office with me, and let us see Norman about it."

So a few minutes later, Edward Norman greeted the minister and young Morris, and Maxwell briefly told the cause of the errand.

Norman's keen gaze was softened by a smile that made it winsome. "I want reporters who won't work Sundays. In fact, I am making plans for a special kind of reporting that I believe you can develop because you are in sympathy with what Jesus would do."

He assigned Morris a definite task, and Maxwell started back to his study.

On his way home he passed by one of Milton Wright's stores. He thought he would simply step in and shake hands with his parishioner and bid him Godspeed in what he had heard he was doing to put Christ into his business. But when he went into the office, Wright insisted on detaining him to talk over some of his new plans. "There is no use to disguise the fact, Mr. Maxwell, that I've been compelled to revolutionize the entire method of my business since I made that promise. I came down here Monday morning after that Sunday and asked myself, 'What would Jesus do in His relation to these clerks, bookkeepers, office boys, day men, salesmen? Would He try to establish some sort of personal relation to them different from that which I have sustained all these years?' Then came the question of what that relation would be and what it would lead me to do. I did not see how I could answer it to my satisfaction without getting all my employees together and having a talk with them. So I sent invitations to all of them, and we had a meeting out there in the warehouse Tuesday night. A good many things came out of that meeting. I kept asking, 'What would Jesus do?' and the more I asked it, the further along it pushed me into the most intimate and loving relations with the men who have worked for me all these years. Every day something new is coming up, and I am right now in the midst of a reconstruction of the motive for conducting business."

Wright eagerly reached up into one of the pigeonholes of his desk and took out a paper.

"I have sketched out what seems to me like a program such as Jesus might go by in a business like mine." He handed the paper to Maxwell.

Henry Maxwell read it over slowly.

What Jesus Would Probably Do
in Milton Wright's Place as a Businessman

1. The primary purpose of the business is glorifying God.

2. He would never regard the money He made as His own.

3. His relations with all the persons in His employ would be the most loving and helpful.

4. He would never do a single dishonest or questionable thing or try to get the advantage of anyone else.

5. The principle of unselfishness and helpfulness in the business would direct all its details.

Maxwell looked up and met Wright's gaze. "Do you believe you can continue to make your business pay on these lines?"

"I do."

"Does your plan contemplate what is coming to be known as cooperation?"

"Yes, as far as I have gone, it does. I am working on those general principles. I must have time to complete the details."

When Maxwell finally left, he was profoundly impressed with the revolution at work in the business. There was no mistaking the fact that Milton Wright's new relations to his employees were beginning to transform the entire business in a very short time. When Maxwell reached his study, he prayed. Then he began the preparation of a sermon on the subject of the saloon in Raymond, as he now believed Jesus would do.

He had never preached against the saloon before. Nevertheless, he went on with his work, and every sentence he wrote or shaped was preceded with the question, "Would Jesus say that?"

❧

The meetings in the Rectangle had intensified with each night, much of it due to Rachel's singing. It cannot be said that up to that Saturday night there was any appreciable lack of oaths and impurity and heavy drinking. But in spite of itself, there was a yielding to a power it had never measured and did not know well enough to resist beforehand.

Gray had recovered his voice so that by Saturday he was able to speak. Gradually the people had come to understand that this man gave his time and strength to give them a knowledge of a Savior out of a perfectly unselfish love for them. Tonight the great crowd was as quiet as Henry Maxwell's decorous audience ever was. The fringe around the tent was deeper and the saloons were practically empty. The Holy Spirit had come at last, and Gray knew that one of the great prayers of his life was going to be answered.

Rachel's singing was the best that Virginia or Jasper Chase had ever known. They came together again tonight, this time with Dr. West. Virginia was at the organ, Jasper sat on a front seat looking up at Rachel, and the Rectangle swayed as one body toward the platform as she sang:

> *"Just as I am, without one plea,*
> *But that Thy blood was shed for me,*
> *And that Thou bidst me come to Thee,*
> *O Lamb of God, I come, I come."*

Gray stretched out his hand with a gesture of invitation. And down the two aisles of the tent, broken, sinful creatures, men and women, stumbled toward the platform. One woman out of the street was near the organ. Virginia caught the look on her face, and for the first time the thought of what Jesus was to the sinful woman came to her with a suddenness and power that was like nothing but a new birth. Virginia left the organ, went to her, looked into her face, and caught her hands in her own. The other girl trembled, then fell on her knees sobbing, with her head down upon the back of the rude bench in front of her, still clinging to Virginia. And Virginia, after a moment's hesitation, knelt down by her, and the two heads were bowed close together.

When the people had crowded in a double row all about the platform, most of them kneeling and crying, a man in evening dress pushed through the seats and came and knelt down within a few feet of Rachel Winslow, who was still singing softly. And as she turned for a moment and looked in his direction, for a moment her voice faltered. Rollin Page! Then she went on:

> *"Just as I am, Thou wilt receive,*
> *Wilt welcome, pardon, cleanse, relieve,*
> *Because Thy promise I believe,*
> *O Lamb of God, I come, I come."*

CHAPTER 10

Gray stayed up long into Sunday morning, praying and talking with a little group of converts who in the great experiences of their new life clung to the evangelist with a personal helplessness that made it impossible for him to leave them.

Virginia and her uncle left about eleven o'clock, and Rachel and Jasper Chase went with them as far as the avenue where Virginia lived. Dr. West had walked on a little way with them to his own home, and Rachel and Jasper had then gone on together to her mother's.

Never had her beauty and her strength influenced Jasper Chase as tonight. While she was singing he saw and heard no one else. It was no secret between them that the heroine of Jasper's first novel had been his own ideal of Rachel and the hero in the story was himself. The names and characters were drawn with a subtle skill that revealed to Rachel the fact of his love for her, and she had not been offended. That was nearly a year ago.

Tonight he recalled the scene between them with every inflection and movement vivid in his memory.

"Rachel, you know I love you as my life. I can no longer hide it from you if I would."

Rachel's arm trembled in his. She allowed him to speak and had turned her face neither toward him nor away from him. She looked straight on, and her voice was sad but firm and quiet when she spoke.

"Why do you speak to me now? I cannot bear it—after what we have seen tonight."

"Why—what—"

Rachel withdrew her arm from his but still walked near him. "Rachel! Do you not love me? Is not my love for you as sacred as anything in all of life itself?"

She walked silently for a few steps after that. They passed a streetlamp. Her face was pale and beautiful. He made a movement to clutch her arm, and she moved a little farther from him.

"No," she had replied. "There was a time— You should not have spoken to me—now."

He had seen in these words his answer. He could not think of pleading with her.

"Sometime—when I am more worthy?" he had asked in a low voice, but she did not seem to hear, and they had parted at her home. No good night had been said.

Now he lashed himself for his foolish precipitance. He had not reckoned on Rachel's tense, passionate absorption of all her feeling in the scenes at the tent that were so new in her mind. When the clock in the First Church struck one, he still sat at his desk staring at the last page of manuscript of his unfinished novel.

❧

Rachel went up to her room and faced her evening's experience with conflicting emotions. Had she ever loved Jasper Chase? Yes. No. But overmastering her emotions Jasper's declaration brought was the response of the wretched creatures in the tent to her singing. The swift, powerful, awesome presence of the Holy Spirit had affected her as never in all her life before.

The moment Jasper spoke her name and she realized that he was telling her of his love, she had felt a sudden revulsion for him. It was not the time to be absorbed in anything less than the divine glory of those conversions. All the time she was singing with the one passion of her soul to touch the conscience of that tent full of sin, Jasper Chase had been unmoved by it except to love her for herself. It gave her a shock as of irreverence on her part as well as on his.

Her mind was busy with the sights she had witnessed in the tent. Those faces, men and women, touched for the first time with the Spirit's glory— what a wonderful thing life was after all! The complete regeneration revealed in the sight of drunken, vile, debauched humanity kneeling down to give itself to a life of purity and Christlikeness was surely a witness to the superhuman in the world! And Rollin Page's face by the side of that miserable wreck out of the gutter!

She recalled Virginia crying with her arms about her brother just before she left the tent, and Mr. Gray kneeling close by, and the girl Virginia had taken into her heart while she whispered something to her before she went out. All these pictures stood out in Rachel's memory now.

"No! No!" she said aloud. "He had no right to speak after all that! I am sure I do not love him—not enough to give him my life!"

❧

The people of Raymond awoke Sunday morning to a growing knowledge of events that were beginning to revolutionize many of the regular, customary habits of the town. Nearly one hundred persons in Henry Maxwell's church had made the pledge to do everything after asking, "What would Jesus do?" The result had been, in many cases, unheard-of actions. As a climax to the week's events had come the spiritual manifestation at the Rectangle, and the announcement of the actual conversion at the tent of nearly fifty of the worst characters in that neighborhood, together with the conversion of Rollin Page, the well-known society and club man.

The First Church of Raymond came to the morning service in a condition that made it quickly sensitive to any large truth. Perhaps nothing had astonished the people more than the great change that had come over the minister since he had proposed to them the imitation of Jesus in conduct. The sermon had become a message. It was brought to them with a love, an earnestness, a passion, a desire, a humility that poured out its enthusiasm about the truth and made the speaker no more prominent than he had to be as the living voice of God. His prayers were unlike any the people had heard before. His great longing to voice the needs and wants of his people made him unmindful of an occasional mistake. It is certain that he had never prayed so effectively as he did now.

The effect of Henry Maxwell's message this morning owed its power to the unusual fact of his preaching about the saloon at all, together with the events that had stirred the people. He spoke now with a freedom that seemed to measure his complete sense of conviction that Jesus would speak so. At the close he pleaded with the people to remember the new life that had begun at the Rectangle. The regular election of city officers was near at hand. The question of license would be an issue in the election. Was not the most Christian thing they could do to act as citizens in the matter, fight the saloon at the polls, elect good people to the city offices, and clean the municipality? His appeal was stronger at this point than he knew. It is not too much to say that the spiritual tension of the people reached its highest point right there. The imitation of Jesus that had begun with the volunteers in the church was working like leaven in the organization, and Henry Maxwell would have been amazed if he could have measured the extent of desire on the part of his people to take up the cross.

The service was over, the great audience had gone, and Maxwell again faced the company gathered in the lecture room as on the two previous Sundays. The after-service seemed now to be a necessity. As he went in and faced the people, his heart trembled. There were at least one hundred present. The Holy Spirit was never before so manifest. He missed Jasper Chase. But all the others were present.

CHAPTER 11

"Your sermon today made clear to me what I have long been feeling I ought to do," Donald Marsh, president of Lincoln College, said as he and Mr. Maxwell walked home. "'What would Jesus do in my place?' I've asked the question repeatedly since I made my promise. I've tried to satisfy myself that He would simply go on as I have done, attending to the duties of my college work, teaching my classes. But I've been able to avoid the feeling that He would do something more. Something I don't want to do, as it will cause me genuine suffering to do it. I dread it with all my soul. But I shall never be satisfied until I carry this cross."

"Yes, I think I know. It is my cross, too. I would almost rather do anything else."

Donald Marsh looked surprised, then relieved. "Maxwell, we've lived in a little world of literature and scholarly seclusion, doing work we have enjoyed and shrinking from the disagreeable duties of citizenship. Our city officials are a corrupt, unprincipled set of men, controlled in large part by the whiskey element and thoroughly selfish so far as the affairs of city government are concerned. Yet I've been satisfied to let them run the municipality and have lived in my little world, out of touch and sympathy with the real world of the people. 'What would Jesus do?' I have even tried to avoid an honest answer. But my plain duty is to take a personal part in this coming election, go to the primaries, throw the weight of my influence, whatever it is, toward the nomination and election of good men, and plunge into the very depths of the entire horrible whirlpool of deceit, bribery, political trickery, and saloonism as it exists in Raymond today."

"You have spoken for me also," replied Maxwell with a sad smile. "All my parish work, all my little trials or self-sacrifices, are as nothing to me compared with the breaking into my scholarly, intellectual, self-contained habits of this open, coarse, public fight for a clean city life. The answer to the question, 'What would Jesus do?' in this case leaves me no peace except when I say Jesus would have me act the part of a Christian citizen. We can do no less than take up this cross and follow Him."

The two men then walked on in silence for a while. Finally, President

Marsh said, "We do not need to act alone in this matter. With all the men who have made the promise, we certainly can have companionship and strength, even, of numbers. Let us organize the Christian forces of Raymond for the battle against rum and corruption, a campaign that will mean something because it is organized righteousness. Jesus would use great wisdom in this matter. He would employ means. He would make large plans. Let us do so."

They talked over the matter a long time and met again the next day in Maxwell's study to develop plans. The city primaries were called for Friday, a public meeting at the courthouse.

In its Saturday edition the evening *News* gave a full account of the primaries, and in the editorial columns Edward Norman spoke with a directness and conviction that the Christian people of Raymond were learning to respect.

Never before in the history of Raymond was there a primary like the one in the courthouse last night. It was a complete surprise to the city of politicians who have been in the habit of carrying on the affairs of the city as if they owned them. A large number of the citizens of Raymond who have never before taken part in the city's affairs entered the primary and controlled it, nominating some of the best men for all the offices to be filled at the coming election.

It was a tremendous lesson in good citizenship. President Marsh of Lincoln College made one of the best speeches ever made in Raymond. The consternation deepened as the primary proceeded and it became evident that the old-time ring of city rulers was outnumbered.

Scores of well-known businessmen and professional men, most of them church members, were present, and it did not take long to see that they had all come with the one direct and definite purpose of nominating the best men possible. Most of those men had never before been seen in a primary. They were complete strangers to the politicians. But they were able by organized and united effort to nominate the entire ticket.

As soon as it became plain that the primary was out of their control, the regular ring withdrew in disgust and nominated another ticket. The News *simply calls the attention of all decent citizens to the fact that the line is sharply and distinctly drawn between the saloon and corrupt management, such as we have known for years, and a clean, honest, capable, businesslike city administration, such as every good citizen ought to want.*

The crisis of our city affairs has been reached. The issue is squarely before us. Shall we continue the rule of rum and bribery and shameless incompetence, or shall we, as President Marsh said in his noble speech, rise as good citizens and begin a new order of things, cleansing our city of the worst enemy known to municipal honesty, and doing what lies in our power to do with the ballot to purify our civic life?

For the first time in its history, Raymond had seen the professional men—the teachers, the college professors, the doctors, the ministers—take political action and put themselves definitely in public antagonism to the evil forces that had so long controlled the machine of the municipal government.

⟡

Saturday afternoon as Virginia stepped out of her house to go and see Rachel, a carriage drove up containing three of her fashionable friends. They wanted Virginia to go driving with them up on the boulevard. The day was too pleasant to be spent indoors.

"Where have you been all this time, Virginia?" asked one of the girls, tapping her playfully on the shoulder with a red silk parasol. "We hear that you have gone into the show business. Tell us about it."

Virginia colored, but she frankly told something of her experience at the Rectangle.

"I tell you, girls, let's go 'slumming' with Virginia this afternoon. I've never been down to the Rectangle. I've heard it's an awful, wicked place and lots to see. Virginia will act as guide, and it will be interesting."

The other girls seemed to be of the same mind with the speaker, and Virginia suddenly saw an opportunity. These girls had never seen the sin and misery of Raymond. Why should they not see it, even if their motive in going down there was simply to pass away an afternoon?

"Very well, I'll go with you, but you must let me take you where you can see the most," she said as she entered the carriage.

CHAPTER 12

"Hadn't we better take a policeman along?" said one of the girls with a nervous laugh.

"There's no danger," said Virginia briefly.

"Is it true that your brother, Rollin, converted?" asked another.

It struck Virginia that all three of her friends were regarding her with close attention as if she were peculiar. "Yes, he certainly is."

"I understand he's going around to the clubs talking with his old friends there, trying to preach to them," said the girl with the red silk parasol.

Virginia did not answer, and as they neared the district, the girls grew more and more nervous. As they entered farther into the district, the Rectangle seemed to stare as with one great, bleary, beer-soaked countenance at this fine carriage with its load of fashionably dressed young women. Frightened and disgusted, the girls felt that instead of seeing the Rectangle, they were the objects of curiosity.

"Let's go back," said the girl sitting with Virginia.

At that moment they were just opposite a notorious saloon and gambling house. The street was narrow and the sidewalk crowded. Suddenly, out of the door of this saloon a young woman reeled. She sang in a broken, drunken sob that indicated she partly realized her awful condition—"Just as I am, without one plea"—and as the carriage rolled past, she leered at it. Virginia recognized the face of the girl who had knelt sobbing the night Virginia knelt beside her, praying for her.

"Stop!" cried Virginia. The carriage stopped, and in a moment she was out and took the girl by the arm. "Loreen!"

The girl looked into her face, and her own changed into a look of utter horror. The saloonkeeper came to the door of the saloon and stood there looking on with his hands on his hips. And the Rectangle, from its windows, its saloon steps, its filthy sidewalk, gutter, and roadway, paused and with undisguised wonder stared at the two girls. Over the scene the warm sun of spring poured its mellow light.

Virginia simply saw a soul that had tasted of the joy of a better life slipping back again into its old hell of shame and death. She asked only one question, "What would Jesus do?" She looked around now as she stood with Loreen, and the whole scene was cruelly vivid to her.

"Drive on; don't wait for me. I am going to see my friend home," she said calmly to the girls in the carriage.

The girl with the red parasol gasped at the word *friend*, but she didn't say anything. The other girls were speechless.

The carriage moved on, and Virginia was alone with her charge. She looked up and around. Many faces in the crowd were sympathetic. The Holy Spirit had softened a good deal of the Rectangle.

"Where does she live?" asked Virginia.

No one answered.

The girl suddenly wrenched her arm from Virginia's grasp, nearly throwing Virginia down. "Leave me! Let me go to hell! That's where I belong!" she exclaimed hoarsely.

Virginia stepped up to her and put her arm about her. "Loreen," she said firmly, "come with me. You do not belong to hell. You belong to Jesus, and He will save you. Come."

The girl suddenly burst into tears.

Virginia looked around again. "Where does Mr. Gray live?" she asked. A number of voices gave the address.

"Come, Loreen. Go with me to Mr. Gray's," she said, still keeping her hold of the swaying, trembling creature, who moaned and sobbed and now clung to her.

So the two moved on through the Rectangle toward the evangelist's lodging place. The sight seemed to impress the Rectangle seriously. The fact that one of the richest, most beautifully dressed girls in all Raymond was taking care of one of the Rectangle's most noted characters, who reeled along under the influence of liquor, was a fact astounding enough to throw dignity and importance about Loreen herself. When they finally reached Mr. Gray's lodging place, the woman who answered Virginia's knock said that both Mr. and Mrs. Gray were out somewhere and would not be back until six o'clock.

Virginia had not planned anything further than a possible appeal to the Grays, either to take charge of Loreen for a while or to find some safe place for her until she was sober. She stood now at the door, at a loss to know what to do. Finally, a thought possessed her that she could not escape. What was to hinder her from taking Loreen home with her? Why should not this homeless, wretched creature, reeking with the fumes of liquor, be cared for in Virginia's own home instead of being consigned to strangers in some hospital or house of charity? "Loreen, come. You are going home with me."

Loreen staggered to her feet and, to Virginia's surprise, made no trouble. She had expected resistance or a stubborn refusal to move. When they reached the corner and took the car, it was nearly full of people going uptown. Virginia was painfully conscious of the stare that greeted her and her companion as they entered. Loreen was lapsing into a state of stupor, and Virginia was obliged to hold fast to her arm. Several times the girl lurched heavily against her. When she mounted the steps of her handsome house, Virginia breathed a sigh of relief, even in the face of the interview with her grandmother, and when the door shut and she was in the wide hall with her homeless outcast, she felt equal to anything that might come.

Hearing Virginia come in, Madam Page came into the hall. Virginia stood there supporting Loreen, who stared stupidly at the rich magnificence of the furnishings around her.

"Grandmother"—Virginia spoke without hesitation and very clearly— "I have brought one of my friends from the Rectangle. She is in trouble and has no home. I am going to care for her here a little while."

Madam Page glanced from her granddaughter to Loreen in astonishment.

"Did you say she is one of your friends?" she asked in a cold, sneering voice.

"Yes." Virginia's face flushed, but she recalled a verse that Mr. Gray had used for one of his recent sermons, "A friend of publicans and sinners." Surely Jesus would do this that she was doing.

"Do you know what this girl is?" asked Madam Page in an angry whisper, stepping near Virginia.

"I know very well. She is an outcast. I know it even better than you do. She is drunk at this minute. But she is also a child of God. I have seen her on her knees, repentant. And I have seen hell reach out its horrible fingers after her again. And by the grace of Christ, I feel that the least I can do is to rescue her from such peril."

Madam Page glared at Virginia and clenched her hands. All this was contrary to her social code of conduct. What would Virginia's action cost the family in the way of criticism and loss of standing? To Madam Page society represented more than the church or any other institution. It was a power to be feared and obeyed. She stood erect and stern and confronted Virginia, fully roused and determined. Virginia placed her arm about Loreen and calmly looked her grandmother in the face.

"You shall not do this, Virginia! You can send her to the asylum for helpless women. We can pay all the expenses. We cannot afford, for the sake of our reputations, to shelter such a person."

"Grandmother, I do not wish to do anything that is displeasing to you, but I must keep Loreen here tonight, and longer if it seems best."

"Then you can answer for the consequences! I do not stay in the same house with a miserable—" Madam Page lost her self-control.

Virginia stopped her before she could speak the next word. "Grandmother, this house is mine. It is your home as long as you choose to remain. But in this matter I must act as I fully believe Jesus would in my place."

"I shall not stay here, then!" said Madam Page. "You can always remember that you have driven your grandmother out of your house in favor of a drunken woman." Then, without waiting for Virginia to reply, she turned and went upstairs.

Virginia called a servant and soon had Loreen cared for.

CHAPTER 13

When the bell rang for tea, Virginia went down, but her grandmother did not appear. A few minutes later Rollin came in. He brought word that his grandmother had taken the evening train for the South. He had been at the station to see some friends off and had by chance met his grandmother as he was coming out. She had told him her reason for going.

"Rollin," said Virginia, "am I wrong?"

"No, dear, I cannot believe you are. If you think this poor creature owes her safety and salvation to your personal care, it was the only thing for you to do. Surely Jesus in our places would do what you have done."

Of all the wonderful changes that Virginia was to know on account of her great pledge, nothing affected her so powerfully as the thought of Rollin's change of life. Truly, this man in Christ was a new creature.

Dr. West came that evening at Virginia's summons and did everything necessary for the outcast. The best that could be done for her now was quiet nursing and careful watching and personal love.

The after-meeting at the First Church was now eagerly established. Henry Maxwell went into the lecture room on the Sunday succeeding the week of the primary and noted again the absence of Jasper Chase. All the others were present, and they were drawn together by a bond of common fellowship that demanded and enjoyed mutual confidences.

In the spirit of very open, frank confession of experience, it seemed the most natural thing in the world for Edward Norman to tell all the rest of the company about the details of his newspaper.

"I have lost a great deal of money during the last three weeks. I am losing a great many subscribers every day."

"What do the subscribers give as their reason for dropping the paper?" asked Mr. Maxwell. All the rest listened eagerly.

"There are a good many different reasons. Some say they want a paper that prints all the crime details, sensations like prizefights, scandals, and horrors of various kinds. Others object to the discontinuance of the Sunday edition. My greatest loss has come from a falling off in advertisements and from the attitude I have taken on political questions. I may as well tell you all frankly that if I continue to pursue the plan which I honestly believe Jesus would pursue in the matter of political issues and their treatment from a nonpartisan and moral standpoint, the *News* will not be able to pay its operating expenses."

He paused a moment, and the room was very quiet.

He went on. "Are there enough genuine Christian people in Raymond who will rally to the support of a paper such as Jesus would probably edit? Or are the habits of the church people so firmly established in their demand for the regular type of journalism that they will not take a paper unless it is stripped largely of the Christian and moral purpose? I may say in this fellowship gathering that owing to recent complications in my business affairs outside of my paper, I have lost a large part of my fortune. It is not necessary for me to go into details. I mention it because I have the fullest faith in the final success of a daily paper conducted on the lines I have recently laid down, and I had planned to put into it my entire fortune in order to win final success. As it is now, unless the Christian people of Raymond—the church members and professing disciples—will support the paper with subscriptions and advertisements, I cannot continue its publication on the present basis."

Virginia followed Mr. Norman's confession with the most intense eagerness. She now asked, "Do you mean that a Christian daily ought to be endowed with a large sum like a Christian college in order to make it pay?"

"That is exactly what I mean. I've laid out plans for putting into the *News* a variety of material in a strong and truly interesting way that it would more than make up for whatever was absent from its columns in the way of unchristian matter. I'm very confident that a Christian daily such as Jesus would approve can be made to succeed financially. But it will take a large sum of money to work out the plans."

"How much, do you think?" asked Virginia quietly.

Edward Norman looked at her keenly. "I should say half a million dollars in a town like Raymond could be well spent in the establishment of a paper such as we have in mind," he answered. His voice trembled a little.

"Then," said Virginia, speaking as if the thought was fully considered, "I am ready to put that amount of money into the paper on the one condition, of course, that it be carried on as it has been begun."

"Thank God!" exclaimed Mr. Maxwell softly. Norman was pale.

Virginia went on, "I have come to know that the money, which I have called my own, is not mine but God's. If I, as a steward of His, see some wise way to invest His money, it is not an occasion for vainglory or thanks from anyone simply because I have proved honest in my administration of the funds He has asked me to use for His glory. I've been thinking of this very plan for some time. The fact is, we need the *News* to champion the Christian side. It would be giving up to the enemy to allow the *News* to fail. I have great confidence in Mr. Norman's ability. If we can keep such a paper going for one year, I shall be willing to see that amount of money used in the experiment. I believe it is what Jesus would do."

No one spoke for a while. Mr. Maxwell, standing there where the faces lifted their intense gaze into his, felt what he had already felt—a strange movement out of the nineteenth century into the first, when the disciples had all things in common and a spirit of fellowship must have flowed freely between them such as the First Church of Raymond had never before known. It had the effect that a physical miracle may have had on the early disciples in giving them a feeling of confidence in the Lord that helped them to face loss and martyrdom with courage and even joy.

CHAPTER 14

Election week followed this Sunday meeting. President Marsh, true to his promise, tore himself out of the scholarly seclusion of years with a pain and anguish that cost him more than anything he had ever done as a follower of Christ. With him were a few of the college professors who had made the pledge in the First Church. Henry Maxwell also plunged into the horror of this fight against whiskey and its allies with a sickening dread of each day's new encounter with it. He staggered under it, and in the brief intervals when he came in from the work and sought the quiet of his study for rest, the sweat broke out on his forehead, and he felt the actual terror of one who marches into unseen, unknown horrors. When Saturday, the election day, came, the excitement rose to its height. An attempt to close all the saloons was only partly successful. The Rectangle boiled and heaved and cursed and turned its worst side out to the gaze of the city.

Gray continued his meetings during the week, and the results had been even greater than he had dared to hope. When Saturday came, it seemed to him that the crisis in his work had been reached. The Holy Spirit and the Satan of rum rose up in a desperate conflict. The saloon men no longer concealed their feelings, making open threats of violence. Once during the week, Gray and his little company of helpers were assailed with missiles of various kinds as they left the tent late at night. Rachel's power in song had not diminished. Rather, with each night, it seemed to add to the intensity and reality of the Spirit's presence.

Gray had at first hesitated about having a meeting that Saturday night. But the Spirit seemed to lead him to continue the meeting, and so Saturday night he went on as usual.

The excitement all over the city reached its climax when the polls closed at six o'clock. Never before had there been such a contest in Raymond. Never before had such elements in the city been arrayed against each other. It was an unheard-of thing that the president of Lincoln College, the pastor of the First Church, the dean of the Cathedral, the professional men living in fine houses on the boulevard, should come personally into the wards and by their presence and their example represent the Christian conscience of the place.

The fight grew hotter every hour, and when six o'clock came neither side could have guessed at the result with any certainty. Both sides awaited the announcement of the result with the greatest interest.

It was after ten o'clock when the meeting at the tent closed. Maxwell had come down again at Gray's request. He was completely worn-out by the day's work, but the appeal from Gray came to him in such a form that he did not feel able to resist it. President Marsh was also present. He had never been to the Rectangle, and his curiosity was aroused. Dr. West and Rollin had come with Rachel and Virginia; and Loreen, who still stayed with Virginia, was present near the organ, in her right mind, sober, with a humility and dread of herself that kept her as close to Virginia as a faithful dog. The returns from the election were beginning to come in, and the Rectangle had emptied every lodging house, den, and hovel into the streets. Once in a while a shout from the large crowd swept into the tent.

In spite of these distractions, Rachel's singing kept the crowd in the tent from dissolving. There were a dozen or more conversions. Finally, the people became restless and Gray closed the service, remaining a little while with the converts.

Rachel, Virginia, Loreen, Rollin, President Marsh, Mr. Maxwell, and Dr. West went out together, intending to go down to the usual waiting place for their car. Outside the tent, they were at once aware that the Rectangle trembled on the verge of a drunken riot, and as they pushed through the gathering mobs in the narrow streets, they realized that they themselves were objects of great attention.

"There he is—the bloke in the tall hat! He's the leader!" shouted a rough voice. President Marsh, with his erect, commanding figure, was conspicuous in the little company.

"How has the election gone? It is too early to know the result yet, isn't it?" He asked the question aloud, and a man answered.

"They say second and third wards have gone almost solid for no-license. If that is so, the whiskey men have been beaten."

"Thank God! I hope it is true!" exclaimed Maxwell. "Marsh, we are in danger here. We ought to get the ladies to a place of safety."

At that moment a shower of stone and other missiles fell over them. The narrow street and sidewalk in front of them was completely choked with the worst elements of the Rectangle.

"This looks serious," said Maxwell. With Marsh and Rollin and Dr. West, he started to go forward through a small opening. Virginia, Rachel, and Loreen followed closely sheltered by the men. "Down with the aristocrats!" shouted a shrill voice, more like a woman's than a man's. A shower of mud and stones followed. Rachel remembered afterward that Rollin jumped directly in front of her and received on his head and chest a number of blows that probably would have struck her if he had not shielded her from them.

Then Loreen darted forward in front of Virginia and pushed her aside, looking up and screaming. It was so sudden that no one had time to catch the face of the one who did it. But out of the upper window of a room, over the very saloon where Loreen had come out a week before, someone threw a heavy bottle. It struck Loreen on the head, and she fell to the ground. Virginia turned and instantly knelt down by her. President Marsh raised his arm and shouted over the howl that was beginning to rise from the wild beast in the mob.

"Stop! You've killed a woman!" The announcement partly sobered the crowd.

"Is it true?" Maxwell asked as Dr. West knelt on the other side of Loreen, supporting her.

"She's dying!" said Dr. West briefly.

Loreen opened her eyes and smiled at Virginia, who wiped the blood from her face and then bent over and kissed her. Loreen smiled again, and the next minute her soul was in paradise.

CHAPTER 15

Sunday morning Loreen's body lay in state at the Page mansion on the avenue. The clear, sweet spring air swept over the casket from one of the open windows at the end of the grand hall. Church bells rang, and people on the avenue service turned curious, inquiring looks up at the great house and then went on.

At the First Church, Mr. Maxwell, bearing on his face marks of the scene he had been through, confronted an immense congregation and spoke to it with a passion and a power that came naturally out of the profound experiences of the day before. All through his impassioned appeal this morning, there was a note of sadness and rebuke and stern condemnation that made many of the members pale with self-accusation or with inward anger.

Raymond had awakened that morning to the fact that the city had gone for license after all. A meager majority won the victory, it was true, but the result was the same as if it had been overwhelming. The Christians of Raymond stood condemned by the result. More than a hundred professing Christian disciples had failed to go to the polls, and many more than that number had voted with the whiskey men.

With a voice that rang and trembled and broke in sobs of anguish for the result, Henry Maxwell poured out upon his people these truths that Sunday morning. And men and women wept as he spoke. President Marsh sat there, his usual erect, handsome, firm, bright, self-confident bearing all gone; his head bowed upon his breast, the great tears rolling down his cheeks, unmindful of the fact that never before had he shown outward emotion in a public service. Edward Norman sat nearby with his clear-cut, keen face erect, but his lip trembled, and he clutched the end of the pew with a feeling of emotion that struck deep into his knowledge of the truth as Maxwell spoke it. The thought that the Christian conscience had been aroused too late or too feebly lay with a weight of accusation upon the heart of the editor. And up in the choir, Rachel Winslow, with her face bowed on the railing of the oak screen, gave way to a feeling that she had not allowed yet to master her, but it so unfitted her for her part that when Mr. Maxwell finished and she tried to sing the closing solo after the prayer, her voice broke, and for the first time in her life, she was obliged to sit down, sobbing and unable to go on.

When the congregation had finally gone and Maxwell entered the lecture room, it needed but a glance to show him that the original company of followers had been largely increased. The meeting was tender; it glowed with the Spirit's presence; it was alive with strong and lasting resolve to begin a war on the whiskey power in Raymond that would break its reign forever. It was a meeting full of broken prayers of contrition, of confession, of strong yearning for a new and better city life.

The Rectangle also felt moved strangely in its own way. Loreen's death was not in itself so remarkable a fact. It was her recent acquaintance with the people from the city that lifted her into special prominence and surrounded her death with more than ordinary importance. Everyone in the Rectangle knew that Loreen was at this moment lying in the Page mansion up on the avenue. Inquirers besieged Gray and his wife, wanting to know what Loreen's friends and acquaintances were expected to do in paying their last respects to her.

So that is how it happened that Monday afternoon Loreen's funeral service was held at the tent before an immense audience that choked the tent and overflowed beyond all previous bounds.

Virginia with her uncle and Rollin, accompanied by Maxwell, Rachel, President Marsh, and the quartet from the First Church, went down and witnessed one of the strangest things of their lives.

A somewhat noted newspaper correspondent passed through Raymond that afternoon. He heard of the service at the tent and went down. His description caught the attention of very many readers the next day.

A very unique and unusual funeral service was held in the slum district known as the Rectangle this afternoon at the tent of an evangelist, Reverend John Gray. The woman, killed during an election riot last Saturday night, had been recently converted during the evangelist's meetings. She was a common street drunkard, and yet the services at the tent were as impressive as any I ever witnessed in a metropolitan church over the most distinguished citizen.

A trained choir sang a most exquisite anthem. But the most remarkable part of the music was a solo sung by a strikingly beautiful young woman, a Miss Winslow. She had a most wonderful manner in singing, and everybody was weeping before she had sung a dozen words. That, of course, is not so strange an effect to be produced at a funeral service, but the voice itself was one of thousands. Miss Winslow sings in the First Church of Raymond and could probably command almost any salary as a public singer.

The service was peculiar. The evangelist, a man of apparently very simple, unassuming style, spoke a few words, and he was followed by a fine-looking man, the Reverend Henry Maxwell, pastor of the First Church of Raymond. He spoke in a peculiarly sensitive manner of the effect of the liquor business on the lives of men and women like this one. Raymond is full of saloons. I caught from the minister's remarks that only recently he had changed his views in regard to license. He certainly made a very striking address, and yet it was in no sense inappropriate for a funeral.

Then followed what was perhaps the oddest part of this strange service. The women in the tent, many of them up near the coffin, began to sing in a soft, tearful way, "I was a wandering sheep." Then while the singing was going on, one row of women stood up and walked slowly past the casket, and as they went by, each one placed a flower of some kind upon it. Then they sat down and another row filed past, leaving their flowers. All the time the singing continued softly like rain on a tent cover when the wind is gentle. It was one of the simplest and at the same time one of the most impressive sights I ever witnessed. There must have been a hundred of these women, and I was told many of them had been converted at the meetings just recently. I cannot describe the effect of that singing. All women's voices, and so soft, and yet so distinct, that the effect was startling.

The service closed with another solo by Miss Winslow, who sang, "There were ninety and nine." And then the evangelist asked them all to bow their heads while he prayed. The last view I caught of the service was of the great crowd pouring out of the tent and forming in open ranks while the coffin was borne out by six of the women. It is a long time since I have seen such a picture in this unpoetic republic.

CHAPTER 16

No one in all Raymond, including the Rectangle, felt Loreen's death more keenly than Virginia. That short week while the girl had been in her home had opened Virginia's heart to a new life. The day after the funeral, Rachel called on Virginia, and they sat in the hall of the Page mansion.

Virginia looked over to the end of the hall where Loreen's body had lain. "I've decided on a good plan, as it seems to me. After talking to Rollin, he and I will devote a large part of our money to help those women to a better life.

"Rachel, I want you to work with me. Rollin and I are going to buy up a large part of the property in the Rectangle. The field where the tent now is has been in litigation for years.

"We mean to secure the entire tract as soon as the courts have settled the title. The money God wants me to use can build wholesome lodging-homes, refuges for poor women, asylums for shop girls, safety for many a lost girl like Loreen. But I don't want to simply dispense the money. I want to put myself into the problem." Virginia suddenly rose and paced the hall. "However, all that limitless money and limitless personal sacrifice can possibly do will not really lessen very much the awful condition at the Rectangle as long as the saloon is legally established there."

Rachel answered with a note of hope in her voice. "It is true. But, Virginia, what a wonderful amount of good can be done with this money! And the saloon cannot always remain here. The time must come when the Christian forces in the city will triumph."

Virginia paused near Rachel, and her pale, earnest face lit up. "The number of those who have promised to do as Jesus would is increasing. If we ever have, say, five hundred such disciples in Raymond, the saloon is doomed. But now, dear, I want you to look at your part in this plan for capturing and saving the Rectangle. You could organize among the girls a musical institute, give them the benefit of your voice training. Did anyone ever hear such singing as that yesterday by those women? You shall have the best of material in the way of organs and orchestras that money can provide. Much can be done with music to win souls into higher and purer and better living."

The thought of her lifework flowed into Rachel's heart and mind like a flood, and the torrent of her feeling overflowed in tears that could not be restrained. It was what she had dreamed of doing. "Yes," she said as she rose and put her arm about Virginia. "Yes, I will gladly put my life into that kind of service." Both girls now paced the hall with enthusiasm.

"Add to the money consecrated personal enthusiasm like yours, and it certainly can accomplish great things," said Virginia, smiling.

Before Rachel could reply, Rollin came in. He hesitated a moment. Then, as he passed out of the hall into the library, Virginia called him back and asked him some questions about his work.

Rollin came back and sat down, and together the three discussed their future plans. Rollin, apparently free from embarrassment in Rachel's presence while Virginia was with them, still treated her with a politeness that was almost cold. He had not forgotten the past, but he was completely caught up for this present time in the purpose of his new life. After a while Rollin was called out, and the girls talked of other things.

"By the way, what has become of Jasper Chase?" Virginia asked the question innocently, but Rachel flushed, and Virginia added with a smile, "I suppose he is writing another book. Is he going to put you into this one, Rachel? You know I always suspected him of doing that very thing in his first story."

"Jasper told me the other night that he—in fact—he proposed to me—or he would, if—" Rachel stopped and sat with her hands clasped on her lap. There were tears in her eyes. "I thought not long ago I loved him, as he said he loved me. But when he spoke, my heart felt repelled, and I told him no. I have not seen him since."

"I am glad for you," said Virginia quietly.

"Why?" asked Rachel, a little startled.

"Because he is too cold and—I do not like to judge him, but I have always distrusted his sincerity in taking the pledge at the church with the rest."

Rachel looked at Virginia thoughtfully.

"I have never given my heart to him, I am sure. I think perhaps if he had spoken to me at any other time than the one he chose, I could easily have persuaded myself that I loved him. But not now."

After Rachel left, Virginia sat in the hall thinking over the confidence her friend had just shown her. Soon Rollin came back, and he and Virginia walked arm in arm up and down the long hall. It was easy for their talk to settle finally upon Rachel because of the place she occupied in their plans for the Rectangle.

"Did you ever know of a girl of such really gifted powers in vocal music who was willing to give her life to the people as Rachel is going to do?"

"It is certainly a very good example of self-sacrifice," replied Rollin a little stiffly.

Virginia looked at him a little sharply but said nothing. The two walked on in silence for the length of the hall.

Then Virginia spoke: "Rollin, why do you treat Rachel with such a distinct, precise manner? I think that she is annoyed by it. You need to be on easy terms."

Rollin suddenly stopped, deeply agitated. He took his arm from Virginia's and walked alone to the end of the hall. Then he returned, with his hands behind him, and stopped near his sister. "Virginia, have you not learned my secret?"

Virginia looked bewildered; then over her face the unusual color crept, showing that she understood.

"I have never loved anyone but Rachel Winslow." Rollin spoke calmly enough now. "That day she was here when you talked about her refusal to join the concert company, I asked her to be my wife. She refused me, and she gave as her reason the fact I had no purpose in life, which was true enough. Now that I have a purpose, now that I am a new man, it's impossible for me to say anything. I owe my very conversion to Rachel's singing. And yet that night while she sang, I can honestly say that for the time being, I never thought of her voice except as God's message." Rollin was silent; then he went on with more emotion. "I still love her, Virginia. But I do not think she ever could love me." He stopped and looked at his sister with a sad smile.

Virginia noted Rollin's handsome face, his marks of dissipation nearly all gone now, the firm lips showing manhood and courage, the clear eyes looking into hers frankly, the form strong and graceful. Rollin was a man now. Why shouldn't Rachel come to love him in time? Surely the two were well fitted for each other, especially now that the same Christian force motivated their purpose in life.

CHAPTER 17

The next day Virginia went down to the *News* office to see Edward Norman and Mr. Maxwell and arrange the details of her part in the establishment of the paper on its new foundation.

"I have written down some of the things that it has seemed to me Jesus would do," said Edward Norman. He read from a paper lying on his desk.

"I have headed this 'What would Jesus do as editor of a daily newspaper in Raymond?'

"1. He would never allow anything in His paper that could be called bad or coarse or impure.

"2. He would conduct the political part of the paper from the standpoint of the advancement of the kingdom of God on earth."

Edward Norman looked up from the reading a moment. "You understand that I am simply trying to answer honestly.

"3. Jesus' aim of a daily paper would be to do the will of God, not to make money or gain political influence.

"4. All questionable advertisements would be impossible.

"5. Jesus' relations to the employees on the paper would be of the most loving character."

"So far as I have gone," said Norman, again looking up, "I am of the opinion that Jesus would use some form of cooperation that represented the idea of a mutual interest in a business where all worked together for the same great end, and expressed not only in personal love and sympathy for the other employees but also in a sharing of the profits of the business.

"6. Jesus would give large space to the work of the Christian world—devoting space to the facts of reform, sociological problems, institutional church work, and similar movements.

"7. He would do all in His power in His paper to fight the saloon as an enemy of the human race and an unnecessary part of our civilization, regardless of public sentiment and regardless of its effect upon His subscription list."

Again Edward Norman looked up. "I state my honest conviction on this point. I believe He would use the influence of His paper to remove the saloon entirely from the political and social life of the nation.

"8. Jesus would not issue a Sunday edition.

"9. He would print the news of the world that people ought to know, but nothing which in any way would conflict with the first point in this outline.

"10. Jesus would secure the best and strongest Christian men and women to cooperate with Him in the matter of contributions.

"11. The main principle that guides the paper is the establishment of the kingdom of God in the world. This large general principle would necessarily shape all the detail.

"This is merely a faint outline. I have a hundred ideas for making the paper powerful that I have not thought out fully as yet. As I have talked it over with other newspapermen, some of them say I will have a weak, namby-pamby Sunday school sheet. If I get out something as good as a Sunday school, it will be pretty good. But the paper will not necessarily be weak because it is good. Good things are more powerful than bad. The question with me is largely one of support from the Christian people of Raymond. There are over twenty thousand church members here in this city. If half of them will stand by the *News*, its life is assured. What do you think, Maxwell, of the probability of such support?"

"I don't know enough about it to give an intelligent answer. The great thing will be to issue such a paper, as near as we can judge, as Jesus probably would. Put into it all the elements of Christian brains, strength, intelligence, and sense, and command respect for freedom from bigotry, fanaticism, narrowness, and anything else that is contrary to the spirit of Jesus."

"Yes." Edward Norman spoke humbly. "I shall make a great many mistakes, no doubt. I need a great deal of wisdom. So I shall continue to ask the question and abide by the results."

"I think we are beginning to understand," said Virginia, "the meaning of that command, 'Grow in the grace and knowledge of our Lord and Savior Jesus Christ.' I am sure I do not know all that He would do in detail until I know Him better."

"That is very true," said Henry Maxwell. "I cannot interpret the probable action of Jesus until I know better what His Spirit is. The greatest question in all of human life is summed up when we ask, 'What would Jesus do?' if we also try to answer it from a growth in knowledge of Jesus Himself. We must know Jesus before we can imitate Him."

Virginia and Edward Norman worked out the details of their arrangement, and Norman found himself in possession of the sum of five hundred thousand dollars to use for the establishment of a Christian daily paper. When Virginia and Maxwell left, Norman closed his door and, alone with the Divine Presence, asked like a child for help from his all-powerful Father.

∾

Early one afternoon in August, after a day of refreshing coolness following a long period of heat, Jasper Chase walked to his window in the apartment house on the avenue and looked out.

On his desk lay a pile of manuscript. Since that evening when he had spoken to Rachel Winslow, he had not met her. His singularly sensitive nature served to thrust him into an isolation intensified by his habits as an author.

All through the heat of summer he wrote. His book was nearly done now. He threw himself into its construction with a feverish strength that threatened at any moment to desert him and leave him helpless.

He had not forgotten his pledge made with the other church members at the First Church. It forced itself upon his notice all through his writing. "Would Jesus do this? Would He write this story?" It was a social novel, written in a style that had proved popular. It had no purpose except to amuse. Its moral teaching was not bad, but neither was it Christian in any positive way. Jasper Chase knew that such a story would probably sell. But he felt that Jesus would never write such a book.

The question obtruded on him at the most inopportune times. He became irascible over it. The standard of Jesus for an author was too ideal. Of course Jesus would use His powers to produce something useful or helpful, or with a purpose. But Jasper wrote for the same reason nearly every writer wrote for—money, money, and fame as a writer. He had no need to write for money. But his desire for fame urged him on. He must write this kind of matter. What would Jesus do? The question plagued him even more than Rachel's refusal.

As he stood at the window, Rollin Page came out of the clubhouse just opposite. Jasper noted his handsome face and noble figure as he started down the street. He went back to his desk and turned over some papers there, then came back to the window. Rollin now walked with Rachel Winslow. Rollin must have overtaken her as she was coming from Virginia's that afternoon.

Jasper watched the two figures until they disappeared in the crowd on the walk. Then he turned to his desk and began to write. When he had finished the last page of the last chapter of his book, it was nearly dark. "What would Jesus do?" He had finally answered the question by denying his Lord, deliberately choosing his course, urged on by his disappointment and loss.

CHAPTER 18

That afternoon when Rollin came upon Rachel Winslow as he turned into the avenue, his heart leaped up at the sight of her. He walked along by her now, rejoicing in a little moment of this earthly love he could not drive out of his life.

"Virginia tells me the arrangements are nearly completed for the transfer of the Rectangle property," Rachel said.

"Yes. It has been a tedious case in the courts. Did Virginia show you all the plans and specifications for building?"

"We looked over a good many. It is astonishing to me where Virginia has managed to get all her ideas about this work."

"Virginia knows more now about Arnold Toynbee and East End London and institutional church work in America than a good many professional slum workers." Rollin felt more at ease talking about the safe, common ground of their coming work of humanity. "What have you been doing all summer? I have not seen much of you," Rachel suddenly asked, and then her face warmed with its quick flush of tropical color.

"I've been busy," replied Rollin briefly.

"Tell me about it," persisted Rachel. "You say so little. Have I a right to ask?"

She put the question very frankly, turning toward Rollin in real earnest.

"Yes, certainly," he replied with a graceful smile. "I am not sure that I can tell you much. I've tried to find some way to reach the men I once knew and win them into more useful lives."

He stopped, almost afraid to go on, but Rachel kept quiet.

"I have made the pledge to do as I believe Jesus would do," continued Rollin, "and it is in trying to answer this question that I have been doing my work."

"It's wonderful to think that you are trying to keep that pledge. But what can you do with the clubmen?"

"That night at the tent," replied Rollin, his voice trembling a little, "I asked myself what purpose I could now have in my life to redeem it, to satisfy my thought of Christian discipleship. And the more I thought of it, the more I was driven to a place where I knew I must take up the cross. The churches look after the poor, miserable creatures like those in the Rectangle; they make some effort to reach working people; they have a large constituency among the average salary-earning people; they send money and missionaries to the foreign heathen. But the fashionable, dissipated young men around town, the clubmen, are left out of all plans for reaching and Christianizing. I know these men, their good and their bad qualities. I've been one of them. So that's what I have been trying to do, reach out to these men for Christ."

Rachel's interest in his plan was larger than mere curiosity. Rollin Page was so different now from the fashionable young man who had asked her to be his wife that she could not help thinking of him and talking with him as if he were an entirely new acquaintance.

They turned off the avenue and headed up the street to Rachel's home—the same street where Rollin had asked Rachel why she could not love him. They fell silent.

Rachel finally spoke. "In your work with your old acquaintances, what sort of reception do they give you? How do you approach them? What do they say?"

"It depends on the man. A good many of them think I am a crank. I've kept my membership up and am in good standing in that way. I try to be wise and not provoke any unnecessary criticism. Many of the men have responded to my appeal. Only a few nights ago a dozen men honestly and earnestly engaged in a conversation over religious matters. I've had the great joy of seeing some of the men give up bad habits and begin a new life. The men are not fighting shy of me, and I think that is a good sign. Also, I have actually interested some of them in the Rectangle work, and when it is started up, they will give something to help make it more powerful."

Rachel again noted the strong, manly tone of his speech as Rollin spoke with enthusiasm. With it all she knew there was a deep, underlying seriousness that felt the burden of the cross even while carrying it with joy. "Do you remember I reproached you once for not having any purpose worth living for?" she asked. "I want to say in justice to you now that I honor you for your courage and your obedience to the promise you have made as you interpret the promise. The life you are living is a noble one."

Rollin trembled, his agitation greater than he could control. Rachel could not help seeing it. At last he said, "I thank you. It is worth more to me than I can tell you to hear you say that." He looked into her face for one moment, noting that her face was more beautiful than ever.

She read his love for her in that look, but he did not speak.

When they separated, Rachel went into the house, and sitting down in her room, she put her face in her hands and said to herself: "I am beginning to know what it means to be loved by a noble man. I shall love Rollin Page after all."

She rose and walked back and forth, deeply moved. Nevertheless, it was evident to herself that her emotion was not that of regret or sorrow. A glad new joy had come to her. She rejoiced, for if she was beginning to love Rollin Page, it was the Christian man she had begun to love; the other never would have moved her to this great change.

CHAPTER 19

Letter from Rev. Calvin Bruce, DD, of the Nazareth Avenue Church, Chicago, to Rev. Philip A. Caxton, DD, New York City.

My dear Dr. Caxton,

It is late Sunday night, but I feel driven to write you now some account of the situation in Raymond as I have been studying it. It has apparently come to a climax today.

You remember Henry Maxwell in the seminary, a refined, scholarly fellow. When he was called to the First Church of Raymond within a year after leaving the seminary, I said to my wife, "Raymond has made a good choice. Maxwell will satisfy them as a sermonizer." He has been here eleven years, in a comfortable berth, with a very good salary, and pleasant surroundings, a not very exacting parish of refined, rich, respectable people.

A year ago today at the close of the service, Maxwell made the astounding proposition that the members of his church volunteer for a year not to do anything without first asking the question, "What would Jesus do?" and, after answering it, to do what in their honest judgment He would do, regardless of what the result might be to them.

The effect of this proposition has been so remarkable that the attention of the whole country has been directed to the movement. Maxwell tells me he was astonished at the response to his proposition. Some of the most prominent members in the church made the promise to do as Jesus would.

One needs to come here and learn something of the changes in individual lives, to realize all that is meant by this following of Jesus' steps so literally. But I can give you some idea perhaps of what has been done as told me by friends here and by Maxwell himself.

The result of the pledge upon the First Church has been twofold. It has brought about a spirit of Christian fellowship, which Maxwell tells me impresses him as being very nearly what the Christian fellowship of the apostolic churches must have been; and it has divided the church into two distinct groups of members. Those who have not taken the pledge regard the others as foolishly literal in their attempt to imitate the example of Jesus. The effect on Maxwell is very marked. I heard him preach in our State Association four years ago. He impressed me at the time as having considerable power in dramatic delivery. His sermon was well written and abounded in what the seminary students used to call "fine passages."

This morning I heard Maxwell preach again. He is not the same man. He gives me the impression of one who has passed through a crisis of revolution. He tells me this revolution is simply a new definition of Christian discipleship.

He certainly has changed many of his old habits and many of his old views. The idea that is moving him on now is the idea that the Christianity of our times must represent a more literal imitation of Jesus, especially in the element of suffering. He seems filled with the conviction that what our churches need today, more than anything else, is this factor of joyful suffering for Jesus in some form.

I can give you some of the results on the individuals who have made this pledge and honestly tried to be true to it, so that you may see that this form of discipleship is not merely sentiment or fine posing for effect.

Take the case of Mr. Powers, who was superintendent of the machine shops of the L&T RR here. When he acted upon the evidence that incriminated the road, he lost his position, and his family and social relations have changed so that he and his family no longer appear in public. The president of the road, who was the principal offender, has resigned. Meanwhile, the superintendent has gone back to his old work as a telegraph operator. I met him at the church yesterday. He impressed me as a man who had, like Maxwell, gone through a crisis in character. Or take the case of Mr. Norman, editor of the Daily News. He risked his entire fortune in obedience to what he believed was Jesus' action and revolutionized his entire conduct of the paper at the risk of failure. To my mind it is one of the most interesting and remarkable papers ever printed in the United States. It is so far above the ordinary conception of a daily paper that I am amazed at the result. He tells me that more Christians in the city are reading the paper. He is very confident of its final success. Then there is Milton Wright, the merchant. He has so revolutionized his business that no man is more beloved today in Raymond.

During the winter, while he was lying dangerously ill at his home, scores of clerks volunteered to watch and help in any way possible, and his return to his store was greeted with marked demonstrations. All this was brought about by the element of personal love introduced into the business. It is a fact, however, that while he has lost heavily in some directions, he has increased his business and is today respected and honored as one of the best and most successful merchants in Raymond.

And there is Miss Winslow. She has chosen to give her great talent to the poor of the city. Her plans include a Musical Institute where choruses and classes in vocal music shall be a feature. In connection with her friend Miss Page, she has planned a course in music which, if carried out, will certainly do much to lift up the lives of the people down there. Miss Winslow expects to be married this spring to a brother of Miss Page who was once a society leader and clubman, and who was converted in a tent where his wife-to-be took an active part in the service. President Marsh of Lincoln College is a graduate of my alma mater, and I knew him slightly when I was in the senior year. He has taken an active part in the recent municipal campaign, and his influence in the city is regarded as a very large factor in the coming election. He impressed me as having fought out some hard questions and as having taken up some real burdens that have caused, and still do cause, that suffering that does not eliminate, but does appear to intensify, a positive and practical joy.

CHAPTER 20

I want to tell you something of the meeting in the First Church today.

As I said, I heard Maxwell preach. His sermon this morning was as different from his sermon at the Association meeting four years ago as if it had been thought out and preached by someone living on another planet. I was profoundly touched. His text was "What is that to thee? Follow thou Me." It was a most unusually impressive appeal to the Christians of Raymond to obey Jesus' teachings and follow in His steps regardless of what others might do.

At the close of the service there was the usual after-meeting that has become a regular feature of the First Church. Into this meeting have come all those who made the pledge to do as Jesus would do, and the time is spent in mutual fellowship, confession, question as to what Jesus would do in special cases, and prayer that the one great guide of every disciple's conduct may be the Holy Spirit.

Maxwell asked me to come into this meeting. I have never felt the Spirit's presence so powerfully.

I asked questions. It is very evident that many of these disciples have repeatedly carried their obedience to Jesus to the extreme limit, regardless of financial loss. There is no lack of courage or consistency at this point.

It is also true that some of the businessmen who took the pledge have lost great sums of money in this imitation of Jesus and may have, like Alexander Powers, lost valuable positions owing to the impossibility of doing what they had been accustomed to do and at the same time what they felt Jesus would do in the same place. Those who still have means have helped those who have suffered in this way. In this respect these disciples have all things in common.

I never dreamed that such Christian fellowship could exist in this age of the world. I was almost skeptical as to the witness of my own senses. I still seem to be asking myself if this is the close of the nineteenth century in America.

But now, dear friend, I come to the real cause of this letter, the real heart of the whole question as the First Church of Raymond has forced it upon me. Before the meeting closed today, steps were taken to secure the cooperation of all other Christian disciples in this country. I think Maxwell took this step after long deliberation. The idea crystallized today in a plan to secure the fellowship of all the Christians in America. The churches, through their pastors, will be asked to form disciple gatherings like the one in the First Church. They will call for volunteers in the great body of church members in the United States, who will promise to do as Jesus would do.

Maxwell spoke particularly of the result of such general action on the saloon question. He is terribly in earnest over this. He told me that there was no question in his mind that the saloon would be beaten in Raymond at the election now near at hand. If so, they could go on with some courage to do the redemptive work begun by the evangelist and now taken up by the disciples in his own church. He convinced his church that the time had come for a fellowship with other Christians.

This is a grand idea, Caxton, but right here is where I find myself hesitating. I do not deny that the Christian disciple ought to follow Christ's steps as closely as these here in Raymond have tried to do. But I cannot avoid asking what the result would be if I ask my church in Chicago to do it.

I am writing this after feeling the solemn, profound touch of the Spirit's presence, and I confess to you, old friend, that I cannot call up in my church a dozen prominent business or professional men who would make this trial at the risk of all they hold dear.

The actual results of the pledge as obeyed here in Raymond are enough to make any pastor tremble, and at the same time long with yearning that they might occur in his own parish. Never have I seen a church so signally blessed by the Spirit as this one.

But—am I myself ready to take this pledge? I ask the question honestly, and I dread to face an honest answer. I know well enough that I should have to change very much in my life if I undertook to follow His steps so closely.

Shall I go back to my people next Sunday and stand up before them in my large city church and say, "Let us follow Jesus closer; let us walk in His steps where it will cost us something more than it is costing us now; let us pledge not to do anything without first asking: 'What would Jesus do?' "

If I should go before them with that message, it would be a strange and startling one to them. But why? Are we not ready to follow Him all the way? What is it to be a follower of Jesus? What does it mean to imitate Him? What does it mean to walk in His steps?

The Reverend Calvin Bruce, DD, of the Nazareth Avenue Church, Chicago, let his pen fall on the table. He had come to the parting of the ways, and his question, he felt sure, was the question of many and many a person in the ministry and in the church. He went to his window and opened it. Oppressed with the weight of his convictions, he felt almost suffocated with the air in the room. He wanted to see the stars and feel the breath of the world.

The night was very still. The clock in the First Church struck midnight. As it finished, a clear, strong voice down in the direction of the Rectangle came floating up to him as if borne on radiant pinions.

"Must Jesus bear the cross alone
And all the world go free?
No, there's a cross for everyone,
And there's a cross for me."

The Reverend Calvin Bruce turned away from the window, and after a little hesitation, he knelt. "What would Jesus do?" That was the burden of his prayer. Never had he yielded himself so completely to the Spirit of Jesus. He was on his knees a long time. He retired and slept fitfully with many awakenings. He rose before it was clear dawn and threw open his window again. As the light in the east grew stronger, he repeated to himself: "What would Jesus do? Shall I follow His steps?"

With this question throbbing through his whole being, Dr. Bruce went back to Chicago, and the great crisis in his Christian life in the ministry suddenly broke irresistibly upon him.

CHAPTER 21

The Saturday afternoon matinee at the Auditorium in Chicago was just over and the usual crowd struggled to get to its carriage before anyone else.

"Now then, 624," shouted the Auditorium attendant; "624!" he repeated, and there dashed up to the curb a splendid span of black horses attached to a carriage having the monogram CRS in gilt letters on the panel of the door.

Two girls stepped out of the crowd toward the carriage. The older one entered and took her seat, but the younger stood hesitating on the curb.

"Come, Felicia! What are you waiting for! I shall freeze to death!" called the voice from the carriage.

The girl outside of the carriage hastily unpinned a bunch of English violets from her dress and handed them to a small boy who stood shivering on the edge of the sidewalk almost under the horses' feet. He took them with a look of astonishment and a "Thank ye, lady!" and instantly buried a very grimy face in the bunch of perfume. The girl stepped into the carriage, the door shut with the incisive *bang*, and in a few moments the coach-man was speeding the horses rapidly up one of the boulevards.

"You are always doing some peculiar thing or other, Felicia," said the older girl as the carriage whirled on past the great residences already brilliantly lighted.

"Am I? What have I done now, Rose?" asked the other.

"Oh, giving those violets to that boy! He looked as if he needed a good hot supper more than a bunch of violets. It's a wonder you didn't invite him home with us."

"Would it be peculiar to invite a boy like that to come to the house and get a hot supper?" Felicia asked the question softly.

"*Peculiar* isn't just the word, of course," replied Rose indifferently. "It would be what Madam Blanc calls '*outré*.' Decidedly."

She yawned, and Felicia silently looked out of the window in the door.

"The concert was stupid and the violinist was simply a bore. I don't see how you could sit so still through it all," Rose exclaimed a little impatiently.

"I liked the music," answered Felicia quietly.

"You like anything. I never saw a girl with so little critical taste."

Felicia colored slightly but would not answer. Rose yawned again and then exclaimed abruptly, "I'm sick of 'most everything. I hope *The Shadows of London* will be exciting tonight. You know we have a box with the Delanos tonight."

Felicia turned her face toward her sister. Her great brown eyes were very expressive and not altogether free from a sparkle of luminous heat.

"And yet we never weep over the real thing on the actual stage of life. Why don't we get excited over the facts as they are?"

"Because the actual people are dirty and disagreeable and it's too much bother, I suppose," replied Rose carelessly. "Felicia, you can never reform the world. What's the use? We're not to blame for the poverty and misery."

"Suppose Christ had gone on that principle," replied Felicia with unusual persistence. "Do you remember Dr. Bruce's sermon on Second Corinthians 8:9 a few Sundays ago: 'For ye know the grace of our Lord Jesus Christ, that, though he was rich, yet for your sakes he became poor, that ye through his poverty might be rich'?"

"I remember it well enough," said Rose with some petulance, "and didn't Dr. Bruce go on to say that there is no blame attached to people who have wealth if they are kind and give to the needs of the poor? Ever since Rachel Winslow wrote about those strange doings in Raymond, you have upset the whole family. People can't live at that concert pitch all the time. You see if Rachel doesn't give it up soon. It's a great pity she doesn't come to Chicago and sing in the Auditorium concerts."

Felicia looked out of the window and was silent. The carriage rolled on past two blocks of magnificent private residences and turned into a wide drive-way under a covered passage, and the sisters hurried into the house. It was an elegant mansion of gray stone furnished like a palace, every corner of it warm with the luxury of paintings, sculpture, art, and modern refinement.

The owner of it all, Mr. Charles R. Sterling, stood before an open grate fire smoking a cigar. He'd made his money in grain speculation and railroad ventures, and was reputed to be worth something over two million dollars. His wife, a sister of Mrs. Winslow of Raymond, had been an invalid for several years. The two girls, Rose and Felicia, were the only children.

Rose was twenty-one years old, fair, vivacious, educated in a fashionable college, just entering society and already somewhat cynical and indifferent. Felicia was nineteen, with a tropical beauty somewhat like that of her cousin Rachel, with warm, generous impulses just waking into Christian feeling, capable of all sorts of expression.

"Here's a letter for you, Felicia," said Mr. Sterling, handing it to her.

Felicia sat down and instantly opened the letter, saying as she did so, "It's from Rachel."

"Well, what's the latest news from Raymond?" asked Mr. Sterling, taking his cigar out of his mouth.

"Rachel says Dr. Bruce has been in Raymond for two Sundays and has seemed very interested in Mr. Maxwell's pledge in the First Church."

"What does Rachel say about herself?" asked Rose, who was lying on a couch almost buried under a half-dozen elegant cushions.

"She is still singing at the Rectangle. Since the tent meetings closed, she sings in an old hall until the new buildings, which her friend Virginia Page is putting up, are completed."

Mr. Sterling lit a new cigar, and Rose exclaimed, "Rachel is so peculiar. She might set Chicago wild with her voice if she sang in the Auditorium. And there she goes on throwing it away on people who don't know what they are hearing."

"Rachel won't come here unless she can do it and keep her pledge at the same time," said Felicia after a pause.

"A very peculiar thing, that," Mr. Sterling said. "I wonder what Dr. Bruce thinks of it on the whole. I must have a talk with him."

"He is at home and will preach tomorrow," said Felicia. "Perhaps he will tell us something about it."

"Oh, well, let's have some tea!" said Rose, walking into the dining room. Her father and Felicia followed, and the meal proceeded in silence. Mrs. Sterling had her meals served in her room. Mr. Sterling was preoccupied. He ate very little and excused himself early.

"Don't you think Father looks very much disturbed lately?" asked Felicia a little while after he had gone out.

"Oh, I don't know! I hadn't noticed anything unusual," replied Rose. After a silence she said, "Are you going to the play tonight, Felicia? Mrs. Delano will be here at half past seven."

"I'll go. I don't care about it. I can see shadows enough without going to the play."

"That's a doleful remark for a girl nineteen years old to make," replied Rose. "If you are going up to see Mother, tell her I'll run in after the play if she is still awake."

CHAPTER 22

When the company was seated in the box and the curtain had gone up, Felicia was back of the others and remained for the evening by herself. Mrs. Delano, as chaperone for half a dozen young ladies, understood Felicia well enough to know that she was "peculiar," and she made no attempt to draw her out of her corner.

The play was an English melodrama full of startling situations, realistic scenery, and unexpected climaxes. One scene in the third act impressed even Rose Sterling.

It was midnight on Blackfriars Bridge. The Thames flowed dark and forbidding below. The figure of a child came upon the bridge and stood there for a moment peering about as if looking for someone. In one of the recesses about midway of the bridge a woman stood, leaning out over the parapet, with a strained agony of face and figure that told plainly of her intention. Just as she stealthily mounted the parapet to throw herself into the river, the child caught sight of her, ran forward with a shrill cry more animal than human, seized the woman's dress, and dragged back upon it with all her little strength.

Then there came suddenly upon the scene two other characters—a tall, handsome, athletic gentleman dressed in the fashion attended by a slim-figured lad who was as refined in dress and appearance as the little girl clinging to her mother, who was mournfully hideous in her rags and repulsive poverty. The gentleman and the lad prevented the attempted suicide, and after the revelation that the man and woman were brother and sister, the scene transferred to the interior of one of the slum tenements in the East Side of London.

Here the scene painter and carpenter had done their utmost to produce an exact copy of a famous court and alley well known to the poor creatures who make up a part of the outcast London humanity. The rags, the crowding, the vileness, the broken furniture, the horrible animal existence forced upon creatures made in God's image were so skillfully shown in this scene that more than one elegant woman in the theater caught herself shrinking back a little as if contamination were possible from the nearness of this piece of scenery.

From the tenement scene the play shifted to the interior of a nobleman's palace. The contrast was startling.

Felicia found herself living the scenes on the bridge and in the slums over and over. This was not the first time she had felt the contrast between the upper and the lower conditions of human life. It had been growing upon her until it had made her what Rose called "peculiar" and other people in her circle of wealthy acquaintants called "very unusual."

Finally, the play was over, the curtain down, and people went noisily out, laughing and gossiping as if *The Shadows of London* was simply good diversion.

Felicia rose and went out with the rest quietly. She was never absent-minded but often thought herself into a condition that left her alone in the midst of a crowd.

"Well, what did you think of it?" asked Rose when the sisters had reached home and were in the drawing room.

"I thought it was a pretty fair picture of real life."

"I mean the acting," said Rose, annoyed.

"The bridge scene was well acted, especially the woman's part. I thought the man overdid the sentiment a little."

"Did you? I enjoyed that. But the slum scene was horrible. I think they ought not to show such things in a play. They are too painful."

"They must be painful in real life, too," replied Felicia.

"Yes, but we don't have to look at the real thing. It's bad enough at the theater where we pay for it."

"Are you going up to see Mother?" asked Felicia after a while.

"No," replied Rose. "I won't trouble her tonight. If you go in, tell her I am too tired to be agreeable."

So Felicia turned into her mother's room as she went up the great staircase and down the upper hall. The light burned there, and the servant who always waited on Mrs. Sterling beckoned Felicia to come in.

"Tell Clara to go out," Mrs. Sterling said as Felicia came up to the bed.

Surprised, Felicia did as her mother bade her and then inquired how she was feeling.

"Felicia," said her mother, "can you pray?"

The question was so unlike any her mother had ever asked before that she was startled. But she answered, "Why, yes, Mother. Why?"

"Felicia, I am frightened. Your father—I have had such strange fears about him all day. Something is wrong with him. I want you to pray."

"Now, here, Mother?"

"Yes. Pray, Felicia."

Felicia reached out her hand and took her mother's. It was trembling. Mrs. Sterling had never shown such tenderness for her younger daughter, and her strange demand now was the first real sign of any confidence in Felicia's character.

The girl knelt, still holding her mother's trembling hand, and prayed. She must have said in her prayer the words that her mother needed, for when it was silent in the room, the invalid wept softly and her nervous tension was over.

Felicia stayed some time. When she was assured that her mother would not need her any longer, she rose to go.

"Good night, Mother. You must let Clara call me if you feel badly in the night."

"I feel better now." Then as Felicia was moving away, Mrs. Sterling said, "Won't you kiss me, Felicia?"

Felicia went back and bent over her mother. The kiss was almost as strange to her as the prayer had been. When Felicia went out of the room, her cheeks were wet with tears.

Sunday morning at the Sterling mansion was generally very quiet. The girls went to eleven o'clock service at church. Mr. Sterling was not a member but a heavy contributor, and he generally went to church in the morning. Today he did not come down to breakfast and finally sent word by a servant that he did not feel well enough to go out. So Rose and Felicia drove up to the door of the Nazareth Avenue Church and entered the family pew alone.

Dr. Bruce walked out of the room at the rear of the platform and went up to the pulpit to open the Bible as his custom was. He proceeded with the service as usual. He was calm and his voice was steady and firm. His prayer was the first intimation the people had of anything new or strange in the service.

No one in Nazareth Avenue Church had any idea that Dr. Bruce, the dignified, cultured, refined doctor of divinity, had within a few days been crying like a little child on his knees, asking for strength and courage and Christ-likeness to speak his Sunday message; and yet the prayer was an unconscious involuntary disclosure of his soul's experience such as the Nazareth Avenue people had seldom heard.

In the hush that succeeded the prayer, a distinct wave of spiritual power moved over the congregation. The most oblivious persons in the church felt it. Felicia, whose sensitive religious nature responded swiftly to every touch of emotion, quivered under the passing of that supernatural pressure, and when she lifted her head and looked up at the minister, there was a look in her eyes that announced her intense, eager anticipation of the scene that was to follow.

CHAPTER 23

"I am just back from a visit to Raymond," Dr. Bruce began, "and I want to tell you something of my impressions of the movement there."

He paused, and his look went out over his people with yearning for them but also uncertainty. Nevertheless, he had been through his desert and had come out of it ready to suffer. He went on now after that brief pause and told them the story of his stay in Raymond.

Dr. Bruce told his people simply and with a personal interest that led the way to the announcement that now followed. Felicia listened to every word with strained attention.

"Dear friends," he said, and for the first time since his prayer, the emotion of the occasion was revealed in his voice and gesture, "I am going to ask that Nazareth Avenue Church take the same pledge that Raymond Church has taken. I know what this will mean to you and me. It will mean what following Jesus meant in the first century, and then it meant suffering, loss, hardship, separation from everything unchristian. Those of us who volunteer in this church to do as Jesus would do simply promise to walk in His steps as He gave us commandment."

Again he paused, and now the result of his announcement was plainly visible in the stir that went up over the congregation. He added in a quiet voice that all who volunteered to make the pledge to do as Jesus would do were asked to remain after the morning service.

He then proceeded with his sermon. His text was "Master, I will follow Thee whithersoever Thou goest." The sermon was a revelation to the people of the definition their pastor had been learning. It was such a sermon as a man can preach once in a lifetime, and with enough in it for people to live on all through the rest of their lives.

The service closed in a hush that slowly broke. People rose here and there, a few at a time. Rose, however, walked straight out of the pew, and as she reached the aisle she turned her head and beckoned to Felicia.

"I am going to stay," she said, and Rose knew that her resolve could not be changed. Nevertheless, she went back into the pew two or three steps and faced her.

343

"Felicia," she whispered, and there was a flush of anger on her cheeks, "this is folly. You will bring some disgrace on the family. What will Father say? Come!"

Felicia looked at her but did not answer at once. She shook her head. "No, I am going to stay. I shall take the pledge. I am ready to obey it."

Rose gave her one look, then turned and went out of the pew and down the aisle.

❧

When Rose reached home, her father stood in his usual attitude before the open fireplace, smoking a cigar.

"Where is Felicia?" he asked as Rose came in.

"She stayed to an after-meeting," replied Rose shortly. She threw off her wraps and was going upstairs when Mr. Sterling called after her.

"An after-meeting? What do you mean?"

"Dr. Bruce asked the church to take the Raymond pledge."

Mr. Sterling took his cigar out of his mouth and twirled it nervously between his fingers.

"I didn't expect that of him. Did many of the members stay?"

"I don't know. I didn't," replied Rose, and she went upstairs, leaving her father standing in the drawing room.

After a few moments he went to the window and stood there looking out at the people driving on the boulevard. His cigar had gone out, but he still fingered it nervously. Then he turned from the window and walked up and down the room. A servant stepped across the hall and announced dinner, and he told her to wait for Felicia. Finally wearied of the walking, he threw himself into a chair and was brooding over something deeply when Felicia came in.

He rose and faced her. Felicia was evidently very much moved by the meeting from which she had just come. At the same time, she did not wish to talk too much about it. Just as she entered the drawing room, Rose came in.

"How many stayed?" Rose asked.

"About a hundred," replied Felicia gravely.

Mr. Sterling looked surprised. Felicia went out of the room, but he called to her. "Do you really mean to keep the pledge?" he asked.

Felicia colored. "You would not ask such a question, Father, if you had been at the meeting." She lingered a moment in the room, then asked to be excused from dinner for a while and went up to see her mother.

❧

That same evening, after the Sunday evening service, Dr. Bruce talked over the events of the day with his wife. They were of one heart and mind in the matter and faced their new future with all the faith and courage of new disciples.

The bell rang and Dr. Bruce, going to the door, exclaimed as he opened it, "It is you, Edward! Come in."

A commanding figure stepped into the hall. The bishop was of extraordinary height and breadth of shoulder but of such good proportions that there was no thought of ungainly or even of unusual size.

He came into the parlor and greeted Mrs. Bruce, who after a few moments was called out of the room, leaving the two men together. The bishop sat in a deep easy chair before the open fire. "Calvin, you have taken a very serious step today," he finally said, lifting his large dark eyes to his old college classmate's face. "I heard of it this afternoon. I could not resist the desire to see you about it tonight."

"I'm glad you came. You understand what this means, Edward?"

"Yes." The bishop spoke very slowly and thoughtfully. He sat with his hands clasped together. Over his face, marked with lines of consecration and service and the love of men, a shadow crept. Again he lifted his eyes toward his old friend.

"Calvin, we have always understood each other. Ever since our paths led us in different ways in church life, we have walked together in Christian fellowship."

"It is true," replied Dr. Bruce with an emotion he made no attempt to conceal or subdue. "Thank God for it. I prize your fellowship more than any other man's."

The bishop looked affectionately at his friend. But the shadow still rested on his face. After a pause he spoke again. "The new discipleship means a crisis for you in your work. If you keep this pledge to do all things as Jesus would do—as I know you will—it requires no prophet to predict some remarkable changes in your parish." The bishop looked wistfully at his friend and then continued. "In fact, I do not see how a perfect upheaval of Christianity, as we now know it, can be prevented if the ministers and churches generally take the Raymond pledge and live it out." There flashed into Dr.

345

Bruce's mind a suspicion of the truth. What if the bishop would throw the weight of his great influence on the side of the Raymond movement? Dr. Bruce reached out his hand and, with the familiarity of lifelong friendship, placed it on the bishop's shoulder. But before he could speak, they were both startled by the violent ringing of the bell.

Mrs. Bruce went to the door and talked with someone in the hall. There was a loud exclamation, and then, as the bishop rose and Bruce stepped toward the curtain that hung before the entrance to the parlor, Mrs. Bruce pushed it aside. Her face was white and she was trembling.

"Oh, Calvin! Such terrible news! Mr. Sterling—oh, I cannot tell it! What a blow to those girls!"

"What is it?" Mr. Bruce advanced with the bishop into the hall and confronted the messenger, a servant from the Sterlings. The man was without his hat and had evidently run over with the news.

"Mr. Sterling shot himself, sir, a few minutes ago. He killed himself in his bedroom. Mrs. Sterling—"

"I will go right over. Edward, will you go with me? The Sterlings are old friends of yours."

The bishop was very pale but calm as always. "Aye, Calvin, I will go with you, not only to this house of death, but also the whole way of human sin and sorrow, please God."

CHAPTER 24

When Dr. Bruce and the bishop entered the Sterling mansion, everything in the usually well-appointed household was in the greatest confusion and terror. The great rooms downstairs were empty, but overhead they heard hurried footsteps and confused noises. One of the servants ran down the grand staircase with a look of horror on her face just as the bishop and Dr. Bruce started to go up.

"Miss Felicia is with Mrs. Sterling," the servant stammered in answer to a question, and then burst into a hysterical cry and ran through the drawing room and out of doors.

At the top of the staircase, Felicia met the two men. She walked up to Dr. Bruce at once and put both hands in his. The bishop then laid his hand on her head, and the three stood there a moment in perfect silence. The bishop had known Felicia since she was a little child. He was the first to break the silence.

"The God of all mercy be with you, Felicia, in this dark hour. Your mother—" The Bishop hesitated.

Answering the bishop's unfinished query, Felicia turned and went back into her mother's room. But both men were struck with her wonderful calm as they followed her.

Rose lay with her arms outstretched upon the bed. Clara, the nurse, sat with her head covered, sobbing in spasms of terror. And Mrs. Sterling lay there so still that the bishop was deceived at first. Then, as the great truth broke upon him, he staggered.

The next moment the house below was in a tumult. Almost at the same time, the doctor came in together with a police officer, both summoned by frightened servants. Four or five newspaper correspondents and several neighbors came in with them. Dr. Bruce and the bishop met this miscellaneous crowd at the head of the stairs and succeeded in excluding all except those whose presence was necessary. With these the two friends learned all the facts ever known about the "Sterling tragedy," as the papers in their sensational accounts the next day called it.

Mr. Sterling had gone into his room that evening about nine o'clock, and that was the last seen of him until, a half hour later, a shot was heard in the

347

room. A servant who was in the hall ran into the room and found him dead on the floor, killed by his own hand. Felicia at the time was sitting by her mother. Rose was reading in the library. She ran upstairs, saw her father as the servants lifted him to the couch, and then ran screaming into her mother's room, where she flung herself down at the foot of the bed in a swoon. Mrs. Sterling at first fainted at the shock, then rallied with a wonderful swiftness and sent for Dr. Bruce. She then insisted on seeing her husband. In spite of Felicia's efforts, she compelled Clara to support her while she crossed the hall and entered the room where her husband lay. She looked upon him with a tearless face, went back to her own room, was laid on her bed, and as Dr. Bruce and the bishop entered the house, she died, with Felicia bending over her and Rose still lying senseless at her feet.

When the facts regarding Mr. Sterling's business affairs were disclosed, they learned that for some time he had been facing financial ruin owing to certain speculations that swept his supposed wealth into complete destruction. Sunday afternoon, he received news that proved to him beyond a doubt the fact of his utter ruin. The very house that he called his, the chairs in which he sat, his carriage, the dishes from which he ate, all rested on a tissue of deceit and speculation that had no foundation in real values. As soon as the truth that he was practically a beggar had dawned upon him, he saw no escape from suicide. Mrs. Sterling's death was the result of the shock. She had not been taken into her husband's confidence for years, but she knew that the source of his wealth was precarious. When she was carried into the room where her husband lay, her feeble tenement could not hold the spirit, and it gave up the ghost, torn and weakened by long years of suffering and disappointment.

The horror of events stupefied Rose for weeks. She lay unmoved by sympathy or any effort to rally. Even when she was told that she and Felicia must leave the house and be dependent on relatives and friends, she didn't seem to understand what it meant.

Felicia, however, was fully conscious of the facts. Mrs. Winslow and Rachel left Raymond and came to Chicago as soon as the terrible news had reached them, and they now planned for Rose and Felicia's future.

So in a few weeks Rose and Felicia found themselves a part of the Winslow family in Raymond. It was a bitter experience for Rose, but there was nothing else for her to do, and she accepted the inevitable, brooding over the great change in her life and in many ways adding to Felicia's and Rachel's burden.

Felicia at once found herself in an atmosphere of discipleship that was like heaven to her in its revelation of companionship. In the spirit of her new life, she insisted upon helping in the housework at her aunt's, and in a short time demonstrated her ability as a cook so clearly that Virginia suggested that she take charge of the cooking at the Rectangle.

Felicia entered upon this work with the keenest pleasure. For the first time in her life, she had the delight of doing something of value for the happiness of others. Her resolve to do everything after asking, "What would Jesus do?" touched her deepest nature. She developed and strengthened wonderfully.

Even Mrs. Winslow was obliged to acknowledge the great usefulness and beauty of Felicia's character. The aunt looked with astonishment upon her niece, this city-bred girl, reared in the greatest luxury, the daughter of a millionaire, now walking around in her kitchen, her arms covered with flour and occasionally a streak of it on her nose, for Felicia at first had a habit of rubbing her nose forgetfully when she was trying to remember some recipe, mixing various dishes with the greatest interest in their results, washing up pans and kettles, and doing the ordinary work of a servant in the Winslow kitchen and at the rooms at the Rectangle Settlement.

Felicia grew into the affections of Raymond people and the Rectangle folks, among whom she was known as the "angel cook." Underneath the structure of the beautiful character she was growing, always rested her promise made in Nazareth Avenue Church. "What would Jesus do?"

CHAPTER 25

Three months of great excitement followed the Sunday morning when Dr. Bruce came into his pulpit with the message of the new discipleship. Rev. Calvin Bruce hadn't realized how deep the feeling of his members flowed. He humbly confessed that the appeal he had made met with an unexpected response from men and women who were hungry for something in their lives that the conventional type of church membership and fellowship had failed to give them.

But Dr. Bruce was not yet satisfied for himself. One evening the bishop joined Dr. Bruce in his study.

They talked for some time about the results of the pledge with the Nazareth Avenue people before the bishop asked his friend, "You know why I've come to you this evening?"

Dr. Bruce shook his head.

"I have come to confess that I have not yet kept my promise to walk in His steps in the way that I believe I shall be obliged to if I satisfy my thought of what it means to walk in His steps."

Dr. Bruce rose and paced his study. The bishop remained in the deep easy chair with his hands clasped, eyes glowing with determination.

"Edward"—Dr. Bruce spoke abruptly—"I have not yet been able to satisfy myself, either, in obeying my promise. But I have at last decided on my course. In order to follow it, I shall be obliged to resign from Nazareth Avenue Church."

"I knew you would," replied the bishop quietly. "And I came in this evening to say that I shall be obliged to do the same thing with my charge."

Dr. Bruce turned and walked up to his friend. "Is it necessary in your case?" asked Bruce.

"Yes. Let me state my reasons. I'm sure they are the same as yours." The bishop paused a moment, then went on with increasing feeling. "Calvin, you know how many years I have been doing the work of my position, and you know something of the responsibility and care of it. I do not mean to say that my life has been free from burden bearing or sorrow. But I have certainly led what the poor and desperate of this sinful city would call a very comfortable, yes, a very luxurious life. And I have been unable to silence the question of late: 'What have I suffered for the sake of Christ?' Maxwell's position at Raymond is well taken when he insists that to walk in the steps of Christ means to suffer. Compared with Paul or any of the Christian martyrs or early disciples, I have lived a luxurious, sinful life, full of ease and pleasure. I cannot endure this any longer. I have not been walking in His steps. Under the present system of church and social life, I see no escape from this condemnation except to give the most of my life personally to the actual physical and soul needs of the wretched people in the worst part of this city."

The bishop rose and walked over to the window. The street in front of the house was as light as day, and he looked out at the crowds passing, then turned, and with a passionate utterance that showed how deep the volcanic fire in him burned, he exclaimed, "Calvin, this is a terrible city in which we live! Its misery, its sin, its selfishness appall my heart. The awful conditions of the girls in some great business places, the fearful curse of the drink and gambling hall, the wail of the unemployed, the countless men who see in the church only great piles of costly stone and upholstered furniture and the minister as a luxurious idler—all this as a total fact in its contrast with the easy, comfortable life I have lived fills me more and more with a sense of mingled terror and self-accusation. What have I suffered for Jesus' sake?" Dr. Bruce was very pale. Never had he seen the bishop or heard him when under the influence of such a passion. There was a sudden silence in the room. The bishop sat down again and bowed his head.

Dr. Bruce spoke at last: "Edward, I do not need to say that you have expressed my feelings also. I have been in a similar position for years. I cannot say that I have suffered any for Jesus. That verse in Peter constantly haunts me: 'Christ also suffered for us, leaving us an example, that ye should follow his steps.' The sin and misery of this great city have beaten like waves against the stone wall of my church and of this house in which I live, and I have hardly heeded them, the walls have been so thick. I have reached a point where I cannot endure this any longer. I am not condemning the Church. I love her. I am not forsaking the Church. I believe in her mission and have no desire to destroy. Least of all in the step I am about to take do I desire to be charged with abandoning the Christian fellowship. But I feel that I must resign my place as pastor of Nazareth Church in order to satisfy myself that I am walking as I ought to walk in His steps. I must come personally into a close contact with the sin and shame and degradation of this great city. And

I know that to do that I must sever my immediate connection with Nazareth Avenue Church."

Again that sudden silence fell over those two men. It was no ordinary action they were deciding. "What is your plan?" The bishop at last spoke gently, looking with the smile that always beautified his face.

"My plan," replied Dr. Bruce slowly, "is to put myself into the center of the greatest human need I can find in this city and live there. My wife is fully in accord with me. We have already decided to find a residence in that part of the city where we can make our personal lives count for the most."

"Let me suggest a place." He went on and unfolded a plan of such far-reaching power and possibility that Dr. Bruce, capable and experienced as he was, felt amazed at the vision of a greater soul than his own.

They sat up late working out the details. Their plan as it finally grew into a workable fact was in reality nothing more than renting a large building formerly used as a warehouse for a brewery, reconstructing it, and living in it in the very heart of a territory where the saloon ruled with power, where the tenement was its filthiest, where vice and ignorance and shame and poverty were congested into hideous forms. The two friends agreed to pool their money to finance the work, most of it going into the furnishing of the Settlement House.

CHAPTER 26

At Nazareth Avenue Church the simple appeal on the part of its pastor to his members to do as Jesus would do had created a sensation that still continued. Then Dr. Bruce came into his pulpit and announced his resignation, and the sensation deepened all over the city. When it became publicly known that the bishop had also announced his resignation and retirement from the position he had held so long in order to go and live himself in the center of the worst part of Chicago, the public astonishment reached its height.

"Why should what Dr. Bruce and I propose to do seem so remarkable a thing?" the bishop asked one valued friend who had almost with tears tried to dissuade him from his purpose. "If we were to resign our charge for the purpose of going to Bombay or Hong Kong or any place in Africa, the churches and the people would exclaim at the heroism of missions. Why should it seem so great a thing if we have been led to give our lives to help rescue the heathen and the lost of our own city in the way we are going to try it?"

But the public continued to talk, and the churches recorded their astonishment that two such men, so prominent in the ministry, should leave their comfortable homes, voluntarily resign their pleasant social positions, and enter upon a life of hardship, self-denial, and actual suffering.

It was fall again when the bishop came out of the Settlement one afternoon and walked around the block, intending to go on a visit to one of his new friends in the district. He had walked about four blocks when he noticed a shop that looked different from the others—a small house close by a Chinese laundry. There were two windows in the front, very clean. Then, inside the window, was a tempting display of cookery, with prices attached to the various articles that made him wonder somewhat, for he was familiar by this time with many facts in the life of the people once unknown to him. As he stood looking at the windows, the door between them opened and Felicia Sterling came out.

"Felicia!" exclaimed the bishop.

"How did you find me so soon?" inquired Felicia.

"Why, don't you know? These are the only clean windows in the block."

"I believe they are," replied Felicia with a laugh that did the bishop good to hear.

"But why have you dared to come to Chicago without telling me, and how have you entered my diocese without my knowledge?" asked the Bishop.

"Well, dear Bishop," said Felicia, who had always called him so, "I was just on my way to see you and ask your advice. I am settled here for the present with Mrs. Bascom, a saleswoman who rents out three rooms, and with one of Rachel's music pupils to whom Virginia Page has given a course of study in violin. She is from the people," continued Felicia, "and I am keeping house for her and at the same time beginning an experiment in pure food for the masses. I am an expert, and I have a plan I want you to admire and develop. Will you, dear Bishop?"

"Indeed I will," he replied.

"Martha can help at the Settlement with her violin, and I will help with my messes. You see, I thought I would get settled first and work out something, and then come with some real thing to offer. I'm able to earn my own living now."

"You are?" the bishop said a little incredulously. "How? Making those things?"

"Those things!" said Felicia with a show of indignation. "I would have you know, sir, that 'those things' are the best-cooked, purest food products in this whole city."

"I don't doubt it," he replied hastily, while his eyes twinkled. "Still, 'the proof of the pudding'—you know the rest."

"Come in and try some!" she exclaimed. "You poor Bishop! You look as if you haven't had a good meal for a month."

So they had an improvised lunch, and the bishop, who, to tell the truth, had not taken time for weeks to enjoy his meals, feasted on the delight of his unexpected discovery and was able to express his astonishment and gratification at the quality of the cookery.

"Felicia, you must come to the Settlement. I want you to see what we are doing. And I am simply astonished to find you here earning your living this way. You don't really mean that you will live here and help these people to know the value of good food?"

"Indeed I do," she answered gravely. "That is my gospel. Shall I not follow it?"

"Aye, aye! You're right. Bless God for sense like yours!"

Felicia went back with him to visit the Settlement. She was amazed at the results of what considerable money and a good deal of consecrated brains had done. As they walked through the building, they talked incessantly. She was the incarnation of vital enthusiasm, and he wondered at the exhibition of it as it bubbled up and sparkled over.

They went down into the basement, and the bishop pushed open a door. It was a small but well-equipped carpenter's shop. A young man with a paper cap on his head and clad in blouse and overalls was driving a plane as he whistled. He looked up as the two entered and took off his cap. As he did so, his little finger carried a small curled shaving up to his hair and it caught there.

"Miss Sterling, Mr. Stephen Clyde," said the bishop. "Clyde is one of our helpers here two afternoons in the week."

Just then the bishop was called upstairs, and he excused himself a moment, leaving Felicia and the young carpenter together.

"We have met before," said Felicia, looking at Clyde frankly.

"Yes, 'back in the world,' as the bishop says," replied the young man, and his fingers trembled a little as they lay on the board he had been planing.

"Yes." Felicia hesitated. "I am very glad to see you."

"Are you?" The flush of pleasure mounted to the young carpenter's forehead. "You have had a great deal of trouble since—since—then," he said.

"Yes, and you also. How is it that you're working here?"

"My father lost his money, and I was obliged to go to work. A very good thing for me. I learned the trade, hoping sometime to be of use. I am night clerk at one of the hotels. That Sunday morning when you took the pledge at Nazareth Avenue Church, I took it with the others."

"Did you?" said Felicia slowly. "I am glad."

Just then the bishop came back, and very soon he and Felicia went away, leaving the young carpenter at his work.

"Felicia," said the bishop, "did you know Stephen Clyde before?"

"Yes, 'back in the world,' dear Bishop. He was one of my acquaintances in Nazareth Avenue Church."

"Ah!" said the bishop.

"We were very good friends," added Felicia.

"But nothing more?" the bishop ventured to ask.

Felicia's face glowed for an instant. Then she looked her companion in the eyes frankly and answered, "Truly, nothing more."

CHAPTER 27

The following week, the bishop was coming back to the Settlement very late when two men jumped out from behind an old fence that shut off an abandoned factory from the street. One of the men thrust a pistol in his face, and the other threatened him with a ragged stake that had been torn from the fence.

"Hold up your hands, and be quick about it!" said the man with the pistol.

He did as he was commanded, and the man with the stake began to go through his pockets.

The bishop was not in the habit of carrying much money with him, and the man searching him uttered an oath at the small amount of change he found. As he uttered it, the man with the pistol savagely said, "Jerk out his watch! We might as well get all we can out of the job!"

"The chain is caught somewhere!" And the other man swore again.

"Break it, then!"

"No, don't break it," the bishop said. "The chain is the gift of a very dear friend."

At the sound of the bishop's voice, the man with the pistol started. With a quick movement of his other hand, he turned the bishop's head toward what little light was shining from the alleyway, at the same time taking a step nearer. Then he said roughly, "Leave the watch alone! We've got the money. That's enough!"

"Enough! Fifty cents! You don't reckon—"

Before the man with the stake could say another word, he was confronted with the muzzle of the pistol turned from the bishop's head toward his own.

"Leave that watch be! And put back the money, too. This is the bishop we've held up."

"And what of it! The president of the United States wouldn't be too good to hold up, if—"

"I say, you put the money back, or in five seconds I'll blow a hole through your head that'll let in more sense than you have to spare now!" said the other.

For a second the man with the stake seemed to hesitate; then he hastily dropped the money back into the rifled pocket.

"You can take your hands down, sir." The man lowered his weapon slowly, still keeping an eye on the other man.

The bishop slowly brought his arms to his sides and looked earnestly at the two men. In the dim light it was difficult to distinguish features.

"You can go on. You needn't stay any longer on our account." The man who had acted as spokesman turned and sat down on a stone. The other man stood viciously digging his stake into the ground.

"That's just what I am staying for," replied the bishop. He sat down on a board that projected from the broken fence.

"You must like our company."

"If you would only allow me to be of any help." The bishop spoke gently.

The man on the stone stared at the bishop through the darkness. After a moment of silence, he spoke slowly.

"Do you remember ever seeing me before?"

"No," said the bishop, "the light is not very good, and I have really not had a good look at you."

"Do you know me now?" The man suddenly took off his hat and, getting up from the stone, walked over to the bishop until they were near enough to touch each other.

The man's hair was coal black except one spot on the top of his head as large as the palm of the hand, which was white.

The minute the Bishop saw that, he started. A memory of fifteen years ago stirred in him.

"Don't you remember one day back in '81 or '82 a man came to your house and told a story about his wife and child having been burned to death in a tenement fire in New York?"

"Yes."

"Do you remember how you took me into your own house that night and spent all the next day trying to find me a job? And how when you succeeded in getting me a place in a warehouse as foreman, I promised to quit drinking because you asked me to?"

"I remember it now. I hope you have kept your promise."

The man laughed savagely. "Kept it! I was drunk inside of a week! But I've never forgotten you or your prayer. Do you remember the morning after I came to your house, after breakfast you had prayers and asked me to come in and sit with the rest? My mother used to pray! I can see her now kneeling down by my bed when I was a lad. I never forgot that prayer of yours that morning. You prayed for me just as Mother used to, and you didn't seem to take 'count of the fact that I was ragged and tough-looking and more than half drunk when I rang your doorbell. My promise not to drink was broken into a thousand pieces inside of two Sundays, and I lost the job you found for me and landed in a police station two days later." The man put his hat back on and sat down on the stone again.

The bishop did not stir. Somewhere a church clock struck one. "How long is it since you had work?" he asked.

The man standing up answered. "More'n six months since either of us did anything to tell of, unless you count 'holding up' work. I call it a pretty wearing kind of a job myself, especially when we put in a night like this and don't make nothin'."

"Suppose I found good jobs for both of you? Would you quit this and begin all over?"

"What's the use?" The man on the stone spoke sullenly. "I've reformed a hundred times. Every time I go down deeper. It's too late."

"No!" said the bishop. And never before had he felt the desire for souls burn up in him so strongly. "No!" the bishop repeated. "What does God want of you two men? He wants just what I do in this case. You two are of infinite value to Him." And then his wonderful memory came to his aid. He remembered the man's name in spite of the busy years that lay between his coming to the house and the present moment.

"Burns," he said, "if you and your friend here will go home with me tonight, I will find you both places of honorable employment. I will believe in you and trust you. Why should God lose you? But if you need to feel again that there is love in the world, you will believe me when I say, my brothers, that I love you, and in the name of Him who was crucified for our sins, I cannot bear to see you miss the glory of the human life. Come, be men! Make another try for it, God helping you. No one but God and you and myself need ever know anything of this tonight. It was the sinner that Christ came to help. I'll do what I can for you. O God, give me the souls of these two men!"

And he broke into a prayer to God that was a continuation of his appeal to the men. His pent-up feeling had no other outlet. The prayer seemed to break open the crust that for years had surrounded them and shut them off from divine communication. And they themselves were thoroughly startled by it.

The bishop ceased. Burns still sat with his head bowed between his knees. The man leaning against the fence looked at the bishop with a face in which new emotions of awe, repentance, astonishment, and joy struggled for expression. The bishop rose.

"Come, my brothers. God is good. You shall stay at the Settlement tonight, and I will make good my promise as to the work."

The two men followed him in silence. When they reached the Settlement, it was after two o'clock. He let them in and led them to a room.

"God bless you, my brothers!" he said, and leaving them his benediction, he went away.

True to his promise he secured work for them. The janitor at the Settlement needed an assistant, owing to the growth of the work there. So Burns was given the place. The bishop succeeded in getting his companion a position as driver for a firm of warehouse dray manufacturers not far from the Settlement. And the Holy Spirit began His marvelous work of regeneration.

CHAPTER 28

Later that afternoon Burns was cleaning off the front steps of the Settlement when he paused a moment and stood up to look about him. The first thing he noticed was a beer sign just across the alley. Immediately opposite were two large saloons.

Suddenly the door of the nearest saloon opened, and a strong odor of beer floated up to Burns as he stood on the steps. He took another step down, still sweeping. The sweat stood on his forehead although the day was frosty. Then he pulled himself up one step and swept over the spot he had just cleaned. Then, by a tremendous effort, dragged himself back to the floor of the porch and went over into the corner of it farthest from the saloon and began to sweep there. He swept in the corner for two or three minutes, his face drawn with the agony of his conflict. Gradually he edged out again toward the steps and began to go down them. He looked toward the sidewalk and saw he had left one step unswept. The sight seemed to give him a reasonable excuse for going down there to finish his sweeping.

He was on the sidewalk now, sweeping the last step, with his face toward the Settlement and his back turned partly on the saloon across the alley. He swept the step a dozen times. The sweat rolled over his face and dropped down at his feet.

He was down in the middle of the sidewalk now, still sweeping. He cleared the space in front of the Settlement and even went out into the gutter and swept that. He took off his hat and rubbed his sleeve over his face. He trembled all over like a palsied man and staggered back and forth as if he were already drunk. His soul shook within him.

He crossed over the little piece of stone flagging that measured the width of the alley, and now he stood in front of the saloon, looking at the sign and staring into the window at the pile of whiskey and beer bottles arranged in a great pyramid inside. He moistened his lips with his tongue and took a step forward, looking around him stealthily. As he laid his fingers on the door handle, a tall figure came around the corner.

The bishop seized Burns by the arm and dragged him back upon the sidewalk. The frenzied man, now mad for a drink, shrieked out a curse and struck at his friend savagely. The bishop picked Burns up as if he had been a child and actually carried him up the steps and into the house. He put him down in the hall and then shut the door and put his back against it.

Burns fell on his knees sobbing and praying. The bishop stood there panting with his exertion, moved with unspeakable pity.

"Pray, Burns—pray as you never prayed before! Nothing else will save you!"

"O God! Pray with me. Save me! Oh, save me from my hell!" cried Burns. And the Bishop knelt by him in the hall and prayed as only he could pray.

After that they rose, and Burns went to his room.

The bishop went out on the porch. The air of the whole city seemed to be impregnated with the odor of beer. "How long, O Lord, how long?" he prayed.

When Dr. Bruce joined him, the bishop asked, "Did you ever make any inquiries about the ownership of the property adjoining us?"

"No, I haven't taken time for it. I will now if you think it would be worth-while. But what can we do, Edward, against the saloon in this great city? It is as firmly established as the churches or politics. What power can ever remove it?"

"God will do it in time, as He has removed slavery," was the grave reply. "Meanwhile I think we have a right to know who controls this saloon so near the Settlement."

"I'll find out," said Dr. Bruce.

Two days later Dr. Bruce walked into the business office of one of the members of Nazareth Avenue Church and asked to see him a few moments. His old parishioner cordially welcomed him into his office.

"I called to see you about that property next to the Settlement where the bishop and myself now are. I am going to speak plainly, because life is too short and too serious for us both to have any foolish hesitation about this matter. Clayton, do you think it is right to rent that property for a saloon?"

The effect of the question on his old parishioner was instantaneous.

The hot blood mounted to the face of the man. Then he grew pale and dropped his head on his hands, and when he raised it again, Dr. Bruce was amazed to see a tear roll over his face.

"Doctor, since I took the pledge that morning with the others, that saloon property has been the temptation of the devil to me. It is the best-paying investment at present that I have. And yet it was only a minute before you came in here that I was in an agony of remorse to think how I was letting a little earthly gain tempt me into a denial of the very Christ I had promised to follow. There is no need, Dr. Bruce, for you to say a word more."

Clayton held out his hand, and Dr. Bruce grasped it and shook it hard. Within a month the saloon next to the Settlement was closed. The saloon-keeper's lease expired, and Clayton not only closed the property to the whiskey men, but offered the building to the bishop and Dr. Bruce to use for the Settlement work, which had now grown so large that the building they had first rented was not sufficient for the different industries that were planned.

Soon, Felicia found herself installed in the very room where souls had been lost, as head of the department not only of cooking but of a course of housekeeping for girls who wished to go out to service.

"Felicia, tell us your plan in full now," said the bishop one evening when, in a rare interval of rest from the great pressure of work, he was with Dr. Bruce, and Felicia had come in from the other building.

"Well, I have long thought of the hired girl problem," said Felicia with an air of wisdom that made Mrs. Bruce smile. "So this is what I propose to do. The old saloon building is large enough to arrange into a suite of rooms that will represent an ordinary house. Once it is arranged, then I'll teach housekeeping and cooking to girls who will afterward go out to service. The course will be six months long. In that time I will teach plain cooking, neatness, quickness, and a love of good work."

"Hold on, Felicia!" the bishop interrupted. "This is not an age of miracles!"

"Then we will make it one," replied Felicia. "I know this seems like an impossibility, but I want to try it. I know a score of girls already who will take the course, and if we can once establish something like an esprit de corps among the girls themselves, I am sure it will be of great value to them."

"Felicia, if you can accomplish half what you propose, it will bless this community," said Mrs. Bruce. "God bless you as you try."

With this blessing, Felicia plunged into the working out of her plan with the enthusiasm of her discipleship, which every day grew more and more practical and serviceable.

CHAPTER 29

The breakfast hour at the Settlement was the one hour in the day when the whole family found a little breathing space to fellowship together. It was an hour of relaxation. This particular morning the bishop read extracts from a morning paper for the benefit of the others. Suddenly he paused, and his face instantly grew stern and sad. The rest looked up and a hush fell over the table.

"Shot and killed while taking a lump of coal from a car! His family was freezing and he had no work for six months. Six children and a wife all packed into a cabin with three rooms, on the West Side. One child wrapped in rags in a closet!"

These were headlines that he read slowly. He then went on and read the detailed account of the shooting and the visit of the reporter to the tenement where the family lived. He finished, and there was silence around the table. "How awful! Where is the place, did you say?" asked Mrs. Bruce.

"It is only three blocks from here. I believe Penrose owns half of the houses in that block. They are among the worst houses in this part of the city. And Penrose is a church member."

"Yes, he belongs to the Nazareth Avenue Church," replied Dr. Bruce in a low voice.

Just as the bishop rose from the table, the very figure of divine wrath, the bell rang and one of the residents went to the door.

"Tell Dr. Bruce and the bishop I want to see them. Penrose is the name— Clarence Penrose."

The family at the breakfast table heard every word. The two men instantly left the table and went out into the hall.

"Come in here, Penrose," said Dr. Bruce, and they ushered the visitor into the reception room, closed the door, and were alone.

Clarence Penrose came from an aristocratic family of great wealth and social distinction. He was exceedingly wealthy and had large property holdings in different parts of the city. Now he faced the two ministers with a look of agitation on his face that showed plainly the mark of some unusual experience. He was very pale and his lips trembled. Penrose turned toward Dr. Bruce. "I came to say that I have had an experience so unusual that nothing but the supernatural can explain it. I was one of those who took the pledge to do as Jesus would do. And I have been living in a perfect hell of contradictions ever since. My little girl, Diana, also took the pledge with me. She's asking me a great many questions lately about the poor people and where they live. One of her questions last night touched my sore! 'Do you own any houses where these poor people live? Are they nice and warm like ours?' I went to bed, but I could not sleep. I seemed to see the judgment day. I was placed before the Judge and asked to give an account of my deeds done in the body. 'What had I done with my stewardship? How about those tenements where people froze in winter and stifled in summer? Did I give any thought to them except to receive the rentals from them? Where did my suffering come in? Would Jesus have done as I had done and was doing? Had I broken my pledge? How had I used the money and the culture and the social influence I possessed? Had I used it to bless humanity, to relieve the suffering, to bring joy to the distressed and hope to the despondent? I had received much. How much had I given?'

"All this came to me in a waking vision as distinctly as I see you two men and myself now. I had a confused picture in my mind of the suffering Christ pointing a condemning finger at me, and the rest was shut out by mist and darkness. Then the first thing I saw this morning was the account of the shooting at the coal yards. I read the account with a feeling of horror I have not been able to shake off. I am a guilty creature before God."

Penrose paused. The two men looked at him solemnly. Into that room came a breath such as before swept over Henry Maxwell's church and through Nazareth Avenue. The bishop laid his hand on the shoulder of Penrose and said, "My brother, God has been very near to you. Let us thank Him."

"Yes! Yes!" sobbed Penrose. He sat down on a chair and covered his face. The bishop prayed. Then Penrose quietly said, "Will you go with me to that house?"

For answer the two men put on their overcoats and went with him to the home of the dead man's family. From the moment he stepped into that wretched hovel of a home and faced for the first time in his life a despair and suffering such as he had read of but did not know by personal contact, he dated a new life.

One afternoon just as Felicia came out of the Settlement with a basket of food that she was going to leave as a sample with a baker in the Penrose district,

Stephen Clyde opened the door of the carpenter shop in the basement and came out in time to meet her as she reached the sidewalk.

"Let me carry your basket, please," he said.

"Why do you say 'please'?" asked Felicia, handing over the basket while they walked along.

"I would like to say something else," replied Stephen, glancing at her shyly and yet with a boldness that frightened him. He loved Felicia more every day since she stepped into the shop that day with the bishop.

"What else?" asked Felicia, innocently falling into the trap.

"Why—" said Stephen, turning his fair, noble face full toward her. "I would like to say, 'Let me carry your basket, dear Felicia.' "

Felicia never looked so beautiful in her life. She walked on a little way without even turning her face toward him. It was no secret with her own heart that she had given it to Stephen some time ago. Finally, she turned and said shyly, while her face grew rosy and her eyes tender, "Why don't you say it, then?"

"May I?" cried Stephen, and he was so careless for a minute of the way he held the basket that Felicia exclaimed, "Yes! But oh, don't drop my goodies!"

"Why, I wouldn't drop anything so precious for all the world, dear Felicia," said Stephen, who now walked on air for several blocks.

Late in the afternoon, the bishop, walking along quietly from the Penrose district, in rather a secluded spot near the outlying part of the Settlement district, heard a familiar voice say, "But tell me, Felicia, when did you begin to love me?"

"I fell in love with a little pine shaving just above your ear that day when I saw you in the shop!" said the other voice with a laugh so clear, so pure, so sweet that it did one good to hear it.

"Where are you going with that basket?" the bishop tried to say sternly.

"We are taking it to—where are we taking it, Felicia?"

"Dear Bishop, we are taking it home to begin—"

"To begin housekeeping with," finished Stephen.

"Are you?" said the bishop. "I hope you will invite me to share. I know what Felicia's cooking is."

"Bishop, dear Bishop!" said Felicia, and she did not pretend to hide her happiness. "Indeed, you shall be the most honored guest. Are you glad?"

"Yes, I am," he replied, interpreting Felicia's words as she wished. Then he paused a moment and said gently, "God bless you both!" and went his way with a tear in his eye and a prayer in his heart, and left them to their joy.

CHAPTER 30

Soon after this, the bishop and Dr. Bruce invited Henry Maxwell of Raymond to come to Chicago to speak to a remarkable gathering at the hall of the Settlement. He brought several people from the First Church with him. It is doubtful if Mr. Maxwell ever faced such an audience in his life. It is quite certain that the city of Raymond did not contain such a variety of humanity.

The audience was respectfully attentive as he told in the simplest language he could command some of the results of obedience to the pledge as it had been taken in Raymond. As Mr. Maxwell went on, faces all over the hall leaned forward in a way seldom seen in church audiences or anywhere except among workingmen or the people of the street when once they are thoroughly aroused.

The bishop and Dr. Bruce, looking on, saw many faces that represented scorn of creeds, hatred of the social order, desperate narrowness, and selfishness. They marveled that so soon under the influence of the Settlement life, the softening process already lightened the hearts of many who had grown bitter from neglect and indifference.

It was the custom at the Settlement for a free discussion to follow any open meeting of this kind. So when Mr. Maxwell finished and sat down, the bishop rose and made the announcement that any man in the hall was at liberty to ask questions, to speak out his feelings, or to declare his convictions, always with the understanding that whoever took part was to observe the simple rules that governed parliamentary bodies and obey the three-minute rule, which would be enforced on account of the numbers present.

As soon as the bishop sat down, two men began to talk at once. The bishop called them to order and indicated which was entitled to the floor. The man who remained standing began eagerly.

"This is the first time I was ever in here, and maybe it'll be the last. Fact is, I am about at the end of my string. I've tramped this city for work till I'm sick. I'd like to ask a question of the minister if it's fair. May I?"

"By all means," replied Mr. Maxwell quickly.

"This is my question." The man leaned forward and stretched out a long arm. "I want to know what Jesus would do in my case. I haven't had a stroke of work for two months. I've got a wife and three children, and I love them as much as if I was worth a million dollars. I've been living off a little earnings I saved up during the World's Fair jobs I got. I'm a carpenter by trade, and I've tried every way I know to get a job. I want to work. I've got to live, and my wife and my children have got to live. But how? What would Jesus do?"

Mr. Maxwell sat there staring at the great sea of faces all intent on his, and no answer to this man's question seemed possible. "O God!" his heart prayed. "What would Jesus do?"

At length Mr. Maxwell spoke. "Is there any man in the room, who is a Christian disciple, who has been in this condition and has tried to do as Jesus would do? If so, such a man can answer this question better than I can."

There was a moment's hush over the room, and then a man near the front of the hall slowly rose. He was an old man, and the hand he laid on the back of the bench in front of him shook as he spoke.

"I think I can safely say that I have many times been in just such a condition. I don't know as I have always asked this question, 'What would Jesus do?' when I have been out of work, but I do know I have tried to be His disciple at all times. Yes," the man went on, with a sad smile that was more pathetic than the younger man's grim despair, "yes, I have begged, and I have been to charity institutions, and I have done everything when out of a job except steal and lie in order to get food and fuel. I don't know as Jesus would have done some of the things I have been obliged to do for a living, but I know I have never knowingly done wrong when out of work."

A silence followed, broken by a fierce voice from a large, black-haired, heavily bearded man who sat three seats from the bishop. The minute he spoke nearly every man in the hall leaned forward eagerly, anxious to hear what Carlsen, the Socialist leader, had to say.

"This is all bosh, to my mind," began Carlsen. His great bristling beard shook with the deep inward anger of the man. "The whole of our system is at fault. What we call civilization is rotten to the core. We live in an age of trusts and combines and capitalistic greed that means death to thousands of innocent men, women, and children. Yet this city, and every other big city in this country, has its thousands of professed Christians who have all the luxuries and comforts, and who go to church Sundays and sing their hymns about giving all to Jesus and bearing the cross and following Him all the way and being saved! I don't say that there aren't good men and women among them, but let the minister who has spoken to us here tonight go into any one of a dozen aristocratic churches I could name and propose to the members to take any such pledge as the one he's mentioned here tonight, and see how quick the people would laugh at him for a fool or a crank or a fanatic. I don't look for any reform worth anything to come out of the churches. What we need is a system that starts from the common basis of socialism, founded on the rights of the common people—"

Carlsen was launching himself into a regular oration, when the man just behind him pulled him down unceremoniously. Carlsen subsided with several mutterings in his beard, while the next several speakers gave their opinions as to the cause of and solutions to the social ills in the city.

Finally, the bishop called time on the free-for-all and asked Rachel to sing.

When Rachel Winslow began to sing tonight at this Settlement meeting, she never prayed more deeply for results to come from her voice.

She chose the words, "Hark! The voice of Jesus calling, follow Me, follow Me!"

Henry Maxwell remembered his first night at the Rectangle in the tent when Rachel sang the people quiet. The effect was the same here. Surely this audience had never heard such a melody. How could it? The men who had drifted in from the street sat entranced by a voice that "back in the world" never could be heard by the common people because the owner of it would charge two or three dollars for the privilege. The song poured out through the hall as free and glad as if it were a foretaste of salvation itself.

CHAPTER 31

Friday morning Henry Maxwell received an invitation from the pastor of one of the largest churches in Chicago to fill the pulpit for both morning and evening service.

He hesitated but finally accepted, seeing in it the hand of the Spirit's guiding power. He would prove the truth or falsity of the charge made against the church at the Settlement meeting.

Sunday morning the great church was filled to its utmost. Henry Maxwell, coming into the pulpit from an all-night vigil in prayer, felt the pressure of a great curiosity on the part of the people. With this curiosity was something deeper, more serious. In the knowledge that the Spirit's presence was his living strength, Mr. Maxwell brought his message to that church that day.

This morning the people felt the complete sincerity and humility of a man who had gone deep into the heart of a great truth.

After telling briefly of some results in his own church in Raymond since the pledge was taken, he went on to ask the question he had been asking since the Settlement meeting. He took for his theme the story out of Luke 18 of the young man who came to Jesus asking what he must do to obtain eternal life. Jesus had tested him. "Sell all that thou hast, and distribute unto the poor, and thou shalt have treasure in heaven: and come, follow me." But the young man was not willing to suffer to that extent. "Is it true," continued Henry Maxwell, and his fine, thoughtful face glowed with a passion of appeal that stirred the people as they had seldom been stirred, "that the church of today, the church that is called after Christ's own name, would refuse to follow Him at the expense of suffering, of physical loss, of temporary gain? The statement was made at a large gathering in the Settlement last week by a leader of workingmen that it was hopeless to look to the Church for any reform or redemption of society. Are the Christians of America ready to have their discipleship tested? How about the men who possess large wealth? Are they ready to take that wealth and use it as Jesus would? How about the men and women of great talent? Are they ready to consecrate that talent to humanity as Jesus undoubtedly would do?

"Would it not be true that if every Christian in America did as Jesus would do, society itself, the business world, yes, the very political system under which our commercial and government activity is carried on, would be so changed that human suffering would be reduced to a minimum?

"What is the test of Christian discipleship? If Jesus were here today, would He not call some of the members of this very church to do just what He commanded the young man, and ask them to give up their wealth and literally follow Him?

"What would be the result if in this city every church member should begin to do as Jesus would do? It is not easy to go into details of the result. But we all know that certain things would be impossible that are now practiced by church members.

"What would Jesus do about the great army of unemployed and desperate who tramp the streets and curse the Church, or are indifferent to it, lost in the bitter struggle for the bread that tastes bitter when it is earned on account of the desperate conflict to get it?

"What would Jesus do? Is not that what the disciple ought to do? Is he not commanded to follow in His steps? What does the age need more than personal sacrifice? Is it true that the Christian disciples today in most of our churches are living soft, easy, and selfish lives, very far from any sacrifice that can be called sacrifice? What would Jesus do?

"It is the personal element that Christian discipleship needs to emphasize. Each individual Christian businessman, citizen, needs to follow in His steps along the path of personal sacrifice to Him. There is not a different path today from that of Jesus' own times. It is the same path. Nothing but a discipleship of this kind can face the destructive selfishness of the age with any hope of overcoming it.

"There is a great quantity of nominal Christianity today. There is need of more of the real kind. We need revival of the Christianity of Christ. We have unconsciously, lazily, selfishly, formally grown into a discipleship that Jesus Himself would not acknowledge. Is it possible for this church to sing with exact truth, 'Jesus, I my cross have taken, all to leave and follow Thee'? If we can sing that truly, then we may claim discipleship. But if our definition of being a Christian is simply to enjoy the privileges of worship, be generous at no expense to ourselves, have a good, easy time surrounded by pleasant friends and by comfortable things, live respectably, and at the same time avoid the world's great stress of sin and trouble because it is too much pain to bear it, surely we are a long way from following the steps of Him who trod the way with groans and tears and sobs of anguish for a lost humanity; who sweat, as it were, great drops of blood; who cried out on the cross, 'My God, my God, why hast thou forsaken me?'

"Are we ready to make and live a new discipleship? Are we ready to reconsider our definition of a Christian? What is it to be a Christian? It is to imitate Jesus. It is to do as He would do. It is to walk in His steps."

When Henry Maxwell finished his sermon, he paused and looked at the people with a look they never forgot. A great silence fell over the congregation. Everyone expected the preacher to call for volunteers who would do as Jesus would do. But Maxwell had been led by the Spirit to deliver his message this time and wait for results to come.

He closed the service with a tender prayer that kept the Divine Presence lingering very near every hearer, and the people slowly rose to go out. Then men and women in great numbers crowded around the platform to see Mr. Maxwell and to bring him the promise of their consecration to the pledge to do as Jesus would do. That was a remarkable day in the history of that church, but even more so in the history of Henry Maxwell. He left the meeting very late. He went to his room at the Settlement, and after an hour with the bishop and Dr. Bruce spent in a joyful rehearsal of the wonderful events of the day, he sat down to think over again by himself all the experience he was having as a Christian disciple.

He knelt to pray, as he always did before going to sleep, and it was while he was on his knees that he had a waking vision of what might be in the world when once the new discipleship had made its way into the conscience and conscientiousness of Christendom. He was fully conscious of being awake, but no less certainly did it seem to him that he saw certain results with great distinctiveness, partly as realities. He saw himself going back to the First Church in Raymond, living there in a simpler, more self-denying fashion than he had yet been willing to live. He saw Rachel Winslow and Virginia Page going on with their work of service at the Rectangle and reaching out loving hands of helpfulness far beyond the limits of Raymond. Rachel he saw married to Rollin Page, both fully consecrated to the Master's use, both following His steps with an eagerness intensified and purified by their love for each other. And Rachel's voice sang on, in slums and dark places of despair and sin, and drew lost souls back to God and heaven once more.

He saw Edward Norman, editor of the *News*, creating a force in journalism that in time came to be recognized as one of the real factors of the nation to mold its principles and actually shape its policy.

He saw Jasper Chase, who had denied his Master, growing into a cold, cynical, formal life, writing novels that were social successes but each one with a sting in it, the reminder of his denial, the bitter remorse that, do what he would, no social success could remove.

He saw Felicia and Stephen Clyde happily married, living a beautiful life together, enthusiastic, joyful in suffering, pouring out their great, strong, fragrant service into the dull, dark, terrible places of the great city, and redeeming souls through the personal touch of their home.

He saw Dr. Bruce and the Bishop going on with the Settlement work. He seemed to see the great blazing motto over the door enlarged, "What would Jesus do?" and by this motto everyone who entered the Settlement walked in the steps of the Master.

And now the vision was troubled. Would the church of Jesus throughout the country follow Jesus? Was the movement begun in Raymond to spend itself in a few churches like Nazareth Avenue and the one where he had preached today, and then die away as a local movement, a stirring on the surface but not to extend deep and far? He thought he saw the church of Jesus in America open its heart to the moving of the Spirit and rise to the sacrifice of its ease and self-satisfaction in the name of Jesus. He thought he saw the motto "What would Jesus do?" inscribed over every church door and written on every church member's heart.

He rose at last with the awe of one who has looked at heavenly things and with a hope that walks hand in hand with faith and love.

The
Pilgrim's Progress

John Bunyan's encounter with God transformed a poorly-educated, blaspheming tinker into a bold preacher of the gospel. As a Christian, Bunyan would also display a genius for writing, authoring more than sixty books including the classic *The Pilgrim's Progress*.

Born at Elstow, Bedfordshire, England in 1628, Bunyan attended school briefly, followed his father's vocation of repairing household utensils, and served in the Parliamentary army during the English Civil War. He then married a woman (whose name has been lost to history) who encouraged him to attend church, where he heard the Gospel. After a long internal struggle, Bunyan surrendered himself to Christ.

He soon began to preach, and the obvious change in his life brought many people out to hear him. Bunyan's messages, however, also drew the attention of government officials, who arrested him in 1660 for preaching without permission of the state church. Bunyan would spend the next twelve years in jail for his "non-conformist" ways.

During his imprisonment, Bunyan wrote some of his best works, including his spiritual autobiography *Grace Abounding to the Chief of Sinners* (1666). Bunyan's masterwork, *The Pilgrim's Progress,* was published in 1678, six years after his release from the "County Gaol."

In the final decade of his life, Bunyan continued to write and serve churches throughout his region. In 1688, on a forty-mile horseback ride to preach in London, Bunyan was caught in a heavy rainstorm and contracted a violent fever which led to his death. He was buried in Bunhill Fields, London.

A man clothed in rags and weighed down by a great burden on his back stood facing away from his own house. He opened the Bible he held in his hand, and as he read, he wept and trembled. Finally, no longer able to contain himself, he cried, "What shall I do?"

In this plight he entered his home and spoke his mind. "Oh, dear wife and children, I am distressed by this burden upon my back. Moreover, I am certain our city will be burned by fire from heaven. We shall all perish unless I find a way for us to escape."

His family was amazed—not because they thought what he said was true, but because they thought he was out of his head. They thought sleep might calm him down, so they got him to bed. But nighttime was as troubling to him as the day, and he spent the night in sighs and tears.

In the morning he declared he was worse than the night before. He spoke to them again, but they didn't want to hear him. Since sleep hadn't helped, they decided to treat his craziness by mocking, scolding, and ignoring him.

He withdrew, often alone in the fields, to pray for them and read his Bible. For some days he spent his time this way.

One day he stood in the fields and cried, "What must I do to be saved?" He looked this way and that way as if he would run, but knew not where.

A man approached. "I am Evangelist. Why are you crying so?"

The man answered, "Sir, I read in this Bible that I am condemned to die, and after that to come to judgment. I find that I am not willing to do the first, nor able to do the second."

Evangelist asked, "Why are you not willing to die, since this life is so full of evil?"

The man answered, "I fear that this burden on my back will sink me to hell. I am not ready to go to judgment. And my thoughts make me despair."

"Why then are you standing still?"

"I don't know where to go!"

"Read this." Evangelist gave him a roll of parchment that said, "Fly from the wrath to come."

The man asked, "Where should I fly?"

Evangelist pointed beyond a wide plain. "Do you see the distant wicket gate?"

"No."

"Do you see the distant shining light?"

"I think I do."

Then Evangelist said, "Follow the light and it will bring you to the gate. When you knock, the gatekeeper will tell you what to do from there."

So the man began to run. Seeing him, his wife and children cried after him to return. But the man put his fingers in his ears and ran on, crying, "Life! Life! Eternal life!"

The neighbors also came out to see him run, and some mocked, others threatened, and some cried after him to return. Two neighbors, Obstinate and Pliable, followed him and overtook him, attempting to persuade him to return with them.

He answered, "You dwell in the City of Destruction. And dying there, you will sink into a place that burns with fire and brimstone. Come along with me."

"What!" said Obstinate. "And leave friends and comforts behind?"

"Yes," answered Christian, for that was now the man's name. "Those are not worthy to be compared with what I seek. I seek an inheritance incorruptible, undefiled, that never fades away. It awaits in heaven, to be bestowed on those who diligently seek it. Read about it in my Bible."

"Phooey on your Bible," said Obstinate. "Will you go back with us or not?"

"No, because I have 'put my hand to the plow.'"

"Come, neighbor Pliable," said Obstinate, "he is a fool and wiser in his own eyes than seven men who can render a reason. Let us go home without him."

Pliable hesitated. "If what good Christian says is true, the things he looks for are better than ours. My heart longs to go with him."

"What? You are a fool, too. I will be no companion of such misled fantasies," said Obstinate and turned back. "Be wise and come back with me."

When Obstinate was gone, Christian and Pliable walked on across the plain.

"Are you certain the words of your book are true?" Pliable asked Christian.

"Yes, the Bible was made by He who cannot lie. There is an endless kingdom to inhabit, and everlasting life. We will be given crowns of glory and garments that will make us shine like the sun."

"These are pleasant thoughts," said Pliable. "What else does your Bible say?"

"There will be no more crying, no more sorrow. We shall be with seraphim, and cherubim, and creatures that will dazzle our eyes. We shall meet with tens of thousands who have gone before us, loving and holy, everyone walking in the sight of God—all well again, and clothed in the garment of immortality."

"But how can we share in that?"

"The Lord has recorded in this Bible," answered Christian, "that if we are willing to have it, He will bestow it on us freely."

"The hearing of this is enough to delight one's heart. Come, let us quicken our pace."

But Christian answered, "I cannot go as fast as I would like because of the burden that is on my back."

Because they were careless, however, they became mired in a bog in the midst of the plain called the Slough of Despond.

Pliable, angry now, cried out to Christian, "Is this the happiness and pleasure you told me about? If the journey starts out this way, what will the rest be like? If I get out of here alive, you can take your journey without me."

He pulled himself out on the side nearest his home, and he lost no time putting Christian behind him.

Christian struggled across the Slough of Despond toward the wicket gate, but he could not get out because of the burden on his back. A man approached from the other side.

"What are you doing here?" the man asked.

"I'm on my way to the gate that I may escape the wrath to come. But I fell into this slough instead."

"Why didn't you look for the steps?" asked the man.

"Fear followed me so hard, I fell in the Slough."

"I am Help." And Help plucked Christian out and bid him on his way, explaining, "The Slough of Despond cannot be mended so that travelers pass safely. It is the accumulation of scum and filth that continually runs from the conviction for sin. Because even though the sinner is awakened to his lost condition, fears and doubts and discouraging apprehensions still run from his soul and settle in the Slough. It is not the pleasure of the King that the Slough remain so bad. There are, by direction of the Lawgiver, certain good and substantial steps, placed evenly through the very midst of the Slough. Yet because of the filth the steps are hardly seen, or if they are, dizzy men fall by the side anyway."

Now Christian, walking across the plain by himself, met Mr. Worldly Wiseman, who dwelt in Carnal Policy, a very great town close to the City of Destruction. Worldly Wiseman had some inkling of Christian, because Christian's departure was already gossip in other places.

Worldly Wiseman greeted Christian and asked where he was going.

"To the wicket gate across the plain," Christian replied. "I've been told that is the entrance to the way to get rid of this heavy burden."

"Will you heed my counsel?" asked Worldly Wiseman.

"If it is good, I will."

"There is no more dangerous and troublesome way in the world than that which Evangelist has directed you. Hear me; you will meet weariness, pain, hunger, peril, sword, lions, dragons, darkness, and, in a word, death."

"But this burden on my back is more terrible to me. I don't care what I meet if I also meet deliverance from my burden."

"How did you get that burden?"

"By reading this Bible."

"I thought so. It has happened to other weak men, too. Remedy is at hand. But instead of the dangers, you will meet with safety, friendship, and content."

"Show me this secret of yours."

"In the next village of Morality, there is a gentleman whose name is Legality. He has the skill to help you rid yourself of your burden. His house is less than a mile away. If he is not at home, his son, Civility, can take care of you as well as his father would. Once you are healed, you can send for your wife and children to join you there, as there are houses standing empty and the cost of living is very reasonable."

Christian, eager to be rid of his burden, thought the advice was sound. "Sir, which is the way to this honest man's house?"

"You must go to that mountain over there. The first house is his."

So Christian went out of his way to go to Legality's house. The burden seemed even heavier, and the mountain soon loomed over the path and burst flashes of fire. Christian quaked with fear and began to be sorry he'd taken Worldly Wiseman's counsel. At that moment he saw Evangelist walking toward him and he blushed for shame.

"What are you doing here, Christian?" asked Evangelist.

Christian stood speechless before him.

"Are you not the man I spoke to outside the walls of the City of Destruction?"

"Yes, sir."

"How do you come to be here? This is out of the way I showed you.'

"A gentleman showed me a better way, short and not so rife with difficulties as the one you sent me on. But when I came to this place and saw the danger of going forward, I stopped for fear. Now I don't know what to do."

Evangelist then spoke. "God said, 'My righteous one will live by faith. And if he shrinks back, I will not be pleased with him.' You have begun to reject the counsel of the Most High. You drew back your foot from the way of peace."

Christian fell down. "Woe is me, for I am undone!"

Evangelist took his right hand. "The Lord says, 'Every sin and blasphemy will be forgiven.' So be not faithless, but believing."

Christian stood up, revived a little.

Evangelist went on, "Worldly Wiseman, who savors only the doctrine of this world, did three terrible things. First, he turned you from the way. Secondly, Worldly Wiseman disparaged the Cross to you. Thirdly, he sent you on the way to death."

Evangelist went on to explain how Worldly Wiseman almost beguiled Christian out of his salvation. The mountain looming over them was Mount Sinai. Then Evangelist called out to the heavens for confirmation.

In bursts of fire, words rumbled from the mountain: "All who rely on observing the law are under a curse, for it is written: 'Cursed is everyone who does not continue to do everything written in the Book of the Law.'"

"And no one is able to obey every law," explained Evangelist.

Christian now called himself a thousand fools for listening to Worldly Wiseman's advice. Thinking there was no hope for him now but death, he asked Evangelist, "Is it possible for me to go back to the wicket gate? Or am I abandoned and sent back in shame? Is my sin too great to be forgiven?"

"Your sin, indeed, is great," Evangelist said. "But it is forgiven. The man at the gate will receive you, for he has goodwill for men. But take heed that you do not turn aside from the way again, or you might perish."

When Evangelist had bid him Godspeed, Christian hurried back, refusing to speak to anyone, and found the way again. In time he found the wicket gate. Over the small narrow gate was written: KNOCK, AND THE DOOR WILL BE OPENED TO YOU.

He knocked, saying: "May I now enter here? Will he within open to sorry me, though I have been an undeserving rebel? Then shall I not fail to sing his lasting praise on high."

At last a serious man came to the gate. "I am Goodwill. Who knocks? From where have you come? What do you want?"

"I am a poor, burdened sinner. I come from the City of Destruction, but I am going to Celestial City, so that I might be delivered from the wrath to come. I am told this gate is the way. Are you willing to let me in?"

"With all my heart." Goodwill opened the narrow gate and yanked Christian inside.

"Why did you do that?" sputtered Christian.

"There is a strong castle near here where the devil Beelzebub is the captain. He and his army shoot arrows at those who come to this gate, in the hope they die before they enter."

"Thank you for your quick action," Christian praised Goodwill.

"Who directed you here?"

"Evangelist. He told me you would tell me what to do."

"Why do you come alone? Did no one know of your coming?"

"Yes, my wife and children saw me first and called after me to return. Then some of my neighbors joined their cry. But I refused to listen and came on my way. Still I allowed myself to stray from the path. It amazes me that I am allowed to enter now."

"We turn no one away, no matter what they have done before they come to us," Goodwill assured him. Then Goodwill beckoned Christian to follow him. "I will teach you about the way you must go. Look before you. Do you see the narrow way? That is the way you must go. It was laid out by the patriarchs, prophets, Christ, and His apostles. It is as straight as a rule can make it."

"But are there no turnings and windings by which a stranger might lose his way?"

"There are many ways that are crooked and wide, but only the right way is straight and narrow."

Then Christian asked, "Would you help me remove the burden upon my back? I have tried to do it myself, but I cannot do it without help."

"Be content to bear it until you come to the place of deliverance. There it will fall from your back of itself."

As Christian prepared to continue his journey, Goodwill told him,

"When you have gone some distance, you will come to Interpreter's home. He will show you many things that will help you on your journey."

Christian went on until he came to a house. He knocked and called out, "I am going to the Celestial City. I was told at the gate that if I called here, the Interpreter would show me excellent things."

The door opened. A man said, "I am the Interpreter. Come in."

His servant lit a candle and Christian followed the Interpreter through the house to a private room where a portrait hung on the wall. The very somber man in the picture had his eyes lifted to heaven, the Best of Books in his hand, and the Law of Truth written on his lips. The world was behind his back and a crown of gold hung over his head. The man seemed to plead with men.

"What does this mean?" asked Christian.

"This man's work is to know and unfold the darkness to sinners. He has put the world behind him for the love he has for his Master's service. I have shown you this picture first because this man is the only guide authorized by the Lord of the place where you are going. Take good heed. In your journey you will meet with some who pretend to lead you the right way, but their way leads to death."

Then Interpreter took Christian by the hand and led him into a very large parlor that was full of dust. He called for a man to sweep, who went about his job so vigorously Christian began to choke on the dust. Then Interpreter called a girl to bring water and sprinkle the room. When she finished, the room was swept and cleaned with pleasure.

"And what is the meaning of this?" asked Christian.

"This parlor is the heart of a man never sanctified by the grace of the Gospel. The dust is original sin and a lifetime of corruptions that pollute the man. The man who swept is the Law. The maiden who sprinkled water is the Gospel. Instead of cleansing the heart by its working, the Law increased sin in the heart, for it does not give power to subdue it. The Gospel vanquished sin, and the heart is made clean, fit for the King of Glory to enter."

The Interpreter took Christian into another room where two children sat in chairs. The older child, Passion, was restless. The younger child, Patience, sat quietly.

Christian asked, "What is the reason for Passion's discontent?"

The Interpreter said they had been told to wait one year for their reward. But Passion wanted it all now, while Patience was willing to wait. Then someone brought Passion a bag of treasure, which caused him to rejoice and scorn Patience. But he squandered the treasure, and it became rags.

"Explain this to me," said Christian.

"Passion is a figure for the men of this world who want everything now. Patience is a figure for the men who await that world which is yet to come. For men like Passion, they believe in the proverb 'A bird in the hand is worth two in the bush.'"

"I see that Patience has the better wisdom because he waits for the best things, and in the world to come he will have much when Passion will only have rags."

"And there is one more benefit," Interpreter added. "The rewards of the next world never wear out, while the joys of this world don't last. For first must give place to last, but last gives place to nothing, for there is not another to follow."

"I see now that it is best to wait for things to come."

"This is truth. 'For what is seen is temporary, but what is unseen is eternal.'"

Then the Interpreter took Christian into a room where a fire was burning on one wall. A fiend stood by, constantly casting water on it. Yet the fire burned ever higher and hotter.

"What does this mean?" asked Christian.

"The fire is the work of grace wrought in your heart. The man trying to extinguish the fire is the devil. Come with me."

The Interpreter led him to the other side of the wall. A figure hidden from the other room constantly cast oil from a flask into the fire.

"What does this mean?" asked Christian.

"This is Christ, who constantly maintains the fire already begun in your heart with the oil of His grace. It is hard for the tempter to see how the work of grace is maintained in the heart."

Then the Interpreter took Christian to a pleasant place with a beautiful, stately palace. Upon the upper balcony, several people, clothed in gold, walked.

"May we go in?" Christian asked.

The Interpreter led him toward the door of the palace. A large group of men stood around the door, wanting to go in but not having the courage to go farther. Off to the side a man sat at a table with a book and an inkwell, waiting to take the name of any who entered. In the doorway stood many armored men resolved to hurt any who attempted to enter the palace.

A bold man approached the man at the table and said, "Write down my name, sir."

With that the bold man drew his sword, donned a helmet, and fiercely fought his way through the armed men at the door. Finally he prevailed and entered the palace. Inside, a pleasant voice sang: "Come in, come in: Eternal glory you shall win." And the man was clothed in many fine garments.

"I know the meaning of that," said Christian. "Let me get on the way."

"No," said the Interpreter. "Not until I have shown you more."

He led Christian into a very dark room, where a man sat in an iron cage. The man's eyes were lowered, his hands folded together, and he sighed as if heartbroken. The Interpreter encouraged Christian to talk with the man.

"Who are you?" asked Christian.

"I am what I was not at one time."

"Then what were you?"

"I once was a successful professor, both in my own estimation and in the eyes of others. Once I thought I was on the path for the Celestial City, and had the joy of anticipation of my arrival there."

"What are you now?"

"I am a man of despair, locked in this iron cage."

"But how did you get into this condition?"

"I sinned against the light of the Word and the goodness of God. I have grieved the Spirit, and He is gone. I tempted the devil, and he is come to me. I provoked God to anger, and He has left me. I have so hardened my heart I cannot repent. Oh, eternity! Eternity!"

Then Christian turned to the Interpreter and asked, "Is there no hope for this man?"

"Ask him," said the Interpreter.

"There is no hope," the man in the iron cage said in answer to Christian's question.

"But the Son of the Blessed is compassionate and merciful."

"I have crucified Him afresh. I have despised His person and His righteousness, I have counted His Blood an unholy thing and have despised the Spirit of grace. Therefore all that remains for me is certain judgment."

"Why did you bring yourself into this condition?"

"For the lusts, pleasures, and profits of this world that brought me much delight. But now they bite me and gnaw at me like a burning worm."

Then the Interpreter said to Christian, "Remember this man's misery and let it be an everlasting caution to you."

Christian said, "God, help me shun the cause of this man's misery. Is it not time for me to go?"

"Wait until I show you one thing more."

The Interpreter led Christian into another room. A man rose from a bed, trembling.

"Why does this man tremble in this way?" Christian asked the Interpreter, who bade the man to answer.

The man said, "I dreamed that the heavens above were black, and it thundered, and the lightning flashed. Suddenly a trumpet blasted. In flaming fire was a Man on a cloud, attended by thousands. A voice said, 'Arise, you dead. Come to judgment.' The rocks broke apart, the graves opened, and the dead that were buried there came to life. Some of them were very glad and looked upward, but some hid themselves under the mountains. Then the Man on the cloud opened a book and bid them all to draw near. But a fierce flame kept the people from drawing too near, so that the distance between was as the distance between the judge and the prisoners. A voice cried, 'Gather together the tares, the chaff, and the stubble. Cast them into the burning lake.' A bottomless pit opened, emitting smoke and hideous noises. 'Gather My wheat into the barn,' cried the voice. Many people were carried away up to the clouds. But I was left behind! I tried to hide myself, but I could not, for the Man that sat upon the cloud kept His eye on me. My sins came into my mind, and my conscience accused me on every side. Then I woke up. . . ."

"But what made you so afraid of the dream?" Christian asked.

"I thought the Day of Judgment was come, and that I was not ready for it. But what frightened me most was that the angels gathered up several others and left me behind. My conscience bothered me, and the Judge constantly watched me, showing indignation in His countenance."

"Have you considered these things?" the Interpreter asked Christian.

"Yes, and they put me in hope and fear."

"Remember them so they will keep you in the way you must go."

Then Christian prepared to continue his journey.

The Interpreter sent him on his way, saying, "The Comforter is always with you, good Christian, to guide you in the way that leads to the Celestial City."

So Christian went on his way, saying:

"Here I have seen things rare and profitable,
Things pleasant, dreadful, things to make me stable
In what I have begun to take in hand;
Then let me think on them, and understand
What it was they showed me, and let me be
Thankful, oh good Interpreter, to see."

The way was fenced on either side by a wall called Salvation. Christian ran, but not without great difficulty because of the burden on his back. He came to a rise, and there stood a cross, and below it a sepulcher. Just as he came to the cross, the burden fell from his back and tumbled into the mouth of the sepulcher.

With a grateful heart, Christian said, "He has given me rest by His sorrow, and life by His death." Then he stood awhile to look and wonder that the sight of the cross had eased his burden so easily.

As he stood looking at the cross and weeping, three Shining Ones came to him. "Peace be with you," they said. And one added, "Your sins are forgiven." Another stripped him of his rags and clothed him in an embroidered coat and other rich garments. The third put a mark on his forehead and gave him a rolled certificate with a seal. "Look at it as you go," said the Shining One, "and present it at the Celestial Gate."

Christian gave three leaps for joy and went on the way singing:

"How far I did come laden with my sin;
Nothing could ease the grief that I was in,
Until I came here: What a place is this!
Can this be the beginning of my bliss?
Is this where the burden falls from my back?
Can this be where the ropes of bondage crack?
Bless'd cross! Bless'd sepulcher! Blessed rather be
The Man who there was put to shame for me!"

When he came to the bottom of the hill, he saw three men fast asleep a little way off the road. Their ankles were chained. Christian cried, "Wake up and flee. I will help you take off your leg irons. The devil prowls like 'a roaring lion.' You will surely become prey for his teeth."

"I see no danger," said the one called Simple.

"After a little more sleep," answered the man called Sloth.

"Every tub must stand on its own bottom," said the third, Presumption. "Leave us alone."

And the men fell asleep again.

Christian went on, troubled that the men had so little regard for his offer of help. Soon he saw two men come tumbling over the wall onto the narrow way. They hurried to catch up with Christian.

"Where did you come from?" Christian asked. "And where are you going?"

"We are Formalist and Hypocrisy," they said. "We were born in Vain-Glory, and we are going to the Celestial City to get praise."

"Why didn't you come in at the gate at the beginning of the way? Don't you know that it is written: 'The man who does not enter by the gate, but climbs in by some other way, is a thief and a robber'?"

They replied, "It's too far away. So our custom for more than a thousand years is to take a shortcut, as you saw."

"But won't it be counted a trespass against the Lord of the Celestial City? Did you not violate His revealed will?"

"Don't trouble yourself," Formalist and Hypocrisy said. "We have tradition on our side, and they had witnesses who could prove they had not strayed from the accepted."

"But will your tradition pass a trial at law?"

"Since the tradition is one of long standing, any impartial judge would now consider it legal. We are on the way, just as you are. So why is your condition any better than ours?"

"I walk by the rule of my Master. You walk by the rude working of your own devices. The Lord of the Way already considers you thieves. So I doubt you will be found true men at the end of the way. You came in by yourselves without His direction, and you shall go out by yourselves—without His mercy."

The two men didn't answer. For a time they went along silently.

"We keep the laws and ordinances as conscientiously as you do," Formalist and Hypocrisy said. "Therefore we don't see how you are different from us, except for your coat. But we understand that some of your neighbors gave it to you to hide the shame of your nakedness."

"But laws and ordinances will not save you, since you didn't come in by the door," Christian explained. "However, the Lord of Celestial City gave me my coat to cover my nakedness. I take it as a token of His kindness to me, for I had nothing but rags. You may not have noticed, but I have a mark on my forehead. One of my Lord's most intimate associates placed it there the day my burden fell off my shoulders. Moreover, they gave me this sealed roll to comfort me by reading it as I go on the way, and when I arrive at the Celestial City, I am to give it back at the gate as a token of my salvation. All these things you lack because you didn't come in at the gate."

The two looked at each other and laughed. As they continued on the way, Christian stayed in front of his two companions. All three continued on the way, with Christian in the front. He often refreshed himself reading in the roll.

Soon they came to a spring at the foot of the Hill of Difficulty. Christian drank from the spring and saw that the narrow way went straight up the hill.

Christian began to go up the hill, saying:

"This hill, though high, I do long to ascend;
To me the difficulty won't offend.
For I perceive the way to life lies here:
Come pluck up, heart, let's neither faint nor fear;
Better, though difficult, the right way to go,
Than wrong, though easy, where the end is woe."

~

Two other paths went around the base of the hill. Supposing that it would lead them back to the path Christian was on, one of the two men following Christian took the path called Destruction. It led him into a wide field full of dark mountains where he stumbled and fell and rose no more. The other took the path called Danger, which led him into a great wood.

As Christian ascended, he fell to clamber on his hands and knees because of the steepness. About halfway up was a pleasant arbor made by the Lord of the Hill for weary travelers. Christian sat down to rest and read his roll for comfort. Pleased, he fell asleep, and the roll slipped from his hand.

When it was almost night, someone found Christian sleeping and startled him from sleep, saying: "Go to the ant, you sluggard; consider its ways and be wise!"

Ashamed, he scrambled all the way to the top of the hill. Two men rushed toward him. "Sirs, what's the matter that you run the wrong way?" cried Christian.

"We were on our way to the Celestial City, but the farther we go, the more danger we meet with," said a man called Timorous. "Therefore we turned around to go back."

"Before us were a couple of lions," said the other man, Mistrust. "We don't know if they were awake or asleep. But we were afraid that if we came within their reach, they would rip us to pieces."

"You make me afraid, too," said Christian. "But where would I flee for safety? Going back to my own country is sure death. It is destined for fire and brimstone, and I will certainly die there. If I can but get to the Celestial City, I am sure to be safe. So to go back is nothing but death. Going ahead is fear of death, and beyond it, everlasting life! I will go forward."

Timorous and Mistrust scurried down the hill. Thinking about what they had told him, Christian felt for his roll for comfort, and he discovered it was gone. In great distress, he tried to think where he might have lost it. Then he remembered falling asleep in the arbor. He fell on his knees and asked God to forgive him for his foolish sleeping. Then he went back to look for his roll, bewailing his sinful sleep: "Oh, what a wretch I am!"

On the way he looked on each side of the path in case it had fallen on the way. Back at the arbor, his sorrow renewed. "How could I sleep in the daytime? Why did I sleep in the midst of difficulty? Why did I indulge the flesh selfishly and take advantage of the arbor the Lord of the Hill erected only for the relief of pilgrims? What a waste of time that I should walk this part of the path three times over, when I should only have done it once!"

Finally he looked under the settee where he sat, and he spied his roll. He picked it up and placed it into his breast pocket for safekeeping.

Who could know his joy at finding his rolled certificate? It was the assurance of his life, acceptance at the Celestial Gate. He thanked God for directing his eye to the roll.

Nevertheless, he went on his way, nimbly climbing the hill once again. But when the sun set, he bewailed his bad fortune that had him walking in the dark. He remembered the story that Timorous and Mistrust had told him about the lions.

Suddenly, he saw ahead a stately palace beside the way. He rushed ahead, hoping to get lodging there. He entered a very narrow passage leading to the porter's lodge, and saw the two lions just ahead. Afraid, he thought of turning around as Timorous and Mistrust had. For now nothing but death was before him. He stopped. Should he go back?

The porter at the lodge, whose name is Watchful, saw that Christian had stopped, and shouted to him. "Is your strength so small? Don't fear the lions. They are chained and are there to test the genuineness of your faith. Keep in the middle of the path, and you will not be harmed."

Trembling, Christian went past the lions. He heard their roars, but they did him no harm. Then he clapped his hands and ran to the porter's gate. "Sir, what palace is this?" he cried to the man who had yelled encouragement.

"This Palace Beautiful was built by the Lord of the Hill for the relief and security of pilgrims," Watchful answered. "Where are you from and where are you going?"

"I come from the City of Destruction, and I'm going to the Celestial City."

"What is your name?"

"My name is now Christian, but my name at first was Graceless."

"The sun is set. Why are you so late?"

After Christian recounted his foolishness in losing his roll, the porter said, "I will call out one of the virgins. If she likes your talk, she will take you in to the rest of the family." He rang a bell.

Out came a beautiful but very serious maiden named Discretion.

"This is Christian, and he is on his way from the City of Destruction to the Celestial City. He has asked for lodging here tonight. After you have talked with him, you can do what seems best, even according to the law of the house."

She asked him many questions. Finally she smiled with tears in her eyes. She called out several more members of her family: Prudence, Piety, and Charity. They, too, questioned him before inviting him into the palace, saying, "Come in, you who are blessed. The Lord of the Hill built this palace for us to entertain the pilgrims along the way."

Then he bowed his head and followed them into the palace. He sat down, and they gave him something to drink. The four women decided to question Pilgrim further while they waited for supper.

Piety asked, "What moved you at first to become a pilgrim?"

"The fear that unavoidable destruction awaited me." And Christian went on to describe his journey.

"But how did it happen that you came out of your country this way?"

"It was under God's control. When I was under the fear of destruction, I didn't know where to turn. But by chance Evangelist sought me out, and he directed me to the wicket gate where I found the way."

"Didn't you come by the house of the Interpreter?" Piety asked.

"Yes," Christian said. "And I saw many things there that will stick with me as long as I live."

"What else have you seen along the way?"

"I went a short way from the Interpreter's house, where I saw One hanging and bleeding on a cross. The very sight of Him made my burden fall off my back."

Piety asked Christian a few more questions about the things he'd seen along the way.

Then Prudence asked him, "Do you not yet bear some worldly desires?"

"Yes, but greatly against my will. My carnal impulses are now my grief," Christian answered. "I would love to never think of these things again. But when I want to do the best things, that which is worst is with me."

"What is it that makes you desire to go to the Celestial City?" asked Prudence.

"Why, I hope to see Him alive who did hang dead from the Cross. I hope to be rid of all those things in me that to this day are an annoyance. There they say there is no death. To tell you the truth, I love Him because He eased my burden. I am weary of my inner sickness. I long to be where I shall never die, with the company that shall continually cry, 'Holy, Holy, Holy is the Lord God Almighty.'"

Charity asked, "Aren't you a married man?"

"I have a wife and four boys."

"Why did you not bring them along with you?"

Weeping, Christian said, "Oh, how I wish I had! But they were against my going on pilgrimage."

"But you should have talked to them and tried to have shown them the danger of being behind," Charity persisted.

"I told them what God had showed to me of the destruction of our city.

But I seemed to them as one that mocked, and they believed me not."

"And did you pray to God that He would bless your counsel to them?"

"Yes, and that with much affection, for you must know that I love my wife and children very much."

"Did you tell them of your own sorrow and fear of destruction?"

"Over and over and over. But still I was unable to persuade them to come with me."

"But what reason did they give for not coming with you?"

"My wife was afraid of losing this world, and my children loved the foolish delights of youth. So they left me to follow this path alone. I know I'm not perfect, but nothing I did or said could persuade them to join me."

After that they sat down to a supper of rich food and fine wine. All their talk was about the Lord of the Hill. They saw Him as a great warrior who had fought and slain he who had the power of death. He did it with the loss of much blood. But that which put glory of grace into all that He did was that He did it from pure love. Some in the household said they had seen Him since He died on the Cross, and no greater love of poor pilgrims was to be found from the east to the west. Thus they talked until late at night.

After they prayed and asked their Lord for protection, they went to bed. Christian slept in a large upper chamber of the Palace Beautiful called Peace.

In the morning he awoke to the rising sun and sang:

"Where am I now? Is this the love and care
Of Jesus, for the men that pilgrims are,
He did provide? That I should be forgiven,
And dwell already the next door to heaven!"

His hosts told him he shouldn't leave until they had showed him the rarities of the palace. In the study they showed him the pedigree of the Lord of the Hill, that He was the Son of the Ancient of Days, from an eternal generation. Here also were recorded more fully the acts He had done, and the names of many hundreds He had taken into His service. Then they read some of the worthy acts His servants had done, how they had "conquered kingdoms, administered justice, and gained what was promised; who shut the mouths of lions, quenched the fury of the flames, and escaped the edge of the sword; whose weakness was turned to strength; and who became powerful in battle and routed foreign armies."

Then they read testimonies that showed how willing their Lord was to receive into His favor all mankind, even though in time past they had offered great affronts to His person and working. There also were several other histories that spoke of things both ancient and modern, together with accounts of the fulfillment of certain prophecies and predictions that brought fear upon His enemies and comfort to His pilgrims.

The next day they took him into the armory and showed him all kinds of armor the Lord had provided for pilgrims: sword, shield, helmet, breastplate, prayer, and shoes that would not wear out. There was enough to outfit as many men for the service of the Lord as there are stars in the heavens. They also showed him Moses' rod; the hammer and nail with which Jael slew Sisera; the trumpets, pitchers, and lamps with which Gideon put to flight the armies of Midian; the ox's goad Shamgar used to slay six hundred men; the jawbone with which Samson fought; the sling and stone with which David killed Goliath; and the sword their Lord will use to kill the Man of Sin in the last days.

On the third day, Christian planned to take up his pilgrimage once more. But the day was clear, and they took him to the top of the palace to show him the view. They told him to look south. When he did, he saw a most pleasant mountainous country in the distance, with woods, vineyards, fruits of all sorts, flowers, and springs and fountains.

"What country is this?" Christian asked.

"Emmanuel's Land," they said. "It is as well known as the Hill of Diffiiculty for all pilgrims. When you get there you'll be able to see the gates of the Celestial City. Any of the shepherds there will be happy to show you."

Again, Christian desired to be on his way.

"But first," his hosts said, "let us go again to the armory." And there they outfitted him from head to foot with armor, to protect him should he meet with assaults on the way.

Thus equipped, Christian walked with his friends Discretion, Piety, Charity, and Prudence down the hill.

As they passed the porter at the gate, Christian asked, "Have you seen any pilgrims pass by the gate?"

"Yes," the porter replied.

"Did you know him?"

"He told me his name is Faithful."

"Oh, I know him," Christian said. "He is a fellow townsman, a near neighbor, from the place where I was born. How far ahead of me is he?"

"He should be at the bottom of the hill by now."

So Christian and his friends went on together till they came to the where the path started downhill.

"It appears to be as dangerous going down as it was coming up," he said.

"Yes," said Prudence. "It is hard for a man to go down into the Valley of Humiliation without tripping. That is why we are going with you."

So Christian began the downhill trek very carefully. Yet he still slipped once or twice.

At the bottom of the hill his good companions gave him a loaf of bread, a bottle of wine, and a sack of raisins.

And Christian went his way.

Christian had gone but a little way in the Valley of Humiliation when he spied a foul fiend coming over the field to meet him. Afraid, Christian anxiously thought about whether to turn back or to stand his ground. But when he realized he had no armor for his back and to turn around would give the fiend the greater advantage to pierce him with his darts, he resolved to stand his ground.

So he went on until the fiend stood before him. The monster was hideous to behold. Scaled like a fish, he had wings like a dragon and feet like a bear. Out of his belly came fire and smoke. His mouth was fanged like a lion.

The fiend looked down on Christian with disdain. "Where do you come from? And where are you going?" demanded the monster.

"I come from the City of Destruction, which is a place of evil, and I am going to the Celestial City."

"By this I perceive you are one of my subjects, for all that evil country is mine. I am Apollyon, the prince and god of that land. Why have you run away from your king? Were it not for the hope that you may do me more service, I would strike you now with one blow to the ground."

"I was born in your dominions, but your service was hard, and your wages were not enough for a man to live on. 'For the wages of sin is death.' So I want to heal myself. I am going to the Celestial City."

"No prince will so lightly lose his subjects. Since you complain about my service and wages, go back to the City of Destruction. What my country can afford, I promise to give you."

"I have given myself to the King of Princes. How can I go back with you?"

"You have done according to the proverb, and exchanged bad for worse. But it is very common for those who have professed themselves His servants to return to me. If you do so as well, all shall be well."

"I have given Him my faith and sworn my allegiance to Him. How can I go back from this and not be hanged as a traitor?"

"You did the same to me," Apollyon said. "Yet I am willing to forget it all if you will turn again and go back."

"What I promised to you was done when I was too young to know better. The Prince under whose banner I now stand is able to absolve me and pardon all I did in compliance to you. Besides, I like His service, His wages, His servants, His government, His company, and His country better than yours. Therefore, leave me alone. I am His servant, and I will follow Him."

"Reconsider your ways with a cool head. Do you not know how many of His servants have been put to shameful deaths? Besides, He never came personally to deliver any who served Him in my country. Yet how many times have I delivered, either by power or fraud, those who have faithfully served me? In the same way will I deliver you."

"He waits to deliver them purposefully, to try their love, whether they will stay with Him to the end. As for the bad end you say they come to, that is glory to their account. His servants don't expect immediate deliverance, preferring to wait until the Prince does come in His glory."

"You have already been unfaithful to Him. Why would you think He will pay you wages for that?"

"When have I been unfaithful to Him?" demanded Christian.

"You almost choked in the Slough of Despond. You tried various ways to rid yourself of your burden when you should have waited until your Prince took it off. You sinfully slept and lost your roll. You almost turned back at the sight of the lions. And when you speak of your journey and what you have heard and seen along the way, you inwardly desire praise in all you say and do."

"All that is true, and much more. But the Prince I serve is merciful and ready to forgive."

Then Apollyon broke out in a terrible rage. "This Prince is my enemy. I hate His person, His laws, and His people. I have come out on purpose to stand against you."

"Apollyon, beware what you do, for I am in the King's highway, the way of holiness. Therefore, take heed to yourself."

Then Apollyon straddled the way. "I am unafraid in this matter. Prepare to die." He threw a flaming spear.

Christian blocked it with his shield. Then spears came as thick as hail. Christian had wounds on his head, hand, and foot. He backed up and Apollyon followed. Christian again took courage and resisted as best he could The combat lasted half a day, Apollyon roaring hideously the whole time. Christian grew weaker and weaker.

Sensing his opportunity, Apollyon rushed Christian to wrestle him. Christian fell, and his sword flew from his hand.

"I am sure of victory now," roared Apollyon.

But as Apollyon drew back for his last blow, Christian's groping hand found his sword. "Do not gloat over me, my enemy! Though I have fallen, I will rise." With that he gave Apollyon a deadly thrust, which made him stumble back as one who had received a mortal blow.

Christian came at him again, saying, "'Nay, in all these things we are more than conquerors through Him that loved us.'"

When the monster saw Christian ready to thrust again, he spread his wings and sped away.

When the battle was over, Christian said, "I will give thanks to Him who has delivered me out of the mouth of the lion." In gratefulness, he sang:

"Great Beelzebub, the captain of this fiend,
Designed my ruin; therefore to that end
He sent the fiend out harnessed, in a rage,
So hellish he did fiercely me engage:
But blessed Michael helped me, and I,
By dint of sword, did quickly make him fly:
To Michael's help, let me give lasting praise,
And thank, and bless His holy name always."

❧

Then came to him a hand with leaves from the Tree of Life. Christian applied them to his wounds, and they healed immediately. He ate the bread and drank the wine that had been given to him at the Palace Beautiful. Then, sword drawn, he left the valley to enter another: the Valley of the Shadow of Death!

Christian had to go through this valley because the way to the Celestial City lay through the middle of it. The prophet Jeremiah described it as a wilderness, a land of deserts and of pits, a land of drought and of the shadow of death, a land that no man but a Christian passes through, a land where no man dwells.

When Christian arrived at the border of the valley, two men ran toward him. "Back! Back!" they cried. "If you prize either life or peace."

"What have you met with?" asked Christian.

"Why, the valley itself, which is dark as pitch. We also saw hobgoblins, satyrs, and dragons of the pit. We heard continual howling and yelling of people in unspeakable misery, bound in irons. Overhead hang clouds of confusion. Death hovers everywhere. It is dreadful—utter chaos."

"But it is the only way to my desired haven," Christian said.

"Fine for you, but we will not choose it for ours," the men said before they parted from Christian.

So Christian went on, with his sword drawn in his hand in case he should be assaulted. On his right hand yawned a very deep ditch, into which the blind had led the blind for all ages. On his left hand there was a very dangerous quagmire with no bottom. The pathway here was very narrow, making it difficult for Christian to stay out of the ditch on the right and the quagmire on the left. Christian sighed bitterly when he frequently encountered such darkness that he could not see where to place his feet as he moved forward.

Soon he came closer to flames and smoke shooting out in such abundance, with sparks and hideous screams, that his sword was no good now. He had another weapon: prayer. He continued on for a long way with the flames reaching toward him. He heard many mourning voices, rushing feet, so that he thought he might be torn in pieces or trodden down in the streets. He cried, "I call 'on the name of the Lord': Oh Lord, save me!"

Coming to a place where he thought he heard a pack of fiends creeping toward him, he stopped. He had half a thought to go back, but knew the danger of going back might be more than the danger of going forward. Yet the fiends came nearer and nearer.

He cried out in a fiery voice, "I will walk 'in the strength of the Lord'!"

The fiends disappeared.

But now Christian was so confused he did not know his own voice. After he passed the burning pit, one of the wicked ones stepped behind him. The fiend suggested wicked blasphemies to Christian, making him believe they came from his own mind. Distressed to think that he could now blaspheme the One he loved so much before, he knew that if he could have helped it, he would not have done it.

After some considerable time, he thought he heard a voice ahead: "Even though I walk through the Valley of the Shadow of Death, I fear no evil, for You are with me."

Christian calmed. Someone else who feared God was in this valley whom he hoped to meet soon. And God was with him. As he walked on, he called to him he had heard but received no answer. When morning came, Christian looked back into the dark to see what he'd gone through. He was deeply moved by his deliverance from such dangers.

Yet as the sun was rising, he could see the valley before him was, if possible, far more dangerous. The way was full of snares, traps, and nets here, and full of pits, steep slopes, and deep holes there. Had it been as dark as it had been the first part of the way, a thousand souls would have been lost there.

Christian said, "His lamp shines upon my head, and by His light I walk through darkness."

In this light Christian came to the end of the valley. At the end of this valley lay blood, bones, ashes, and mangled bodies of men who had gone this way before.

Then he sang:

"Oh, world of wonders! (I can say no less)
That I should be preserved in the distress
That I have met with here! Oh, blessed be
The hand that from it has delivered me!
Dangers in darkness, devils, hell, and sin
Surrounded me while I was in this glen:
Yes! Snares and pits and traps and nets did lie
About my path, so worthless silly I
Might have been snared, entangled, and
*   cast down:*
But since I live, let Jesus wear the crown."

&

Now as Christian topped a small rise, he saw ahead of him a pilgrim.

Christian yelled, "Wait up, and I will be your companion."

Faithful looked behind him but did not stop. So Christian called again for him to wait.

But Faithful called back: "I cannot pause—the Avenger of Blood is behind me."

Christian exerted himself and ran him down. As he went ahead of Faithful, Christian tripped and fell and couldn't rise again until Faithful came up to help him.

Christian said, "I am glad that I have overtaken you and that God has so changed our spirits we can be companions on this pleasant path."

"I had hoped, dear friend, to have your company directly from our town. But you got the start on me. Therefore, I was forced to come this far of the way alone."

"How long did you stay in the City of Destruction before you set out after me?"

Faithful said, "Until I could stay no longer. There was much talk in town about your desperate journey, for that is what they call your pilgrimage. But I believed, and still do, fire and brimstone from above will destroy our city. Therefore, I made my escape."

"Did you hear no talk of neighbor Pliable?"

"He has been had in great derision. Hardly anyone will give him work. He is seven times worse off than if he had never gone to the Slough of Despond. People mock and despise him as a turncoat!"

"But why are they so against him, since they also despise the way that he forsook?"

"They call him a turncoat, saying he was not true to his profession. I think God has stirred up even his enemies to hiss at him and make him a proverb because he has forsaken the way."

"Did you talk to him before you left?"

"He crosses the street to avoid me. He is ashamed of what he did. So I never spoke to him."

"Well, when I first set out, I had hopes of that man. But now I fear he will perish in the overthrow of the city. For it has happened to him according to the true proverb, 'A dog returns to its vomit.' But let us leave him and talk of things that more immediately concern ourselves. What have you met on the way?"

"I escaped the slough that I heard you fell into, and got to the gate without that danger. I was sorely tempted by a woman named Wanton at the wicket gate, but I went my way."

"What did she do to you?"

"You cannot imagine what a flattering tongue she had. She promised me all manner of content if I would turn aside."

"But she did not promise you the content of a good conscience."

"No, so I shut my eyes so that I would not be bewitched with her looks. Then she scolded me, and I went away."

"Did you meet with no other assault as you came?"

"When I came to the foot of the Hill of Difficulty, I met an old man named Adam the First. He lives in the town of Deceit and offered to pay me if I would live with him. I asked him what work he had for me, and he said his work was many delights. And he would make me his heir. He offered me his three daughters: Lust of the Flesh, Lust of the Eyes, and Pride of Life. And I was inclined to go until I saw written on his forehead: PUT OFF THE OLD MAN WITH HIS DEEDS. And it came burning into my mind that he was going to make me a slave. So when I refused and pulled away, he pinched me so hard I thought he had a piece of my flesh. When I got halfway up the Hill, a man overtook me and beat me until I thought I was dead. He said he served Adam the First."

"That was Moses," said Christian. "He does not know how to show mercy to those who break the Law."

"Yes. He would doubtless have killed me, if someone had not stopped him."

"And who was that?"

"I did not know Him at first, but soon saw the holes in His hands and side. I was saved by the Lord of the Hill."

"Did you see the Palace Beautiful?"

"Yes, and the lions, too, but they were asleep. However, because I had so much of the day before me, I passed by the porter and came down the hill."

"He told me about it. But I wish you had called at the palace. They would have showed you so many rarities that you would scarce have forgotten them to the day of your death. Who did you meet in the Valley of Humiliation?" asked Christian.

"I met Discontent. He told me the valley was without honor. And if I were to wade through this valley, I would offend all our friends: Pride, Arrogance, Self-Conceit, and Worldly Glory. I told him they were indeed relatives of mine, for they are according to the flesh. But since I became a pilgrim, they disowned me. And I reject them. Moreover I told him he had misrepresented the valley, because before honor is humility and a haughty spirit before a fall. Therefore, I told him, I'd rather go through this valley to the honor received from the Wise One than choose that which Discontent esteemed most worthy of our affections."

"Who else did you meet?"

"Shame. He said religion is a pitiful, low, sneaking business for a man to care about, a tender conscience is unmanly, and a man who watches his words and ways is to be ridiculed. He also said that few of the mighty, rich, and wise were ever of this opinion. It is shameful to repent or make restitution after a sermon. It is shameful to ask forgiveness for a petty fault. Religion alienates a man from the great because of a few vices, though he called those vices by much finer names."

"What did you say?"

"At first I couldn't think of what to say. Then I remembered that which man holds in high esteem is an abomination to God. I said he only told me what men are. He told me nothing about God or the Word of God. On the Day of Judgment, life and death are not determined by the world but by God's wisdom and law. So what God says is best, even though all men in the world reject it. So I told him to leave me because God prefers His Word and a tender conscience, declares those who make themselves fools for the kingdom of heaven as truly wise, and makes the poor man who loves Christ richer than the greatest man in the world. I said he was an enemy to my salvation, and I refused to have anything to do with him. But still he attempted to point out other weaknesses of religion. At last I told him that it was useless for him to continue with his accusations because in those things he disdained, I saw the most glory. And when I was rid of him at last, I sang:

"The trials that those pilgrims meet withal,
Who are obedient to the heavenly call,
Are many kinds and suited to the flesh,
And come, and come, and come again afresh.
So now, or sometime else, we by them may
Be taken, overcome, and cast away.
Oh, let the pilgrims, those astride the way,

Be vigilant, behave like saints today."

❧

"I'm glad you withstood the villain so bravely," said Christian. "I think he has the wrong name. He attempts to make pilgrims ashamed before all men, but he has no shame in his audacity. He promotes the fool. The wise will inherit glory, but shame promotes fools."

"We must cry to Him for help against Shame, for He would have us be valiant for truth upon the earth."

"Well said," Christian said. "Who else did you meet in the valley?"

"No one. I had sunshine all the rest of the way through the Valley of Humiliation, and also through the Valley of the Shadow of Death."

Christian then spoke of his battle with Apollyon and the darkness in the Valley of the Shadow of Death.

The path became very wide, and walking beside them was a man who at first appeared tall and handsome, yet became homelier the closer he got to them.

"Are you going to the Heavenly Country?" called Faithful.

"The same place," answered the man.

"May we have your good company? We will talk of things that are profitable."

"To talk of things that are good is very acceptable to me," answered the man. "With you or anyone else. I'm glad that I have met with those who desire such a good thing. Too many talk of things of no profit. This is a problem for me."

"I agree it is a problem," Faithful said. "For what is a worthier use of men's tongues and mouths than the things of the God of heaven?"

"I like you very well, for your speech is full of conviction. I will add, what is so profitable as to talk of the things of God? What things are so pleasant? And if a man loves to talk of the history or the mystery of things, miracles, wonders, or signs, where shall he find things so sweetly penned as in the Holy Scripture?"

"That's true," Faithful replied. "We should strive to gain profit from such things in our conversations."

"As I said, to talk of such things is most profitable. A man may get knowledge of many things, such as the emptiness of earthly things and the benefit of things above. More particularly, by conversation a man may learn the necessity of the new birth, the insufficiency of good works, and the need of Christ's righteousness. A man may learn what it is to repent, to believe, to pray, to suffer, or the like. By this also, a man may learn what are the great promises and consolations of the Gospel, to his own comfort. Even more, a man may learn to refute false opinions, to vindicate the truth, and also to instruct the ignorant."

"All this is true, and glad am I to hear these things from you."

"Indeed, few understand the necessity of a work of Grace in their soul in order to gain eternal life, but live ignorantly in the works of the Law, by which no man can obtain the kingdom of heaven."

"By your leave," added Faithful, "heavenly knowledge such as this is the gift of God. No man can hope to attain them by works or only the talk of them."

"All this I know very well. For a man can receive nothing except it be given him from heaven. All is of grace, not of works. I could give you a hundred scriptures to confirm this truth," the man replied.

"So what is the one thing that we shall talk about at this time?"

"Whatever you want. I will talk of heavenly or earthly things, moral or evangelical, sacred or profane, past or future, things foreign or domestic, essential or circumstantial," the man said. "Provided that all that is said or done is for our profit."

At this, Faithful began to wonder about their companion, and turning to Christian, he whispered, "What a brave companion have we got? Surely this man will make a very excellent pilgrim!"

Christian smiled and said, "This man, with whom you are so taken, will beguile twenty strangers with his tongue."

"Do you know him?" asked Faithful.

"Better than he knows himself."

"Who is he, then?"

"His name is Talkative," Christian answered. "He dwells in our town. I'm surprised that you don't know him."

"Who is his father? Where in town does he live?"

"He is the son of Say-Well. He lived in Prating-Row. He's well known in that part of town. In reality, he's a pitiful man, in spite of his glib tongue."

Faithful said, "Well, he seems to be a very pleasant fellow."

"He is to those who don't know him well. He reminds me of the work of the Painter, whose pictures show best at a distance but unpleasing when viewed close at hand."

"I think you must jest, because you smiled just now."

"God forbid that I should jest in this matter or that I should accuse any falsely. Talkative adapts to any company or talk. He talks as well in a tavern. He has no religion in his heart or his home. They are as empty of religion as the white of an egg is of flavor. Religion is only on his tongue."

"Then I am greatly deceived."

"Remember: 'The kingdom of God is not a matter of talk but of power.' This man talks of prayer, repentance, faith, and the new birth. But he knows only to talk of them. I have been in his family and have observed him both at home and about town. What I say of him is the truth. His house is as empty of religion as the white of an egg without flavor. He neither displays any indication he prays or repents of his sin. Talkative is the shame of religion. A brute serves God better than he.

"The people who do know him say he is 'a saint abroad, and a devil at home.' I know his family finds that proverb true. He is so rude and unreasonable his servants have no idea how to do their jobs or speak to him. Men who have had business dealings with him say that he goes beyond all others in fraud, deception, and unscrupulous behavior. And he's bringing up his sons to be as him. He has caused many men to stumble and fall. And if God doesn't prevent it, he will be the ruin of many more."

Said Faithful, "I am inclined to believe you, not only because you say it but also because you've made this report as a Christian man. I can't imagine why you would say these things out of ill will."

"If I hadn't known him, I might have thought of him as you first did," Christian assured his friend. "In fact, if the enemies to religion had given this assessment of Talkative's character, I would have thought it slander. But all I have spoken about him I can prove him guilty of. Good men are ashamed of him because they can call him neither brother nor friend. Just his name makes them blush if they know him."

"Well, I see that saying and doing are two things. From now on I will better observe this distinction."

"The very soul of religion is the practical part: 'Pure religion and undefiled before God and the Father is this, To visit the fatherless and widows in their affliction, and to keep himself unspotted from the world.' But Talkative thinks that hearing and saying will make a good Christian. He deceives his own soul. Hearing is just the sowing of the seed, and talking is not sufficient to prove that the fruit of the seed is in the heart and life. The end of the world is compared to our harvest with our fruit. There nothing can be accepted that is not of faith."

"I am not fond of him now. What shall we do to be rid of him?" Faithful asked.

"Take my advice, and do as I bid you," Christian answered. "You will find that he'll be sick of your company, too, unless God touches his heart and turns it."

"What shall I do?"

"Go to him and enter into some serious discourse about the power of religion. Ask him plainly whether religion is set up in his heart, house, or conversation."

Then Faithful called to Talkative, "How does the saving grace of God manifest itself, when it is in the heart of a man?"

"So we speak about the power of things? It's a very good question, and I'm happy to answer you. First, where the grace of God is in the heart, it causes a great outcry against sin. Secondly—"

"Wait a moment," interrupted Faithful. "I think it shows itself by inclining the soul to abhor its sin."

"Why, what's the difference between crying out against sin and abhorring sin?"

"Oh, a great deal: A man may cry out because of a law against it, but he cannot abhor it unless he has a godly antipathy against it. What was your second point?"

"Great knowledge of the Gospel mysteries."

"That is also false. Great knowledge may be obtained in the mysteries of the Gospel and yet not work as grace in the soul. Consequently he would not be a child of God. A man may know like an angel, and yet be no Christian; therefore your sign is not true. Indeed, to know is a thing that pleases talkers and boasters; but to do is that which pleases God. Not that the heart can be good without knowledge, for without that, the heart is nothing. There is therefore knowledge and *knowledge*—knowledge that rests in the bare speculation of things, and knowledge that is accompanied with the grace of faith and love—which puts a man upon doing even the will of God from the heart. The first of these will serve the talker, but without the other, the true Christian is not content. If a man 'can fathom all mysteries and all knowledge' but has not love, he is nothing," countered Faithful. "What is another point?"

"None. I see we shall not agree."

"Well, if you won't give another point, will you give me permission to do it?"

"You may use your liberty."

"A work of grace in the soul shows, either to him who has it or to others who observe it. To the one who has it, it gives him conviction of sin, especially whatever defiles his nature and the sin of unbelief. Because of his sinful condition and the battle between it and grace, he finds the Savior of the world revealed in him. According to the strength or weakness of his faith in his Savior, so is his joy and peace and love for holiness, as well as his desire to know Him more and to serve Him in this world. Others see in his life an inner abhorrence to sin, a desire to promote holiness in the world, not by talk only but by a practical subjection in faith and love to the power of the Word. Now, sir, if there is anything you object to in what I've spoken, please do so. If not, then give me permission to offer a second question for discussion."

"My part is not to object now, but to hear. Let me have your second question."

Faithful said, "It is this: Do you experience the first part of the description of it? And does your life and conversation testify the same? Or is your religion based in word or conversation, and not in deed and truth? Please, if you decide to answer me in this, say no more than you know the God above will say amen to and also nothing but what your conscience can justify in you."

Talkative flushed angrily. "You now speak of experience, conscience, and God, and to appeal to Him for justification of what is spoken. This kind of discourse I did not expect, nor am I disposed to give an answer to such questions, because I'm not bound by it. I refuse to make you my judge. But please tell me why you ask me such questions."

"Because of your willingness to talk, and because I didn't know if you had anything else but empty words. Besides, to tell you all the truth, I have heard of you that you are a man whose religion lies in talk, and that your conversation gives your mouth-profession the lie. They say that religion fares the worse for your ungodly conversation, that some already have stumbled at your wicked ways, and that more are in danger of being destroyed because of your words. The proverb is true of you, which is said of immoral women: she is a shame to all women. So you are a shame to all followers."

"Since you are ready to listen to gossip and to judge so rashly as you do, I cannot but conclude that you are some irritable, dismal man. You are not my judge. You are not fit to be talked to. Good-bye."

Christian joined Faithful. "I told you how it would happen. Your words and his lusts could not agree. He would rather leave your company than re-form his life. But he is gone. Let him go," said Christian. "The loss is no one's but his own. He has saved us the trouble of leaving him. Besides, the Apostle says, 'From such withdraw thyself.'"

Faithful said, "I am glad we have had this conversation with him. It may happen that he will think of it again. I have dealt plainly with him and so am clear of his blood if he perishes."

"You did well to talk so plainly as you did. Men to whom religion is only a word make religion stink in the nostrils of many," said Christian. "I wish all such men could be dealt with as you have dealt with Talkative. Religion would enter their hearts, or the company of saints would be too hot for them."

Faithful sang:

"How Talkative at first lifts up his plumes!
How bravely does he speak. How he presumes
To overwhelm all minds near! But as soon
As I did speak of heart, like waning moon,
He shrivels to an ever smaller part:
And so do all, but those who know the heart."

࿇

Thus they talked of what they had seen on the way, and so made the way easy, instead of tedious. For now they went through wilderness. They were almost out of the wilderness when they saw someone coming after them.

"It is my good friend Evangelist," said Christian.

"And mine, too," said Faithful, "for he showed me the way to the gate."

"Peace be with you, dearly beloved," called Evangelist, "and peace be with your helpers."

"Welcome, my good Evangelist," Christian said. "Seeing you brings to my remembrance your ancient kindness and unwearied labor for my eternal good."

"And a thousand times welcome," said Faithful. "Your company, O sweet Evangelist, is beneficial to us poor pilgrims!"

"How has it fared with you, my friends, since our last parting? What have you met with, and how have you behaved yourselves?"

Christian and Faithful told him of all the things that had happened to them on the way.

"Right glad I am," said Evangelist, "that you have been victors. The day is coming when both he who sows and they who are reaped shall rejoice together. The crown is before you, and it is an incorruptible one. So run that you may obtain it. Be careful that no one comes in and takes it from you. Hold fast. You are not out of gunshot of Beelzebub. Let the kingdom be always before you and believe steadfastly concerning things that are invisible. Let nothing that is on this side of the other world get within you. And above all, look well to your own hearts and to the lusts thereof, for they are deceitful above all things, and desperately wicked. Set your faces like a flint. You have all power in heaven and earth on your side."

Christian said, "We well know you are a prophet. Tell us what is going to happen to us."

"My sons, you have heard in the words of the truth of the Gospel that you must go through many tribulations to enter into the kingdom of heaven. And that in every city, bonds and afflictions abide in you. You cannot expect that you should go long on your pilgrimage without them, in some sort or other. You have found something of the truth of these testimonies upon you already, and more will immediately follow. For now, as you see, you are almost out of this wilderness. You will soon come into a town, and you will be beset with enemies who will strain hard to kill you. One or both of you will seal your testimony with blood. But be faithful unto death, and the King will give you the crown of life. He who shall die there, although his death will be unnatural and his pains perhaps great, will arrive at the Celestial City sooner and escape many miseries of the rest of the journey. So when you are come to the town and shall find fulfilled what I have here related, then remember your friend, and quit yourselves like men, and commit the keeping of your souls to your God, as unto a faithful Creator."

When Christian and Faithful came out of the wilderness, they entered the town of Vanity. The town had kept a fair the year around and called it Vanity Fair because the town is lighter than vanity and everything sold at the fair is vanity.

Almost five thousand years ago, Beelzebub, Apollyon, and Legion with their companions set up the fair because Vanity was on the way to the Celestial City. At the fair, pilgrims could find houses, lands, trades, places, honors, promotions, titles, countries, kingdoms, lusts, pleasures, and delights of all sorts—whores, wives, husbands, children, masters, servants, lives, blood, bodies, souls, silver, gold, pearls, precious stones, and whatnot. To be seen were juggling, games, plays, fools, apes, knaves, and rogues. And for nothing there were thefts, murders, adulteries, cheats, and slanders. Every pilgrim to the Celestial City had to go through this town. Even the Prince of Princes went through the town to His own country. Beelzebub would have made Him Lord of the fair, would He have revered him as He went through the town. He was such a person of honor the devil showed Him all the kingdoms of the world that he might entice Him to cheapen and buy some of his vanities. But the Blessed One left Vanity without spending one penny.

Christian and Faithful entered the city, and they attracted intense interest. Their garments were like none other at the fair, made out of material that couldn't be found there. The people watched them closely, casting judgment. Some said they were fools, some called them madmen, and others said they were from a strange place. Their speech set them apart from the people of Vanity, and only a few could understand them. They naturally spoke the language of Canaan, holy things, but those who kept the fair were men of this world. As they walked past the many booths, Christian and Faithful didn't even look at the wares. When someone called on them to buy, they put their fingers in their ears and cried, "Turn away my eyes from seeing vanity." They kept their gazes upward, and they indicated their trade and wares were in heaven.

On seeing the way Christian and Faithful carried themselves through the town, one seller mockingly said, "What will you buy?"

But they looked gravely at him and said, "We buy the Truth."

At that, many openly despised the pilgrims the more—some mocking, some taunting, some speaking reproachfully, and some calling upon others to smite them. The confusion in the fair was so great, all order was destroyed. Word reached Beelzebub, who quickly came down and had some of his most trusted friends bring in the men for interrogation.

Those who examined them asked, "Where did you come from? Where are you going? And why are you in Vanity, wearing such unusual clothing?"

Christian and Faithful said they were pilgrims going to their heavenly Jerusalem. They hadn't given any reason to the men of the town or the sellers at the fair to ridicule them, except to say, when asked what they would buy, that they would buy Truth.

The interrogators did not believe them and said the two were either madmen or troublemakers. They beat them and smeared them with dirt. They put them in a cage, so they would be a spectacle at the fair. They lay for some time and were made the objects of any man's sport, malice, or revenge, laughing still at all that befell them.

The two remained patient, giving good words for bad, kindness for injuries.

Some less prejudiced people at the fair thought the men were treated unfairly. Angered, the merchants let fly at their accusers again, counted them as bad as the men in the cage, and told them that they seemed allies and should be made partakers of their misfortunes. The other replied that for all they could see, the men were quiet and sober and intended nobody any harm. They pointed out that there were many who traded in their fair who were more worthy to be put into the cage, and pillory, too, than were the men they abused. Thus, after many words had passed on both sides, they fell to some blows among themselves and did harm one to another.

Even though Christian and Faithful were quiet and calm throughout the fights, they were again brought before their examiners for more questioning. They were charged with being guilty of the latest hubbub in the fair. So the two poor men were beaten and marched in leg irons to terrorize the others, lest any more should further speak in their behalf or join them. But Christian and Faithful behaved themselves yet more wisely and received the humiliation and shame that was put on them with such meekness and patience that it won to their side several of the men in the fair.

This put the other party yet into a greater rage, insomuch that they concluded the death of these two men. Wherefore they threatened that neither cage nor irons should serve their turn, but that they should die for the abuse they had done, and for deluding the men of the fair. This time they were threatened with death. So they were sent back to the cage and their feet put into stocks until further order should be taken with them.

While they remained in the cage, they remembered what they had heard from their faithful friend Evangelist, and they were the more confirmed in their ways and sufferings because of what he told them would happen to them. They also now comforted each other, that whose lot it was to suffer, even he should have the best; therefore each man secretly wished that he might have that advancement. But contentedly committing themselves to Him who rules all things, they lived in the condition in which they were until they should be otherwise disposed of.

On the day that was set, they were brought to trial before their enemies and arraigned. They were indicted on these charges: that they were enemies to the people and disturbers of their trade; that they were the cause of the civil unrest and divisions in the town; and that they had followers to their most dangerous opinions in contempt of the law of their prince.

Judge Hate-Good made Faithful the first prisoner of the bar.

In answer to the charges against him, Faithful said that he had only set himself against that which had set itself against Him who is higher than the Highest. "As for disturbance, I make none, being myself a man of peace. The followers who chose to follow us were won by beholding our truth and innocence and are only turned from the worse to the better. As for the king you speak of, since he is Beelzebub, the enemy of our Lord, I defy him and all his angels."

Then a proclamation was made that they who had anything to say for their lord the king against the prisoner at the bar should come forward with their evidence. Then three witnesses were sworn in: Envy, Superstition, and Opportunist. They were then asked if they knew the prisoner at the bar and what they had to say for their king against him.

Envy testified first. "My lord, I have known this man a long time. This man is one of the vilest men in our country. He has no regard for prince or people, law or custom. He does all he can to persuade all men of his principles of faith and holiness. I heard him say Christianity and the customs of our town are diametrically opposite, and could not be reconciled. By which saying, my lord, he does at once condemn not only all our laudable doings, but also us in the doing of them. I could say much more, but I don't want to bore the court. If any charge be lacking, I will be glad to enlarge my testimony against him."

The judge requested him to stand by until the rest of the testimony was heard.

Superstition was then called and testified. "I have no great acquaintance with this man, nor do I desire to have further knowledge of him. However, I do know that he is a pestilent fellow from some of the discourse I had with him the other day in this town. I heard him say that our religion was nothing and that it could by no means please God. In fact, his saying was that the people of Vanity worship in vain, are in sin, and shall be damned!"

Then the third witness was sworn in and testified. "I have known this fellow for a long time," said Opportunist. "I have heard him speak things that ought not be spoken. He not only has railed against our noble Prince Beelzebub, but also has spoken contemptibly of our prince's honorable friends the Lord Carnal-Delight, the Lord Luxurious, the Lord Vain-Glory, my old Lord Lechery, and Sir Greedy. Moreover, he has said that if all men were of his mind, there is not one of these noblemen should have any place in this town. He has not been afraid to rail on you, my lord. He called you, Judge, an ungodly villain and many other vilifying terms."

"Renegade! Heretic! Traitor!" yelled Judge Hate-Good to Faithful. "Have you heard the charges by these honest gentlemen?"

"May I speak a few words in my defense?" asked Faithful.

"You don't deserve to live any longer, and you will be slain immediately after the proceedings. Yet, so all men may see our gentleness to you, let us hear what you have to say."

"In answer to Envy's charge, I only said that any prince or people or law or custom against the Word of God is also against Christianity. If this is spoken amiss, convince me of my error, and I am ready to recant before you. As to Superstition's charge, I said that in the worship of God there is required a divine faith, but there can be no divine faith without a divine revelation of the will of God. Therefore, whatever is thrust into the worship of God that is not agreeable to divine revelation cannot be done but by a human faith which will not profit to eternal life. Finally, in response to Opportunist, ignoring the part where he said I 'railed,' I say that the prince of this town along with all the rabble, the attendants Opportunist named, are more fit for hell than for this town and country. Lord, have mercy on me."

Then the judge spoke to the jury. "Gentlemen of the jury, you see this man about whom so great an uproar has been made in this town. You have also heard what these worthy gentlemen have witnessed against him. Also you have heard his reply and confession. It now lies in your breasts to hang him or save his life, but I think it appropriate to instruct you in our law.

"There was an act made in the days of Pharaoh, servant to our prince, that in case those of a contrary religion should multiply and grow too strong for him, their males should be thrown into the river. There was also an act made in the day of Nebuchadnezzar, another of his servants, that whoever would not fall down and worship his golden image should be thrown into a fiery furnace. There was also an act made in the days of Darius, that whoever called upon any God but him should be cast into the lions' den. Now the substance of these laws this rebel has broken, not only in thought but also in word and deed.

"Pharaoh's law was made to prevent mischief, no crime being yet apparent; but here is a crime apparent. For the second and third, you see he disputeth against our religion, and for the treason he has confessed. He deserves to die."

Then the judge sent the jury out. In its chamber they deliberated. Everyone gave his private verdict against Faithful among themselves, and afterward they unanimously concluded to bring him in guilty before the judge.

The jury foreman, Blind-Man, said, "I see clearly this man is a heretic."

No-Good said, "Rid the earth of this fellow."

"I hate the very looks of him," agreed Malice.

Love-Lust added, "I could never endure him."

"Nor I," Live-Loose said. "He would always be condemning my ways."

"Hang him. Hang him," reasoned Brainy.

High-Mind muttered, "A sorry scrub indeed."

"My heart is black toward him," snarled Enmity.

"He is a rogue," said Liar.

Cruelty insisted, "Hanging is too good for him."

Hate-Light said, "Let's get rid of him."

Implacable had the final opinion: "If I had all the world given to me, I could not be reconciled to him. Let's vote him guilty of death."

Therefore Faithful was condemned to be put to the cruelest death that could be invented.

They therefore brought Faithful out to punish him according to their law. First, they scourged him. Then they beat him. Then they stabbed him with knives. After that they stoned him. Then they slashed him with swords. Then they burned him to ashes at the stake. Thus, Faithful died.

Unseen to the multitude, a chariot and a couple of horses stood behind the crowd, waiting for Faithful. As soon as he died, Faithful was put in the chariot and was carried up through the clouds to the sound of trumpets and off to the Celestial Gate.

Christian was given a short reprieve and sent back to prison where he remained for a while. And He who rules all things brought it about that Christian escaped his cage.

And Christian left Vanity mourning:

"Well, Faithful, you have faithfully professed
Unto your Lord, with Him you shall be blessed;
When faithless ones, with all their vain delights,
Are crying out under their hellish plights:
Sing, Faithful, sing, and let your name survive;
For though they killed you, yet are you alive."

As Christian fled Vanity, a man named Hopeful joined him. And hopeful he was, made so by beholding the words and behavior of Christian and Faithful in their sufferings at the fair. Thus, one died testifying to the truth; another rose from his ashes to accompany Christian in his pilgrimage. Hopeful told Christian many more people at the fair would follow on the pilgrimage, but it would take time.

The two pilgrims soon overtook a man. "How far do you go this way? And where are you from?" they asked.

"I'm going to the Celestial City. I'm from the town of Fair-Speech."

"Fair-Speech?" Christian asked. "Is there any good that lives there?"

"Yes," the man said, "I hope."

"What is your name, sir?" Christian asked.

"I am a stranger to you and you to me. If you're going this way, I shall be glad of your company. If not, I must be content."

Christian said, "This town of Fair-Speech, I have heard of it. As I remember, they say it's a wealthy place."

"Yes, it is," the man agreed.

"Who are your relatives there?"

"Almost the whole town. I have many rich relatives there. In particular Lord Turn-About, Lord Time-Server, and Lord Fair-Speech himself. Also

Smooth-Man; Facing-Both-Ways; Anything, the parson of our parish; and Two-Tongues, my mother's brother. To tell the truth, I have become a gentleman of good quality. And to think my grandfather was just a waterman, looking one way and rowing another. I earned most of my wealth in the same way."

"Are you married?" Christian asked.

"Yes, and my wife is a very virtuous woman from a very honorable family, daughter of Lady Feigning. My wife has arrived at such a fineness of breeding that she knows how to maintain her composure with every social level from prince to peasant. It's true we differ in religion from those of a stricter sort, yet only on two small points. First, we never strive against wind and tide. Secondly, we are most zealous when religion goes in his silver slippers. We love to walk with him in the street, if the sun shines and people applaud him."

Then Christian stepped closer to Hopeful to speak to him privately. "I'm pretty sure that this is By-Ends of Fair-Speech. If so, we have as deceitful a man with us as dwells in all these parts."

Hopeful said, "Ask him. I don't think he should be ashamed of his name."

Christian turned to the other man and asked, "Sir, you talk as if you knew something more than all the world does. And I believe I know who you are. Is not your name By-Ends?"

"That is not my name. It is a nickname given to me by those who cannot stand me. I must be content to bear that reproach. I never gave an occasion to earn the name."

"But did you never give a reason for men to call you by this name?"

"Never! Never! The worst that ever I did to give them a reason was that I have always been lucky, that's all. I count it a blessing, and don't allow the malicious to reproach me."

"I thought indeed that you were the man that I've heard of. However, I believe this name belongs to you more properly than you are willing to believe."

"Well, I can't help what you think. You'll still find me fair company, if you will still accept me as your associate."

"If you go with us, you must go against wind and tide, which is against your opinion. And you must be loyal to religion in rags as well as silver slippers. You must be ready to stand by him whether he is bound in irons or walks the streets with everyone's applause."

"You must not impose your faith," said By-Ends, "nor lord it over my faith. Let me go with you in freedom."

"Not a step farther, unless you will do as we believe," said Christian.

"I won't desert my principles, since they are harmless and profitable. If I can't go on with you, then I will go on by myself. I'll wait until someone comes along who will be glad of my company."

So Christian and Hopeful left By-Ends behind and kept their distance ahead of him. But before long, they noticed that three men following By-Ends came up with him. The men gave him a very low bow in greeting. By-Ends welcomed them since they were former schoolmates: Hold-the-World, Money-Love, and Save-All. Their schoolmaster had taught them the art of getting either by violence, fraud, flattery, lying, or religion.

Money-Love said to By-Ends, "Who are they upon the road before us?"

"They are a couple of far countrymen who are going on pilgrimage according to their own way."

"Why did they not stay that we might have had their company? Are we not all on the same pilgrimage?"

"We are, indeed," said By-Ends. "But the men in front of us are so rigid and so love their own notions and lightly esteem the opinions of others that if a person doesn't believe the same way in all things, they thrust him out of their company."

Save-All spoke: "That's bad. But we read of some who are overly righteous. Such rigidness makes them judge and condemn all but themselves. But in what did you differ?"

"They conclude that it is their duty to keep going on the way in all weather, and I wait for wind and tide. They are willing to hazard all for God, while I am for taking all advantages to secure my life and estate. They will hold their beliefs even if everyone is against them, but I am for religion that is in keeping with the times and doesn't hazard my safety. They are for religion that will keep them in poverty and makes them hold in contempt all others. However, I am for him when he walks in his golden slippers in the sunshine and gives me praise."

Hold-the-World said, "Stay with your beliefs, By-Ends. Those men are fools who, having liberty to hang on to the pleasures of this world, instead let go of them. Let us be content to take the fair weather with us and not the rain. I like that religion best that will give us the security of God's blessing. Why would God withhold any good thing from us and keep them for Himself?'

With that, the four men agreed with one another and spoke no more of the two men in front of them.

By-Ends then asked innocently, "Then let's look for a better diversion from things that are bad. Suppose a minister or a tradesman had an opportunity to get the good blessings of life, but only if he had to become very zealous on some point of religion he never bothered with before. May he not get the blessings and still be an honorable man?"

Money-Love spoke right away: "I see what you are getting at, and I'm willing to shape an answer. Let's take the minister first. If he can benefit from such a small alteration of principle, I see no reason why he can't do it and still be an honest man. After all, the desire for blessings is lawful and the opportunity is set before him by Providence. Besides, his desire makes him a more studious, a more zealous preacher and a better man before God. His people won't mind if he denies to serve them some of his principles. That will prove he has a self-denying temperament and a sweet and winning personality, making him even more fit for the ministry. So I conclude that a minister who changes a small for a great should not be judged as covetous, but rather, since he is improved in his parts and industry, he pursues his call and the opportunity to do good.

"Now as to the tradesman, suppose such a one has a poor business, but by being religious, he can improve his market, maybe even get a rich wife. I see no reason why this is not lawful. To become religious is a virtue. Nor is it unlawful to get a rich wife. By becoming good himself, he gets a good wife and good customers and good profit."

The others applauded Money-Love for a wholesome and advantageous answer. They decided that because Christian and Hopeful were still within sight and hearing they would ask them the same question. So they called after the two men before them, who stopped and waited for them.

After greeting the two men, Hold-the-World gave out the original question. Then he asked, "What do you think, Christian?"

"A babe in religion could answer that. Only heathens, hypocrites, devils, and witches would make Christ and religion a stalking-horse to get worldly riches. To answer the question affirmatively, as I perceive you have done, and to accept as authentic such an answer is heathenish, hypocritical, and devilish. Your reward will be according to your works."

With that reprimand, the four men grew sullen and fell behind.

"If they cannot stand before a man, how will they stand before God? And if they are mute when dealt with by vessels of clay, what will they do when they shall be rebuked by the flames of a devouring fire?" asked Christian.

Christian and Hopeful went far ahead until they came to a narrow plain called Ease to come to a hill called Lucre. In that hill was a silver mine, which because of its rarity had lured many pilgrims to leave the path to investigate it. But the ground around it was not stable, and the pilgrims fell into the pit and perished. Those who didn't die bore permanent injuries and could not be their own selves again.

A man at the side of the road called to them, "Come over here, and I will show you a silver mine. With a little sweat, you may get rich."

"Let us go and see," said Hopeful.

"Not I," said Christian. "I have heard of this place. Many have died here. And the treasure is a snare to those who seek it, for it keeps them from their pilgrimage." And he called to Demas, "Is not the place dangerous?"

"Only to those who are careless," answered the man, blushing.

Christian said to Hopeful, "Let's not stir a step but keep on our way."

"I'll guarantee you that if By-Ends receives the same invitation, he will turn aside to see," said Hopeful.

"No doubt," Christian agreed. "His principles will lead him that way, and he will die there."

The man called out again, "But will you not come over and see?"

"You are an enemy to the righteous ways of the Lord, Demas," called Christian. "And you have already been condemned by one of His Majesty's judges for your own turning aside. Why do you seek to bring us into like condemnation?"

"But I also am a pilgrim. If you will wait a little, I will walk with you."

"Is not your name Demas?" Christian asked.

"Yes, that is my name. I am the son of Abraham."

"I know you," Christian said. "You have trod in the steps of Gehazi and Judas. It is an evil prank you use. Your father was hanged for a traitor, and you deserve no better reward. Be assured that when we come to the King, we will give Him word of your behavior."

So Christian and Hopeful went on their way. And Christian sang:

"By-Ends and Silver Demas both agree;
One calls, the other runs, that he may be

A partner in his Lucre; thus such fools
Are lost in this world that the devil rules."

&

The pilgrims came to a place where a monument stood by the side of the way. When they saw it, they were both disturbed, for it seemed as if a woman had been transformed into a pillar. Hopeful saw written above the head the words REMEMBER LOT'S WIFE.

Christian said, "This comes opportunely after the invitation from Demas."

"I am sorry I was so foolish. I wonder, what difference is there between her sin and mine? She only looked back, and I had a desire to go see. Let grace be adored, and let me be ashamed that ever such a thing was in my heart."

"Let us take notice of what we see here for our help for time to come. This woman escaped one judgment, the destruction of Sodom. Yet she was destroyed by another."

"True, and she may be to us both caution and example—caution that we should shun her sin; example to beware. But above all this, I wonder how Demas and his fellows can stand so confidently yonder to look for that treasure when this woman, just for looking behind her, was turned into a pillar of salt. Especially since she stands within sight of where they are. They can't help but see her if they look up."

"It is something to wonder about. It argues that their heart is grown desperate in this case. It is said of the men of Sodom that they were sinners exceedingly because they were sinners before the Lord. That is, in His eyesight and notwithstanding the kindnesses that He showed them, they provoked Him the more to jealousy and made their plague as hot as the fire of the Lord out of heaven could make it. It leads to the conclusion that despite such visible examples set continually before them to caution them to the contrary, they must be partakers of the severest of judgments."

"What a mercy it is that I myself was not made this example," Hopeful said. "She is a caution to both of us. We should thank God, fear Him, and always 'remember Lot's wife.'"

They went on their way and soon reached a pleasant river. It seemed David's River of God, John the Baptist's Water of Life. Their way lay on the bank of this river, and they walked with great delight. The pilgrims drank of the water, which was pleasant and enlivening to their weary souls. On both banks of the river were green trees with all kinds of fruit. The leaves of the trees were good for medicine, and the fruit was delicious. On either side of the river was a meadow, beautified by lilies. It was green all year long. Here they slept safely. When they awoke, they gathered fruit and drank the water of the river. This they did for several days and nights.

They sang:

"Behold, you, how these crystal streams do glide
To comfort pilgrims by the highway side.
The meadows green besides their fragrant smell,
Yield dainties for them: And he who can tell
What pleasant fruits and leaves these trees do yield,
Will soon sell all, so he can buy this field."

❧

When Christian and Hopeful decided to continue on their way, they ate and drank and left the peaceful meadow. They had not journeyed far when the river and the path they followed parted. They were sorry to leave the river behind, but they dared not go out of the way. However, the way from the river was rough and their feet were tender because of their travels. So the souls of the pilgrims were discouraged, and they wished for a better way.

A little way ahead of them, on the left side of the road, was By-Path Meadow. In the meadow a path went along the way.

"Why shouldn't we walk over there?" asked Christian as he climbed onto the stile to look into the meadow. "Come, Hopeful, that path is easier going."

"But what if the path should lead us out of the way?"

"That's not likely. Does the path not parallel the way?"

So they crossed a stile that spanned the fence and walked the path in the meadow. Ahead of them walked a man. Christian called, "Who are you? And where does this path go?"

"I'm Vain-Confidence. This path goes to the Celestial City," replied the man.

"Didn't I tell you so?" Christian asked Hopeful.

When night came, it grew very dark, and they could no longer see the man ahead.

Vain-Confidence, not seeing the way before him, fell into a deep pit, which was on purpose there made by the prince of those grounds to catch fools in it. He was dashed in pieces with his fall.

But the pilgrims heard him fall, then heard only groaning. So they called out to know what was the matter, but no one answered.

"Where are we now?" asked Hopeful. "Let's stop."

But Christian was silent, afraid that he had led Hopeful out of the way. Now it began to rain and thunder and lightning in a dreadful way. Water rose around them.

Hopeful groaned and cried, "Oh that I had kept on my way!"

Christian answered, "Who could have thought that this path should have led us out of the way?"

"I was afraid of it from the very first and therefore gave you that gentle caution. I would have spoken plainer, but you are older than I."

"Good brother, be not offended. I am sorry I have brought you out of the way and that I have put you into such imminent danger. Please forgive me. I didn't do it with evil intent."

"Be comforted, my brother, for I forgive you. And I believe that this shall be for our good."

"I am glad I have with me a merciful brother. But we must not stand here. Let's try to go back again."

"Let me go before," Hopeful offered.

"No, let me go first, so that if there is any danger, I will be the first one in. It's my fault that we are both gone out of the way."

"No, you shall not go first, for your mind is troubled, and it may lead you out of the way again."

Then they heard a voice say, "Let your heart take you to the way again."

By this time the waters were very high, and the way of going back was very dangerous. Even so, they tried to go back. But it was so dark and the flood so high that they could have drowned nine or ten times.

So at last they found a little shelter, and they sat down to wait for day to break. Being tired, they fell asleep. Not far from the place where they were lay a castle. The owner, Giant Despair, got up early that morning, and while walking his grounds, he caught Christian and Hopeful asleep on his grounds.

With a grim and surly voice he woke them. "Where are you from and what are you doing on my land?"

"We are pilgrims who have lost their way."

"You are trespassing by trampling in and lying on my grounds of Doubting Castle! You must come with me."

Despair was a giant! So they were forced to go because he was stronger than they. They also had but little to say, for they knew themselves to be at fault.

He prodded them to his castle, where he threw them down into a very dark dungeon, nasty and stinking. Here they lay from Wednesday morning until Saturday night, without one bit of bread or drop of drink or light or any to ask how they did. Far from friends and acquaintances, no one knew where they were. In this place, Christian had double sorrow because it was his unadvised haste that brought them here.

When Despair went to bed, he told his wife, Diffidence, what he had done and how the two prisoners in his dungeon had gotten there. When he asked for her advice, she counseled him to beat the prisoners without mercy.

So when he arose the next morning, he got a large crabtree cudgel and went down to the dungeon to them. There he cudgeled them fearfully, so that they were unable to help themselves. When Despair was done, he withdrew and left them there to their misery.

All that day they spent the time in nothing but sighs and bitter lamentations.

When Diffidence learned that the pilgrims still lived, she advised Despair to counsel his prisoners to do away with themselves. So in the morning, he went to the dungeons irritated. He saw they were very sore from the beating.

"Why live?" asked Despair. "Life holds only bitterness. I'll give you a choice of a knife, a rope, or poison."

They begged the giant to let them go, but seized by a fit brought on by sunshine, he threw them back in the dungeon and withdrew.

Christian said, "What shall we do, brother? The life we now live is miserable! As for me, I don't know whether it is best to live this way or to die. My soul chooses strangling by rope rather than life. The grave is easier for me than this dungeon! Shall we be ruled by the giant?"

"Indeed our present condition is awful, and death would be far more welcome to me than to live like this forever. But yet the Lord of the country to which we are going has said, 'You shall not murder,'" replied Hopeful. "And for one to kill himself is to murder body and soul at once. And have you forgotten the hell that awaits murderers? Also, think of this. Not all the law is in the hand of the giant Despair. Others have been taken by him, as well as we, and they have escaped out of his hands. Who knows but that God, who made the world, may cause the giant to die, or that at some time or other he may forget to lock us in? Or he may have another of his fits before us and may lose the use of his limbs. If that ever happens again, I am resolved to pluck up my courage and try my utmost to get from under his hand. I was a fool that I did not try to do it before. However, my brother, let's be patient and endure awhile. The time may come that we will find a happy release. But let us not be our own murderers." With that, Hopeful changed Christian's mind.

As evening drew near, the giant went down into the dungeon again to see if his prisoners had taken his counsel. But when he got there, he found them alive. Barely. They'd had no bread or drink in all the time they'd been there, and with the wounds they received from their beating, they could do little more than breathe. Despair fell into a terrible rage and told them that since they had disobeyed his counsel, it would be worse with them than if they had never been born.

At this the pilgrims trembled greatly, and Christian fell into a swoon. When he came a little to himself again, they renewed their discourse about the giant's counsel and whether they should take it or not. Christian seemed to be for doing it again, but Hopeful tried to dissuade him again.

"My brother, do you remember how valiant you have been before now? Apollyon could not crush you, nor could all that you heard or saw or felt in the valley of the Shadow of Death. What hardship, terror, and consternation you have already gone through, and are you now nothing but fear? You see that I am in the dungeon with you, a far weaker man by nature than you are; also, this giant has wounded me as well as you, and has also cut off the bread and water from my mouth, and with you I mourn without the light. But let's exercise a little more patience. Remember how you played the man at Vanity Fair, and were neither afraid of the chain nor cage, nor yet of bloody death. Let us at least avoid the shame that a Christian shouldn't bear and hold up with patience as well as we can."

That night after the giant and his wife were in bed, she asked him concerning the prisoners, and if they had taken his counsel.

He replied, "They are sturdy men who choose to bear all hardships rather than to make away themselves."

Then said she, "Take them into the castle yard tomorrow and show them the bones and skulls of those that you have already killed, and make them believe that before a week comes to an end, you also will tear them in pieces, as you have done their fellows before them."

The next day Despair took them into the castle yard and showed them bones and skulls of his victims. "These were pilgrims who trespassed on my grounds as you have done. I tore them into pieces. Within ten days I will tear you apart, just as I have done to these pilgrims before you." And he beat them all the way back into the dungeon.

All day Saturday they lay in the dungeon in a horrible state.

That night in bed, the giant and his wife again discussed the fate of the prisoners. The giant wondered that he could not bring them to an end no matter what he did.

His wife replied, "I fear that they live in hope that some will come to relieve them, or that they have picklocks about them which they hope will help them escape."

"Now that you mention it, my dear, I will search them in the morning."

At midnight on Saturday they began to pray, and they prayed until just before daybreak.

A little before daybreak, Christian, half stunned at a sudden thought, said, "What a fool I've been to lie in this stinking dungeon when I could walk away free! I have a key in my bosom called Promise that is supposed to open any lock."

"That is good news, brother. Pluck it out of your bosom and try."

Christian used his key to unlock the door to the cell, then the door to the castle yard, then the great iron gate to the castle. But that lock was very hard. It did open. But when they thrust open the gate, it creaked so loudly, Despair ran out in the sunshine to pursue them; but he was seized by a fit, and his limbs were too weak to allow him to give chase.

The men ran all the way back and found the stile that led to the way again. Once over the fence they were out of the giant's jurisdiction, and therefore were safe. To prevent other pilgrims from making their mistake, they erected a pillar with a warning: "Over this stile is the way to Doubting Castle, which is kept by Giant Despair, who despises the King of the Celestial City and seeks to destroy His holy pilgrims." That done, Christian and Hopeful continued on the way, singing:

"Out of the way we went, and then we found
What it was like to tread forbidden ground.
And let those who come after note today,
Lest carelessness makes them, too, leave the way,
Lest they, for trespassing, his prison bear,
Whose castle's Doubting, and whose name's Despair."

❧

They went until they came to the Delectable Mountains. They climbed up into the mountains to see gardens and orchards, vineyards, and fountains of water. They drank and washed themselves and freely ate of the vineyards. At the tops of the mountains by the side of the road, four shepherds were feeding their flocks.

Christian and Hopeful went to them, and as they leaned on their staves, Christian asked, "Whose Delectable Mountains are these? And whose sheep feed upon them?"

"These mountains are Emmanuel's Land," answered a shepherd. "They are within sight of His City. These sheep belong to Him. He laid down His life for them."

"Is this the way to the Celestial City?"

"You are in your way," the shepherd agreed.

"How far is it to get there?" Christian asked.

"Too far for all but those who persevere."

"Is the way to the Celestial City safe or dangerous?" asked Christian.

"Safe for some. 'But the rebellious stumble' in the way."

"Is there in this place any rest for the weary?"

A shepherd replied, "The Lord of these mountains told us, 'Do not forget to entertain strangers.' Therefore the good of the place is yours."

Then the four shepherds asked Christian and Hopeful many questions, such as, Where did you come from? How did you get into the way? By what means have you so persevered in your journey? They saw few pilgrims, because most didn't make it that far. When the shepherds heard their answers, they were pleased and looked lovingly on them.

"Welcome to the Delectable Mountains," said one. "We are Knowledge, Experience, Watchful, and Sincere." They took Christian and Hopeful by the hand and led them to their tents. They made them eat of that which was ready at the moment.

And they said, "We would like you to stay here awhile, to come to know us, and most importantly to be comforted with the good of these Delectable Mountains."

Christian and Hopeful said they were content to stay. They all went to bed soon after that because it was very late.

The next day the shepherds took them walking. They had a pleasant view to behold on every side. Then the shepherds decided to show them some wonders. So they first took them to the top of the mountain called Error, which was very steep on its far side. When the shepherds bid them to, the pilgrims looked down a precipice to see several men dashed to pieces from a fall they had from the top.

"What happened?" asked Christian.

"These men listened to Hymenaeus and Philetus, who said the resurrection of the faithful had already taken place," answered a shepherd. "They lie unburied from that day until now as a warning to take heed how they clamber too high or how they come too near to the brink of the mountain."

Next they topped the mountain of Caution. In the distance they saw men walking up and down among the tombs that were there. And they saw the men were blind because they stumbled against the tombs and never found their way out of the graveyard.

"What does this mean?" asked Christian.

A shepherd answered, "Did you see a little below these mountains a stile that led into a meadow on the left-hand side of the way?"

"Oh yes."

"From that stile there goes a path that leads directly to Doubting Castle, which is kept by Giant Despair, and these men came on the pilgrimage at one time, as you do now, until they came to the stile. Because the path is rough in that spot, they chose to go out of it into the meadow and were carried off by the giant and cast into the dungeons at the castle. He ripped out their eyes and led them among those tombs to wander to fulfill the proverb: 'A man who strays from the path of understanding comes to rest in the company of the dead.'"

Then Christian and Hopeful looked at one another with tears streaming down their faces, but yet said nothing to the shepherds.

Next the shepherds led them into a valley where there was a door in the side of a mountain. As one shepherd opened the door, they bid the pilgrims to look in. When they did, they saw that within it was very dark and smoky. They also thought that they heard a rumbling noise as of fire and a cry of some of the tormented. The odor of smoke and brimstone nearly overwhelmed them.

"What is it?" asked Christian.

"A detour to hell," answered a shepherd. "For hypocrites, mainly, like Esau, who sold his birthright; or like Judas, who sold his Master; or like Alexander, who blasphemed the Gospel; or like the liars Ananias and Sapphira."

"Each one had started the pilgrimage like us, did they not?" asked Hopeful.

"Yes," said the shepherds. "And held it a long time, too."

"How far might they go on pilgrimage in their day, since they were thus miserably cast away?" asked Hopeful.

"Some farther, and some not so far as these mountains."

"Then we have need to cry to the Strong One for strength."

"Ay, and you will have need to use it when you have it," agreed the shepherds.

By this time, the pilgrims had a desire to go forward on their journey. So the shepherds walked them to the end of the mountains, intending to show the pilgrims the gates of the Celestial City. On the mountain of Clear they let the pilgrims look toward the Celestial City through a telescope.

As they tried to look, the remembrance of the last thing the shepherds had shown them made their hands shake so they could not look steadily through the glass. Yet they thought they could make out something like the gate and some of the glory of the place.

As they departed, one of the shepherds gave them a "Note of the Directions of the Way."

Another cautioned, "Beware of the Flatterer."

The third warned, "Take heed not to sleep on the Enchanted Ground."

The fourth bid them, "Godspeed!"

Then they went away, singing this song:

"Thus by the shepherds secrets are revealed,
Which but for pilgrim eyes are kept concealed:
Come to the shepherds, then, if serious
To see things hidden and mysterious."

The pilgrims headed down the mountains along the way toward the City. A little below the mountains on the left hand lay the country of Conceit. From that country there comes into the way in which the pilgrims walked a little crooked lane. Here they met with a very energetic lad who came out of that country. His name was Ignorance.

"From what land do you come?" called Christian. "And where do you go?"

"I am Ignorance," replied the lad. "I come from Conceit. I'm going to the Celestial City."

"You may have some difficulty there getting in the Gate."

"As other good people do," answered Ignorance.

"But what rolled certificate do you have to show at the Gate?"

"I know my Lord's will," replied Ignorance. "I have lived a good life. I pay my debts. I pray, fast, pay tithes, give alms. And I have left my country for the Celestial City."

"But you didn't come in at the wicket gate that is at the head of the way," worried Christian. "I fear you will not get into the City. Instead you will be charged 'a thief and a robber.'"

"Gentlemen, you are utter strangers to me. I don't know you. Be content to follow the religion of your country, and I will follow the religion of mine. I hope all will be well, and as for the wicket gate that you talk of, all the world knows that it is a great way off. I cannot think that any men in all our parts do so much as know the way to it. Nor need it matter whether they do or not, since we have, as you see, a fine pleasant green lane that comes down from our country the way into it."

When Christian saw that the man was wise in his own conceit, he whispered to Hopeful, "There is more hope of a fool than of him. As Solomon the wise man says, 'Even as he walks along the road, the fool lacks sense and shows everyone how stupid he is.' Shall we talk further with him now or go ahead of him and leave him to think about what he's already heard? Later we could join up with him and see if by degrees we can do him any good."

"Let us pass him and talk to him later, if he can bear it," said Hopeful. "It is not good, I think, to say all to him at once."

So they went on and Ignorance stayed behind them on the way. When they had gotten ahead of Ignorance a ways, they entered a very dark lane. Off the way they saw a man bound by seven strong cords to a pole carried by seven devils. They carried him to a door set on the side of the hill. Christian began to tremble, as did Hopeful. As the devils led away the man, Christian looked to see if he knew him.

"The doomed man looks like Turn-Away from Apostasy," whispered Christian.

"Inscribed on the man's back are the words 'Wanton Professor and Damnable Apostate,'" whispered Hopeful.

"Now I remember something that was told me of a thing that happened to a good man hereabout," Christian said. "The name of the man was Little-Faith, but a good man, and he lived in Sincere. At the entrance of this passage there comes down from Broad-Way-Gate a lane called Deadman's Lane, so called because of the many murders that are commonly done there. Little-Faith was on pilgrimage, as we are now, and chanced to sit down there and fell asleep. About that time three men, sturdy rogues, came down that lane. They were three brothers, Faint-Heart, Mistrust, and Guilt. They saw Little-Faith where he was asleep and came running. Now the good man had just awakened and was getting up to continue his journey. The three came to him and with threatening language told him to stand. Little-Faith looked as white as a sheet and had neither power to fight nor fly.

"Faint-Heart said, 'Give me your purse,' but Little-Faith made no haste to do it.

"Mistrust ran up to him and thrust his hand into his pocket and pulled out a bag of silver.

"At that Little-Faith cried out, 'Thieves, thieves!'

"Then Guilt, with a great club that was in his hand, struck Little-Faith on the head, and with that blow felled him to the ground where he lay bleeding.

"The thieves stood near until they heard someone on the road. Fearing that it might be Great-Grace who lives in the city of Good-Confidence, they ran away and left Little-Faith to fend for himself. After a while, Little-Faith came to himself and hobbled on his way."

"But did they take from all he ever had?" asked Hopeful.

"No. They missed the place where his jewels were. But, as I was told, the good man was much afflicted for his loss, for the thieves got most of his spending money. He had a little odd money left, but not enough to bring him to his journey's end. He was forced to beg as he went, to keep himself alive.

Still he spent many times hungry all the rest of the way to the Celestial City."

"Is it not a wonder they didn't get his certificate by which he was to receive admittance at the Celestial Gate?"

"It is a wonder, but they didn't get it. Not through his own cunning, for he hadn't any time to hide anything. So that was more of providence than his endeavor."

"But it must be a comfort to him that the thieves did not get that."

"It might have been a comfort to him if he had used it. But after the attack he made very little use of it the rest of the way because of the dismay that the thieves had got his money. In fact, he forgot most of the rest of his journey. Any memory that came to mind that comforted him, he lost when he had fresh thoughts of his loss. And those thoughts swallowed the comfort."

"Poor man! This could not be but a great grief to him."

"Ay, a grief indeed. It is a wonder he did not die with grief. I was told that he scattered almost all the rest of the way with nothing but doleful and bitter complaints."

"But, Christian, I am persuaded that these three fellows are a company of cowards. Otherwise would they have run as they did at the noise of one coming onto the road? And why didn't Little-Faith dig up some courage? I thought he might have stood up to them and yielded when there was no other choice."

"They are cowards. They are no better than journeymen thieves, serving under the king of the bottomless pit who will come to their aid if they need it. And his voice is like a roaring lion. When I was attacked by these three men, I, too, almost gave in when their leader roared. But I was dressed in the Armor of Proof. I still found it hard work to finish the work as a man."

"But they ran," Hope pointed out, "when they suspected that Great-Grace was coming."

"No marvel that they ran. Great-Grace is the King's champion. But put some space between Little-Faith and His champions. All the King's subjects are not His champions. Nor can they, when tried, do such feats of war as He. Some are strong, some are weak, some have great faith, some have little. This man was one of the weak; therefore he went to the walls.

"For such footmen as you and I are, let's never desire to meet with an enemy, nor vaunt as if we could do better when we hear of others who have been tricked and failed. But when we hear that such robberies are done on the King's highway, we have two things we can do: First, go out fully clothed in armor, including the shield; second, we must desire the King to go with us. Let us pray we can do better. Even Peter, who said he could stand firmer for his Master than all other men, was foiled by the villains."

So they went on with Ignorance following until they came to a place where they saw a way put itself into their way. It seemed to lie as straight as the way that they should go. They didn't know which of the two to take, for both seemed straight before them. So they stood still to consider.

A man in a white robe appeared on the other way.

"Where are you going?" he asked.

"To the Celestial City, but now we're not sure which is the right way," answered Christian.

"Follow me," said the man. "This is the way."

So they followed the man, who applauded everything the pilgrims said. Christian was confused. Did this new way ever so slowly depart from the way they had been on? Suddenly they were trapped inside a net, so entangled they didn't know what to do. The white robe fell off the man. He was a devil. And the pilgrims knew they were being led to hell. They lay crying for some time, for they could not get themselves out.

"Do you remember the proverb: 'Whoever flatters his neighbor is spreading a net for his feet'?" Christian asked Hopeful. "Did not the shepherds warn us about flatterers?"

"They also gave us a 'Note of Direction for the Way,' which we forgot to read," lamented Hopeful. "And now we are on the path of the destroyer."

They prayed for mercy. As they lay in the net, a Shining One appeared, carrying a small whip. When he came to where they were, he asked where they came from and what they were doing there. They told him they were poor pilgrims on the way to the Celestial City. A devil in a white robe had tricked them out of the true way.

"It is Flatterer, a false apostle," said the Shining One. "He changes himself into an Angel of Light."

He ripped the net and let them out. Then he said, "Follow me that I may set you on your way again." So he led them back to the way.

Then he asked them, "Where did you lie last night?"

"With the shepherds upon the Delectable Mountains."

"Did they not give you a 'Note of Direction for the Way'?"

"Yes."

"But did you pull it out and read it when you were resting?"

"No."

"Why?"

"We forgot about it."

"Well then, didn't the shepherds tell you to beware of the Flatterer?"

"Yes, but we didn't even imagine that this fine-spoken man had been he."

But before the Shining One left them, he commanded them to lie down, and when they did he whipped them severely and scolded them for forgetting the directions of the shepherds. "As many as I love, I rebuke and chasten. Be zealous, therefore, and repent."

So they thanked the man for all his kindness, and as they continued carefully on the right way, they sang:

"Now listen, you who walk along the way,
To hear how pilgrims fare who go astray:
Ensnared they were, entangled in a net,
Because good counsel did the two forget.
It's true one rescued them, but yet you see
He whipped them too: Let this your caution be."

After a while they saw a lone man coming carefully toward them.

Christian said to Hopeful, "There is a man with his back toward the Celestial City, and he is coming to meet us."

"I see him. Beware of another flatterer," whispered Hopeful.

So the man drew nearer and nearer, and at last came up to them.

"Where are you going?" asked the stranger.

"To the Celestial City," answered Christian.

The stranger laughed mightily. "What ignorant fellows you are, to take upon yourselves such a tedious journey. You'll get nothing for your pains, or my name isn't Atheist."

"Do you think we will not be received?"

"Received! There is no such place as you dream of in all this world."

"But there is in the world to come."

"I have been seeking this City for twenty years, but have found no more of it than the day I first set out."

"We both have heard and believe that there is such a place to be found."

"If I hadn't believed before I started out, I wouldn't have come this far to seek. But having found nothing, even though I should have if there was such a place, I'm going back again. I'll seek to refresh myself with the things I cast away before my fruitless quest."

"Do you think he speaks truth?" Christian asked Hopeful.

"Be careful," Hopeful said. "He is one of the flatterers. Remember what it has already cost us for listening to one of these fellows. What? No Celestial City? We saw the Gate of the City from the Delectable Mountains. We walk in faith. We are not of those who shrink back and are destroyed, but of those who believe and are saved. We will go on."

"My brother, I didn't ask the question because I doubted the truth of our belief myself, but to test you and to fetch from you a fruit of the honesty of your heart. As for this man, I know that he is blinded by the god of this world. Let you and I go on, knowing that we have belief in the truth and no lie is of the truth."

"Now I do rejoice in hope of the glory of God," Hopeful said.

And they turned away from the man. He laughed at them and went his way.

They went on the way until they entered a land whose air naturally tended to make one drowsy if he was a stranger in the land. Hopeful began to feel very dull and heavy of sleep. He said to Christian, "I am so drowsy. I can scarcely hold my eyes open. Let's lie down here and take a nap."

"By no means, unless you never want to wake up again," Christian said.

"Why, my brother. Sleep is sweet to the laboring man. We may be refreshed if we take a nap."

"Do you not remember the shepherds warning us of the Enchanted Ground? He meant that we should beware of sleeping. So let's not sleep as so many others do. Let us watch and be sober."

"I acknowledge my fault," Hopeful said. "Had I been here alone I might have died. The Wise Man said, 'Two are better than one.' Even before now, your company has been my mercy."

"Now then," said Christian, "to prevent drowsiness in this place, let us have a lively conversation."

"With all my heart."

"Where shall we begin?"

"Where God began with us, but you go first, please," said Hopeful.

So Christian sang this song:

"When saints grow sleepy, let them come to us,
And hear how lively pilgrims do discuss.
Yes, let them learn of what we did devise
To keep agape our drowsy, slumbering eyes;
Saints' fellowship, if it be managed well,
Keeps them awake, and that in spite of hell."

❧

Then Christian said, "I will ask you a question. How came you to think at first of doing as you do now?"

"Do you mean, how came I at first to look after the good of my soul?"

"Yes, that is what I meant."

"I continued a great while in the delight of those things that are seen and sold at our fair, things that I now believe would have drowned me in perdition and destruction."

"What things were they?"

"All the treasure and riches of the world," Hopeful said. "Also I delighted much in revelry, partying, drinking, swearing, lying, uncleanness, Sabbath-breaking, and whatnot that tended to destroy the soul. But I realized at last, by hearing and considering of things that are divine, which indeed I heard from you and Faithful, that the end of these things is death. For these things the wrath of God comes on the children of disobedience."

"Did you presently fall under the power of this conviction?"

"No, I wasn't willing to know the evil of sin nor the damnation that follows on the commission of it. Instead I endeavored, when my mind at first began to be shaken with the Word, to shut my eyes against the light of it."

"But what was the cause of your carrying of it to the first working of God's blessed Spirit on you?"

"I was ignorant that this was the work of God on me. I never thought that my new awareness of sin was a result of God's seeking my conversion. Yet sin was very sweet to my flesh, and I didn't want to leave it. I didn't want to part with my old companions because their presence and actions were so desirable to me. But the hours when I was convicted of my sin were so troublesome and frightening that I couldn't bear to remember them."

"But sometimes you got rid of your trouble?"

"Yes, but it would come into my mind again, and it was worse than before."

"Before the journey, what brought your sins to mind?" Christian asked.

"Many things brought my sins to mind. If I met a righteous man in the street. If anyone read the Bible. If my head ached. If I heard a neighbor was sick. If I heard the bell toll for the dead. If I thought of dying myself. If I heard of someone else's sudden death. If I thought I myself might come to sudden judgment."

"What did you do about it?" asked Christian.

"I endeavored to change my life. Not only turning away from my own sin, but putting the sinful company behind me, too. I prayed, read the Bible, wept for sin, and told the truth to my neighbors. But trouble returned."

"Why? Were you not reformed?"

"Several things brought it to me. Especially such sayings as 'All our righteousnesses are as filthy rags.' Because 'A man is not justified by Law, but by faith in Jesus Christ.' I finally came to the conclusion it was foolish to think of heaven by the law. If a man runs a hundred pounds into the shopkeeper's debt, and after that pays for all he buys, his old debt still stands in the shopkeeper's book unpaid. The shopkeeper may sue him and cast him into prison till he pays the debt."

"So how did you apply that to yourself?"

"Why, I thought this: I have by my sins run a great way into God's Book, and my now reforming will not pay off that score. Therefore I should think still, under all my present amendments. But how should I be freed from that damnation that I brought myself in danger of by my former sins?"

"A very good application."

"Another thing that has troubled me," Hopeful went on, "even since my late amendments, is that if I look narrowly into the best of what I do now, I still see sin, new sin, mixing itself with the best of that which I do. So now I'm forced to conclude that I have committed sin enough in one duty to send me to hell, even if my former life had been faultless."

"What did you do then?" Christian asked.

"I didn't know what to do until one day in Vanity I spoke my mind to Faithful. For we were well acquainted. He told me that unless I could obtain the righteousness of a man who had never sinned, neither my own nor all the righteousness of the world could save me."

"Did you think he spoke truth?"

"Not before I saw my own weakness to sin. But since I've seen the sin that cleaves to my best performance, I've been forced to agree with him.'

"But did you think, when at first he suggested it to you, that there was such a man to be found? Someone of whom it could truly be said, 'This man never committed sin'?"

"At first it sounded strange, but after a little more talk and time spent with Faithful, I had full conviction about it."

"Did you ask him, 'What man is this?' and how you must be justified by him?"

"Yes, and he told me it was the Lord Jesus who dwells on the right hand of the Most High. 'So,' he said, 'you must be justified by him, even by trusting to what He has done by Himself in the days of His flesh and suffered when He did hang on the tree.' I asked him how *that* Man's righteousness could be that powerful as to justify another before God. And he told me that He was the Mighty God, and He did what He did and died the death also, not for Himself but for me. His doings and their worthiness before God would be imparted to me if I believed on Him."

"What did you do then?" Christian asked.

"I listed my objections against my believing because I thought He was not willing to save me."

"What did Faithful say to you then?"

"He bid me to go to Him and see. I said that was presumption, and Faithful said no, I was invited to come. Then he gave me a copy of the Book of Jesus that spoke of His invitation to men, to encourage me to go to Him more freely. Then I asked Faithful what I must do when I came. And he told me I must pray on my knees with all my heart and soul, and the Father would reveal Him to me. Then I asked him what to say in my supplication when I came to Him, and Faithful taught me this prayer for salvation:

"God, be merciful to me, a sinner, and make me to know and believe in Jesus Christ. For I see that if His righteousness had not been, or I have not faith in His righteousness, I will be utterly cast away. Lord, I have heard You are a merciful God, and have ordained Your Son, Jesus Christ, the Savior of the world. Moreover, I have heard You are willing to

bestow on such a poor sinner as I Your grace in the salvation of my soul,
through Your Son, Jesus Christ. Amen."

"Did you do as you were bidden?"

"Yes, many times."

"Did the Father reveal His Son to you?"

"Not at first, nor for several times after that."

"What did you do then?"

"I didn't know what to do!"

"Had you thought of not praying anymore?"

"Oh yes. A hundred times and more."

"Why didn't you?"

"I believed that all was told me was true. I needed Christ's righteousness to live, and I thought if I quit praying for it, I would die in my sin. Then this verse came to mind: 'If it tarry, wait for it, because it will surely come, and it will not tarry.' So I continued to pray until the Father showed me His Son."

"How was He revealed to you?" asked Christian.

"One day I saw Him—not with my eyes but with my heart. The Lord Jesus looked down from heaven on me, saying, 'Believe in the Lord Jesus, and you will be saved.' And I replied, 'Lord, I am a very great sinner.' He answered, 'My grace is sufficient for you.' And my heart was full of joy, my eyes full of tears, my love running over in the ways of Jesus Christ. If I had a thousand gallons of blood in my body, I could spill it all for the sake of the Lord Jesus."

"This was a revelation of Christ to your soul indeed. But tell me specifically what effect this had on your spirit."

"It made me see that all the world is in a state of condemnation. It made me see that God the Father, though He be just, can justify the sinner who comes to Him. I was greatly ashamed of the vileness of my former life, and I was confounded at the sense of my own ignorance. Until I saw the beauty of Jesus Christ, I didn't have love for the holy life. Now I long to do something for the honor and glory of the name of the Lord Jesus."

Just then Hopeful looked back and saw Ignorance. "Look how far the youngster loiters behind us."

"Ignorance does not care for our company."

"Let's wait for him."

When Ignorance came closer, Christian yelled, "Why do you stay so far behind?"

"I take greater pleasure walking alone," replied Ignorance.

"Come on up," Christian encouraged the young man. "Let us talk away the time in this lonely place. How do things stand between God and your soul?"

Ignorance drew closer. "I hope well, for I am always full of good thoughts that come into my mind to comfort me as I walk."

"What are these thoughts?"

"Of God and heaven."

"So do devils and damned souls," commented Christian.

"But I desire God and heaven," countered Ignorance.

"So do many who are never likely to go there. The soul of the sluggard desires and has nothing. Why are you persuaded you have left everything for God and heaven?"

"My understanding tells me so," said Ignorance.

"The Wise Man says, 'He who trusts in himself is a fool.'"

"This is spoken of an evil heart. But mine is good."

"How can you prove that?"

"It comforts me in the hope of heaven."

And thus they bantered back and forth, Christian answering each of Ignorance's assumptions with truth from the Bible.

"This faith of yours is nowhere in the Bible. True faith takes refuge in Christ's righteousness, not your own."

"What! Would you have us to trust what Christ has done without us? You would have us sin all we want, because we may be justified by Christ's personal righteousness as long as we believe in it?"

"Ignorance is your name, and so you are," said Christian. "You are ignorant of the true effects of faith in this righteousness of Christ, which is to commit your heart to God in Christ and to love His ways."

"Have you ever had Christ revealed to you from heaven?" Hopeful asked Ignorance.

"What? You are a man for revelations! I believe that what both you and all the rest of you say about that matter is but the fruit of distracted brains."

"Why? Christ is so hid in God from the natural understanding of all flesh that He cannot by any man be known in salvation unless God the Father reveals Him to them."

"That is your faith, but not mine. I don't doubt mine is as good as yours," answered Ignorance.

"Give me leave to put in a word," Christian said. "You ought not to speak so lightly of this matter. I boldly affirm that no man can know Jesus Christ but by the revelation of the Father. Yes, and faith, too, by which the soul lays hold upon Christ, must be worked by the exceeding greatness of His mighty power. I perceive you are ignorant of the working of faith. So wake up, see your own wretchedness, and fly to the Lord Jesus. For by His righteousness, which is also the righteousness of God, you will be delivered from condemnation."

"I can't keep up with you," Ignorance said. "Go on ahead."

Christian and Hopeful chanted:

"Well, Ignorance, are you so foolish to
Reject good counsel, ten times given you?
And if you yet refuse it, you will know,
Too soon, the evil of your doing so.
Remember, man, in time: Yield. Do not fear.
Good counsel taken well saves; therefore hear.
But if you yet reject it, you will be
The loser, Ignorance, we guarantee."

&

"Come, Hopeful," Christian said. "I see that you and I must walk by ourselves again."

So they went on ahead as before, and Ignorance came hobbling after. Then Christian said, "I'm sorry for this poor man. It certainly will go badly for him at the end."

"Alas! There are an abundance in our town in his condition. Whole families, whole streets, pilgrims, too. And if there be that many in our parts, how many, do you think, must there be in the place where he was born?"

Moments later, Christian asked, "What do you think of such men? Do they have no conviction of sin, and as a consequence no fear of their dangerous condition?"

"Sometimes they may be fearful."

"And yet they don't know that such conviction of sin and consequent fear tend to their good. They try to stifle their fear. But 'The fear of the Lord is the beginning of wisdom.'"

"How do you describe right fear?" Hopeful asked.

"True or right fear is revealed in three things. First, it comes with a saving conviction of sin. Also, it drives the soul to lay hold of Christ for salvation. And finally, it births and continues in the soul as a great reverence of God, His Word, and His ways by keeping the soul tender and making it afraid to turn from these things to anything that would dishonor God, break its peace, grieve the Spirit, or cause the enemy to speak reproachfully."

"Well said. I believe you have the truth," Hopeful said. "Are we now almost past the Enchanted Ground?"

"Why?" Christian asked. "Are you weary of our discourse?"

"No, not at all. I just want to know where we are."

"We have about two miles farther to go. But let's return to our topic. Those who are ignorant of the things of God do not know that these convictions that tend to put them in fear are for their good, so they seek to stifle them."

"How?"

"They think that those fears are worked by the devil, and so they resist them as things they need to overthrow. They also think that these fears tend to spoil their faith, and they harden their hearts against them. They think they shouldn't fear, so they take on a false confidence. Then, too, they see that these fears take away their self-holiness, and so they resist them with all their might."

"I knew something of this myself. It was so with me before I knew myself."

"Well, let's leave our neighbor Ignorance by himself for now. Let's talk of something else. Did you know a man assertive in religion named Temporary?"

"Yes!" answered Hopeful. "He dwelt in Graceless, two miles from Honesty. He lived under the same roof as Turn-Back."

"Well, Temporary was awakened to his sins once. He even told me he was resolved to go on the pilgrimage. But after he grew acquainted with Save-Self, he became a stranger."

"He was a backslider," agreed Hopeful. "There were four reasons, I think. Although his conscience was awakened, his mind was unchanged. So when the power of guilt wore away, the things that provoked him to be religious faded away. So as his sense and fear of hell and damnation cooled, so his desires for heaven and salvation also cooled. And he was held by the world; he didn't want to lose everything, especially what others thought of him.

He didn't want to bring unnecessary trouble his way. A third reason was the shame he felt for religion. Being proud and haughty doesn't go with religion, which is low and contemptible in his thinking. And lastly, he hated the feelings of guilt and hardened his heart. He chose ways to harden his heart more and more. And now you tell me how a man backslides."

"They block all thoughts of God, death, and judgment. Then by degrees they cast off their private duties of prayers, curbing their lusts, ogling, and guilt. They shun the company of Christians. They cast off public duties of hearing, reading, and conferring. Then they begin to make fun of the godly, so they feel better about leaving religion." Christian went on to describe the final slide into the company of evil men and carnal pleasures, first secretly, and finally openly.

Suddenly the two pilgrims realized the Enchanted Ground was behind them.

"Beulah Land!"

The air was sweet and pleasant, and their way lay directly through it. Here they heard continually the singing of birds, and saw every day new flowers appear in the earth. In this country the sun shone night and day because this was beyond the Valley of the Shadow of Death. It was also out of reach of Giant Despair. Here they were within sight of the City they were going to. Here they met some of the inhabitants of the country. The Shining Ones commonly walked in this land because it was on the borders of heaven. In this land the contract between the bride and the bridegroom was renewed. There was no want of corn and wine, for in this place they met with abundance of what they had sought in all their pilgrimage.

As they walked in this land, they had more rejoicing than in parts more remote from the Kingdom to which they were bound. And drawing near to the City, they had a more perfect view of it. It was built of pearls and precious stones. Also, the streets were paved with gold, so that by reason of the natural glory of the City and the reflection of the sunbeams upon it, Christian fell sick with desire to dwell there. Hopeful also had a bout or two of the same disease.

But being strengthened after a rest, they were better able to bear their sickness, and they walked on their way and came yet nearer and nearer. Orchards, vineyards, and gardens opened their gates onto the way. "Whose goodly vineyards and gardens are these?" called the pilgrims to a gardener standing in the way.

"They are the King's, planted here for His delight—and the solace of His pilgrims."

The gardener had them enter and invited them to refresh themselves. They ate delicacies and strolled the King's walks and arbors. And they slept. The pilgrims relaxed and took solace there for many days.

Finally the pilgrims no longer desired food or wine or sleep. They had to go on to the City. They could scarcely look at the City except through an instrument made for that purpose because the pure gold was so dazzlingly bright.

Two Shining Ones in golden robes met them. They asked the pilgrims where they came from. They also asked where they lodged along the way, what difficulties and danger they encountered, what comforts and pleasures they had met on the way. And the pilgrims answered all their questions.

Finally the Shining Ones said, "You have but two more difficulties and you are in the City."

Christian and Hopeful asked the men to go along with them.

"We will," they agreed. "But you must obtain it by your own faith."

So they went on together until they came within sight of the Gate.

Between them and the Celestial Gate was a river. There was no bridge, and the water was very deep. At the sight, the pilgrims were astounded, but the men with them said, "You must go through, or you cannot come to the Gate."

"Is there no other way to the Gate?" the pilgrims asked.

"Yes," the Shining Ones answered, "but only two, Enoch and Elijah, have been allowed to tread that path since the foundation of the world. And no one else will until the last trumpet sounds."

The pilgrims were despondent at this difficulty before them and tried to discover a way they could escape the river.

"Is the river all one depth?" asked Christian.

"You will find it deeper or shallower, as you believe in the King of the City," was the answer.

Then the pilgrims entered the water. Christian began to sink. He cried out to his good friend Hopeful, "The water is going over my head!"

"Be of good cheer, brother," said Hopeful. "I feel the bottom, and it is good."

"The sorrows of death have me, my friend. I shall not see the land that flows with milk and honey." Darkness and horror held Christian so that he could not see before him. In a great measure he lost his senses so that he could neither remember orderly talk nor any of the sweet refreshments he had met with along the way of his pilgrimage. He feared that he should die in that river and never obtain entrance at the Gate. Also he was troubled at the thought of the sins he had committed, both before and since he began his pilgrimage. He saw hobgoblins and evil spirits.

Hopeful had an awful time to keep his brother's head above water. Sometimes Christian would completely sink under the water, and then arise above it half-dead.

"Brother, I see the Gate and men standing by to receive us," encouraged Hopeful.

"It is you they are waiting for. You were always hopeful. But for my sins He has brought me into this trap and left me."

"You have quite forgotten the Bible," said Hopeful. "The wicked 'have no struggles at their death. . . . They are free from burdens' carried by good men. The troubles that you have in these waters are no sign that God has forsaken you, but are sent to test you. Will you call to mind His goodness that you received before today? Be of good cheer. Jesus Christ will make you whole!"

"Oh, I see Him now! And He tells me, 'When you pass through the waters, I will be with you, and through the rivers, they shall not overflow thee,'" cried Christian.

Then they both took courage. After that the hobgoblins and evil spirits were as silent as stones. He felt bottom. The river was shallow.

When they reached the far bank of the river, they were met by the two Shining Ones. They said, "We are ministering spirits sent forth to those who shall be heirs to salvation."

So they went on toward the Gate. They sped upward, though the foundation upon which the City was grounded was higher than the clouds. But the pilgrims went up the hill with ease because they had these two men to lead them up by the arms. They had left the mortal garments behind in the river. So they went up, sweetly talking as they went, being comforted because they safely crossed over the river and had such glorious companions to attend them.

The Shining Ones said, "You are going now to the paradise of God. You will see the Tree of Life and eat its imperishable fruit. You shall be given robes of light, and you will walk and talk every day with the King, for all eternity. You will see no sorrow, no sickness, no affliction, no death. These former things have passed away. You are going now to Abraham, Isaac, and Jacob, and to the prophets."

"But what must we do in the Holy Place?" asked Christian.

"You shall receive comfort for all your toil, and joy for all your sorrow. You reap what you have sown, even the fruit of your prayers and tears and sufferings for your King along the way. You must wear crowns of gold and enjoy the perpetual sight of the Holy One, for there you shall see Him as He is. There you shall serve Him continually with praise, with shouting, and with thanksgiving. Your eyes shall be delighted with seeing, and your ears with hearing the pleasant voice of the Mighty One. There you shall enjoy your friends again who have gone before you, and there you shall with joy receive even every one who follows into the Holy Place after you. When He shall come with sound of trumpet in the clouds, as upon wings of the wind, you shall come with Him. And when He sits upon the throne of judgment, you shall sit by Him. For whether it be angels or men, you shall have a voice in that judgment because they were His and your enemies. You will be forever with Him."

Now as they were drawing toward the Gate, a throng of Heavenly Hosts came out to surround them.

The two Shining Ones said, "These are the men who have loved our Lord when they were in the world, and they have left all for His Holy Name. He has sent us to fetch them and we have brought them this far on their journey."

The Heavenly Hosts gave a great shout and cried, "Blessed are those who are invited to the wedding supper of the Lamb! Blessed are they who do His commandments, that they may have the right to the Tree of Life, and may go through the Gate into the City."

Several of the King's trumpeters, clothed in white and shining raiment, made the heavens echo with their melodious and loud noises. They saluted Christian and Hopeful with ten thousand welcomes from the world.

After this, they surrounded the pilgrims and continually sounded the trumpets as they walked on together. Christian and his brother were amazed at the welcome they felt as more and more trumpeters joined the crowd around them. The pilgrims were swallowed up with the sight of angels and with the melodious notes. Now they had the City itself in view, and they thought they heard all the bells therein to ring in welcome. Thus they came to the Gate.

Over the Gate was written in letters of gold, "Blessed are they who do His commandments, that they may have right to the Tree of Life and may enter through the gates into the City."

After the Shining Ones instructed them, Christian and Hopeful cried to the Gate, "We call upon the Gatekeepers: Enoch, Moses, and Elijah."

Above the Gate three saints appeared. "What do you want?" they asked.

"These pilgrims come from the City of Destruction," cried the Shining Ones, "for the love they bear to the King of this place."

"Bring their certificates," commanded a voice from above.

Then the pilgrims handed the attendants the certificates that they had received in the beginning of their pilgrimage. The attendants carried the certificates to the King, who when He had read them said, "Where are these men?"

"They are standing without the Gate."

Then the same voice boomed through the heavens, "Open the Gate that the righteous may enter, those who keep faith!"

All the bells in the City rang again for joy. Christian and Hopeful entered, to be transfigured, crowned with glory, and adorned in garments that made them shine like the sun. Hovering were seraphim, cherubim, and creatures too dazzling to recognize. And the whole Heavenly Host cried, "Holy, Holy, Holy is the Lord God Almighty." And Christian and Hopeful joined them in immortality to gaze upon the Holy One.

After the Gate closed after the pilgrims, Ignorance came up to the river on the other side. But he soon got over, and without half the difficulty that the other two men met with. For it happened that there was then in that place one Vain-Hope, a ferryman, who with his boat helped him over. So Ignorance ascended the hill and came up to the Gate, alone. No one met him with the least encouragement. When he was come up to the Gate, he looked up to the writing that was above, and then began to knock, supposing that entrance should be quickly given to him.

But the men who looked over the top of the Gate asked, "Where have you come from? And what do you want?"

He answered, "I have eaten and drunk in the presence of the King, and

He has taught in our streets."

Then they asked him for his certificate that they might go in and show it to the King.

So he fumbled in his bosom for one and found none.

Then said they, "Do you have one?"

But the man answered never a word.

So they told the King, but He would not come down to see him but commanded the two Shining Ones, who conducted Christian and Hopeful to the City, to go out and take Ignorance and bind him hand and foot and have him away.

Then they took him up and carried him through the air to the door in the side of the hill and put him in there. It was a way to hell, even from the gates of Heaven.

☙

Meanwhile, back in the City of Destruction, Christian's wife was in torment. Losing her husband had cost her many a tear. She remembered his restless groans, his tears, his burden. After Christian went over the river and she could hear of him no more, her thoughts began to work in her mind.

She considered herself and whether her unbecoming behavior toward her husband was one reason she saw her husband no more. And that because of her he was taken away. Then came into her mind, by swarms, all her unkind, unnatural, and ungodly behavior toward her friends. These clogged her conscience and loaded her with guilt. She remembered how she hardened her heart against all his entreaties and loving persuasions he used with both her and their sons to go with him. All Christian said or did assaulted her memory and ripped her heart in two. His bitter cry, "What shall I do to be saved?" rang in her ears.

Finally she said to her four boys, "Sons, I have sinned against your father. I would not go with him, and I have robbed you of everlasting life."

Then the boys all fell into tears and cried out to go after their father.

"Oh," said the woman, "if only we had gone with your father. Then it would have been well with us. But now it is likely to be a very difficult journey without him. Even though I foolishly thought that your father's troubles proceeded from a silly fancy he had, or that he was overtaken with depression, yet now I cannot get them out of my mind. Now I believe they sprang from another cause—the light of eternal life was given him. And with that light's help he has escaped the snares of death."

Then they all wept again.

That night she dreamed. A parchment was unrolled before her, in which was recorded all her ways, and they were black indeed. She cried out, "Lord, have mercy on me, a sinner." And her children heard her.

Almost immediately, two foul-looking creatures were beside her bed, saying, "What shall we do with this woman? If she continues this, we will lose her as surely as we lost her husband. We must by one way or another seek to take her off from the thoughts of what should be after this life, else all the world cannot stop her from becoming a pilgrim."

Next morning she awoke in a great sweat, and she started to tremble. But after a while she fell asleep again. When she dreamed this time, she saw Christian, her husband, in a place of bliss among many immortals. He had a harp in his hand, and he stood and played it before One who sat on a throne with a rainbow about His head. She also saw Christian bow his head, placing his face on the pavement under the Prince's feet, saying, "I heartily thank my Lord and King for bringing me into this place." Then shouted a company of them who stood round about and harped. But no living man could tell what they said.

Later, she got up, prayed to God, and talked with her children awhile. When there was a hard knock on the door, she called, "If you come in God's name, come in."

A man answered, "Amen." He opened the door and greeted her: "Peace be to this house. Do you know why I come?"

Then she blushed and trembled, and her heart grew warm with desire to know where he came from and what his business was with her.

"My name is Secret. I dwell with those on high. They tell me you are now aware of your sin done to your husband when you hardened your heart to his way and in keeping your children in ignorance. Also, that you have a desire to go to the place where I live. The Merciful One has sent me to tell you that He is a God ready to forgive, and that He takes delight the more pardons He gives. He invites you to come into His presence, to His table, and He will feed you with the fat of His house and with the heritage of your father.

"Christian, your husband, is there with legions more of his companions. They always behold the face that ministers life to the beholders. And they will all be glad when they hear the sound of your feet step over your Father's threshold."

The woman was disconcerted and embarrassed. She bowed her head to the ground.

The visitor continued to speak. "Here is a letter for you from the King."

She took it and opened a perfumed letter. Letters of gold read: "I want you to come as your husband did on the way to the Celestial City, and dwell in My presence with joy forever."

"Oh, sir," she cried, quite overcome. "Won't you carry me and the boys with you, so that we may worship the King?"

"The bitter comes before the sweet," he answered. "You must go through troubles, as he did who went before you, before you enter the Celestial City. I advise you to do as Christian did. Go to the wicket gate over beyond the plain, for that is the entrance to the way you should go. Keep the letter with you. Read it often to yourself and to your children until you have learned it by heart. It is one of the songs that you must sing while you are in this house of your pilgrimage. You must deliver it at the Celestial Gate."

Then she called the boys. "My sons, I have been under much stress in my soul about the death of your father; not that I doubt at all of his happiness, for I am satisfied now that he is well. I have also been much affected with the thoughts of my own state and yours, which is miserable by nature. My behavior to your father in his distress is a great load to my conscience, for I hardened both my own heart and yours against him and refused to go with him on pilgrimage.

"The thoughts of these things would now kill me outright but for a dream which I had last night and for the encouragement that Secret has given me this morning. Come, my children, let us pack up and be gone to the gate that leads to the Celestial City, that we may see your father and be with him and his companions in peace, according to the laws of that land."

The boys burst into tears of joy. Secret then left, and they began to prepare for their journey.

Soon there was another knock on the door.

"If you come in God's name, come in," answered the wife of Christian, who now called herself Christiana.

Two stunned neighbors entered: Mrs. Timorous and the maiden Mercy. They were unused to hearing this kind of language from Christiana.

"Why are you packing?" asked Mrs. Timorous.

"I am preparing for a journey," Christiana answered.

"What journey?"

"To follow my good husband." Christiana burst into tears.

"Oh, I hope this isn't true, good neighbor. For your children's sake, don't cast yourself away."

"They are going with me. Not one of them is willing to be left behind." Christiana went on to tell her everything, even reading the letter from the messenger.

"Oh, the madness that possesses you and your husband to run yourselves upon such difficulties," replied Mrs. Timorous. "You have heard, I am sure, what your husband did meet with, even in a manner at the first step that he took on his way. We also heard how he met with the lions, Apollyon, the Shadow of Death, and many other things. Nor can you forget the danger that he met with at Vanity Fair. For a man, he was so hard put to it, what can you, being but a poor woman, do? Have you even considered that you are not only being so rash as to cast yourself away, but you are planning to do it to your children as well? If for nothing else, stay home for the sake of your sweet children."

"Don't tempt me, my neighbor," said Christiana. "I have now a price put into my hand to get gain, and I should be a fool of the greatest size if I should have no heart to strike in with the opportunity. And for all these troubles you speak of that I am likely to meet in the way, they are so far off from being to me a discouragement that they show I am in the right. The bitter comes before the sweet and makes the sweet even sweeter. Please leave. You did not come here in God's name. I don't need you to disturb me further."

"Come on, Mercy!" snapped Mrs. Timorous. "This fool scorns our counsel."

But Mercy said, "Since this is Christiana's farewell, I will walk a little way with her."

Mrs. Timorous said, "I suspect you are thinking of going with her. Well, take heed: we are out of danger here in the City of Destruction. I can't wait to talk to Mrs. Bats-Eyes, Mrs. Inconsiderate, Mrs. Light-Mind, and Mrs. Know-Nothing. They know I'm right."

Christiana and the boys were soon on the way, and Mercy went along with her.

Christiana said, "Mercy, I take this as an unexpected favor, that you should set foot out of doors with me, to accompany me a little in my way."

Then young Mercy said, "If I thought it would be to a good purpose to go with you, I would never go near the town anymore."

Christiana said, "Cast your lot with us, Mercy. I know well what will be the end of our pilgrimage. For I am sure not all the gold in Spain could make my husband sorry he is there in that place. You won't be rejected, even if you go along with me as my servant. We will have all things in common between us if only you go along with me."

"But how do I know that? If I had this hope from one who could tell, I would make no stick at all, but would go, though the way was never so tedious."

"Well, loving Mercy, I will tell you what you shall do. Come with me to the wicket gate. There I will inquire further for you. See if you are allowed to enter. If you aren't given encouragement to continue, then I will be content to let you return to your house. I will also pay you for your kindness you've shown to me and my children in accompanying us in our way as you're doing."

"Then I will go that far with you and will take what shall follow. Lord, grant that my lot will fall with you," prayed Mercy.

Christiana was glad in her heart that not only did she have a companion, but she had prevailed with this poor maiden to fall in love with her own salvation.

As they went along, Mercy began weeping. "My poor relatives remain in our sinful town, and there is no one to encourage them to come."

"Your leaving will encourage them, just as Christian's encouraged me. The Lord gathers our tears and puts them into His bottle. These tears of yours, Mercy, will not be lost. For the Truth has said that they who sow in tears shall reap in joy and singing, bearing precious seed. And they shall doubtless come again with rejoicing, bringing his sheaves with him."

Then Mercy said:

"Let the Most Blessed be my guide,
If 't be His blessed will,
Into His gate, into His fold,
Up to His Holy Hill.
And let Him gather those of mine
Whom I have left behind."

ॐ

When they came to the Slough of Despond, Christiana stopped. "This is the place in which my dear husband was nearly smothered with mud." She also saw that in spite of the King's command to make this place good for pilgrims, it was worse than before.

But Mercy said, "Come, let us venture in, only let us be careful."

So they did not plunge straight in but found the steps.

As soon as they had crossed the slough, they heard someone speaking. He said, "Blessed is she that believes, for there shall be a performance of the things that have been told her from the Lord."

As they went on again, Mercy said to Christiana, "Had I a good reason to hope for a loving reception at the wicket gate as you, I think no Slough of Despond would discourage me."

"You know your affliction and I know mine, and, good friend, we shall all have enough evil before we come to our journey's end. For it can be imagined that the people who desire to attain such excellent glories as we do and who are so envied the happiness we have can expect to meet with what fears and scares, troubles and afflictions those who hate us can possibly assault us with."

Soon Christiana, Mercy, and the boys approached the wicket gate. They had a discussion as to how to approach the gate and what should be said to the gatekeeper. Then Christiana, since she was the oldest, knocked on the gate. She knocked and knocked, but no one answered.

Then they heard a dog barking at them. It sounded like a very large dog, and it made the women and children afraid to knock anymore for fear the mastiff should fly at them. Now they weren't sure what to do. They didn't want to knock for fear of the dog. Nor did they want to turn away, in case the gatekeeper did finally come to the gate and be offended with them for knocking and walking away.

Just as they were thinking of knocking again, the gatekeeper said, "Who is there?"

The dog quit barking, and the gatekeeper opened the narrow gate.

Christiana bowed low before the gatekeeper and said, "Let not our lord be offended with his handmaidens because we have knocked at his princely gate."

"Where do you come from? What do you want?" he asked.

Christiana said, "We come from the same place Christian came from, and we're on the same errand as he. We want to be admitted through this gate to the way that leads to the Celestial City. I am Christiana, the wife of Christian, who is now gone above."

"What?" marveled the keeper. "Are you now a pilgrim, who once despised that life?"

She bowed her head and said, "Yes, and these are my sweet children also."

He waved her in and the boys, too, saying, "Let the little children come to me." A trumpet sounded for joy, and the gatekeeper shut the gate.

All this time, Mercy stood outside the gate, trembling and crying for fear that she was rejected. But when Christiana gained admittance for herself and her boys, then she made intercession for Mercy. "My lord, I have a companion of mine who is still standing outside the gate. She has come for the same reason as myself. She is dejected because she thinks that without the King sending for her, she cannot come in."

Just then Mercy came to the end of her patience, for each minute felt like a hour that she waited for Christiana to intercede for her. So she knocked at the gate herself. And she knocked so loud that Christiana started. "It is my friend," she told the gatekeeper.

So the gatekeeper reopened the gate and looked out. But Mercy had fainted with fear that no gate would be opened to her.

Then the gatekeeper took her by the hand and said, "Girl, I bid you arise."

"Oh, sir" she said, "I am faint. There is scarcely any life left in me."

But the gatekeeper said, "Don't be afraid. Stand up and tell me why you have come."

Mercy blurted, "I am come even though I was never invited as my friend Christiana was. Hers was from the King, and mine is from her. But I fear to presume."

"Did she desire that you come with her to this place?"

"Yes, and as you see I have come. If there is any grace and forgiveness of sins to spare, please let me in, too."

Then he took her by the hand and gently led her in. "I take all who believe in to me, by whatever means they come to me." Then he called on his servants to bring a bundle of myrrh for Mercy to smell in order to stop her fainting.

Inside, all six pilgrims said they were sorry for their sins and begged his forgiveness. He granted them pardon and told them that along the way they would see what deed saved them. He continued to speak words of comfort and gladness to them, and they were greatly encouraged.

So he left them for a while in a summer parlor where they talked by themselves.

Christiana spoke first. "How glad I am that we are here!"

"So well you may, but I of all of us have reason to leap for joy," Mercy said.

"I did think as I stood outside the gate that all our work was for nothing, especially when that dog made such a heavy barking against us."

"My worst fear was after you and the boys were taken into the gate-keeper's favor and I was left behind. I thought the scripture was fulfilled when it says, 'Two women shall be grinding together; the one shall be taken, and the other left.' It was all I could do to keep from crying out, 'Undone! Undone!' I was so afraid to knock anymore, but when I looked up to what was written over the gate, I took courage. It was either knock again or die. So I knocked. But I'm not sure how, because my spirit then struggled between life and death.

"I was in such a state! The door was shut on me, and there was a most terrible dog somewhere about. Who wouldn't have knocked as I did with all their might? Tell me, what said my lord about my rudeness? Wasn't he angry with me?"

"I believe what you did pleased him well enough, for he showed no sign to the contrary. But I am surprised that he keeps such a dog. If I'd known that, I'm afraid I may have not had the heart to venture forth. But now we are in, and I am glad with all my heart."

"I will ask the gatekeeper why he keeps such a dog the next time we see him. I hope he won't take it wrong."

"Yes, do ask," said the children. "We are afraid he will bite us when we leave this place."

At last the gatekeeper came down to them again. Mercy fell to the ground on her face before him and worshipped and said, "Let my lord accept the sacrifice of praise which I now offer unto him with my lips."

He said to her, "Be at peace and stand up."

"Why do you keep such a cruel dog?" asked Mercy, still shaken.

"He belongs to Beelzebub, to frighten pilgrims from the way. He has frightened many honest pilgrims. But there is nothing I can do. He hopes to keep pilgrims from knocking at the gate for entrance. Sometimes the dog has broken out and scared those I love. But I take it all patiently. I also give my pilgrims timely help so they are not delivered up to his power to do whatever his doggish nature would prompt him to."

Then Mercy said, "I confess my ignorance. I spoke of what I didn't understand. You do all things well. I should have known better."

Then Christiana began to speak of the journey and to inquire after the way. So the gatekeeper fed them, washed their feet, and set them in the way of his steps, much the same as he dealt with Christian.

So the pilgrims went on the way, between the walls of salvation. Suddenly Christiana saw the two foul-looking creatures she had seen in her dream. They came toward her as if to embrace her.

"Stand back or pass peaceably," she warned them.

But they didn't listen and tried to lay hands on the women. But Christiana, very angry now, kicked at them. Mercy also followed Christiana's example.

Again Christiana spoke to them: "Stand back and be gone. We have no money to lose since we are pilgrims."

"We don't want your money. If you will grant one small request that we ask, we will make women of you forever," they replied and tried to embrace Christiana and Mercy. But they tried again to walk around the men. But they blocked the way against Christiana and Mercy.

"You would have us body and soul. I know this is why you have come. But we would rather die on the spot than suffer ourselves to be brought into such snares that will harm our well-being forever." Then both Christiana and Mercy screamed, "Murder! Murder!" But the men still would not leave the women alone. So they cried out again.

Several in the gatekeeper's house heard the screams and came to investigate. They found the women in a great scuffle with the men while the children looked on crying.

"Would you make my lord's people sin?" demanded one of the men who appeared on the way.

The man attempted to take the other men, but the two fiends jumped the wall and escaped into the realm of Beelzebub. They were seen joining the cruel mastiff.

"I marveled when you came in the gate that you did not ask our lord for a protector," said the man. "He would have granted you one."

"We felt so blessed by present blessing we forgot all future danger," said Christiana. "Should we go back and ask for one?"

"No. Go ahead. I will tell him of your confession. But remember: 'Ask and it will be given to you.'" And the man went back to the gate.

Mercy said, "I thought we were past all danger and that we should never sorrow again. What happened?"

"I am to blame," said Christiana. "I was warned in a dream these two fiends would try to prevent my salvation."

"Well, we have had a chance to see our imperfections. And the Lord has taken the occasion to reveal the riches of His grace. He has delivered us from the hands of those who were stronger than us."

When they had talked away a little more time, they came near a house by the way. As they came closer, they heard a lot of talking within the house, and thought they heard Christiana's name spoken.

Word of Christiana's pilgrimage with her children went before them. It was pleasing news, especially to those who knew she was Christian's wife.

So they stood at the door and listened to the talk within. Finally, Christiana knocked on the door.

A maiden opened the door. "To whom do you wish to speak?"

"We understand this is a privileged place for pilgrims. I am Christiana, the wife of Christian, who some time ago traveled this way. These are his four children. The maiden is my companion and is also going on pilgrimage. We pray that there is room for us, for the day is nearly over, and we don't wish to continue any farther at night."

The maiden ran inside, yelling, "Christiana and her children are at the door!" The pilgrims heard rejoicing inside the house. Soon the master, the Interpreter, came to the door. "Come in, daughter of Abraham. Come, boys. Come, maiden Mercy."

So when they were within, they were bidden to sit down and rest. Those who had attended Christian came into the room to see his family. They all smiled for joy because Christiana had become a pilgrim.

After a while, because supper wasn't ready, the Interpreter took them into his significant rooms. Soon they saw all the things Christian had seen: the picture of Christ, the devil trying to extinguish grace, the man in the cage, and the rest.

Then the Interpreter took them into another room. There was a man who could look no way but down. He held a rake in his hand. One stood over the man's head with a celestial crown in his hand. He offered to give him the crown for his rake, but the man neither looked up nor acknowledged the other man. Instead he raked the straws, the small sticks, and dust on the floor toward him.

"Is this the figure of the man of the world?" asked Christiana.

"Yes," said the Interpreter. "The rake is his carnal mind. He is so intent on raking straw and dust and sticks he doesn't see God. Heaven is but a fable to some, and the things of this earth are the only substantial things. The man can only look down. It is to show that when earthly things control a man's mind, his heart is carried away from God."

Then they went into a sumptuous room. "What do you see here? Anything profitable?" asked the Interpreter.

Christiana was quick to see a large spider on the wall. But Mercy saw nothing. The Interpreter told Mercy to look again. "There is nothing here but a big, ugly spider who hangs on the wall."

"Is there but one spider in all this spacious room?"

Then the water stood in Christiana's eye. "This shows how the ugliest creatures full of the venom of sin belong in the King's house. God has made nothing in vain."

"You have said the truth," Interpreter said to her. This made Mercy blush, and the boys covered their faces, for they all began to understand the riddle.

He then took them into another room where a hen and her chickens were. One of the chickens went to the trough to drink, and every time she drank, she lifted up her head and her eyes toward heaven. "See what this little chick does," said the Interpreter. "Learn of her to acknowledge from where your mercies come, by receiving them with looking up."

As they watched more, they saw that the hen walked in a fourfold method toward her chickens. She had a common call, a special call she only used sometimes, a brooding note, and an outcry.

"Now compare this hen to your King and the chickens to His obedient ones. The King walks toward His people with His common call in which He gives nothing, his special call with which He always has something to give, His brooding voice for those under His wing, and an outcry to give the alarm when He sees the enemy coming."

The Interpreter went on to show them more riddles, and then he gave them one wise saying after another. "The fatter the sow is, the more she desires the mire; the fatter the ox is, the more gamesomely he goes to the slaughter; and the more healthy the lusty man is, the more prone he is to evil. There is a desire in women to go neat and fine, and it is a comely thing to be adorned with that. That in God's sight is of great price."

When he was done with the wise sayings, the Interpreter took them out into his garden and showed them a tree whose inside was all rotten and gone. Yet it grew and had leaves.

Mercy asked, "What does this mean?"

"This tree whose outside is fair and whose inside is rotten is to which many people could be compared who are in God's garden. With their mouths they speak high in behalf of God, but indeed will do nothing for Him. Their leaves are fair, but their heart is good for nothing but to be tinder for the devil's tinderbox."

Now supper was ready, the table spread, and all things set on the board. So they sat down and did eat after one had given thanks. It was the Interpreter's custom to entertain those who lodged with him with music at meals. So the minstrels played. One who sang had a very fine voice. His song was like this:

"The Lord is only my support,
And He that doth me feed;
How can I then want anything
Whereof I stand in need?"

࿐

After the music, the Interpreter asked Christiana and Mercy to tell him of their reasons for starting the pilgrimage. Though each had a different story to tell, he commended them for their good start and for already showing courage along the way. Later, Mercy could not sleep for the joy the Interpreter's words to her had inspired. At last her doubts were gone, so she lay blessing and praising God who had such favor for her.

In the morning they arose with the sun and bathed. They came out not only sweet and clean, but enlivened and strengthened. They donned fine linen, white and clean. The Interpreter called for his seal and marked their faces, so they looked like angels. And each accused the other of being fairer because they could not see their own glory.

Then the Interpreter called for a manservant of his. A huge man appeared.

The Interpreter said, "Take your sword, helmet, and shield, Great-Heart, and escort these pilgrims to the Palace Beautiful." And to the pilgrims he said, "Godspeed."

The pilgrims departed, singing:
"This place has been a pleasant stage,
Here we have heard and eyed
Those good things that are age to age
Hid from the evil side."

&

Great-Heart went before them. They soon came to the Cross, where Christian's burden had tumbled into the sepulcher. Here they made a pause, and here they blessed God.

Christiana said, "Now I remember the gatekeeper told us we would come to the word and deed by which we are pardoned. By word, which is by the promise, and by deed, which was in the way our pardon was obtained. I know something of the promise, but of the deed and how it should be obtained, I don't know. Mr. Great-Heart, if you know, please, let us hear your discourse thereof."

"We are redeemed from sin at a price," said Great-Heart. "And that price was the blood of your Lord, who came and stood in your place. He has performed righteousness to cover you and the spilt blood to wash you in."

"But if He parts with His righteousness to us, what will He have for Himself?"

"He has more righteousness than you have need of, or than He needs Himself."

"Now I see that there was something to be learned by our being pardoned by word and deed. Good Mercy, let us labor to keep this in mind. And, my children, you remember it also. But, sir, was not this that made my good Christian's burden fall from off his shoulder and that made him give three leaps for joy?"

"Yes, it was the belief of this that cut out those strings that could not be cut by other means."

"My heart is ten times lighter and more joyous now," said Christiana, "yet it makes my heart ache to think He bled for me."

"There is not only comfort and ease of a burden brought to us by the sight and consideration of these things, but an endeared affection that is born in us by it. For who can but be affected with the way and means of redemption and so with the Man who worked it for him?"

"It makes my heart bleed to think that He should bleed for me," said Christiana. "You deserve to have me: You have bought me. You deserve to have me all, for You have paid for me ten thousand times more than I am worth."

"You speak now in the warmth of your affection," said Great-Heart. "I hope you always will be able to."

They went on until they came to the place where Simple, Sloth, and Presumption lay and slept when Christian went by. Now they came upon the three men hanging by the way in irons.

"Who are these men?" asked Mercy. "What did they do?"

Great-Heart answered, "They are Simple, Sloth, and Presumption. They had no intention to be pilgrims but only to hinder the pilgrims who passed by. They turned several out of the way: Slow-Pace, Short-Wind, No-Heart, Linger-after-Lust, Sleepy-Head, and Dull."

Christiana said, "They got just what they deserved, then."

After that they came to the foot of the Hill of Difficulty. The spring where Christian refreshed himself, which was once so pure, was now muddy. Great-Heart explained, "The evil ones do not want pilgrims to quench their thirst. Put it in a vessel and let the dirt settle. It will be pure again."

The two byways, Destruction and Danger, had been barred by chains. "'The way of the sluggard is blocked. . .but the path of the upright is a highway,'" quoted Christiana of the wise man Solomon.

"Yet some pilgrims still take the byways," said Great-Heart, "because the hill is very hard."

So they went forward and began to go up the hill. Before they reached the top, Christiana began to pant and said, "I daresay, this is a breathing hill. No marvel if they who love their ease more than their souls choose for themselves a smoother way."

Then said Mercy, "I must sit down."

Then the smallest child began to cry.

"Come, come," said Great-Heart, "don't sit down here. A little bit farther on is the Prince's arbor." Then he took the boy by the hand and led him up to the arbor.

When they came to the arbor, they were all willing to sit down and rest because of the pelting heat.

Mercy said, "How good is the Prince of pilgrims to provide such resting places for them! I have heard much of this arbor. Let's beware of sleeping, for as I have heard it cost poor Christian dearly."

As they rested, Christiana set out food to refresh their bodies. After a while, Great-Heart said, "The day is wearing away. If you think good, let us prepare to get going." So they got up to go.

But Christiana forgot to take her bottle of spirits with her, so she sent one of the boys back to fetch it.

Then Mercy said, "I think this is a losing place. Here Christian lost his roll, and here Christiana left her bottle behind her. Sir, what is the cause of this?"

"The cause is sleep or forgetfulness. Some sleep when they should keep awake, and some forget when they should remember. And this is the reason why often at the resting places, some pilgrims come off losers. Pilgrims should watch and remember what they have already received under their greatest enjoyments. But because they don't do so, many times their rejoicing ends in tears and their sunshine in a cloud."

After they topped the Hill, Great-Heart gathered them beside him to walk between the lions. The boys, instead of leading the way as they had done, lined up behind Great-Heart. He drew his sword with the intent to make a way for the pilgrims in spite of the lions.

Suddenly a giant appeared beyond the lions. He called out to Great-Heart, "Guide, what is the cause of your coming here?"

Great-Heart called, "These are pilgrims, and this is the way they must go."

"I am Grim. Some call me Bloody-Man. This is no longer the way.'

"I see now the path is overgrown with grass," said Great-Heart angrily. "You must be stopping pilgrims." He lunged at Grim with his sword. "This is the King's highway, and these women and children will follow it."

His sword came down on the giant's helmet and brought him down The giant writhed on the ground, dying.

When the giant was dead, Great-Heart said to the pilgrims, "Come now, and follow me. No hurt shall happen to you from the lions."

They therefore went on, but the women trembled as they passed by the lions. The boys also looked as if they would die, but they all got by without further hurt.

It was getting dark, so they made haste to the porter's gate. Soon Great-Heart knocked on the gate to a palace. He had only to say, "Porter, it is I," and the gate opened. But the porter did not see the women and children standing behind Great-Heart.

The porter asked, "What is your business here so late tonight, Great-Heart?"

"I have brought some pilgrims here, where by my lord's commandment they must lodge. I would have been here sooner if I had not been opposed by the giant who used to back the lions. But after a long and tedious combat with him, I have cut him off and have brought the pilgrims here to safety."

"Will you not go in and stay till morning?"

"No, I will return to my lord tonight."

Then the pilgrims realized Great-Heart was going back to the Interpreter's house. They begged him to stay. "I know not how to be willing you should leave us in our pilgrimage. You have been so faithful and so loving to us. You have fought so stoutly for us. You have been so hearty in counseling us that I shall never forget your favor toward us," Christiana said.

Mercy said, "Oh that we might have your company to our journey's end! How can such poor women as we hold out in a way so full of troubles as this way is without friend or defender?"

"I am at my lord's command," he replied. "You should have asked him to let me go all the way with you. He would have granted your request. For now, I must return. Good-bye."

Then the porter, Mr. Watchful, asked Christiana of her country and kindred. She told him she came from the City of Destruction. "I am a widow. My husband is dead. His name was Christian."

The porter then rang the bell. A maiden answered the door to the palace. Upon learning Christiana was the wife of Christian, she rushed back inside where there followed the sound of rejoicing. The pilgrims received a great welcome. They met Prudence, Piety, and Charity. They feasted on lamb and ended supper with a prayer and a psalm. Christiana asked to spend the night in the same room where her husband had slept.

"Little did I think once," said Christiana, "that I should ever follow my husband, much less worship the Lord with him."

Next morning the pilgrims sent a message back to the Interpreter's house requesting Great-Heart for their escort on the rest of the journey.

After about a week at the palace, Mercy had a visitor who pretended some goodwill to her. His name was Mr. Brisk, a man of some breeding who pretended to religion, but a man who stuck very close to the world. So he came once or twice or more to Mercy and offered love to her. Now Mercy had a fair countenance and was very alluring.

Her mind also was always busying herself in doing, from when she had nothing to do for herself, she would make hose and garments for others and would give them to others as had need. Mr. Brisk, not knowing where or how she disposed of what she made, seemed to be greatly taken, for he never found her idle. He thought she would be a good housewife.

Mercy then revealed the business to the maidens of the household and inquired of them concerning Mr. Brisk, for they knew him better than she. So they told her that he was a very busy young man, one who pretended to religion, but was really a stranger to the power of that which is good.

"No, I will look no more on him," said Mercy. "For I have purposed never to have a clog to my soul."

Prudence then replied, "You don't need a great matter of discouragement. Just continue doing as you have for the poor. That will quickly cool his courage."

So the next time he came, he found her at her work, making things for the poor.

"What, always at it?" he asked.

"Yes," she said, "either for myself or for others."

"What do you earn in a day?"

"I do these things that I may be rich in good work, laying up in store a good foundation against the time to come that I may lay hold on eternal life."

"What do you do with them?"

"Clothe the naked," she said.

His countenance fell. And he didn't come to see her again. When asked as to the reason why, he said that Mercy was a pretty lass but troubled with ill conditions.

After a month had passed, the family where Christiana was saw that they had a purpose to go forward. They called the whole house together to give thanks to their King for sending them such profitable guests as these.

Then they said to Christiana, "We shall show you something that we do to all pilgrims. It is something you can meditate on when you are on the way."

So they took Christiana, her children, and Mercy into the closet and showed them one of the apples that Eve did eat of and then gave to her husband. They asked Christiana what she thought the object was.

Christiana said, "Food or poison. I don't know which."

So they opened the matter to her, and she held up her hands and wondered.

Then they took her to a place and showed her Jacob's ladder. They watched the angels ascending and descending while they watched. They saw many other things their hosts wanted to show them.

Finally Great-Heart arrived. And when the porter opened the door and let him in, what joy there was at being reunited with their friend.

Then said Great-Heart to Christiana and to Mercy, "My lord has sent each of you a bottle of wine, and also some parched corn, together with a couple of pomegranates. He has also sent the boys some figs and raisins to refresh you in your way."

Then they put their attention to their journey, and Prudence and Piety went along with them. When they came to the gate, Christiana asked the porter if anyone came by lately.

"No, the only one was awhile ago, but he told me that there had been a great robbery committed on the King's highway as you go. But he said the thieves were taken and will shortly be tried for their lives."

Christiana and Mercy were afraid until Matthew reminded them of Great-Heart. So the little group left the palace and went forward to the brow of the hill. Piety then remembered something she'd planned to give to Christiana and her companions. So she went back to get it. While she was gone, Christiana thought she heard in a grove a little way off on the right hand a very curious melodious note.

Christiana asked Prudence about the one making the curious notes. "They are our country birds. I often keep them tame in our house. They are very fine for company when we are melancholy. They make the woods and groves and solitary places desirable to be in."

By this time Piety had returned. So she said to Christiana, "Look here, I have brought you a scheme of all those things that you saw at our house. You may look on this when you find yourself forgetful and call those things again to remembrance for your edification and comfort."

Then the pilgrims descended into the Valley of Humiliation. It was steep and slippery, but they were careful, so they got down pretty well.

"This valley is a most fruitful place," reassured Great-Heart. "See how green the valley. See how beautiful the lilies. Listen to the shepherd boy over there."

The pilgrims heard the boy sing:

"He who is down, need fear no fall;
He who is low, no pride.
He who is humble, ever shall
Have God to be his guide.
I am content with what I have,
Be it little or much:
And, Lord, yet more content I crave,
because You save such.
Fullness to those, is all a blight,
Who go on pilgrimage:
Here little, and after delight,
Is best from age to age."

&

Great-Heart went on to tell of the features of the valley. "Did I say our Lord had his country house here in former days? He loved to walk here. To the people who live here, He has left a yearly revenue to be faithfully paid them at certain seasons for their maintenance and for their further encouragement to go on their pilgrimage."

Soon the pilgrims came to a pillar that read:

Let Christian's slips, before he came here, and the battles he met with in this place, be a warning to those who come after.

"Forgetful Green here is the most dangerous place in all these parts," explained Great-Heart. "This is where pilgrims have trouble if they forget favors they have received and how unworthy they are. This is where Christian fought Apollyon. Christian's blood is on the stones to this day. Look. There are Apollyon's broken arrows. When Apollyon was beaten, he retreated into the next valley, which is called the Valley of the Shadow of Death."

As they entered the Valley of the Shadow of Death, they heard groaning, as if from great torment. The ground shook and hissed. A fiend approached them, then vanished.

"'Resist the devil, and he shall flee from you,'" remembered one of the pilgrims.

They heard a great padding beast behind them. Its every roar made the valley echo. When Great-Heart turned to face it, it too vanished. Then a great mist and darkness fell, so that they could not see. They heard the noise and rustling of the enemies.

"Many have spoken of the Valley of the Shadow of Death," said Christiana, "but no one can know what it means until they come into it themselves. 'Each heart knows its own bitterness, and no one can share its joy.' To be here is a fearful thing."

Great-Heart added, "This is like doing business in great waters, or like going down into the deep. This is like being in the heart of the sea, and like going down to the bottoms of the mountains. Now it seems as if the earth, with its bars, surrounds us forever. But let them who walk in darkness, and have no light, trust in the name of the Lord, and stay upon their God. For my part, as I have told you already, I have gone often through this valley, and have been much harder put to it than now I am; and yet you see I am alive. I would not boast, for that I am not my own savior. But I trust we shall have a good deliverance. Come, let us pray for light to Him who can rebuke all the devils in hell."

So they cried and prayed, and God sent light and deliverance, for there was now no obstruction in their way. Then they were stopped with a pit. Yet they were not through the valley, so they went on still, and behold great stinks and loathsome smells, to the great annoyance of them. Then said Mercy to Christiana, "It is not so pleasant being here as at the gate, or at the Interpreter's, or at the house where we lay last."

"Oh but," said one of the boys, "it is not so bad to go through here, as it is to abide here always. For all I know, one reason why we must go this way to the House prepared for us is that our home might be made the sweeter to us."

"Well said, Samuel," said the Guide. "You have now spoken like a man."

"Why, if ever I get out here again," said the boy, "I think I shall prize light and good way better than ever I did in all my life."

Then said the Guide, "We shall be out by and by."

So on they went, and Joseph said, "Can't we see to the end of this valley yet?"

Then said the Guide, "Look to your feet, for you shall presently be among snares." So they looked to their feet and went on, but they were troubled much with the snares. Now when they had come among the snares, they saw a man cast into the ditch on the left hand, with his flesh all rent and torn.

Then said the Guide, "That is one Heedless, who was going this way. He has lain there a great while. There was one Take-Heed with him, when he was taken and slain; but he escaped their hands. You cannot imagine how many are killed hereabouts, and yet men are so foolishly venturous as to set out lightly on pilgrimage, and to come without a guide. Poor Christian! It was a wonder that he here escaped. But he was beloved of his God. Also he had a good heart of his own, or else he could never have done it."

They continued on. Ahead of them was an old man. They knew he was a pilgrim by his staff and his clothes. The old man turned defensively.

"I am a guide for these pilgrims to the Celestial City," explained Great-Heart.

"I beg your pardon. I was afraid you were of those who robbed Little-Faith some time ago."

"And what could you have done if we had been of that company?" puzzled Great-Heart.

"Why, I would have fought so hard I'm sure you couldn't have given me the best of it. No Christian can be overcome unless he gives up himself."

"Well said," marveled Great-Heart. "What is your name?"

"My name is Honest. I only wish that was my nature." When Honest learned who the pilgrims were, he gushed to Christiana, "I have heard of your husband. His name rings all over these parts of the world for his faith, his courage, his endurance, and his sincerity."

As they walked, Honest and Great-Heart discussed a pilgrim whom they both knew: Fearing.

"What could be the reason that such a good man should be so much in the dark?" asked Honest.

"The wise God will have it so. Some must pipe, and some must weep. Though the notes of the bass are woeful, some say it is the ground of music."

As they continued on their way, they found a giant holding a man, rifling his pockets. Great-Heart attacked the giant. After the ebb and flow of much fighting, Great-Heart beheaded the giant with his sword.

Christiana asked Great-Heart, "Are you wounded?"

"A small wound, proof of my love to my Master and a means by grace of increasing my final reward."

"Weren't you afraid?" asked Christiana.

"It is my duty to distrust my own ability, so I may rely on Him who is stronger than all."

"And what of you?" Christiana asked of the man Great-Heart had rescued.

"Even after the giant Slay-Good took me," said the man, "I thought I would live. For I heard that any pilgrim, if he keeps his heart pure toward the Lord, will not die by the hand of the enemy."

"Well said," agreed Great-Heart. "Who are you?"

"Feeble-Mind." He seemed reluctant to continue on the way with the others. "You are all lusty and strong. I will be a burden." Just then a man approached on crutches. "And what of him?"

"I am committed to comfort the feebleminded and to support the weak," said Great-Heart.

As they continued in the way, there came one running to meet them. He said, "Gentlemen, and you of the weaker sort, if you love life, shift for yourselves, for the robbers are before you."

They stayed alert, searching all the turnings where they could have met the villains. But they never came to the pilgrims.

About this time Christiana wished for an inn for herself and her children because they were very tired. Then Honest said, "There is one a little before us where a very honorable disciple, Gaius, lives."

So they all decided to turn in there because the old gentleman gave him so good a report. So when they came to the door, they went in. Then they called for the master of the house, and they asked if they might lie there that night.

"Yes," said Gaius, "if you speak truth. My house is for none but pilgrims."

So gladdened that the innkeeper loved pilgrims, they called for rooms. While the servants prepared a late supper, they had good conversation with the innkeeper.

The company and conversation were so good, the group stayed for a month at the inn, getting refreshment they needed after their various trials. While there, Matthew and Mercy were married, and Gaius gave his daughter Phebe to James as his wife.

Finally the day came to leave the inn. Gaius refused payment, saying that he received all he needed from the Good Samaritan. As they all went on, they neared Vanity. Knowing the trials Christian and Faithful faced in that town, they discussed how they should pass through the town. Finally Great-Heart said, "I have, as you know, often been a conductor of pilgrims through this town. I know of a man at whose house we may lodge. If you think good, we will turn in there."

They all agreed, and as they came to the town, evening fell. But Great-Heart knew the way and they were soon settled into the house with their host, Mnason.

Because of the fellowship they found in that house, the group stayed there for a long time. Before they left, Mnason gave his daughter Grace to Samuel to wed, and his daughter Martha to Joseph. During the time they stayed in Vanity, the pilgrims came to know many of the good people of the town and did them what service they could.

While they were there, a monster came out of the woods and slew many of the people of the town. It carried away their children. No man in the town dared to face this monster. All the men fled when they heard the noise of his coming.

The monster had a body like a dragon with seven heads and ten horns. Now Great-Heart, together with those who came to visit the pilgrims at Mnason's house, made a covenant to destroy the beast. They went to battle against the monster so many times, they wore the beast down through multiple wounds, so that they expected the monster to die. This made Great-Heart and his companions greatly famed throughout the town.

Finally the time came for the pilgrims to resume their pilgrimage. So they prepared for their journey. They sent for their friend, conferred with them, and committed each other to the protection of their Prince. So they went forward on their way.

Soon they came to the place where Faithful was put to death. They stopped and thanked Him who had enabled him to bear his cross so well. Thus they passed through the fair.

They passed the hill of Lucre where the silver mine claimed By-Ends and others. They passed the pillar of salt that had been Lot's wife. There they considered how intelligent men could be so blinded as to turn aside here. Only as they considered again that nature isn't affected with the harms men meet up with, then they could understand the attracting virtue upon the foolish eye.

They went on till they came to the river that was on this side of the Delectable Mountains. Here they committed their little ones to Him who was Lord of this meadow. Beyond the River of God they came to By-Path Meadow where the stile led to Doubting Castle. Great-Heart halted at the warning left by Christian. Here they discussed what was best to do.

"I have a commandment to 'fight the good fight of the faith.' And who is a greater enemy of faith than the giant Despair?" Suddenly Great-Heart led the others off the way and over the stile to find Doubting Castle. When they approached the castle, they knocked for entrance with an unusual noise.

Despair rushed out, yelling, "Who are you?" His wife, Diffidence, followed.

"Great-Heart, one of the King's protectors for pilgrims to the Celestial City. I demand of you that you open your gates for my entrance. Prepare yourself for battle, for I am come to take away your head and to demolish Doubting Castle."

"I have conquered angels," bragged Despair. So he put on his armor and went out to fight.

Yet Great-Heart assaulted him so savagely, Diffidence came out to help. Honest cut her down with one blow. Despair fought hard, with as many lives as a cat, but died when Great-Heart cut off his head. It took the pilgrims seven days to destroy the castle. Yet Great-Heart warned:

"Though Doubting Castle is demolished,
And the giant Despair has lost his head,
Sin can rebuild the castle, make it remain,
And make Despair the giant live again."

They took the giant's head with them when they went back to join the rest of their group. They had a party to celebrate the end of the giant Despair, his wife Diffidence, and Doubting Castle. When they left the area, Great-Heart put the giant's head on a pillar that Christian erected to warn pilgrims who came after him. Then he wrote under the head on the marble,

This is the head of him, whose name only
In former times did pilgrims terrify.

His castle's down, and Diffidence his wife
Brave Master Great-Heart has bereft of life.
Despondency, his daughter Much-Afraid,
Great-Heart, for them also the Man has play'd.
Who hereof doubts, if he'll but cast his eye
Up hither, may his scruples satisfy.
This head also, when doubting cripples dance,
Doth show from fears they have deliverance.

Then the company moved forward along the way. When the pilgrims reached the Delectable Mountains, they were welcomed by the shepherds Knowledge, Experience, Watchful, and Sincere. The pilgrims feasted, then rested for the night. The next morning, with the mountains so high and the day clear, the shepherds showed them many things. On one mountain they saw Godly-Man, clothed in white, being pelted with dirt by two men, Prejudice and Ill-Will. The dirt would not stick to his clothes. On another mountain a man cut clothes for the poor from a roll of cloth, yet the roll of cloth never got smaller.

The pilgrims left singing. Along the way was a man with sword drawn and face bloody. "I am Valiant-for-Truth," he said. "I was set upon by three men: Wild-Head, Inconsiderate, and Pragmatic. They gave me three choices: become one of them, go back on the way, or die. I fought them for hours. They fled when they heard you coming."

"Three to one?" marveled Great-Heart.

"'Though an army besiege me, my heart will not fear,'" replied Valiant-for-Truth.

"Why did you not cry out?"

"Oh, I did—to my King."

Then said Great-Heart to Valiant-for-Truth, "You have behaved yourself worthily. Let me see your sword."

So Valiant-for-Truth showed him the blade. Great-Heart studied it for a while, then said, "Ha! It is a right Jerusalem blade."

Valiant-for-Truth said, "It is so. The man who holds it need not fear it. Its edges will never blunt. It will cut flesh and bones and soul and spirit and all."

"You have done well," Great-Heart said.

Then they took Valiant-for-Truth and washed his wounds and gave him of what they had to refresh him. And so he joined the company of pilgrims.

By the time they were better acquainted with Valiant-for-Truth, they now walked the Enchanted Ground, where the air made them drowsy. Then a great darkness fell over them, and they walked blindly. Thorns tore them, bushes tripped them, and they lost shoes in the mud. All about them was mud, purposely made to smother pilgrims. Yet with Great-Heart leading and Valiant-for-Truth bringing up the rear, they made their way.

They reached an arbor, warm and cozy. A soft couch was there for weary bones. Great-Heart warned them, however, that it was a temptation, a trap. At the next arbor they found two men, Careless and Too-Bold, fast asleep. They could not be awakened. The Enchanted Ground was very deadly because it was so near Beulah that pilgrims thought they were at last safe.

They came upon a man on his knees. Honest knew him. "He is Standfast, a right good pilgrim. What happened, Standfast?"

"A woman of great beauty came to me. She spoke soothingly and smiled at the end of every sentence. She offered me her body, her purse, and her bed. I am very lonely; I am very poor; and I am very weary; but I turned her down several times. And yet she persisted: If only I would let her rule me, she said, she would make me so happy. She said she is the mistress of the world, Madam Bubble. I fell to my knees as you see me now and prayed to Him above who could help me. She only just left me."

"She is a witch," said Great-Heart. "It is her sorcery that enchants this ground. Anyone who lays his head down on her lap lays it on the chopping block."

The pilgrims trembled, yet sang for joy:

"What danger is the pilgrim in?
How many are his foes?
How many ways there are to sin, no living mortal knows.
Some do escape the ditch, yet can fall tumbling in the mire.
Some though they shun the frying pan do leap into the fire!"

෴

After this, they came into the land of Beulah, where the sun shines night and day. Here, because they were weary, they betook themselves awhile to rest. And because this country was common for pilgrims, and because the orchards and vineyards that were here belonged to the King of the Celestial City, they were licensed to make bold with any of His things. But a little while soon refreshed them here, for the bells did so ring and the trumpets continually sounded so melodiously that they could not sleep. And yet they received as much refreshing as if they had slept their sleep never so soundly.

One day a messenger came to Feeble-Mind. The Master wanted him to cross the river to the Celestial City. The entire company went with him to the river. His last words as he entered the river were, "Welcome, life."

Honest departed next. His last words were, "Hold out, faith and patience."

As he departed, Christiana said, "'Here is a true Israelite, in whom there is nothing false.' I wish you a fair day and a dry river when you set out for the Celestial City, but as for me, come wet or dry, I long to go."

One by one over the weeks the pilgrims left. Valiant-for-Truth said, "Death, where is your sting?" as he entered the river, then, "Grave, where is your victory?" as he crossed over.

One day a messenger brought Christiana a letter:

Hail, good woman! I bring you tidings: the Master calls for you, and expects you to stand in His presence, clothed in Immortality, within ten days.

When the day came that Christiana must go, the road was full of people to see her take her journey. The banks beyond the river were full of horses and chariots, which had come down from above to accompany her to the City Gate.

So she came and entered the river with a beckon of farewell to those who followed her to the riverside.

As she entered the river, she said, "I come, Lord, to be with You, and bless You." Behind her, her children wept, but Great-Heart clashed the cymbals for joy.

It would be many, many years before the Lord called for Christiana's sons, who with their wives greatly increased the church in Beulah.